WHAT PEOPLE ARE SAYING ABOUT *WILLOW GROVE*

"Bet you will laugh a little, cry a little and remember a lot."
—Dean W. Moore, author of *Washington's Woods,* college instructor, Cincinnati, Ohio

"[The author] has given us a heartfelt, nostalgic look at what life was like on a working family farm post World War II."
—Rob Benson, retired business owner, Historic Landmark Commission member, and Ravenswood, West Virginia, history buff

"A heartfelt memoir by a farming family's son in West-by-God Virginia during the Baby Boomer years..."
—Spencer Dreischarf, a Boomer with West Virginia roots, Flowery Branch, Georgia

"Interesting. Informative. Well-done, humorous, very descriptive of farm machinery and farm life."
—Peg Lyons, classmate and lifelong citizen of Ravenswood, West Virginia

"...*Willow Grove* will put a tear in your eye and a smile on your face at the same time."
—Mark McComas, Vice President, Jackson County Historical Society, Millwood, West Virginia

"I've just finished your book and really enjoyed it. I'm amazed at how clear your memories are of your time at Willow Grove."
—Kay Plumer, Frederick, Maryland

"Growing up on a rural dairy farm comes to life as Larry Suek milks his homespun tale of youthful adventure. A life with few luxuries but countless days of joy within a hardworking and loving family. Cozy up to his journey and absorb the fresh country air for yourself.

This book reinforces the idea that farm families form the bedrock of America. They exhibit an unyielding work ethic and strength of character that should be recognized and cherished. They feed our collective belly as well as our soul."
—John Shanahan, novelist and author of *The Last Raven*, Lakewood Ranch, Florida

"*Willow Grove* is a delightful account of Mr. Suek's memories of growing up on his family's dairy farm in rural West Virginia during the 1940s-1950s."
—Kathy White, Mountain Heritage Books, St. Marys, West Virginia

Willow Grove
A Boy, A Family, A Farm

Willow Grove
A Boy, A Family, A Farm

Edmond Lawrence Suek

Copyright 2023 by Edmond Lawrence Suek

All rights reserved. Published in the United States. First print edition, April 2023.

ISBN-13: ISBN: 978-1-951158-08-8
Larry may be contacted via LarrySuek.com.

Published by OrangeBlossomPublishing.com, Sarasota, Florida.

Unless otherwise noted, illustrations are courtesy of the Suek family.

Dedication

To

Margaret (Peggy) Faye Suek
My Adored Wife

and

Conrad Morgan McCoy
Revered Uncle and Dedicated Teacher

Without their sacrifice and wisdom, this book would never have been written.

Disclosure

As specified by my great-great-grandfather in 1846, the correct pronunciation of my ancestral surname, spelled initially "Sück," rhymes with "book." In the English language, the phonic spelling is "Sook." That is, one syllable enunciated just as the short and fast-spoken English word "book."

When my ancestors came to America in the mid-1800s from Germany, the umlaut over the ü in Sück had to be dropped since the English language does not have the equivalent German characters ä, ö, and ü in its alphabet. The bare vowels, a, o, and u, have different pronunciations than their umlauted counterparts in German.

To assist the reader in the correct pronunciation of my familial surname, I have chosen to use the umlauted version in my book, even though the umlaut was not used by the core Sück family in Jackson County, West Virginia. Neither by family members who settled in Frederick, Maryland, and Allentown, Pennsylvania. However, anecdotally, a few family members did! My great-grandfather's youngest brother, Leopold Sück, settled in Los Angeles at a young age in the latter part of the 1800s. His son Leo Edward used the umlauted last name to identify Sück family relatives on the back of vintage photographs gifted to my parents by Leo Edward's niece, Carrie M. Sück Grodevant.

Disclaimer

The content of this book is based mostly on my own research and many hours of discussion with my mother, Kathrine Genevieve Barber Sück. I have sincerely attempted to be as accurate as possible regarding many details in this book. Please note that I have deliberately used defining adjectives to flag where I am uncertain about a topic but suggest that my hypothesis or summation is correct or at least highly probable. I used the word *anecdotally* a few times in my writing. Notwithstanding, I suspect some details are worthy of additional research, which I would welcome.

Preface

Initially, I had intended to highlight the narratives in this book only for myself. The genesis took root and slowly morphed over several years when I worked for Mobil Chemical Corporation in Edison, New Jersey.

In 1981, Dr. Charles Lancelot, an admirable gentleman and colorful scientist, invited me to come to the Garden State to help market a new plastic material, which had huge potential in the vast petrochemical industry. This plastic had so much potential that the scientists and marketing manager at the prestigious Mobil Chemical Company Research Center forecast sales of hundreds of millions of pounds. Mobil was eager to commercialize the unique thermoplastic domestically and, soon afterward, internationally. The plastic was potentially destined to displace polystyrene, a large-volume global commodity introduced to the United States market in the late 1930s.

All of the excitement at the Mobil Chemical Research Center about the marketing of para-methyl styrene polymer, Mobil Poly-PMS, commenced in the early 1980s, which was also during an economic recession. While many blue-chip petrochemical companies were laying off employees, Mobil Chemical was simultaneously attracting and hiring successful scientists and engineers from high-profile companies in the plastics industry.

As a humble country boy from rural Jackson County, West Virginia, I soon learned that I had entered a fast-moving coterie of highly educated and decidedly experienced colleagues, which inexorably blossomed into an intensely competitive business climate.

Competitive it was! I quickly realized that a thick skin was necessary to survive Wall Street's hardened, profit-motivated entrepreneurs. Even if I got through the moat in front of the executive's dark walnut office door, I still had an uphill battle to garner a return appointment. Often, I left an executive's office totally exhausted but, fortunately, I usually found a way to leave behind a few crumbs. A hook, which made the next visit a lot easier.

During my late-afternoon return to the office, jostling my way among six lanes of bumper-to-bumper traffic in New York City and metropolitan New Jersey, I would hearken back to my years growing up in the farming communities of Silverton and Willow Grove, West Virginia. My parents, grandparents, uncles, aunts, and dedicated elementary and high school teachers all engendered such great memories that my perpetual enthusiasm was reset by the time I got to my destination. My family had instilled integrity, hard work, and perseverance. I was so fortunate to have such ardent teachers, especially in my formative elementary school years. The deep roots planted in the Ravenswood Elementary classrooms enabled well-grounded students to survive happily in the most demanding professional situations. I am deeply indebted to my family, many cousins, and all of my earnest teachers and friends in Jackson County, West Virginia!

This book, *Willow Grove: A Boy, A Family, A Farm* is the first of two historical memoirs. Though published after *Willow Grove*, the companion memoir, *Silverton,* will focus on my earliest years and my family's history, and I anticipate publishing *Silverton* in 2024.

Table of Contents

Chapter One: The Beginning..........................1
   First Day...3
   Willow Grove..23
   A Day in Paradise..45
   Fall Butchering...54
   Farms Can Be Dangerous, Part 1....................63
   Gored!..71
   Milk and Money..72
   Love Pecks..80
   Confessions of a Calf Conductor....................84
   Mousers..88
   Digging a Hole...90
   Scaredy-Cat..92
   Ravenswood Elementary..............................96
   Second Grade...99
   Jamesway to the Rescue.............................101
   Bedtime Sheriff...108
   The Hump..118
   Fun and Games with Bob.............................127
   Pay Now or Pay Later.................................130

Chapter Two: Too Young..........................133
- Muck Brawl!..135
- Harvesting Hair....................................147
- Willow Switches...................................149
- Make do or do Without.......................151
- Country Boy meets City Girl...............158
- First Winter...173
- First Summer......................................175
- Handsome Chariot..............................177
- Farmall M..188
- Milking Tilly..189
- Third Grade...191
- Packet Virginia....................................197
- Knapping Rock....................................201
- Tatterdemalion....................................203
- Pulling Teeth.......................................210
- Aunt Jack Arrives................................212
- Surprised by Snuff!..............................222
- Midnight Pebbles.................................224
- Fourth Grade.......................................230
- Playing with Ravenswood Marbles......232
- Bullies Beware!....................................238
- Dr. Monroe, Ravenswood's Beloved Doctor.......240

Chapter Three: Still Too Young..............245
- Ode to the Mighty Sycamore..............247
- Aunt Dee, Meet Outhouse...................251
- Run Over!..258
- Another Cautionary Tale.....................261
- Fifth Grade..264
- Train Whistle Averts Disaster!............275
- In One Ear...281
- Wasp Warfare......................................282
- Evening Fun..285

Dewey Gene Strikes Again!..............................289
1949 Family Reunion..295
Pony Antics..302
Uncle Conrad Bears ALL..................................310
Black Snake!..318
Rattlesnake!...319
The Seasonal Rhythm of the Farm...................328
Multi-Talented Uncle Homer.............................332
A Pig in a Blanket in a Car................................338
Dad's Summer Birthday....................................340
A Pox on Christmas..342
An Idyllic Life..347
John and Uncle Everett go for a Walk..............349
The Land of Karo..351
Big Top, Big Trouble...354
Beware Dewey Gene!.......................................356
Outrunning Indians...359
Sixth Grade..363
Very Fine Land...372
World War II on our Silverton Farm..................374
The Ladies of the Farms..................................382

Chapter Four: Old Enough..........................385

Grandpa's Chauffeur..387
Whitewashed Eyes!..392
Sundays at Willow Grove.................................395
Grandpa, Draft Horses, and Nancy..................400
Dewey Gene, at it Again!.................................404
Calf Lady..410
Farm Chores: Watermelon...............................413
High Standards Start at Home.........................415
High School..418
Coach Bill...423
Coach Jones..427
Half-Time Entertainment by Mart Moore..........432

 Scarred for Life..433
 While the Sun Shines...436
 Little Go-Getter..459
 Brother Bob..464
 Binder Twine..467
 Farms Can Be Dangerous, Part 2......................469
 Mastery...473
 Sunday Visitors..476
 Dinner with Robert Park and His Family..........482
 Fertilizer Pit...484
 Family of the Year!...489
 Happy Story..490

Chapter Five: The End..................................497
 Kaiser..499
 Humble Stranger..501
 RIP of the Mighty Sycamore...............................507
 Last Day..507
 Parkersburg..511

Family Trees..521

Maryland Family Reunion............................525

Acknowledgments...529

For further reading.......................................537

Chapter One: The Beginning

Willow Grove: A Boy, A Family, A Farm

First Day

It was dawn, September 2, 1946, and the first day of school for my younger brother Robert and me. We were dressed in identical khaki overalls and matching T-shirts. The crystal-clear sky indicated that it was going to be a beautiful fall day in Jackson County, West Virginia. It was also going to be an extraordinary day for me! In addition to going back to school after the summer break, I was anxiously looking forward to an unusual journey, which my brother and I would undertake at the end of our first school day.

Bob and I had just finished breakfast and said farewells to our mother and baby brother, John. We were on our way to the bus stop along the county road, which linked our home in Silverton to the nearby community of Wilding. We would cross over Straight Fork Creek on a swinging bridge and, for the last time, follow the path up the side of an embankment to the bus stop. I was destined for the second grade, while Robert—"Bob"—was just entering his first year at Ravenswood Elementary. We were both eager for the first day of school, yet I was more apprehensive than Bob. Alone, I had made this same trek through the grassy field every

Willow Grove: A Boy, A Family, A Farm

school day during my first year in elementary school. However, today would be my brother's *first* and *last* trip from our Silverton home to school, because today was moving day! Today my family would move from Silverton to our new farm at Willow Grove.

After Bob and I had walked a short distance, we hesitated and looked back toward our home, where Mom and John were watching from inside the woven wire fence. We both waved vigorously as we embraced our new, fresh-smelling school supplies. Mom and John saw us waving and acknowledged by waving back. Our two-story white farmhouse was perched on a knoll overlooking the entire creek bottom, which spanned the length of our farm. From that elevation, our mother could easily see every step we took, even though, in some spots, the orchard grass along the single-file path was nearly as high as our heads. While we were walking, I would occasionally turn around and take in another mental portrait of our house and the accompanying white barn. I wanted to memorize the serene picture because it would be the last one I would be able to savor of our historical family home!

The walk across the flat field was a convenient shortcut to the Silverton-Wilding County Road, plus the swinging bridge was the only practical way to cross the small but sometimes treacherous creek. The journey across the bottom became especially interesting for young kids once they reached the stream. At the edge of the creek, Bob and I climbed

First Day

up several steps onto the swinging bridge, which extended across the shallow ravine. On the opposite side, a footpath snaked its way up to the bus stop at the top of the embankment.

Our mother paid close attention to every step that Bob and I took until we were safely on the other side of the wobbly bridge. The bridge was fun to cross, and Mom knew we would likely stop about halfway and procrastinate. Our mother wouldn't leave the front yard until she could see us standing at the bus stop.

Twenty minutes after we boarded the school bus, the driver parallel parked along the wide sidewalk in front of the two-story, red-brick structure. We had arrived at the Ravenswood Elementary School, which my brother and I would attend through grade six.

Before the school bus came to a complete stop, I motioned to Bob to remain in his seat until all the other kids had exited. The moment the last kid stood up, we followed close behind until we reached the front of the bus. I said to the driver, who was still in his seat, "Excuse me, sir. I want to let you know that my brother and I won't be going back home on your school bus. We are moving to a brand-new farm, so after school we will be riding a different bus." The driver thanked us for letting him know, and off we went down the steps onto the sidewalk.

All day during school, I daydreamed about Willow Grove. I tried to envision what the new farm would look like based on all the family discussions

Willow Grove: A Boy, A Family, A Farm

and images that I had memorized over the past several weeks. Even though Mom had assured me that Bob and I would enjoy living in Willow Grove, I was excited about seeing our new farm with my very own eyes and could hardly wait until the school day was over.

As soon as the bell rang, I hastily gathered up my books and hurried to meet my brother at the school's main entrance. All of the big yellow buses were neatly lined up and ready to take students home. What I didn't know was that my brother and I had plenty of time: Our school bus ferried kids to nearby North Ravenswood first, then returned to pick up the remaining students who lived in distant Millwood and the several communities between Ravenswood and Millwood.

I was a little uneasy about finding our new farm, even though our mother had explained several times how I would know when we arrived at the right bus stop. As it turned out, I knew precisely which school bus to board since all 10 of the McCoy kids on the bus were first cousins. There were 11 counting their first cousin Don King. I knew Bob and I would remain on the bus until cousin James Conrad got off at his home in Pleasant View. In addition, I also knew we would arrive at our bus stop very soon after Richard, Dave, and Ann McCoy got off at their farm. Richard and Dave were twins, and both were in Mrs. Smith's second-grade class with cousin James Conrad and me. Afterward, Bob and I would ride approximately three more miles before we would

First Day

reach our destination. Hazel and Buzzy Casto and Phyllis, Sharon, and Jimmy McCoy lived on the next two farms after our farm, which James Conrad said was within eyesight of our bus stop. So, with our mother's in-depth instructions and assistance from our older cousins and schoolmates, I had no reason to be uneasy about identifying the right farm.

We had been waiting in front of the elementary school for about half an hour when the empty school bus returned from North Ravenswood. Even though I was having fun talking and joking around with my cousins and other classmates, I was anxious to board the bus, which would take us to our new farm. Our grandparents, parents, and little brother, John, were already there. It would be strange, but exciting, to see everyone in a new environment, nestled alongside the mighty Ohio River.

The younger kids were lined up single-file while the older boys stood back, like hungry bears, ready to climb onboard. Girls sat on the left side behind the driver; boys on the right. All the elementary kids sat in the front seats only, reserving the back seats for the really big kids: the senior high students who would board the bus at its next stop. Even though I was one of the younger kids and could be first in line, I purposely stayed back with the older boys so I could be one of the last to board the bus. I wanted to tell the school bus driver who I was and that my brother and I needed to get off at the big Gordon Kyle farm in Willow Grove. Luckily,

Willow Grove: A Boy, A Family, A Farm

while we were waiting, the driver stepped off the bus and stood not far from where I was standing.

I introduced myself and told him that my family had just moved from Silverton to Willow Grove and that my brother and I needed to get off the bus at the Gordon Kyle farm. I asked him if he knew where the farm was and would he let me know when we got there? The bus driver replied assuredly, "Of course! I certainly do know where the Kyle farm is, and, in fact, your new farm is where I park the school bus every night after I take all the students home." I immediately liked the bus driver and felt confident that Bob and I were in good hands.

After the last student boarded and was safely seated, the super-long yellow bus pulled out from where it had been parked on Henry Street in front of the elementary school. In less than 30 seconds, the bus turned left at the end of the block onto Sycamore Street, where you could see the high school directly ahead on the right side of the street. As soon as the bus stopped, the high school students began piling onto the bus. Girls first and then the boys. Nearly every seat was occupied after all the high school kids were on the bus.

As soon as everyone was seated, the bus driver made an immediate left turn directly in front of the high school onto Henrietta Street. Two short blocks later, we crossed over Walnut Street, one of only two main streets in all of Ravenswood. At the eastern edge of town, Walnut Street turned into West Virginia State Route 56, which headed east to Silverton. Walnut continued westward through a

First Day

residential section of Ravenswood to the town's business district. The single business street, aptly named Washington Street, after our first president, ran north-south and parallel with the Ohio River.

A minute or so after we crossed Walnut Street, the bus passed through a cluster of several residences in the very southeast quadrant of Ravenswood. The backsides of the homes on the right side of the street were all lined up along the rim of a deep embankment that descended down to a creek called Sand Creek. The place where Sand Creek flowed into the Ohio River was within eyesight of where the school bus crossed over the creek on its way out of Ravenswood.

The passageway over the creek was a single-lane steel bridge with a flimsy plank floor. The roadbed changed to gravel at the opposite end of the rickety bridge. The bus would follow this country road to our new farm and onward to the remote village of Millwood. Much of the way, the gravel road ran parallel to the Ohio River.

The distance from Ravenswood to the end of the school bus route at Millwood was about 12 miles. In a few spots, the road was too narrow for vehicles to safely pass each other unless both drivers slowed down considerably and were very cautious. Happily, my brother and I would ride the bus only eight miles before we reached our destination. Eight miles doesn't seem far in today's age of paved highways and interstates, but traveling on a countryside gravel road during the mid-1940s in a school bus, which made frequent stops...eight miles

9

Willow Grove: A Boy, A Family, A Farm

can easily amount to 45 minutes or more, even in the best of weather conditions.

Soon after the bus crossed the single-lane bridge over Sand Creek, it passed through a span of perfectly flat farming ground. A couple of minutes later, the bus came to the first farm south of Ravenswood. The property belonged to Blaine Hughes. The county road passed between the Hughes' white frame farmhouse on the right and their dairy barn and barnyard on the left. The front lawn of the family residence extended from the front porch to the berm of the road.

After leaving the Hughes' farm, the flat land abruptly disappeared, and the surrounding terrain became quite rough and steep. The road traced a gentle climb up alongside a rocky hillside and soon leveled out before continuing its parallel path along the Ohio River. The Baltimore & Ohio Railroad—B&O—was at a much lower elevation and incredibly close to the main road on the right side. The Ohio River was only slightly further down the steep embankment beyond the B&O tracks, and was mostly hidden from view by trees along the short stretch of road beyond the Hughes' farm.

On the left side of the road was a prominent rock cliff near the top of a steep hill. At the base of the rock cliff, the county road and railroad track snuggled close to each other, not far from the river. On October 29, 1770, a soon-to-be famous American, while floating down the Ohio River with his surveying party, saw the same prominent rock cliff and noted: "About a mile or a little better below

First Day

the mouth of the creek, there is another pavement of rocks on the east side in a kind of sedgy ground." The 38-year-old surveyor was George Washington, who would become the first president of the United States. The observation was from the diary he kept while on mission down the Ohio River at the behest of Governor Robert Dinwiddie of the British Commonwealth of Virginia. The creek that George Washington referred to in his diary was Sand Creek, the same stream which we had crossed over on the rickety bridge. I had a more personal connection to this very spot: nearly 200 years later, during road construction below the very same escarpment, a large boulder came tumbling down the hillside and slammed into the passenger side of the vehicle that my mother was driving. Brother John was with her, since he was too young for public school. The boulder hit the car so hard it shoved it off the road and close to the steep embankment descending to the railroad tracks. Amazingly, neither Mom nor brother John was hurt, though it was necessary to use construction equipment to pull the car back from the treacherous bank. Though the side of the car was heavily dented, it was drivable.

Even with the section of the road tucked between the base of the rock cliff on the left and the embankment on the right, there was still enough space for a postage-sized house. The frame house had a miniature front yard, while the back section of the house, which faced the Ohio River, extended perilously out over the edge of a steep bank and very close to the railroad track. The rear portion of the house was supported by several pylons, which were anchored into the side of the slope above the railroad track.

The school bus stopped at the house and let one student off—the first since we left Ravenswood High. By the time the driver reached out to manually close the twin bus doors, the young boy had already stepped out of the bus, opened a gate, run across the lawn, and bounded up onto the front porch.

Just beyond the tiny house, the bus came to a wide spot alongside the road. The spot was large enough for a driver to pull off the road and absorb an unobstructed panoramic view of the grand Ohio River and an impressive view of Great Bend, Ohio. The distant span of wide-open acreage showed a farming community of several hundred flat farmland acres, just beginning to show its fall colors.

From this same vantage point, you could see the beginning of a gigantic aerial sculpture formed by the Ohio River. The sculpture depicts a near-perfect outline of a mid-calf boot. The Great Bend community is situated inside the heel of the boot. The boot's insole, toe, and vamp are fashioned further down the river.

The big X in the accompanying diagram symbolizes Big Bend, Ohio, and the famous "great bend" in the Ohio River.

First Day

Winding Ohio River Forms a Near Perfect Boot

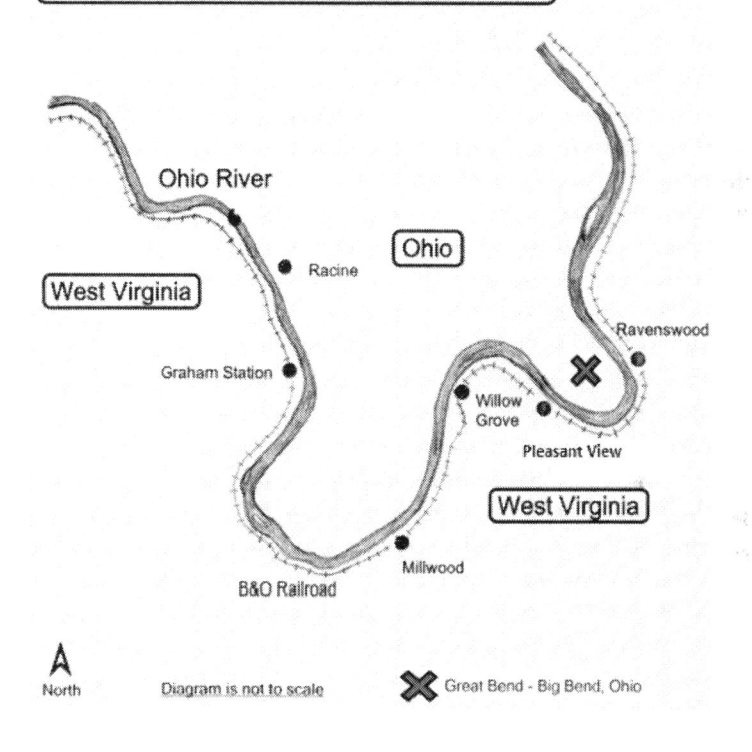

Ohio River
West Virginia
Racine
Ohio
Ravenswood
Graham Station
Willow Grove
Pleasant View
West Virginia
Millwood
B&O Railroad

North
Diagram is not to scale
✖ Great Bend - Big Bend, Ohio

Immediately after the observation area, the road made a 90-degree turn to the left, away from the river, and headed inland toward a rural community consisting of small farms and a few secluded homes. One of the larger parcels of land was a neatly manicured farm owned by Sammy Williams, an elderly gentleman about the same age as my

Willow Grove: A Boy, A Family, A Farm

grandfather. Sammy and his wife lived in their two-story farmhouse, nestled among huge shade trees around its perimeter. Later, my grandfather and Sammy became good friends, and sometimes when we were not in a hurry, grandfather and I would stop by and visit with Sammy and his wife.

Not much more than a stone's throw beyond Sammy Williams' farmhouse, the bus came to a quaint country church, Cedar Run Church, in the fork of the road. The bus driver took the right fork and followed the winding road through densely wooded countryside. Occasionally, you would see a tiny speck of flat land along a ravine where a farmer cultivated crops.

The gravel road traveled crookedly for almost a mile before arriving at the next bus stop. This family farm was owned by Wayne Hughes, brother of Blaine Hughes, whose farm was the first one we had passed shortly after leaving the fringe of Ravenswood.

On the right side of the bus, the scenic Ohio River came back into plain view for the first time since we passed the Great Bend observation overlook. Once again, the county road wasn't far from the Ohio River, but now was at a much lower elevation than at the observation post. The distance to the river was a five-minute walk across Mr. Hughes' wide-open cornfield. Right beside the road —not more than 50 feet—the B&O track continued its parallel course with both the public road and the Ohio River.

First Day

Ravenswood, Big Bend, Ohio & Willow Grove Farming Community

[Map showing: East To Silverton, Route 56, Sandy Creek, Ravenswood, Blaine Hughes, Rock Cliff, Sammy Williams, Big Bend Ohio, Rock Quarry, Cedar Run, Wayne Hughes, Cedar Run Church, Conrad McCoy, County Road, Rome Paar Farm, Pond, Spring Creek, Ohio River, Vernon McCoy, Raymond Casto, John Miller, South To Millwood, Dan McCoy, Wolverton Farm, B&O Railroad, Willow Grove Family Farm. Note: Schematic is close to scale.]

Leslie Hughes stepped down onto the edge of the road, crossed over in front of the bus, and commenced running up a short lane toward the dairy barn and family residence, which was partially obscured among shade trees in the front yard. Younger brothers Lyle and Butch were standing in the lane next to the dairy barn, watching Leslie as the school bus pulled away.

Willow Grove: A Boy, A Family, A Farm

At a modestly lower level than the road, the perfectly flat river bottom between the railroad track and river stretched over a quarter of a mile along the main road. The long rectangular-shaped field comprised all the land from the railroad track to the bank of the river. At the far end of the Hughes' cornfield was a ravine, which drained the unruly pasture fields and hills on the left side of the road into the Ohio River. This gully was also the property line between the Hughes farm and the next, equally attractive river bottom, one that I easily recognized. The river bottom was part of Pleasant View Farm, my cousins' home: John Paul, Eddie, Dottie, and James Conrad.

As the bus approached Pleasant View, the driver gradually raised his foot up off the throttle, and soon the bus whined to a complete stop. The bus driver waited a few seconds to open the door, giving the whirling dust bowl that had been chasing us time to sprint ahead of the bus and scatter. In hot weather, all of the windows were lowered, which allowed gulps of scratchy dust to spread throughout the inside of the bus. Open windows constituted the bus's only "air conditioning," and kids sitting beside the windows inhaled and tasted more than their share of brownish air.

From the left side of the bus, I could see the McCoy farmhouse perched majestically on a knoll well above the elevation of the bus stop. Just as the family's dog was waiting eagerly on the side of the road for the school bus to arrive, the handsome house seemed equally anxious for the safe return of

First Day

its energetic, hungry minors, who would soon increase the hustle and bustle in the house by several decibels. I could almost smell Aunt Edra's freshly baked bread from her country kitchen in the back of the house all the way to the bus stop. Thick slices of warm homemade bread smothered with a generous amount of homemade butter and grape jelly didn't have a chance after the cousins scurried through the kitchen door and greeted their smiling mother.

The front part of Uncle Conrad and Aunt Edra's house, the portion facing the bus stop, was built in 1847 and was originally occupied by Andrew Flesher, a West Virginia state senator and the first postmaster for the Pleasant View community. For the past 173 years, the occupants of the historical house have had a marvelous view of the Ohio River and the steamboats moving slowly up and down the river between Pittsburgh and New Orleans. From the front lawn all the way to the dairy barn, the massive Great Bend, Ohio, farming community was in full view on the opposite side of the river. On a quiet summer day, anyone sitting on the front porch could watch and hear the murmur of an occasional automobile across the river in Ohio, crawling slowly like a distant ant on the lone countryside road.

After all the cousins exited the bus, the driver continued south, still driving parallel with the Ohio River. The B&O railroad track on the right side of the bus remained slightly lower than the main road and was so close that a student could easily toss a marble underhand onto the railroad track from one of the windows. The continuous strip of tillable river bottom, which had commenced way back at the Hughes' bus stop, was in full view for one and a half miles.

The left side of the road was hillside pasture and completely fenced along the road from the cousins' bus stop to the furthermost end of their parents' farm. Here, the fence turned sharply away from the gravel road and continued at a near 90-degree angle up the side of a hillside pasture. At the same boundary point, the tillable river bottom ended with an abrupt beginning of a solid line of trees.

The terrain on both sides of the road was quite steep and heavily populated with mature hardwoods and water maples. For nearly a quarter of a mile, the trees on both sides of the road were so dense that they formed a continuous canopy above the road. The Ohio River was barely visible.

By now, the remaining kids on the bus were ready to get home. The road was dusty, and every time an automobile passed in either direction, all the passengers except the bus driver made a conscious effort not to inhale too much swirling grit before it settled on their books and clothing.

We were still traveling under the canopy of trees when the bus driver completely backed off the accelerator, pushed the clutch clear to the floorboard, and manually shifted the bus into a lower gear. Soon the bus's speed dwindled to practically a crawl. It was descending a slight bend

First Day

in the road toward a skinny, one-lane bridge that crossed over a wide and deep-shaded canyon. From a distance, the long steel bridge looked sturdy enough. Yet, the driver was gingerly coaxing the bus across the bridge at a snail's pace. I soon realized why the bus was sneaking across the spooky bridge. Looking straight down over the side of the bridge, I could see we were high above a gorge splattered with large, jagged boulders at the bottom. The wood planks on the bridge floor made an assortment of crackling, grinding, and grunting sounds as the front and dual rear wheels rolled over the end of one quivering plank onto the beginning of the next. I held my breath until the bus reached the opposite end of the bridge and its rear wheels were safely on solid ground.

I was glad when we had conquered the creepy bridge. It wouldn't be much longer before we would arrive at our Willow Grove bus stop.

After leaving the bridge, the bus had to climb a long incline. During the slow ascent to the top of the gorge, the driver had to keep the bus in its lowest gear and the gas pedal smashed against the floorboard. By the time we reached the top of the incline, it was obvious that the old groaning yellow bus had just endured a strenuous workout.

Halfway up the incline, bright sunshine suddenly lit up the inside of the bus, which signaled the tree-covered roadway and rough terrain were behind us. We were now entering wide-open, unobstructed farmland. Knowing that we were getting closer to the Gordon Kyle farm, I began

Willow Grove: A Boy, A Family, A Farm

to carefully scrutinize the surrounding farmland, ahead and on both sides of the school bus.

The Rome Paar farm was just beyond the peak of the incline at the top of the canyon. The farm's topography was totally flat. There wasn't much evidence of activity at the Paar farm, but there were indications that Mr. Paar took good care of his livestock and farm buildings. Just as at the Blaine Hughes farm, the Paar residence and cattle barns were strategically located close to and on opposite sides of the main road.

From the left side of the bus, I had a perfect view of Mr. Paar's weather-beaten cattle barn and a smattering of black Angus beef cattle roaming inside the corral next to the barn. Mr. and Mrs. Paar were sitting on the shaded front porch of their two-story frame home. As the bus accelerated toward the open countryside, the bus driver waved to the elderly couple. Mr. Paar answered by thrusting his cane high above his head.

The expanse of farmland visible through the bus's windshield was enormous. The land was level, and vigorous farming activity was evident in all directions. Immediately beyond the Paar residence, the road made a gentle turn to the right and then continued due west for about a mile. The cornfields on both sides were huge, and the road ahead was as straight as a broom handle. There was one large, stately shade tree in an enormous field on the left side of the road; otherwise, there were no visible trees anywhere, save those off in the distance, which lined and highlighted the east bank of the

First Day

Ohio River. Both sides of the road were fenced with barbwire to keep roaming cattle out of the tempting cornfields.

From the Paar farm, acres upon acres of hardy field corn populated both sides of the road. At the end of the mile-long straightaway, the road began a gradual curve to the left. At the very beginning of the lazy turn was a thriving dairy farm that I soon realized belonged to Vernon McCoy, my Uncle Conrad's brother. When I saw Richard and Dave reach for their schoolbooks, I knew the bus would be stopping at their farm. Ann, their older sister, was the first to bid the bus driver a cordial goodbye and step down off the bus. It would take Ann and the twins three or four minutes to walk to the front door of their home. The family's farmhouse was nestled gracefully amongst several shade trees at the end of a short lane—just beyond the barnyard. A handsome dairy barn, a tall silo, and adjacent farm buildings embellished the left side of the private lane.

The next bus stop was less than a quarter of a mile after the 90-degree bend in the road, which commenced at the McCoy's bus stop. Ray and Roy Rhodes were the next lucky students to arrive at their homes. As soon as their feet hit the ground, Ray kicked the front gate open, and the two boys sprinted across the front yard. The first one to grab the handle on the screen door was probably the hungriest. The brothers' two little sisters, Stella and Della, were standing inside the fenced yard beside the front gate, with their heads tilted back as they peered toward the open windows on the bus. Younger sister Della marveled at the sight of the big yellow bus as the driver closed the door and continued down the road.

Shortly after the school bus pulled away from the Rhodes' home, I saw the bus driver glance in the rear-view mirror directly above his head. The driver looked directly at me and with a warm smile nodded his head. His friendly gesture assured me that the next stop would be where Bob and I would get off. When I saw him glance in the rear-view mirror, my heart was thumping with excitement. I motioned to my brother to get his books and be ready. The driver muscled the long lever, which opened the two exit doors beside his seat. I was halfway out of my seat when the bus came to a complete stop. Bob and I carefully maneuvered ourselves down the center aisle. When I reached the front of the bus, I hesitated, turned, and looked directly into the bus driver's eyes: "Sir, thank you very much!" I would later learn that Bob and I were related to the bus driver. My paternal grandmother's mother was a Shockey, which was also the surname of the bus driver.

Bob and I scampered down the two giant steps at the front of the bus and walked a few steps away from the bus. Both of our faces were plastered with broad smiles. We waved to the bus driver as he closed the folding doors, and then stood motionless for a few moments, watching as the bus lurched forward each time the driver shifted into a higher gear.

First Day

Still standing in the middle of the lane beside the county road, I was captivated by the spectacular view all around us. In every direction, the flat terrain was enchanting. There was absolutely no doubt in my mind that Willow Grove was going to be a joyful place. We had definitely arrived at a new frontier!

Willow Grove

Shortly after the end of World War II, while visiting with his daughter Edra and her husband, Conrad McCoy, my grandfather learned that Conrad and his brother Dan were contemplating buying a large farm in the Willow Grove farming community, presently owned by Gordon Kyle, a furniture entrepreneur in the state capital of Charleston, West Virginia. Uncle Conrad asked grandfather if he would be interested in partnering with him and his brother. The discussion eventually developed into a partnership between Conrad and Grandpa when Dan decided not to participate, since he already owned an excellent farm within eyesight of the Kyle property.

Grandpa and Uncle Conrad owned the Kyle farm for about six months before they sold one-third of the farm to my parents. Dad and Grandpa purchased Uncle Conrad's one-third interest in the Willow Grove farm two years later.

The Willow Grove farm was an incredible investment and a rewarding endeavor for my parents and grandparents. Our new Willow Grove

Willow Grove: A Boy, A Family, A Farm

farm occupied 211 acres and was one of nearly a dozen magnificent, similar-sized farms, all with ample shorelines along the grand Ohio River. My parents had described it as a big farm with several buildings and a bountiful amount of idyllic flat land, perfect for growing corn and hay crops for a herd of dairy cattle. Because my grandfather's health was poor, all day-to-day operations and physical management of the farm fell on my father's shoulders and on the hired help, who occupied three tenant houses on the farm.

The only practical access to the Willow Grove community was a public road, and, when we traveled north to Ravenswood or south to Millwood, it was easy to appreciate the outstanding farming characteristics of every one of the individual farms we could see on our trip. At an early age, I recognized that all the Willow Grove properties had one vitally important attribute: large acreages of pancake-flat fertile soil, ideal for growing hay and corn crops. In addition, all the dairy farms had proud, committed owners and loyal farmhands who contributed to the profitability of the farms. Like my father, the ardent and devoted landowners knew how to manage their farms and, along with the help of their diligent employees, they understood and faithfully applied what it took to properly care for herds of prime dairy cattle.

Though Dad was responsible for the actual physical operation of the Willow Grove farm, Grandma handled the bookkeeping duties for the farm business. Grandpa advised and consulted

Willow Grove

with my father regarding any capital for new equipment and special projects that needed to be addressed during the typical workday. As usual, my mother took care of her multiple obligations as a homemaker, plus she always had additional tasks outside the kitchen. Whenever necessary and if no one else was available, she would also help my father around the barnyard, in the hayfields, and, on many occasions, run important and unanticipated errands to Ravenswood or Ripley. Growing up on the Willow Grove farm with my parents, brothers, grandparents, and grandmother's sister—all living harmoniously in a 1900s historic brick home—was truly remarkable and so important during my formative years.

Pleasant View is a rolling hill farming community along the Ohio River three miles north of Willow Grove. Before the "horseless carriage," steamboats delivered passengers, mail, and retail dry goods to the Pleasant View and the Willow Grove general stores. The two general stores were about a half-hour apart via a horse and buggy ride over an inland dirt road. Post offices were conveniently located inside the general stores at their respective steamboat landings.

When my family moved to Willow Grove in 1946, the Willow Grove and Pleasant View communities had a dozen large farms, of which eight were successful dairy farms and four were beef and crop farms. All the dairy and crop farms had perfectly flat river bottoms along the Ohio River. Three of the eight dairy farms were owned and operated by brothers Conrad, Dan, and Vernon McCoy, and their sister, Constance, and her husband, Matson King, owned a fourth dairy farm.

Three of the eight dairy farms were located north of our farm, and four were south. The northern farms were owned by brothers Vernon and Conrad McCoy and Wayne Hughes. The dairy farms south of our farm were owned by Raymond Casto, Dan McCoy, John Miller, and Matson King.

Bob and I had just stepped down onto the edge of the road. We watched as the school bus drove away and continued on to Millwood, the last stop on the bus route. The translucent clouds of roiling dust from behind the bus had almost disappeared as it approached the next bus stop. We could see several large shade trees in the yard of a white, two-story Victorian farmhouse where Hazel and Buzzy Casto lived. Slightly hidden and tucked in behind the Casto house was the home of Sharon, Phyllis, and Jimmy McCoy.

Standing in the middle of the lane, Bob and I stopped to appreciate the spectacular view all around us. In every direction, the view was more than I could ever have imagined! A cluster of buildings in the distance revealed a red barn, a tall white silo, and several adjacent buildings. Beyond the red barn and silo was a group of large trees and the roofline of another structure, which I correctly surmised was our new home. My parents said the house was a large two-story brick with lots of spacious rooms. I could see the roof was decked with several chimneys. The scene from the bus stop

Willow Grove

was sensational, and I knew right away that my brothers and I were going to love living on our new farm. I couldn't wait to explore every building, one by one, and walk every acre of the land. Life couldn't have been more exciting than it was at that moment.

With our schoolbooks tucked tight under our arms, Bob and I began running. We hadn't run very far before we spotted our mother standing beside the big red barn. She had watched us get off the school bus and was waiting to walk together down the lane to our new house.

The closer we got to the farm buildings, the more excited I became about our new Willow Grove farm. All I could think about was exploring every structure within eyesight. As we approached our mother and the array of farm buildings, my eyes were pulled toward the sky-high barn on the left side of the lane. The barn was fewer than 100 feet from the edge of the lane and lengthwise was parallel with the road we were walking on. I hadn't realized how many different structures were huddled around the huge barn. I could see a shed, two circular corn cribs next to a wood fence, and a concrete silo at the end of the big barn. They were precisely what a storybook farm would look like. A short distance from the barn was a concrete block pump house, which provided cool running water for all the farm buildings and the two primary residences. As we walked past the barn, I had a clear view of the two-story red brick house in the distance and a single-story, matching brick

Willow Grove: A Boy, A Family, A Farm

residence located just to the left of the main dwelling. Aesthetically, the smaller brick house, where my grandparents would live, was in complete harmony with the main house and likely had been built at the same time with the same homemade, unfired orange bricks. Several mature shade trees accented both houses. Beyond the houses, I could see the other side of the wide Ohio River and the edge of a seemingly miniature road crowded up against a wall, dwarfed by a tall, vertical rock cliff.

Our farm at Willow Grove.
Note the "little house" to the right.

As we approached the brick house, I was struck by its charm. The handsome building had such a warm and inviting appearance, appropriate for a mid-1800s Virginia plantation. Our happy faces

Willow Grove

were adorned with broad pearly white smiles. Everything was so different from our previous home at Silverton! So magnificent and exciting! Willow Grove was going to be a great playground for my brothers and me.

My first impression of the main house's interior was as grand as it was earlier from the outside. We entered the house through a side door directly off a patio that opened into Mom's new kitchen. Mom had worked very hard for days, cleaning, painting, and organizing her new workspace. The spacious room had two tall windows. One window above the kitchen sink faced south out over a concrete patio that connected our big house with my grandparents' house. The other tall window in the kitchen faced eastward toward the dairy barn and silo. The kitchen table was conveniently centered in the middle of the room. The Warm Morning wood stove, refrigerator, and the cupboards for dishes and cookware were all neatly arranged along the walls.

The kitchen was connected to another large room with an efficient early American fireplace. This would be our family room. Right beside the doorway from Mom's kitchen were two other identical doors. One opened into a king-sized laundry room with its own wood-burning fireplace and lavatory. Directly outside the washroom was a hefty porch that stepped down to the concrete patio between our house and my grandparents' house.

This side porch, with its swing sofa and several cushioned wrought iron chairs, would become one of my father's favorite summertime places to relax in the evening after supper. The porch was a perfect spot to take in a cool breeze as it marched across the patio from the shade trees out in the yard and an excellent place to watch the sun disappear behind the hills on the other side of the Ohio River.

There were seven fireplaces in the house—all with painted white mantles. Four rooms on the first floor had fireplaces. Directly above the outside wall fireplace in Mom's family room on the first floor was a matching fireplace in my parents' bedroom on the second floor. Three of the five bedrooms had fireplaces.

The five bedrooms and full bath on the second floor of the main house were quite spacious. At one time, the landing at the bottom of the staircase leading to the bedrooms had a second door that opened outdoors onto the roomy side porch outside the laundry room. The entry had been very convenient for the servants, who could quietly enter

Willow Grove

the second-floor bedrooms and fulfill their house cleaning duties, completely unnoticed by the occupants in the active downstairs living quarters. When we lived at Willow Grove, the door had been eliminated and the space filled in with brick. The entire house comprised approximately 3600 square feet.

Willow Grove Second Floor Bedrooms

- Bob, Jr. Bedroom
- Full Bath
- Aunt Jack Bedroom
- Parents, John Bedroom
- Closet
- Front Foyer
- Guest Bedroom Klingbergs Family Winter 1950
- Guest Bedroom Summer Bedroom Grandparents
- Cousin Dewey Gene Summers
- Fire Place
- Small Oil Stove

North

Courtesy of John E. Suek

Bob and I shared the bedroom directly above our mother's kitchen. We had the most practical bedroom in the house. It was at the end of an open hallway overlooking the back staircase and, most important, next to a bathroom that was kept toasty warm during frigid winter weather. It was a bathroom that anyone living in the early 1900s, whether in an urban or rural community, would appreciate. The full bathroom was always wonderfully comfortable, thanks to an efficient oil stove that burned night and day in the winter months. Everyone in the family appreciated the rare, modern convenience during cold weather! It was certainly a luxury!

Willow Grove farmhouse from the side.

After a quick tour of both floors of our new home, I changed into my everyday clothes and hurried out to find my father. He was working somewhere around the barnyard, and I was anxious to see him and begin exploring.

Before I left to go find Dad, Mom took Bob and me next door to see our grandparents in their new house. The kitchen doors of both homes faced each other, and both opened out onto the handy concrete patio. The two kitchen doors would host nearly all of the foot traffic for both houses since the formal front doors, which faced the Ohio River, were not nearly as convenient for the numerous daily trips to and from the dairy barn. Mom's

Willow Grove

kitchen door was also convenient for Mom to keep an eye on me and my brothers while we were playing in the side yard, as well as providing quick access to our vegetable gardens.

After seeing my grandparents, I headed straight for the barn to find Dad. It was a historic day for me, and from now on I could look forward to living every day with my grandparents, parents, and brothers on a large, wonderful farm. As I ran toward the barn, my head was constantly twisting from one side of the lane to the other, taking in all the new sights. I didn't want to miss anything!

On the left side of the lane, about halfway between the pump house and our new home, was the largest sycamore tree that I'd ever seen. The branches on the gigantic tree extended clear out over the lane on one side and way out into a pasture field on the opposite side. Moreover, it was at least 30 feet from the ground to the first ring of massive branches around the tree. When I reached the massive sycamore tree, I looked up and marveled at how far it was from the ground to the lowest branch and how far out the limbs extended above my head. The branches shaded a healthy portion of the distance from the side yard to the pump house. The tree was truly a colossal monument that I would admire every day during the great nine years that we lived in Willow Grove.

I raced up the lane past the pump house, ran diagonally across a perpendicular side road, and then slowed down when I reached an open door at the end of the barn. A lot of work would have to be

Willow Grove: A Boy, A Family, A Farm

done before Dad could begin milking our dairy herd at Willow Grove. Dad was busy ripping out heavy, decades-old boards from horse stalls so he could pour concrete and install individual iron pipe stanchions for the Holstein dairy cows. The barn was partitioned with roomy, individual wood stalls for huge draft horses, which previous owners used in the 1800s and early 1900s to till the land and harvest crops. It wasn't built or equipped to milk dairy cows. The entire ground floor of the barn would have to be completely gutted and a row of individual stanchions installed along both sides for the dairy cows. In addition, a new milk house would have to be built adjacent to the ground floor entrance to the barn.

After talking with Dad, I began scouring the inside of the barn and soon found a rugged wooden ladder in the center of the barn that led up to an opening in the floor of the hayloft. The wide-open hayloft was enormous. It was separated in the middle by a clear path, where loose hay was unloaded from horse-drawn wagons. I soon realized that the open space in the center of the loft would be an excellent place for a basketball net. It wasn't long before Bob and I cut the bottom out of a bushel basket and nailed it on the inside of the barn. We spent many hours shooting baskets in the hayloft on rainy summer days and cold winter afternoons.

The Willow Grove farm was 211 acres of farmland configured in the general shape of a rectangle. The west end of the farm bordered the

Willow Grove

Ohio River and, from the river, extended eastward for over a mile. The substantial rolling pasture field was embellished with a large pond filled with largemouth bass. Most of the land was premium, flat acreage nestled between the farm dwellings and hill pasture.

From the hayloft, I ran outside through a wide opening in the side of the barn. I continued down an earthen slope onto a semicircular driveway, which extended from one end to past the other end of the barn. The crescent-shaped driveway linked up on both ends with the lane that ran from the main county road past the farm buildings and stopped just beyond the main house at the railroad track. Close by the semicircular driveway were two circular metal corn cribs and a tool shed, which I explored to see what tools and farm machinery had been left behind by the previous owner.

Everything about the Willow Grove farm was ideal for a knowledgeable dairy farmer. The size of the farm was large enough to yield an abundance of good corn and hay, which together comprised the primary sustenance for dairy cattle. Every acre of the farm could be fully utilized. All the farm buildings, including the two primary farmhouses, were wisely concentrated on the northwest corner of the farm. Both main houses faced the Ohio River and were at an elevation high enough that floodwater wouldn't be an issue. Also, the dairy barn, barnyard, and various farm buildings were perfectly huddled a short distance from the farmhouses, leaving all the surrounding acreage

Willow Grove: A Boy, A Family, A Farm

Willow Grove, WV Farming Community

Courtesy of Hazel Casto Parsons

Willow Grove

Willow Grove: A Boy, A Family, A Farm

uninterrupted for three large contiguous hay- and cornfields. All the tillable ground was gravel and sand sub-soil covered with rich topsoil. The gravel functioned as a sponge that lessened water puddles from forming on the topsoil during heavy summer rains.

I was only seven years old when we moved from Silverton to Willow Grove, yet I was quite cognizant of the characteristics that constituted a high-quality farm. I had gone on many trips with my father and grandfather to visit a number of different farms, and had listened to the adults discuss different topographies and what made one farm more attractive than another. Our new farm in Willow Grove was one of those ideal properties, which, even as a youngster, I could readily appreciate the moment my brother and I stepped off the school bus and saw the marvelous landscape for the first time. From the fall of 1946 to the spring of 1955, my family would cultivate and take excellent care of the farm, which prospered due to my father's long hours of hard work during those nine extraordinary years. Every year bumper crops of field corn grew higher than the year before. The Willow Grove farm was a prime piece of land, and my family wasn't the first to recognize the superior value of thousands of acres at Willow Grove.

On October 20, 1770, George Washington, the future first president of the United States, left Pittsburgh with a group of men on a surveying trip

Willow Grove

down the Ohio River. Along the way, Washington recorded his comments about several exceptional pieces of flat land on both sides of the Ohio River. Washington specifically described attractive sections of fertile land at Washington Bottom, Ravenswood, Belleville, Millwood, and Point Pleasant, West Virginia, and Long Bottom, Ohio. Washington was impressed with these parcels and recorded his observations using laudatory comments, such as "...through a fine piece of land that was very good in appearance,..." for the Belleville parcel. Moreover, when Washington described the 4,000-plus acres of land near Millwood, he was even more laudatory and used words like VERY FINE, EXCEEDINGLY VALUABLE, and EXCEEDINGLY RICH to draw special attention to the land that would eventually become the Willow Grove-Millwood farming community.

About three years later, in 1773, George Washington asked for and was granted by King George III of England ownership of a dozen parcels of land totaling some 40,000 acres which Washington described as "choice land." One of four parcels granted to Washington was 4,395 acres above Millwood that Washington was so impressed with and subsequently was referred to as Warth's Bottom. Later, in the early 1900s, the same land was known as Willow Grove. The other nearby parcels were Washington Bottom, Ravenswood, and Point Pleasant.

In the book *Washington, The Making of the American Capital*, George Washington described "...

Willow Grove: A Boy, A Family, A Farm

and more than twenty thousand acres on the Ohio and Great Kanawha rivers, in present-day West Virginia, 'the cream of the country.'" Later, during the French and Indian War, George Washington took advantage of the "bounty lands" given to colonial enlistees by King George III to fight for Great Britain "...and parlayed it into tremendous personal holdings in the Ohio [Valley]."

After George Washington died in 1799, the parcel of land at Willow Grove was inherited by his niece, Harriet Washington Park, and her husband, Andrew. Sometime after 1803, the same vast acreage of prime land was acquired by John Warth, an influential citizen of nearby Ravenswood. During the time Warth lived in Willow Grove, he served as justice of the peace and school commissioner. Throughout this same period in his life, the enterprising young man lived and worked on his farm at Willow Grove. On March 1, 1831, Jackson County was formed, and Willow Grove was chosen as its temporary county seat. On May 23 of the same year, the very first county court meeting was held in John Warth's home in Willow Grove, which at the time was also commonly referred to as "Warth's Bottom."

While John Warth lived in Willow Grove, the rural community became a popular landing spot for flatboats and eventually steamboats going up and down the Ohio River. The farming community had its own post office, general store, and later passenger train service. The stately brick home that I was so fortunate to live in for nearly a decade was

Willow Grove

less than a hundred yards from all three of the public services. Anecdotally, the John Warth residence would have been built on the same spot as my family's stately home.

Before paved roads, rural residences and accompanying farm buildings were commonly built as close as reasonably possible to public service roads, for very practical reasons. Freezing and thawing weather cycles in early spring effectively transformed countryside roads into passages that were difficult and sometimes risky to navigate. Additionally, private roads could become impossible to navigate in a motor vehicle, so walking or riding a horse wasn't uncommon.

Ravenswood Landing, with Grandfather's brother, George Earnest, in the car.

When we moved to Willow Grove, the dwellings, barns, and ancillary structures of all 12 farms in

Willow Grove: A Boy, A Family, A Farm

the farming community were located right beside or very close to the public road, which was inland, a considerable distance from the Ohio River. That is, all except two farms: my family's farm and the Wolverton farm, our next-door neighbor to the north.

Due to the strategic location of the river landing and, later, the general store at Willow Grove, these two early residences and their respective clusters of farm buildings embraced land near the Ohio River instead of land close to an interior public road. The landing at Willow Grove was the most practical doorway to the farming community for keelboats and later steamboats going up and down the river.

The Willow Grove landing was at the leading edge of a half-moon-shaped river bottom of a few hundred acres. The beginning and end of the mile-long river bottom were close to and equidistant from the Ohio River. However, the terrain at the southern end of the arc was steep and impractical to navigate compared to the northern or upper end of the river bottom. By far, the upper end of the crescent was the best path from the river to a higher, non-flood plain and, consequently, a prime riverboat landing for Willow Grove. When George Washington and his surveying crew were floating down the Ohio River, the same spot on the upper end of the crescent would have been the best place to disembark to survey the "very fine land." I wrote the text to explain why George Washington very likely landed his canoes at that particular spot and why it was a practical and logical spot for a future

Willow Grove

Willow Grove landing and the birth of a new farming community. George Washington stopped and surveyed Willow Grove in October 1770. His diary was reprinted in detail in the "Ravenswood News" in 1900 and again in Dean Moore's book *Washington's Woods*, published in 1971.

On a macro scale, the Willow Grove landing was about midway through the farming community, convenient for citizens in both the northern and southern parts of the community.

The part of our lane, which was straight as an arrow and about three-fourths of a mile in length, ran from the railroad crossing to an iron gate at the entrance to the daytime hill pasture. The lane was snug up against the northern property line between our farm and the Wolverton and Walker farms. At the lane's midpoint and intersection with the county road at the school bus building, our property line with our Wolverton neighbor ceased and continued on the other side of the road with the Walker farm. The length of our farm from the Ohio River to the rear boundary was over a mile.

At the entrance to the daytime pasture field, the road veered slightly to the right and away from the previously perfectly straight road. At the iron gate, the front portion of the pasture field was flat for a short distance before the road dipped down into a shallow stream, which flowed across the entire width of the pasture. The creek was clean water for thirsty animals grazing in the front part of the pasture. It was also an excellent place for a refreshing drink of pure water—providing you didn't drink downstream from where a few of the cattle were standing in the creek. Upstream was okay! The water was as crystal clear as a Wyoming trout stream.

Slightly beyond the creek, the road commenced up the side of a high ridge, which spanned the whole width of the farm and ran parallel to the ravine. From the top of the ridge, you could look back toward the west and see all our tillable farmland, farm buildings, tree-lined Ohio River, and the state of Ohio on the horizon. The bird's eye view from the top of the hill was a remarkable sight every time we descended the steep hill in an automobile or on one of the farm tractors.

The scene toward the north was a panoramic view of our northern neighbors: the Rome Paar farm, Bill Walker's farm, and, way in the distance along a bend in the Ohio River, was the Vernon McCoy dairy farm. The farm buildings and residence of Raymond Casto, our immediate neighbor to the south, were equally visible from the top of the hill, as was Dan McCoy's residence—the next farm below the Casto farm.

The best part of our hill pasture was on the east or far side of the ridge. The cattle preferred the spacious backside of the pasture because the terrain was gentler and produced more lush grass than the front part. The rolling hillside was sprinkled with a few shade trees, where the cattle would stand or lie under after filling their stomachs with green grass. Moreover, there was a three-acre body of freshwater that was one of the finest farm ponds in Jackson County. The pond provided our animals with a second source of fresh drinking water and a perfect spot to cool off during hot weather.

View of our farm pond.

A Day in Paradise

The Willow Grove farm was a dairy farmer's dream. The land was eminently suitable for the operation of a successful dairy business. In 1770, George Washington, our first president, was among

Willow Grove: A Boy, A Family, A Farm

the first to recognize and record the value of the fertile land along the Ohio River. From 1946 to 1955, the Willow Grove farm prospered and generated a good standard of living and a healthy lifestyle for three full-time families. During the busy summer and fall harvesting seasons, income from the farm also paid the salaries of additional employees. The farm's income was substantial enough to accommodate quarterly mortgage payments on the $40,000 loan used to purchase the farm in 1946. By 1955, the loan was all but paid off—a mere nine years later. And notwithstanding the perfect topography and richness of the land, the financial success of the Willow Grove farm was principally due to the unrelenting, consistently hard work of my father—seven days a week, 365 days a year.

My father's dedication to the family dairy business was solid to the core. During the years we lived in the acclaimed Willow Grove farming community, my father was in partnership with his father. Dad worked long hours to ensure that the income from the sale of raw milk was sufficient to meet the farm's weekly payroll. At least three families, sometimes more, depended on the farm income. Money was also needed to cover general farm operating expenses and make the quarterly mortgage payments. The extra income was used to maintain existing machinery and buy new farm equipment, such as a new tractor, wagon, or hay rake.

A Day in Paradise

For 10 years, Dad and Grandpa worked side by side, along with their wives, to ensure the success of the family farm. Early on, Grandfather's declining health prohibited him from doing any physical labor. This left my father, more than ever, wholly responsible for making sure all farm work was completed and in a manner that met his father's strict work ethics and high quality standards. Nearly every evening, Grandpa would walk into Mom's kitchen while we were eating supper and chat with Dad about specific jobs completed during the day. Occasionally, Dad would humbly disagree with his father's advice, but never did he say anything that would contradict his father. Instead, he listened politely and, without any reluctance, followed through with his father's wishes. They would end their discussion by reviewing special projects that needed to be contemplated within the next day or so.

My father's responsibilities at Willow Grove were generally the same as they had been since he was a young man working with his father on their dairy farm at Silverton. His task was to make sure that every routine chore was completed by the end of the day. Year-round, the quantity of daily work on the farm was too much for one man to handle. Dad always had at least one good, dependable adult to help him keep up with the chores. He worked alongside the hired help and provided guidance when necessary. Dad would employ extra men during the summer months when farm work and harvesting were the heaviest. The farm had three small houses, which were occupied by full time and seasonal employees and their families. Not once did I ever witness any friction between Dad and any of the hired men. The men were treated like family and, in turn, were loyal workers. Dad maintained an excellent rapport with all the men he worked with and supervised. Furthermore, he never expected any of the men to do anything he wouldn't do. If a chore was tough, sensitive, or required experience, Dad would take the lead and perform the job himself. Dad knew what jobs needed to be done, and if necessary, he would work late into the night. At the end of the day, "the buck stopped" with Dad.

    The principal income from the farm came from the sale of whole milk to a milk-processing company in Charleston. The amount of money we received for our milk was based on both butter-fat content and the total pounds of milk shipped each day to the Valley Bell creamery. Ten-gallon cans of milk were picked up early every day and transported by truck.

    It was imperative that the farm ship as many pounds of milk as possible. Dad made sure the farm was effectively managed to support a sizable herd of dairy cattle. He knew how important it was that every dairy cow was as productive as possible. Dad rose every morning before five to start his daily routine. While the hired help rounded up the dairy cows in the nearby night pasture by the Ohio River, Dad assembled the milking equipment. Afterward, he would help herd the dairy cows from the

A Day in Paradise

barnyard into the dairy barn, where each one would be manually fastened in individual stanchions.

After all the cows were milked, and breakfast was over, Dad would return to the barn and complete additional daily chores, chores that were essential to properly care for the dairy cattle and prepare them for the subsequent, late afternoon milking. During the middle part of the day, Dad and the men would work around the farm and in the fields until a little before four in the afternoon, when he and one employee would get ready to milk the dairy cows for the second time that day. On a typical day, Dad would return to the kitchen for supper by around six o'clock. Except for a quick breakfast and an hour break at noon for dinner—today's contemporary lunch—Dad worked this same schedule every day except Sunday. The Sunday slice of the day after the morning and before the late afternoon milking was for relaxation and family time. Short of any unforeseen problems that required immediate attention, Grandpa was adamant about not working on Sunday! Except for milking the cows and caring for the farm animals, he would not allow anyone to work on the Sabbath.

Dad's only time off to relax and spend time with his family was on Sunday. There were occasions when his casual time was interrupted, and he ended up working most of the day. Something unexpected would happen, such as a neighbor might call and report that some of our cattle had broken through the property line fence and were wandering around on his property, or the conveyor

Willow Grove: A Boy, A Family, A Farm

chain broke on the automatic manure cleaner system, making it impossible to clean out the dairy barn without first repairing the broken link. Replacing a broken link in the manure conveyor chain was time-consuming and not an easy repair.

My father worked for the Jackson County Agriculture Extension Service for several years during his free time on Sundays. Large and small farmers throughout the county would telephone during the week and schedule an appointment with Dad to come to their farm and artificially inseminate one or more milk cows. During the early 1950s, there were over 130 dairy farms in Jackson County, and on many Sundays, Dad would have multiple appointments. In addition to making a little extra money for the family, artificial insemination performed a public service for the county. It was also a good way for Dad to obtain expensive semen from certified bulls worth thousands of dollars. Over a short period, Dad utilized the valuable semen to build up a large herd of highly productive Holstein dairy cows.

During the decade that we lived at Willow Grove, I can only recall two occasions when my father failed to get up in the morning to milk our herd of dairy cows. In one instance, he was so sick and weak with the flu that he couldn't get out of bed. Happily, his teenage nephew John Paul McCoy came to the rescue and milked our dairy cows for a few days. On the other occasion, my parents, brothers, and I were on a real vacation. I think this was the only vacation my parents ever took when

A Day in Paradise

we lived at Willow Grove. We went to Rock Creek, in northeast Ohio, to visit Dad's Aunt Ollie and her family. During the brief vacation, we drove a little further north and dipped our toes in Lake Erie. Seeing the huge lake was a big deal for all of us.

During the trip, the bottom of the heel on my left foot became abscessed. The pain was excruciating, and the only relief was to elevate the foot. Mom made a bed in the back of our Chevy station wagon for me on our long trip home. We stopped at the doctor's office in Ravenswood before we continued home. The doctor X-rayed and lanced the abscess. The tip of my heel bone was broken, which explained why my foot had been painful for several weeks. The abscess resulted from walking on the broken bone, caused most likely from jumping barefoot out of the dairy barn hayloft onto the wood floor.

Other than those two occasions, Dad personally made sure that every animal on the farm was properly cared for and that the dairy cows were milked twice each day. The vacuum pump that ran the automatic milking equipment was turned on precisely at 6:00 a.m. and 4:00 p.m. Dad understood how vital it was to keep the dairy cattle on a strict schedule since the amount of milk shipped each day to the Valley Bell creamery was our sole source of income. Farmers who consistently adhered to a strict regimen for their dairy cattle were usually successful. In contrast, undisciplined dairy farms of the same size, same topography, and same resources often failed

Willow Grove: A Boy, A Family, A Farm

financially, ending up in various forms of disarray. Sometimes bankruptcy!

I remember trying to reach up with one hand to touch the silver tassels on top of corn stalks in our cornfield at Willow Grove. To come close, I had to stand on top of the rear tire of our Farmall C tractor. I never actually measured the height of the corn stalks, but I know they were unusually high. In David McCullough's book *The Pioneers*, in 1787, Rufus Putman saw corn stalks 14 feet high at Marietta, Ohio. I would not be surprised if our corn at Willow Grove didn't reach that height.

Every year, the alfalfa and orchard grass fields were heavier and more luscious than the year before. Some years the hay was so high and thick that Dad had to drive the tractor in low gear to mow the field. There were times, after Dad baled heavy windrows of dry hay, when the compacted bales lying on the ground were so close to one another that I could almost cross the entire hayfield by jumping from one hay bale to the next—never touching the ground.

More bountiful crops year after year allowed Dad to increase the size of our dairy herd. More dairy cows meant more milk, and more milk meant more revenue. The acreage, texture, richness of the soil, and the topography were magnificent!

The Willow Grove farm was certainly a prime piece of land. Uncle Conrad, Grandpa, and my father were not the first to recognize the attributes of the Willow Grove land. The indigenous Indians

A Day in Paradise

and later, in October 1770, a young surveyor named George Washington were among the first!

It was a long walk from the barnyard to the hill pasture. The cattle knew the routine, and every morning after milking they were ready to make the 20-minute trek. As soon as the vacuum pump on the automatic milking machines was shut off and all of the dairy cows unlatched from their individual stanchions, the cows would begin to crowd together inside the closed barnyard gate. Once the gate was opened, the herd would move spiritedly through the gate and head down the lane. As soon as the first cow reached the main road, whoever was walking in front of the cattle would check to see if any cars were approaching from either direction. Most of the time, there wasn't a vehicle in sight, and when one did appear, the considerate driver would stop at a safe distance to keep from spooking the herd. Once across the main road, it was a short distance to the hill pasture entrance. The cows would graze and rest under the shade trees until it was time to reverse the daily routine and drive the cattle back to the barnyard. The switch for the vacuum pump was turned on, and the first of three automatic Surge milking machines was placed on the first cow at exactly four o'clock.

The main house and adjacent tenant house faced the Ohio River and overlooked the northern tip of our triangular-shaped river bottom. The front lawn of the main residence covered at least a half-acre from the house to the edge of the railroad track. The mild slope in the front yard toward the

Willow Grove: A Boy, A Family, A Farm

B&O Railroad tracks was so slight it was barely noticeable. And since the track itself was on a lower plane than the front yard, the railroad tracks didn't detract from the splendid panoramic view of the Ohio River.

My brothers and I loved to stand on the top of the embankment at the edge of the front yard and watch as a freight train approached and billowed vast plumes of jet-black coal smoke high into the sky. We stood and watched as a gigantic B&O engine lumbered ponderously past our house, pulling a hundred or more hopper cars piled high with chunks of glistening, bituminous coal. As the mighty locomotive passed in front of us, my brothers and I were at eye level with the engineer, who was seated comfortably with his arm resting on the padded bottom of the open window.

Fall Butchering

Butchering was always a big annual event at Willow Grove. Every fall, as soon as the daytime temperature was consistently on the chilly side and the nights remained crispy cool, Grandpa and Dad would butcher several hogs and at least one full-grown steer. Both day and nighttime temperatures needed to be on the cool side because afterward, the butchered sides of meat had to hang outdoors.

Butchering was an event in which everyone was involved. Each person had a special job to perform to preserve as much fresh meat as possible. These activities included Grandpa, Dad, the hired help,

Fall Butchering

and support from my mother, grandmother, and Aunt Jack. The women had to synchronize their jobs with the men so that cuts of meat and organs weren't wasted because of improper handling. Most of the fresh cuts of pork and beef were wrapped in heavy white paper and packed in two top-loading freezers.

Other family members and friends would come to the farm to help with butchering tasks that commenced well before daybreak and lasted late into the evening. Seventeen long hours of arduous, non-stop work were not uncommon. It would be close to midnight before Mom could stop, sit down, and relax a few quiet moments before she would retire to the upstairs bedroom. Pleasantly exhausted, everyone else was in bed and would sleep sound after working all day, cutting and packaging fresh pork and beef!

My grandfather had decades of experience, so when he advised the family that it was time to butcher, the countdown began. It would take a day or two to round up empty 55-gallon drums, gather firewood, sharpen all the various butchering knives, and locate several horse singletrees, rope, pulleys, and other pertinent supplies.

A couple of specialized items were necessary before the actual butchering could begin. First, two A-frames had to be constructed using long, sturdy wood poles. The A-frames were held together at the top by a stiff horizontal pole. The pole and A-frames had to be strong enough to support the weight of three or four pigs, each of which could weigh 220 to

Willow Grove: A Boy, A Family, A Farm

280 pounds. Next, three 55-gallon drums filled to the top with water had to be stationed close to one of the A-frames. Two of the drums were set on top of concrete blocks, high enough off the ground to build a fire underneath both drums. A third 55-gallon drum was placed under a tripod with a pulley dangling from the peak of the tripod. Nearby, a long table would serve as a workstation for cutting and segregating different cuts of meat.

    The evening before butchering day, Grandpa went to a designated drawer in the house and gathered his butchering tools, including various knives, saws, meat cleavers, and sharping stones. Grandpa and his brother John, visiting with his wife, Mary, from Pittsburgh, sat around the kitchen table and socialized while they checked each tool and made sure all the knives were razor sharp and ready. Grandma would gather all of her large pots, pans, and ancillary containers, and make certain they were ready. She would also locate plenty of rags and long white cloths for the men to use to keep their tools clean, and to dry their hands during the butchering process. Large swaths of worn-out bed sheets and buckets of clear, cool water were necessary to wash residual blood from inside the hanging carcasses after all the internal organs were removed.

    Everyone was up before dawn on butchering day. The weather was perfect. No rain was in sight or forecast and the early morning air was clear, dry, and crisp. The adults were chipper and shuttled laughingly around the house in a happy mood.

Fall Butchering

They were ready to get the beautiful fall morning underway.

Our instructions were to stay out of the way of the men. Any help that Bob and I participated in had to be safe and productive since some situations could get us or one of the men injured. Any breach of their instructions would get us remanded to the yard. Not being able to watch our grandfather, Dad, and the other men butcher the hogs would be a terrible punishment. Accordingly, we stood back and watched every move the men made. Occasionally, we would anticipate that a particular item would be needed and subsequently run and retrieve it, sometimes before the men even realized the tool wasn't handy.

After a big breakfast, Grandpa, his brother, John, and Dad left the house with their hands full of tools, pans, containers, and clean clothes. Elmer Scarberry and Clarence, who would help butcher, had finished their breakfast and were leaning against the gate that opened into the pigpen. Five hogs would be butchered before the day was over. Grandpa and Uncle John were standing outside the pigpen fence, and together decided not to tackle the largest hog first, instead choosing one of the smaller ones. As soon as Grandpa pointed to the sow standing alone by the fence, Dad and Elmer opened the gate and walked slowly into the pigpen. The idea was not to frighten the pigs any more than necessary. Dad was carrying a rifle and Elmer was gripping a shiny, six-inch knife. Clarence was standing outside the pigpen next to a flatbed wagon, which was hooked to one of the farm tractors. He was holding a perilous-looking hay hook in each hand. The scene was unsettling for the pigs.

Dad and Elmer, slowly and cautiously, shooed the other hogs away and carefully isolated the smaller hog, the one Grandpa had selected from the brood. The two men stood quietly as the curious pig stopped and stared directly into the barrel of the .22-gauge rifle. Dad was steadying the gun against his right shoulder. *Bang!* With one crack of the gun, the pig's two front legs buckled at the knees, and its body fell sideways on the ground. It is vital that the pig's heart pump as much blood as possible out of the carcass before the animal completely succumbs. Elmer immediately moved up beside the pig and with one quick, deliberate swipe of the sharp knife, slit the pig's throat. With a bullet in the pig's brain and its jugular vein severed, the pig died instantly.

The sow's legs stopped kicking. Elmer and Clarence snagged the dead hog in the mouth with their hay hooks and pulled the animal across the barnyard, through the gate to the flatbed wagon. The men tugged and wrestled the heavy carcass up onto the wagon. After the pig was on board, Dad jumped on the seat of the tractor and drove to the spot where Grandpa and Uncle John would do the butchering. As soon as the wagon stopped, Grandpa used one of his sharp knives to cut a slit in the ankles of both hind legs. Next, the men inserted the ends of a wood singletree in each of the

Fall Butchering

two slits. The large ring on the singletree was tied to the end of a rope that ran up and through the pulley at the apex of the tripod. Together, Clarence and Elmer pulled on the opposite end of the rope and hoisted the upside-down pig above the 55-gallon drum of boiling water, placed directly under the tripod. Dad used his hands to help steady and guide the hog's body while the men, hand over hand, pulled on the rope. They raised the pig up in the air without any part of the dead animal touching the ground. The men stopped pulling as soon as the singletree was within a few inches of the pulley at the top of the tripod.

The hog was then slowly lowered headfirst into the barrel, until all but its hind ankles was completely submerged in the scalding lye water. After a few seconds, Grandpa motioned with an upward twirl of his index finger, and the men quickly hoisted the pig entirely out of the scalding water. Grandpa wanted to see if the pig's hide was scalded enough to allow the bristles to be scraped from its skin. With a couple of quick drags of his knife across the hot skin, Grandpa could tell that the hog needed more exposure in the boiling lye water and directed the men to lower the pig back down into the drum. After the third scalding, Grandpa deemed the hide ready for the bristles to be scraped from the animal's carcass.

The carcass was moved to the nearby long table, where Grandpa and Uncle John, in a long smooth motion of their knives, scraped the sow's scalded skin. The hot bristles came off easy and clean. Perfect! While the hide was still hot, the men rolled the animal over so the opposite side could be scraped. Once the skin cooled, the bristles became more challenging to remove and the hog would have to be dunked once again.

After the bristles were removed, Uncle Homer, Clarence, and Elmer lugged the heavy hog to the A-frame, where it would be hung upside down by its hind legs. The animal's head was about two feet off the ground. Grandpa cut off the hog's head behind its ears with a single, circular cut. The severed head fell into a container resting on the ground under the hanging carcass. After the head was removed, the belly was slit from top to bottom. The two sides were spread apart and each of the internal organs was segregated in separate containers. Lastly, any residual blood still left in the wide-open, empty carcass was sponged away with splashes of cool water and wiped dry with white rags.

Even to a young person, it was evident that Grandpa knew exactly what he was doing every time he made a cut. The effortless way Grandpa handled his sharp knives revealed that he'd butchered hundreds of hogs during his lifetime. Grandpa kept his tools carefully arranged and perfectly honed throughout the entire time he was working on the sides of pork and beef.

Before nightfall, all five heavy carcasses were moved to one of the enclosed farm buildings, where they would hang overnight in the cool, crisp air. The hanging slabs of meat needed to be protected

Fall Butchering

from inclement weather and safe from any wandering animals that are always looking for an easy and tasty feast during the night.

It took the men most of the day to butcher the five sows and steer. By 3:30, most of the strenuous work was done, which was good, because in about one-half hour the vacuum pump in the barn would be turned on. This familiar sound signaled that it was time to milk the dairy cows waiting patiently in the barn. In the meantime, Grandpa and Uncle John would hand-wash and dry all the butchering knives and tidy up from the busy day.

Years earlier, on Grandpa's Silverton farm, I had watched him preserve large slabs of hams, bacon, shoulders, et al., by rubbing the meat with copious amounts of saltpeter and various herbs, and afterward, hang the coated meat on hooks in the smokehouse. Making sausage was an especially interesting process. After several days of smoldering in hickory smoke, the sausage, bacon, and hams were well preserved. Besides preserving, the hickory smoke added a nice flavor to the different cuts of pork. The saltpeter that Grandpa hand-rubbed and packed on the surface of the hams and sides of bacon before smoking provided a protective layer that bacteria couldn't penetrate. The hickory and apple smoke that penetrated the meat through the saltpeter heightened the protection and added flavor. Afterward, anytime Grandma needed sausage for breakfast, Grandpa would go to the smokehouse and return with a link or two. Slices of sausage from the smoked crockpot were fried in a skillet as well.

The second day of butchering was also exciting and fun for Bob and me, but not as interesting as the first.

Neither Bob nor I ever had a close attachment to any of the animals, except the ponies. We understood what was happening and why! Bob and I understood that butchering was just an accepted part of our livelihood and the food chain we used to obtain pork, beef, and chicken for the breakfast, lunch, and dinner tables. We enjoyed and valued all of the baby animals born on the farm: baby calves, baby lambs, puppies, new kittens, rabbits, and ponies. One thing about growing up on an active farm, kids (boys and girls) learned about the birds and bees at a very young age. As a young kid I witnessed many births and deaths of a variety of animals. I witnessed animals that were suffering and had to be shot.

I recall once when my father and I were on one of the farm tractors, driving up the steep hill on the dirt road in the pasture field. We were about a mile from the barnyard. Near the top of the hill, we saw a large fox in the middle of the road. It was foaming at the mouth. The fox was very sickly looking, could hardly walk, and was wobbling toward us. The fox made no effort to escape and was not fearful of us, which was very unusual. The fox was dying of rabies.

Dad turned the tractor around and went back to our farmhouse to get his rifle. We returned and

Fall Butchering

Dad shot the fox. I can't recall what we did with the body, but we probably burned it with gasoline and then buried it. Rabies is very contagious. We couldn't risk some other animal digging it up and eating the dead carcass.

In fact, brother Bob was bitten by a wild animal on his farm about 20 years ago. He couldn't wait to catch the animal to find out if it was truly rabid. Early on there are no symptoms, no way to tell whether an animal is rabid or not. The doctor had to act quickly. I believe Bob had to have a dozen or more painful shots in his stomach over a period of time.

Farms Can Be Dangerous, Part 1

Life on an active farm can be dangerous enough, even for an experienced adult, let alone an inquisitive, spirited, young boy. By the time my father was five years old, he was able to help with a few of the easier chores around the farm, such as feeding the calves, chickens, and pigs.

Dad had watched his older siblings, Edra and James, help their father milk the dairy cows by hand many times in the morning and late afternoon. During the months when school was in session, Edra and James would help their father milk the cows, after which they would dress for school, have a quick breakfast, and accompany their father in his Maple Lawn Dairy milk delivery truck to Ravenswood. After Grandpa dropped his children off at school, he would deliver bottles of fresh milk to his customers in town before he returned to the Silverton farm. Even though Dad was too young to be of much help, he witnessed how hard his whole family worked and was only too happy and proud to eventually share some of the heavier chores.

Dad with his pet chickens and puppy.

Years later, my brothers and I were with Dad in the hayfield. We were working around several exposed and rapidly moving parts on the New Holland hay baler. The occasion prompted Dad to recall a time when loose, flowing clothing or a seemingly trivial piece of dangling cloth almost led to severe injury or fatal accident.

Farms Can Be Dangerous, Part 1

The year was 1926, and the following incident occurred at the family Silverton farm. Dad was six years old. He and his mother had just returned from shopping in Ravenswood. He was wearing a brand-new pair of bib overalls and was eager to show his new clothes to his father.

As soon as Dad jumped out of the car, he headed straight to the barnyard, where his father and other men were filling the silo with corn silage. When he arrived at the silo, his father and one of the hired men were standing near the corn-cutter with their backs toward the extremely noisy machine. The two adults were busy trying to communicate above the tremendous clatter emanating from the corn cutter's many clanking metal parts and the roar of the tractor's engine running at full throttle. Standing behind his father, Dad waited patiently for him to finish his conversation and turn around, so he would see his son in his brand-new clothes. In the meantime, Dad got too close to the floppy metal slats that continuously conveyed bundles of corn stalks across a horizontal platform into sharp, whirling blades on the corn harvester-blower. A portion of Dad's new pants got tangled on one of the wide cross-members on the conveyor belt, which quickly snatched him up over the end of the table and pulled him toward the rotating, razor-sharp blades at the opposite end of the machine's platform. The length of the horizontal platform was about the length of a corn stalk, or about six feet. In a matter of seconds, my father would have been sliced into pieces—pieces no larger than the size of a silver dollar. During all the commotion, his father was still facing the opposite direction and had no idea what was happening a few feet behind his back. Even if one of the men in the barnyard had seen that my father was in trouble, it would have been extremely difficult for him to act fast enough to save Dad's life.

Dad told us that as his body approached the end of the silage cutter, the only thing he could do was position his feet against the vertical side of the blower housing, which partially shielded the high-speed, rotating blade. Thankfully, Dad was astute enough to stiffen his body with both feet against the blower housing and, with all his strength resist being pulled feet first into the cutter. He gripped the sides of the conveyor table with both hands while holding his buttocks up off the moving conveyor chain beneath him. In the interim, the overwhelming force began to shred his new overalls. Strip after strip of fabric from his new denim pants was ripped off his body until he could free himself. In a matter of seconds, Dad was standing on the ground with nothing on but his skimpy underwear, a tattered shirt, and fragments of his new overalls hanging mostly around his upper torso. No one witnessed the near disaster. Grandpa did not realize what had just occurred until he turned around and saw his son standing there with his clothes torn to threads. I cannot fathom the fear that must have gone through my grandfather's mind when he saw his son frightened beyond belief.

Farms Can Be Dangerous, Part 1

Someone was truly looking after my father. And this horrible event wouldn't be the last time Dad would need help from the angels above!

Dad with his pony.

Any kid fortunate enough to grow up on an active dairy farm knows that unexpected events can occur at almost any time. Notwithstanding, there were special annual events that would keep any kid starry-eyed and entertained for hours. Each spring, one special occasion occurred when my father dehorned all the young heifers. Both horns needed to be cut off before the heifers were old enough to procreate and join the active herd of older dairy cows. Horns of any size and shape could be lethal for the men who worked daily around the animals.

Willow Grove: A Boy, A Family, A Farm

Also, cattle will periodically get into a minor scuffle, and when they do, they lower their heads to butt and shove each other around. If the spirited animals had sharp horns, they could do permanent damage to one another, rendering them unable to remain in the dairy herd. Too often, an injured dairy cow never completely recovers from her wounds and must be sold at an auction. If the cow was an above-average producer, the loss of income was significant.

Before the weather became too warm in the spring, my father would round up a dozen or so frisky young heifers with small, yet lethal horns and drive them to one of the two pasture fields, where they would mix with the older, docile dairy cows. The next time the dairy herd was moved from the pasture field to the barn to be milked, the heifers instinctively trailed along with the large group of milk cows. Once the group reached the barnyard, all the cattle, including the young heifers, were confined inside the fenced barnyard. A day or two later, after the herd was milked and ready to be driven to the daytime pasture field, the young heifers were segregated from the core group of dairy cattle. The men would make sure none of the young heifers left the barnyard with the main herd. The challenge was to intercept and force back the young heifers that tried to sneak through the open gate while sandwiched between two older cows moseying out of the barnyard. As soon as all the milk cows were out of the barn lot, the gate was closed. The restless heifers left behind would

Farms Can Be Dangerous, Part 1

huddle nervously in the northeast corner of the barnyard, where they could watch the older cows making their way to the hill pasture. The young heifers rightly surmised that being left behind was not a good omen!

Dad gathered several clean rags, a large glass bottle of a purple liquid disinfectant, a ball of binder twine, a bucket of freshly shelled corn cobs, and the gargantuan dehorner that had been in the family for generations. The dehorner was analogous to a five-foot-long pair of scissors, except that one of the cutting edges was in the shape of a hook and the other cutting edge was a thin, sharp disk. The hook helped position the cutting disk around the base of the heifer's horn. The long handles enabled the man using the dehorner to generate plenty of leverage to cut through the animal's tough horn in one swift, smooth motion.

One at a time, the heifers were driven into a narrow holding pen. Once inside, the pen was so narrow an animal could not turn around, move forward, or move backward. The animal was completely constrained! Horizontal boards on the sides of the pen were spaced far enough apart that the heifer was visible from all four sides and were high enough that the average farm animal couldn't leap over the top and escape. The top of the pen was completely open.

Normally, the young heifers were dehorned without any problems. Once the heifer was wedged in the holding pen, Dad would tie baling twine tight around the base of both horns. Then he shoved corn cobs up under the taut baling twine on the heifer's forehead. The corn cobs tightened the string even more and cut off circulation in the arteries that supplied blood to the horns. After both horns were cut off, liquid disinfectant was sponged liberally over the top of the heifer's head and around the rim of both openings from the severed horns. A few days later, after the soreness subsided, the dehorned heifers rubbed their heads on the ground or against a tree, which knocked off the corn cob and twine.

The pen was tall enough and perfect to dehorn animals. Yet, I have seen terrified heifers jump and only halfway clear the top railing, ending up straddling the side of the pen, with both front legs dangling over the top and outside, while the hind legs were still on the floor inside the pen. Another time, I saw a frightened heifer kick the sideboards off and escape into the barnyard, with one horn cut off and one remaining intact. A single stream of bright red blood spurted high in the air from the open hole in the skull that once housed the missing horn.

Another heifer kicked and bucked so hard that boards splintered and were utterly destroyed. The frightened heifer stampeded away and, in the process, nearly collided with one of the men in its path. When something like that happened—it was every man for himself! A copious amount of blood would be spurting like mini geysers out of both openings on top of the animal's head.

Farms Can Be Dangerous, Part 1

Even though dehorning was hard work and sometimes unexpectedly dangerous, it was a task that had to be done every year. It was imperative for the heifers' safety and security and for everyone who worked among the cattle.

Gored!

This story about my mother's unfortunate encounter with the Guernsey cow and her newborn is a prime example of why every animal in the dairy herd had to be dehorned. It was after four o'clock in the afternoon. Bob, John, and I were not yet home from school, and Dad and Elmer Scarberry were busy in the dairy barn milking the cows. Grandpa needed Mom's help to corral one of the dairy cows that had just given birth out in the open pasture field. The white-spotted Guernsey and her newborn were in the pasture between the two main houses and the dairy barn. Lille, the Guernsey's moniker, and her still wobbly calf needed to be driven from the fenced pasture field to the barnyard. The chore was much easier with two people: one to herd the reluctant dairy cow toward the barnyard and the other to open and close both pasture field and barnyard gates. New mothers can be obstinate and overly protective, especially whenever the newborn cannot keep up with its mother.

Grandpa and Mom were slowly coercing the pair toward the barn. The new calf was straggling well behind its mother when, all of a sudden, the 1,200-pound Guernsey turned completely around and raced back to where my mother was following behind with the new calf. The enraged animal lowered her head and, with a powerful thrust, heaved my mother up in the air. Mom fell to the ground and landed flat on her back. Instead of retreating, the angry cow continued butting, pushing, and goring Mom in the middle of her stomach. Each time the Guernsey butted Mom, the force from the animal's head pushed Mom's body several feet backward on the ground. As soon as Grandpa saw what was happening, he rushed toward Mom and the irate cow. As soon as the angry mother saw Grandpa, she promptly twisted and darted back toward her calf.

Mom was in excruciating pain and bruised with both external and internal injuries. Some of the repercussions from the attack stayed with her for the rest of her life. This incident underscores why farmers always dehorn all their dairy cattle at a young age. Mom's injuries would have been much more severe and possibly even fatal if the angry Guernsey had brandished a pair of sharp horns.

Milk and Money

The following illustration is something the reader might likely posit as information a person doesn't need to know, doesn't care to know, and deems insignificant. Even so, I'm eager for the reader to grasp and fully appreciate why my father rose from his restful bed—very early—every day—365 days—a year. Why he was so meticulous about

Milk and Money

when and how the cows were milked each day and why he endeavored to maintain, as much as possible, a strict milking schedule and a tranquil environment for his herd of dairy cattle. This will explain why my family never took a vacation.

The quality and quantity—*pounds*—of milk produced by a dairy cow each day is, for the purpose of this narrative, reasonably analogous to the quality and quantity of work performed by any average employee of a typical business enterprise. That is to say, both the cow and the employee have to produce a *high-quality* product and both have to produce an acceptable *quantity* of the high-quality product. If the dairy cow doesn't meet the minimum quality and quantity benchmarks established by its owner, if the cost of feeding and housing a dairy cow is greater than the profit derived from the sale of milk from that particular cow, the farmer must get rid of the animal. In the same manner, if an employee's salary, benefits, and collateral costs of employment are higher than the productivity realized from the employee, the company must act decisively.

In both cases, if early corrective action is not taken it would be analogous to an employer buying a shovel on one side of the street for a dollar and then crossing over to the other side of the street and reselling the same shovel for 50 cents. If the employer keeps this up, it won't be long before the company's negative profitability will force the business to entertain bankruptcy. It is that simple! If either the dairy cow or employee's productivity do not meet the employer's minimum requirements, which enables the employer to make a reasonable profit, the cow will eventually be sold at the local stockyard and the employee will be given notice to clean out his desk or pack up his tools. An employer just can't afford to continue to subsidize the negative contribution of the dairy cow or the employee.

Work with me just a little longer on this topic. I have a key point that I want to make regarding my father and the analogy that I'm using between the dairy cow and an employee's quality and quantity of work. Bear in mind that both are literally and readily applicable to so many facets of each of our own individual lives.

The *quantity* of milk is the pounds of milk that the corresponding cow produces each day. The *quality* of milk from a given dairy cow is simply the butterfat content of the milk. The higher the butterfat content, the higher the price paid to the farmer for his milk. A good Jersey dairy cow can have a butterfat content of six percent or higher, whereas a Holstein dairy cow will have a butterfat content closer to four percent. If a dairy farmer sells 100 pounds of Jersey milk and an equivalent amount of Holstein milk, the farmer will receive more revenue from the Jersey milk than the Holstein milk because of higher butterfat content in the Jersey milk. The best price that the creamery paid for the farmer's milk was based on the quality or butterfat content.

Milk and Money

In order to support three full-time families living on the Willow Grove farm, and simultaneously pay off a $40,000 mortgage, the Willow Grove dairy herd had to not only produce high quality milk, the herd had to produce a large volume of milk.

My father's expansive knowledge of animal husbandry and his persistent hard work impelled him to *personally* milk the dairy herd, twice a day, every single day of the year. Without exception! As I mentioned earlier, a valuable, productive dairy cow responds best to a strict routine in a tranquil atmosphere. The dairy cows must be milked at the same time each day and, as well, it is extremely important that the dairy cattle are *milked each day* by the *same individual*. When the same person cares for the herd, the dairy cattle become familiar with the individual's milking habits, which produces the soothing and desirable environment that is absolutely imperative for the highest quality and quantity of milk production.

Every individual dairy cow can be thought of as a single, complex, milk-producing piece of equipment. Like any precision instrument or machine, it will produce its best results if the apparatus is properly cared for. Conversely, if the machine is not properly maintained, it will slow down, malfunction, and eventually break down, sometimes with catastrophic results. Comparatively, a valuable and productive dairy cow can be injured or completely ruined in a very short period of time. It can happen subtly and quickly. If the dairy herd is milked by an inexperienced

Willow Grove: A Boy, A Family, A Farm

person, *regardless of how conscientious the individual might be*, he or she can unwittingly bestow great harm on a good herd of dairy cattle. In essence, a significant number of productive cows could be temporarily harmed or irretrievably ruined in a matter of just a few days—innocently by an inexperienced person. This is why a dairy farm that was once successful might suddenly become unprofitable in a relatively short period of time. My father knew this fact all too well, and this is the primary reason why he made sure that he was the only one who milked our dairy herd.

I would like to explain in more detail, why and exactly how a good dairy cow can be seriously injured or literally destroyed in such a short time.

Before the arrival of electricity in rural America, every dairy cow had to be milked by hand, which limited the number of cows a farmer could milk twice a day. With the advent of electricity and automatic milking machines, the dairy farmer instantly had far more flexibility regarding how many cows he could milk per day. As with most inventions, whether a new pharmaceutical drug or the automatic milking equipment, there is typically a side-effect or downside risk associated with each innovation. With automatic milking machines, the benefit was the capability to milk more cows and, in turn, sell more milk. The automatic milking machine enabled the farmer to produce more milk —in less time and with less manpower.

A high-producing milk cow is the result of superior artificial breeding and excellent care by its

Milk and Money

farmer. Conversely, the risk to a dairy cow is the susceptibility of the cow's udder to injury from leaving the automatic milking equipment on any one of the cow's four teats too long or not long enough. The difference between too long and not long enough can be as little as a minute or so—and this margin is extremely important. On average a good Holstein dairy cow will produce roughly two to three gallons of milk in a span of three to seven minutes using automatic milking equipment. Even though three to seven minutes is a big difference in time to thoroughly milk one cow versus another, the time it takes to milk a cow also will be longer in the morning than during the late afternoon milking. Too, the time that it takes to milk each cow will vary and will decrease during the nine-month lactation period that the cow produces milk. Moreover, the time it takes to milk a dairy cow decreases subtly because the amount of milk that a dairy cow produces each day will gradually taper off during the nine-month lactation cycle.

And something else that makes milking a cow even more complex and delicate is that each of the four quarters of a cow's udder will empty its respective quantity of milk at *different rates* and thus each quarter will finish at *different times*. And the time for each quarter keeps changing over time. The point is...to successfully milk 70 Holstein dairy cows, a person must instinctively know all of the individual times that it takes to empty all of the milk from 280 teats, i.e., *70 cows multiplied by four quarters per cow equals 280!* If all 280 exact times are not known, the person milking a cow will run the risk of leaving the milking equipment on each quarter too long—or not long enough.

At Willow Grove, my father milked three cows at a time, using three automatic Surge milking machines. Milking our herd with three machines kept my father comfortably busy. For nearly two hours he would constantly check and examine each quarter of every cow that was milked. He knew his herd well enough that he could anticipate and know within a matter of few seconds when a certain pulsating rubber component attached to the teat on one of the cow's four quarters should be removed. If the pulsating unit was left on even one teat too long, that particular teat and quarter could easily be bruised and become vulnerable to a costly infection, called mastitis. Anytime a dairy cow got mastitis in one or more quarters, the only remedy was treatment with expensive antibiotics. The antibiotics would be in the cow's system for several days, which mandated that the milk from the infected quarter or quarters be discarded until the infection was entirely gone. Sometimes, several gallons of milk would have to be discarded before the infection cleared up. And if the infection was too chronic, there was a very good possibility that the cow wouldn't return to the level of milk production before the infection. Every pound of milk that had to be discarded was literally "good money down the drain" that the farm would not receive in the next check from the dairy company. Superimposed on top of less revenue is the cost of

Milk and Money

antibiotics, extra work, and attention it took to nurse the animal back to good health.

    I hope it is apparent to the reader why my father was a successful dairy farmer. He was an expert, a specialist. He was a skilled professional. Because he was the youngest male in the family, it was only natural for him to remain at home and help his father manage his dairy farm. He was already accustomed to long hours of hard work, and to be truly successful he would have to work diligently every day of the week. Unlike other types of farming, a dairy farm is operational the year round. It never shuts down. And a valuable herd of dairy cattle under the care of the wrong person for two or three days could damage the herd so much that it could take months to repair. This is why my father only took one short vacation during the nearly 10 years that we lived at Willow Grove. His only "hobby" was his family, since he was generally so busy that he actually didn't have extra time to enjoy the usual hobbies that so many men enjoy who work five days a week. I never, ever saw my father turn a page in a hardback book. He literally did not have the time to enjoy reading, other than short articles in *Hoard's Dairyman* magazine. His goal was to be a successful dairy farmer, raise his family, and help his parents, brother, sisters and other family and friends in any way he could. To this end, my father was victorious.

Willow Grove: A Boy, A Family, A Farm

Love Pecks

My mother was a housewife and an attentive, engaged mother of three energetic boys. She was a loyal daughter-in-law, a good on-site nurse, a chauffeur for her father-in-law, a spontaneous errand runner, a ready helper, and a willing confidant for anyone who solicited her advice. She prepared three full meals a day and took care of multiple chores inside the house and in the vegetable gardens. Mom could often be found in the hayfields driving a truck or tractor or helping my father with farm chores when an extra pair of hands was imperative. Mom was the most versatile and flexible member of our Willow Grove farm family. Mom was the catalyst that made living in Willow Grove a huge success!

In addition to my mother's inside household chores, she had daily tasks outside of the house. One was "chicken patrol": watering, feeding, and gathering eggs from dozens of chickens that Mom raised from biddies purchased from the Ravenswood hatchery. The large brood of hens produced extra eggs to sell, adding cash to the family budget. Once Mom decided I was old enough, I was given responsibility for gathering the eggs, twice a day. When Mom handed me the egg basket, I would take off for the chicken house, which was located just inside the pasture field at the end of our lane.

Inside the chicken house were several rows of cubicles stacked on top of each other a few feet up

Love Pecks

from the floor, though not so high that the chickens would have difficulty fluttering up from the floor to one of the cubicles in the very top row. A cubical in the top row was typically about the height that an adult could peer into and easily extend one arm inside while standing flat-footed.

The technique for gathering eggs was easy enough. Yet, it could be daunting and icky for a youngster in the beginning. Like most things in life, it became easier after you "learned the ropes," which required a little experience.

The best time to gather eggs was when most of the hens were out of their straw nests, scratching around in the pasture field looking for insects and grubs or eating shelled field corn scattered freely on the bare ground. With the hens outside of the chicken house, I could easily reach inside each of the lower cubicles and gingerly place each egg in the cane egg basket. Mom kept a wooden crate in the chicken house specifically for me to stand on for the upper row. After I inspected all the cubicles, I cautiously carried the fragile bounty back to the house so Mom could wash and inspect each egg.

One morning, when I handed the egg basket to Mom, she looked at the contents, hesitated, and turned toward me. She had a puzzled look on her face. "Junior, are these all of the eggs you could find?"

"Yes!" I said.

Mom pondered for a few moments and then asked: "Did you look in all of the nests?"

"Uh-huh."

Willow Grove: A Boy, A Family, A Farm

Mom was still puzzled. She knew how many eggs the chickens laid each day. My basket was obviously short at least a dozen eggs, potentially even more. Fewer eggs meant less money for her grocery budget.

Mom wasn't through with her questions. "Were there any chickens in the nests?"

"Uhhhhhhhhh," and, after some hesitation, I said, "I think so."

"How many?" Mom queried.

Meekly, I struggled but eventually stammered, "Uhhhhhh...uhhhhhh...I'm not sure."

Mom's face morphed into a relaxed grin. She knew exactly where the missing eggs were! They were still in the nests under the chickens.

As soon as Mom emptied the egg basket, she handed it back to me. "Go back and gather the rest of the eggs. Check under every chicken...in *all* of the nests."

Now...I was the one who was concerned! Not happy at all, and with my chin buried in my chest, I slowly forced my way back to the chicken house.

Now the procedure for gathering eggs wasn't so simple and easy! The hens were sitting on their eggs, and the only way to retrieve the eggs was to reach back underneath each of the squatting chickens and feel around for any potential eggs. As I stood in front of one cubicle, the occupant's two beady eyes were focused like a laser beam directly between my twitching eyes and dire-looking countenance. With the empty egg basket tight in my fist, I turned my head slightly to one side,

Love Pecks

closed my eyes, and shoved my extended right arm —at a snail's pace—toward the bottom of the nesting chicken. With my eyes still closed, I kept pushing my hand back under the hen's warm body until I felt a familiar object. Yes! Yes! I pulled my arm back out from under the hen at a rapid pace. When I opened my eyes, I was immediately proud of my bravado. It felt grand to place the warm egg in my basket. I was ready to move on to the next occupied cubical when I hesitated. Was there only one egg under the chicken? Not sure? Reluctantly, I decided I'd better check and make sure. Back I went, and it was a good thing! There were two more eggs under the same chicken. The old hen and I had done an admirable job. My mother will be proud of both of us!

Off to the next occupied nest. I thought to myself that this wasn't bad at all! The smell in the hen house wasn't the best, but I wouldn't be long, anyway! As before, I reached toward the squatting chicken, though this time at a faster and more confident pace. Just as my hand touched the front of the chicken, its beady eyes darted toward me, and I was immediately rebuffed with a quick peck on the top of my hand. The sharp tap startled me. Instinctively, I hastily pulled my hand back out from under the crazy bird! I immediately realized that this stupid chicken didn't like me! Even though the pinprick didn't hurt that much, it was still troubling! What should I do now? Maybe there weren't any eggs under the unfriendly, ugly beast anyway, and I should just move on. But, then again, there might be one...or two...just maybe even three eggs in the nest. Mom wouldn't be happy with me if I didn't find out for sure! Besides, I'm not a coward, and I really shouldn't be afraid of a bully chicken that wants to peck me on my hand. Suddenly, it dawned on me! That's it! I bet it's just a little love peck! Of course! *Of course!*

All I could do now was—be brave! I closed my eyes and pushed my hand back under the chicken. The old hen followed through with two more quick love pecks, which weren't too bad at all. I found one egg and felt around to see if there were any more. No! There was only one egg. I pulled my hand out and thought to myself, *This chicken isn't going to badger me! At least not* today! I checked under all the nesting chickens in the hen house and found several more eggs. In fact, I found more than a dozen eggs that I knew would make my mother happy. This time when I showed Mom the egg basket, she rewarded me with a nice compliment: "Now that's more like it!"

Confessions of a Calf Conductor

Before we were old enough to go to school, Bob and I were assigned a chore that was our sole responsibility. We were also given various other intermittent tasks, with which our mother charged us regularly. Bob had to feed the pigs morning and evening, year-round, except in the morning when we had to go to school.

Confessions of a Calf Conductor

Just as Bob cared for the hogs, I mixed a commercial powder concentrate with water twice each day and fed the warm supplement to all our baby calves. New calves are never allowed to nurse from their mother. They are immediately fed the supplement, which is cheaper than milk; plus, Dad didn't want to risk any potential injury to the mother's udder from over-nursing or butting by the lively newborn. The number of calves averaged four or five, and even more in the spring during heavy birthing. Each newborn would imbibe the nourishment through a large rubber nipple affixed to the side of a galvanized pail, designed explicitly for feeding baby calves.

Baby calves that are a few days old are much easier to feed than newborns. Whenever I entered the calf barn with multiple pails of warm milk replacement, the frisky, hungry calves butted each other to be the first in line. I was their ringmaster, and sometimes I had to discipline one of the unruly calves with a handy snap on the nose with my magic baton, which I kept hanging by the door to the calf barn. I would tap their tender noses just enough to sting a little and remind the rambunctious calf who the boss was in this four-corner, calf-pen circus.

A one- or two-day-old baby calf can be incredibly challenging to feed. Too often, one of the newborns wouldn't drink its nourishment, and I would have to report this uncooperative behavior to my father. After Dad finished milking the cows, he would mix up more warm supplement, and together we would walk to the calf barn. He would set the pail of warm supplement on the floor inside the calf pen and straddle the neck of the baby calf with his knees tight against the calf's neck. Then with his left hand, he would press on the top of the calf's head, hard enough to force its nose against the surface of the warm liquid. At the same time, he inserted his right index and middle finger inside the mouth of the baby calf. Instantly, the newborn would taste the liquid mixture and start nursing on Dad's fingers. Dad would then retract his fingers from the calf's mouth and allow the animal to keep drinking. After a couple of feedings, the newborn no longer needed coaxing to nurse on the flexible nipple on the side of the bucket. Now, just as with the older calves, I could hook the pail on the fence railing and stand in the middle of the calf pen, watching the little animals while they guzzled down their nourishment.

I monitored the feeding from the middle of the pen and made sure each of the calves drank their pail of sustenance. After the first calf finished and the pail was empty, my job became more demanding. I had to make sure the calf, always one of the older ones, didn't crowd in on the smaller calves still feeding in one of the other corners. I was the ringmaster of the feeding circus, and with my suitable little conductor's stick, I trained each of the calves to remain in their designated corner until all the calves had drained their assigned pail.

Regrettably, during one feeding, I unintentionally disciplined one older calf too

Confessions of a Calf Conductor

harshly, and I knew immediately that I would be in a heap of trouble as soon as my father and grandfather learned what I had done. The obstinate older calf wouldn't give up trying to butt in and interfere with one of the smaller calves, which was still nursing its pail. To remedy the problem, I hit the crown of the calf's head with my stick, and the animal dropped like a rock, just as if it had been shot in the head with a pistol. I was sure the calf was dead! Luckily, I had only temporarily knocked the calf unconscious. After a few minutes, the stunned calf began to shake off my punishment—and finally wobbled to its feet. Still befuddled and head bowed, the dazed calf struggled back to its corner in the calf pen. The reader cannot imagine how relieved I was when the calf recovered and showed symptoms of being okay. I bent down, wrapped my arms around the calf's neck, and hugged the little rascal with joy! After that, the beautiful black and white Holstein calf and I were simpatico! All I had to do was point my stick at the calf's nose, and she would stop dead in her tracks, back up, and return sheepishly to her corner.

Baby calves become heifers, and ones sired from high milk-producing mothers and blue-ribbon bulls become productive milk cows after their first calf. The loss of a female calf is a significant financial matter! Even more so if the financial loss was due to a stupid mistake. Like mine!

Since that near-disastrous event in the calf pen 70 years ago—mum has been the word! Until now!

Willow Grove: A Boy, A Family, A Farm

Mousers

Cats are an important asset on every farm. A healthy feline hunts rats and mice, which helps to manage the rodent population in and around the farm buildings. In inclement weather, our cats found perfect shelter in the dairy barn.

During frigid nights, the cats nestled together in the hayloft. They entombed themselves underneath loose hay where their own body heat kept them comfortable. If the night was unusually cold and windy, the cats found their way to the first floor of the barn, where they would spend the night in the middle walkway in front of the milk cows. With all of the doors and windows closed, the mere presence of the large herd was enough to keep the barn warm. Whenever the cats wanted extra heat, they would scoot forward just close enough to feel the breath from the dairy cows.

The cats mostly fended for themselves and didn't need much in the way of commercial cat food. They also had multiple sources of water all year long.

Anytime I was visiting with cousin James Conrad and it was milking time, we could always find his father somewhere inside the spacious dairy barn. After the men finished milking a cow Uncle Conrad would follow close behind, and personally scrutinize all four quarters on every dairy cow in the barn. He would strip any residual milk left behind from the milking machine. Hand stripping allowed him to assess the present health of every cow, as well as rescue a few extra pounds of valuable milk. It only took Uncle Conrad a minute or two to strip each cow—time well spent and so important to sustain the health of his herd.

Shortly before milking time, the cats would congregate at the barn. A few minutes after the vacuum pump was turned on, they would quietly mosey in behind the Holstein that Uncle Conrad was stripping. From one cow to the next, Uncle Conrad carried his three-legged stool in one hand and a small, shiny stainless steel milk pail in the other. The cats followed him and positioned themselves directly behind the same cow, where Uncle Conrad was sitting on his stool. They knew the routine and would patiently wait their turn.

At a leisurely pace, Uncle Conrad would strip several cows, all the while enjoying the stoic presence of the two dutiful mousers. Without tipping his hand, Uncle Conrad would turn and squeeze a six-foot stream of fresh milk toward one of the cats, which was why they had been waiting so patiently. Uncle Conrad would angle the cow's teat away from the milk pail and with a long, constant squeeze, propel a miniature six-foot firehose of warm milk toward the cats' wide-open mouths. Both cats would move forward and jostle for the airborne nourishment. After several long squirts, both had devoured their share of the morning ration. By the time Uncle Conrad ceased spraying the cats with milk, each cat's head looked like it had been submerged in a bucket of milk. The whiskers and fur on their faces would be covered and dripping with droplets of milk. Satisfied, the cats would trot out of the barn, find a sunny spot on the concrete breezeway and cleanse the lingering milk from their whiskers and face. After a short nap, the hunters would reward Uncle Conrad and take care of unwelcome rodents around the barn and milk house.

Digging a Hole

Sometimes, it is crazy what you remember! Dad and I were sitting in the side yard under a shade tree. We were passing time, waiting for a family event to begin. I don't recall the exact occasion, but my clothes were still as clean as a whistle, and I was getting a little bored waiting for my cousins to arrive. In the interim, I recalled a recent discussion in my science class at school. The topic centered on density and why extra soil was always left over after a fresh hole was dug in the ground. That is, you couldn't get the same quantity of dirt that came out of a hole, back into the hole.

Believing that I knew something that Dad might not know, I looked at him and asked, "Why is it that when you dig a hole and afterwards try to put the same dirt back, you can't get all of the dirt back in the hole?" I was confident that I could outwit my father. Dad started to reply, but before I let him answer, I said: "I'll bet you that I can dig a hole and after I refill the hole, there will be dirt left over." Dad said, "Okay, I'll take your bet."

Digging a Hole

After finding a spoon, I spent a few minutes digging a reasonably sized hole along the sidewalk where we were sitting. I wanted to make sure I won the bet and planned to have plenty of dirt lying around the hole, readily visible after my demonstration. After the hole was dug, I started shoveling the loose dirt back into the hole. It looked like I was going to have plenty of dirt left over, when suddenly Dad said, "Wait! Slow down." He followed, "Now, take a little of the dirt back out of the hole." Which I did. He handed me a nice sturdy stick and said, "Now tamp down the dirt already in the hole." I obliged and immediately tamped the loose dirt as lightly as I could. After a few tamps I started to add more dirt to the hole. Again, Dad stopped me and instructed, "No, not yet; tamp some more and tamp a little harder."

I started twisting and squirming and quietly moaning under my breath.

Dad maintained a straight face. He recognized my increasing anguish as I continued tamping the loose dirt down in the hole. Every time I stopped tamping or tried to add more dirt, he would again counsel: "No, not yet" or "Okay, now you can add a little more." All the while I was tamping, Dad was grinning and loving every minute of my discomfort. He couldn't help but chuckle. In the end, Dad made sure that I returned every last speck of black dirt back into the original hole. Afterwards, we both had a good laugh.

Willow Grove: A Boy, A Family, A Farm

Scaredy-Cat

Female calves are vital for the future prosperity of the farm. They will replace the older dairy cows that eventually will be culled from the herd. My job was to make sure all newborns were kept healthy, so they would ultimately join the main herd in a couple of years. At a young age, I learned an important life-long lesson from my grandfather about caring for farm animals. One blustery winter evening, I was stretched out on the couch in front of the fireplace in the family room when Grandpa walked in and asked me about the general condition of the baby calves housed in the calf barn. I commented that I fed the calves and made sure the door was thoroughly latched and the light was off when I left the calf barn. He then asked me, "Did you spread plenty of fresh straw in all of the pens?" Grandpa continued. "It is going to be extremely cold and windy tonight, and fresh straw is all the calves have to keep warm." After a short pause, I replied. "No, I forgot." Grandpa was disappointed with my lame excuse, and his response was simply, "You are warm and comfortable in front of the fireplace. Put your coat on and go back to the barn! Make sure every one of the calves is as comfortable and as warm as you are."

There was no heat in any farm buildings, and consequently, the animals had only their body heat to keep warm. The sides of the calf barn were wide plank boards nailed vertically side by side, with

Scaredy-Cat

narrow cracks between the boards. The cracks were acceptable, functional, and even desirable in the summer. On blistering hot days, the tin roof created a lot of heat in the building, and the cracks allowed hot air inside the calf pen to escape through the spaces between the boards. Similarly, cold air whistled through the same gaps in the winter.

On very cold nights, the calves huddled together in a group. Yet, they still needed a copious pile of fresh, dry straw to curl up on. I knew Grandpa was correct and that plenty of clean, dry straw in each of the pens would bestow more warmth for the animals during the blustery, freezing night.

I immediately got up off the couch and went to the laundry room, where I put on my heavy work jacket and boots, found a flashlight, and hurried out into the pitch-black darkness. I wanted to take care of the calves as quickly as possible and get back to our cozy living room before the icy winds penetrated my clothing.

As I ran up the gravel lane toward the barn, I waved the flashlight beam between both edges of the road and toward the farm buildings in the distance. I was constantly looking for any danger that might be crouched in the tall grass or lurking behind the huge sycamore tree along the lane. Except for the winds whistling between the dairy barn and silos, the pitch-black night was devoid of any strange noises. Yet, the silent backdrop of the farm buildings still presented a creepy setting.

Willow Grove: A Boy, A Family, A Farm

The calf barn was located less than a hundred feet from the silo on the back corner of the barnyard, behind the dairy barn. Hurriedly, I opened the wooden gate beside the steel silo and raced across the frozen ground. Walking, let alone running, was treacherous on the ruffled, frozen mud in the barnyard. However, it was easier than in soggy winter weather when I was too lazy to fasten the buckles on my rubber boots. More than once, I completely stepped out of one of my boots and, before I could catch myself, ended up with one foot stuck in mud up over my ankle. This is not a wholesome feeling, especially during a moonless winter night. After I salvaged the empty muddy boot, the rest of the slog to and from the calf building was made with only one warm foot.

After opening the door to the calf barn, I flipped the switch for the single 100-watt light bulb, scrambled up a ladder, and stepped off onto the floor of the hayloft. By now, all the calves were awake and staring at me. One stood up and wobbled as if she was just stretching her legs. I grabbed four bales of straw and threw them over the railing into the two calf pens below. Two parallel rows of twine on each 50-pound bale had to be cut so the sheaves of straw could be flaked apart and scattered evenly over the floor of both pens. The thick layer of fresh straw would provide a dry and insulated cushion for the calves to lie on. The extra straw that I scattered ensured that the little animals would be protected from penetrating cold wind.

Scaredy-Cat

Satisfied that the baby calves were happy and settled in for the night, I shut the door and headed back across the barnyard toward the gate near the big dairy barn. The only light I could see besides my flashlight was the subdued reflection from the flickering embers in our family room fireplace, and the soft light emanating through Mom's kitchen window. As soon as I closed the barnyard gate and rushed past the silos onto the gravel pit road, I raced as fast as my feet would carry me past the pumphouse...never looking back to see what evil monster was nipping at my heels. Any unusual noise was a sure indication that whatever-it-is was close behind me. I wouldn't be out of danger until I bolted up onto the front porch, completely ignoring the three broad steps that would only slow my entrance to our family room. Only after I felt the doorknob in my hand turn and the door slightly ajar would I look back to see what had been "chasing" me. And even if I hadn't heard any actual snarling sounds in the darkness, it didn't matter. I just knew monsters were out there, watching and waiting patiently—to pounce!

One summer night, a desperado growled furiously and lunged at me from a dark spot between the two silos. It scared the holy oatmeal out of me! Another time the boogeyman was lurking in a bed of grass beside the sycamore tree. It was dark outside, and I had just left in haste from the calf barn, escaped past the silos, and was running full throttle around the pumphouse at the intersection of the gravel-pit road and the lane to the house. Suddenly, a gigantic monster lurched out from behind the mighty sycamore with both arms raised high. It screamed like a wounded hyena. The raging, faceless silhouette pounced on me in the middle of the lane. I was sure that I was a "goner"!

Thankfully, the fear of quick capture or sudden death quickly subsided after I realized the monster was my brother Bob. He had been waiting for the right moment to scare the living daylights out of me. Which he certainly did! Immediately, Bob and I had a gigantic laugh together, sitting in the middle of the road, after which he took off running toward the house with me right on his tail. I attempted to swoop down on Bob and wrestle him vigorously until one of us reluctantly grumbled "Uncle," the officially recognized password for "I give up!"

Ravenswood Elementary

One of the reasons I wanted to write this book was to convey how much I value the sacrifices that my family made so that their future generations could enjoy a good, if not better, standard of living. In addition to my immediate family and ancestors, I am indebted to the Ravenswood Elementary School teachers. The teachers who I was privileged to have were conscientious and caring educators, dedicated to their profession. The discipline, education, and grounding that all my elementary teachers taught in their classrooms have motivated and encouraged me, and endured throughout my lifetime!

Ravenswood Elementary

The main entrance to the circa 1887 elementary school was up a few steps from the sidewalk on Henry Street. Up a few more steps, a short hallway opened into a big intersection in the center of the building. Students could readily access four first-floor classrooms and two very wide staircases from this open area, which also ascended to four identical corner classrooms on the second floor. Wide stone steps on opposite sides of the first floor led down to two separate playgrounds.

Principal John Hall and all the elementary school teachers created a superb atmosphere for the healthy development of their students. The first directive that all elementary students received from Mr. Hall on the first day of school, was that "The fence around the school is for your safety, and under no circumstances is it to be breached!" Mr. Hall's strict delivery left no question in the minds of the young students about what the consequences would be if one of us were caught on the outside of the iron pipe fence. The principal was a stern, impeccably dressed gentleman who rarely left his secluded and daunting office without his suit jacket. One frosted lens in the principal's bifocals indicated his partial blindness, and his spotless and perfectly pressed dark suits accentuated his marine-sergeant erect posture.

John Hall was proud of his school. He was always immaculately dressed, and when he walked the hallways, he did so in a stately manner. His mere presence in the hallway radiated regal authority and all the students in the school acknowledged his complete command of the elementary school. Classroom appearances by the principal were exceedingly rare. However, anytime Mr. Hall walked into a classroom to speak privately with the teacher, every student would sit motionlessly and focus on being as quiet as a "church mouse."

A very narrow flight of metal stairsteps on the second floor led up to the principal's office, which was located beneath the bell tower. Large windows on the front of the school building provided plenty of natural light in the second-floor open area, where shafts of beaming sunlight highlighted and drew attention to Mr. Hall's office. The eerie aura that radiated from the staircase and elevated watchtower office prompted a fuzzy feeling for tentative elementary students. Students rarely had any reason to be on the steep staircase. But,

Ravenswood Elementary

whenever they did find themselves climbing the off-limit steps, it was usually not for a good reason.

On a couple of occasions—which I recall all too vividly—I had the misfortune of climbing the steep stairs and knocking on the only door that opened into the principal's office. The door's upper half was frosted glass, which enabled Mr. Hall to see and grant permission to enter without getting out of the swivel chair behind his desk. Sitting on one of the hard armless chairs in front of his commanding desk, waiting for the principal to say something, was an unforgettable experience. My classmate and I had been inappropriately mischievous in the classroom. More about this awkward and embarrassing matter later.

Second Grade

I began second grade the day we moved to Willow Grove. My second grade teacher was Mrs. Smith. Mrs. Smith's second-grade class was on the first floor, facing the big boys playground at the back of the school. I don't remember much about Mrs. Smith except she was the youngest teacher in the school. My second grade, unqualified guess, is that she was half the age of all the other elementary teachers. Mrs. Smith was an attractive, stern lady, and always flawlessly dressed. Her demeanor in the classroom seemed so rigid for an elementary school teacher, especially for the second grade. She was aloof in a good, noble way, almost as if she were teaching a class of unfamiliar adults. Yet, the fact

Willow Grove: A Boy, A Family, A Farm

that I remember this detail reveals that her method of teaching caught my attention and has stuck with me. In retrospect, she might have been a new teacher or merely following her own strict teaching standards. Mrs. Smith would likely have taught a high school sophomore class just as she taught her second-grade class. My picayune opinion.

I was three days younger than my first cousin and best friend, James Conrad McCoy. At family gatherings, both boys and girls played with kids their own age. James Conrad and I always teamed up and played together until it was time to depart for home. After we entered grade school, we were in the same classes and sought out each other on the playground. We were always within eyesight of each other. Beginning in the fifth grade, we were assigned to different classrooms. I'm not sure why! I don't think we interrupted the class. Disrupting the teacher or class was something that James Conrad would never instigate or participate in. Though, I can't say the same thing for myself.

Notwithstanding being best friends and enjoying each other's company, James Conrad and I were competitive all during our adolescent years. Especially James Conrad. We were constantly challenging each other, such as who could throw a softball the furthest. Who could kick a football the highest...straight up? Who could make the most basketball shots in a row? The endeavors were mostly athletic and never academic. James Conrad was slightly taller and weighed a little more than me and would usually win our competitions, except

Second Grade

where quickness was involved or shooting free-throw basketball shots.

For the decade that James Conrad and I went to school together, we never talked about girls. We had an unspoken pact that we weren't going to bother with girls. Anytime I goofed and happened to mention a girl's name, James Conrad would roll his disappointed eyes and shoot me a few effective but harmless daggers. All with a grimaced look. We were too busy having shared fun and when we became old enough to work in the fields, we enjoyed ourselves being productive on the farm every time we were together.

Jamesway to the Rescue

One of the primary challenges for the dairy farmer is keeping bacteria at an extremely low or acceptable level. At almost any time during the year, a farm that produces milk for public consumption can expect a surprise visit by the State Health Inspector. A state health inspector will show up at the farm unannounced and immediately commence a cleanliness inspection of the milk house, dairy barn, and barnyard premises. These inspections ensure that the dairy farmer complies with all government standards related to sanitation in the milk house, dairy barn, and general environment in which the dairy cattle occupy in the outside barnyard. If the milk inspector finds fault with how clean the farmer keeps his milk house or is concerned about the overall cleanliness inside the dairy barn, any situation that might negatively affect the health and hygiene of the dairy cattle, the farmer can be prohibited from shipping his milk for commercial processing.

The overall cleanliness of the milk house would be scrutinized, top to bottom, and given a passing, warning, or failing grade. The inspector would start inside the milk house, where he checked the stainless-steel milking pails, twin wash and rinse tubs, and all ancillary equipment. Bacteria are found in the milk house as an invisible film, referred to as milkstone, similar to the plaque removed by a dentist. This stealthy bacterium is unacceptable by health department standards. Over time, milkstone can build up on any stainless-steel surface that regularly encounters fresh, warm milk.

The inspector also checks for cracks in the concrete floor and screen doors that didn't close properly or had holes in the screens that would allow flies to enter the milk house. An example of a minor violation would be a small tear at the bottom of one of the milk house screen doors, which the farmer hadn't noticed or had time to repair. In all the years that my father produced and sold milk, he never had to deal with any issues except a few minor ones.

My book, *Willow Grove,* is the summation of a lot of research and conversations with my parents' generation of aunts and uncles. During a trip in August of 1994 to see family in West Virginia I talked with my Aunt Edra about some details for

Jamesway to the Rescue

my book. Aunt Edra provided me with the names of family members in an old picture that I have included in Willow Grove. She also shared a story with me about a visit from the State Health Inspector who found an infraction that was not even listed on his official West Virginia State Inspection list for milk houses and dairy barns. I think you will find the story interesting and amusing.

My Aunt Edra, Edra Francis Sück, my father's sister, and Conrad Morgan McCoy were married on March 19, 1933, the same month and day of both of their birthdays. Conrad had graduated from West Virginia Tech, where he studied education. At the time of their marriage, Conrad was teaching in the one-room elementary school in Pleasant View, a community along the Ohio River, upriver three miles from Willow Grove and approximately the same distance downriver from Ravenswood. Soon after their marriage, each of the couple's parents gave them a dairy cow. With these two animals, Conrad began his long and successful career as a dairy farmer, businessman, and later Jackson County School Board member.

For several years after their marriage, Uncle Conrad continued to teach public school at Pleasant View and, at the same time, milked a few dairy cows for extra income for his growing family. Uncle Conrad milked his dairy cows in the morning before going to school and then again in the late afternoon after teaching all day. Before electricity, the dairy cows were milked by hand, a job that required muscular arms, hands, and determination. During milking time, Aunt Edra carried their two sons to the dairy barn, where she would construct a playpen with bales of hay, so my cousins John Paul and Eddie would be safe and visible while she helped her husband with the chores. At one point, my aunt and uncle, along with hired help, milked 30 head of cattle twice a day.

Uncle Conrad, about the time he taught school.
Photo courtesy of Joyce McDermott McCoy.

During one such surprise visit by a State Health Inspector to their barn, things seemed to be going well. Satisfied that everything was okay inside the milk house, the inspector nodded his approval. He had just finished with the inside of the dairy barn and was walking toward the main door to exit the barn when his detective's eyes noticed something very unusual. Oh my! Unacceptable! Lying beside a

Jamesway to the Rescue

hay bale was an incredible infraction, which wasn't even on his checklist! It was a baby diaper! Even worse, it was a *soiled* baby diaper! Uncle Conrad was warned about the "questionable violation" while the inspector scribbled his findings on an official inspection report. The infraction was quickly dealt with and didn't happen again...even though Aunt Edra continued carrying the babies to the dairy barn during milking time. And a short stack of clean cloth diapers was always close by! Somewhere!

Another constant source of bacteria in a dairy barn is cow manure. Bacteria is present anywhere there is a speck of cow manure. All manure must be collected and the walkway directly behind the stanchions must be disinfected every day by sweeping it clean with white alkaline lime powder. Removing the waste was done manually with a wide, flat shovel and wheelbarrow.

Daily cleaning of the barn manure trenches was not the most popular chore on the farm. During school days, the job was completed by my father and the hired help. On weekends and during summer vacation from school, the job was outsourced to me and brother Bob—once we were old enough to manage a shovel full of manure and successfully hoist it up over the side of the wheelbarrow. Over the years, Bob and I had watched our father clean the barn and, when we were old enough to help out, Dad's instructions were simple: "You boys go clean out the barn." There were no waivers with this chore and "on-the-job training" wasn't necessary. Those seven words encompassed our basic and advanced job training.

After public school was over for the summer, Dad's teenage nephew, Dewey Gene Davis, would spend much of his summer break at Willow Grove. Dewey Gene was named after Thomas E. Dewey, because, as his sister informed me, their father was interested in history. Happily, Bob and I offered to award this high-tech shovel and wheelbarrow job to our cousin. After a lot of verbal jostling, Dewey Gene, being older and wise to our shenanigans, wouldn't bite and refused to agree to any of our proposals.

In addition to cleaning out the manure trenches, we had to sweep both walkways inside the barn with a generous amount of lime. Also, all the stainless-steel pails, milk cans, and automatic milking equipment had to be scoured, disinfected, and rinsed with clean water. The milk house chore was not an easy one, either. It required a lot of vigorous elbow grease. Dad had new alfalfa lying on the ground and he couldn't wait until Dewey Gene, Bob, and I negotiated how to allocate the three chores, which had to be finished before we could depart for the hayfield. Dad solved the problem by mandating the three of us "take turns."

For any dairy business to prosper, the farmer needs to periodically invest in new equipment and grow the size of his dairy herd. Both are necessary to increase productivity and revenue. This is the reason my family was so frugal and spent their hard-earned profits on investments that were

Jamesway to the Rescue

necessary to increase farm income—and hardly ever on items we *wanted* but did not *need*.

After a few years at Willow Grove, the shovel and wheelbarrow chore succumbed to the same eventual demise as the buggy whip. The unpopular, essential job of shoveling manure by hand was undoubtedly the premise for a wonderful invention: an automatic manure removal system.

Dad's brother James was a distributor for Jamesway, a major machinery company that manufactured manure handling systems. With Uncle Jim's assistance, a brand-new unit was installed in our dairy barn. The Jamesway system consisted of an endless steel conveyor, which automatically "shoveled" all the manure from the trenches on both sides of the barn. The manure in the barn magically disappeared once the endless conveyor belt made one complete revolution. With the simple push of a nickel-sized green button, the Jamesway automatic handling system did its job every day of the year. Everyone, especially Bob and me, was so pleased that Jamesway had come to our rescue. Watching the manure slowly disappear from the barn was a remarkable sight for two country boys. Productivity on the farm had just made a significant, positive jump. Jamesway freed up manpower, enabling everyone to head for the hayfield earlier than usual.

Willow Grove: A Boy, A Family, A Farm

Bedtime Sheriff

Every evening at 8:10 p.m., when the lumbering B&O freight train passed by our house, the noise and vibration from the train's mammoth engine would be so thunderous that conversation would cease until after the locomotive passed the crossing, on its way north to Ravenswood and beyond. Railroad route schedules were very exact, *to the minute*, and train engineers and conductors all over our great nation maintained and adhered to strict departure and arrival schedules. They were so precise that after the arrival of the early steam locomotives in the early 1800s, rural farmers in America's northeastern states would set their watches by the daily whistle from a distant locomotive.

Dad was out of bed, dressed in his work clothes, and inside the milk house before daylight. While he was assembling the milking equipment, Jimmy Ice was in the night pasture below the railroad track rounding up the dairy cows that he would drive up the lane beside our yard to the barnyard. The cows were hungry for their first meal of the day, and just as soon as the barn door was opened, they would swiftly file one by one into the barn. Sometimes two hasty cows would attempt to go through the narrow door at the same time and end up getting stuck together in the barn doorway. Dairy cattle are creatures of habit and have their own internal timetable.

Bedtime Sheriff

Accordingly, at 6:00 a.m., a familiar sound could be heard in the peaceful stillness of the early morning hours. The quarter-sized recessed green button on the electrical box, located just inside the barn door, was pushed in, and the unique mellow sound from the vacuum pump motor would permeate the early morning cool air. The dairy cows were accustomed to the tranquil sound, which was a signal to "let down their milk." The continuous monotone would last for over an hour before the hum would cease, announcing that the last of the three automatic Surge milking machines had just been removed from the udder of the last dairy cow that would be milked...until late afternoon when the same routine would be repeated. Dad always had a long workday, and the only time he had to relax was after supper and before his bedtime.

In essence, if Mom and Dad were going to enjoy any quiet time together, it would have to be after my brothers and I were in bed for the night. Eight o'clock bedtime was a rigid rule around our house, and my brothers and I knew better than to even think about questioning Mom's edict. Any effort would be hopeless. The stringent rule was sometimes relaxed in late spring after the school term was over and during nice summer evenings. Mom would either agree in advance or telegraph some subtle hint that my brothers and I could stay up a little later than usual. For us, knowing the rule was relaxed for the evening was especially important—which I will explain shortly.

Willow Grove: A Boy, A Family, A Farm

But first, the reader needs to appreciate the background and the role that the B&O Railroad played in easily persuading my brothers and me to have our bedroom lights out before the struggling freight train huffed and puffed at a snail's pace past our home at precisely 8:10 p.m. every evening.

Our Willow Grove farm was located alongside a lengthy section of the Ohio River that is in the shape of a near-perfect horseshoe. Visualize our Willow Grove farm at the top and on the outside of a horseshoe. The two ends at the top of the horseshoe compose the heel. The distance across the heel of the horseshoe, as the crow flies, is about three miles, whereas the distance the river water flows between the same two points is close to 13 miles. The B&O Railroad track, which parallels the Ohio River all the way around the *outside* of the

Bedtime Sheriff

horseshoe, is in the state of West Virginia. All the land *inside* the horseshoe is in the Buckeye State.

While playing in the front yard, evidence of the regularly scheduled B&O freight train's eventual arrival at Willow Grove could be heard 30 minutes in advance. On any calm evening, we could hear the muted chugging sound of the B&O steam locomotive as it departed from Graham Station Junction, seven miles away, across the heel of the horseshoe. The chugging sound gradually became louder as the monster freight train traveled eastward. Before the freight train reached the bottom of the horseshoe, the mighty locomotive's familiar sound would slowly dissipate and eventually totally disappear.

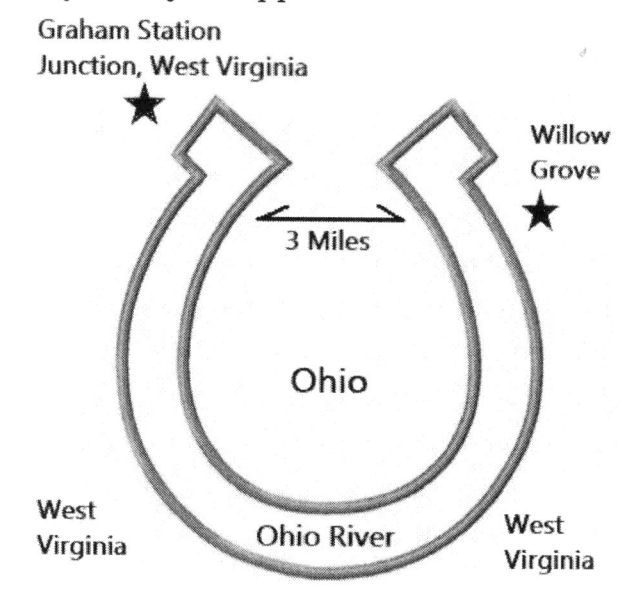

Willow Grove: A Boy, A Family, A Farm

A little while later, we would once again hear a faint muffled sound from the same slow-moving freight train as it approached Willow Grove from the south, after having traveled down the opposite side and across the toe or bend of the horseshoe. Whistles, bells, and heavy panting from the giant steam engine could easily be heard in the distance. Often, the length of the freight train would be over 100 railroad cars. After leaving Graham Station Junction, it took 52 minutes for the locomotive and its long string of coal cars to arrive at Willow Grove Crossing.

The powerful locomotive pulling the coal cars was mammoth, and as it rounded the slight curve between our front yard and night pasture, the engine would bellow giant puffs of jet-black smoke high up into the spotless sky. Every burst of black smoke was accompanied by a familiar *huffing-puffing* cadence, which exemplified just how hard the locomotive labored to pull the string of railroad cars—each piled high with football-size chunks of bituminous coal from southern West Virginia. The heavy engine would shake and shudder so much that chunks of coal would topple off the piles heaped high above the sides of the coal cars. Even the ground under our home would quiver as the train passed by. The vibrations were easily felt lying in bed as the freight train groaned past the Willow Grove Crossing. Occasionally, a bedroom window frame would chime in with a tiny, intermittent rattle, which would only stop after the freight train was slightly beyond the train track crossing.

Bedtime Sheriff

I would lie in bed, listen attentively with my eyes closed, and count the number of cars loaded with coal as they passed the front yard. The rails were long sections of solid steel, and the space between each rail produced its own specific and identifiable sound. If the ends of the rails were snug against each other, the wheels on the railroad cars would quietly pass over the cracks and result in a soft, clicking noise. However, two rails with a wider gap between them would produce a much louder, distinguishable sound as the steel wheels rolled over the wide crack. An identical *clickity-clack, clickity-clack* sound emerged each time the rear wheels on one coal car and the front wheels of the following car passed over a "fish plate," which bolts the ends of the rails together.

Consequently, all a person had to do was count the number of *clickity-clacks* from the first coal car to the last. The count total would equal the exact number of coal cars pulled by the freight train. It was easy to tell when the caboose passed over the wide crack. The *clickity-clack* sound would immediately cease. The house would gradually stop quivering, and the loud puffing sound from the steam engine would grow fainter and fainter until it disappeared into the night. Many times, I counted more than 100 coal cars. It would take a few minutes for so many coal cars to pass by our home, and, more times than not, I would fall asleep before the counting was complete. The never-ending *clickity-clack, clickity-clack, clickity-clack* quickly lulled my tired body to sleep—no matter how hard I tried to stay awake.

The B&O Railroad never knew the role its train played in persuading my brothers and me to be in bed at eight o'clock every night. Eight o'clock and not a minute later!

The 8:10 p.m. daily arrival of the huffing, puffing, chugging locomotive served my mother's objective exceptionally well by encouraging my brothers and me to be in bed by 8:00 p.m. Dad went to bed at about nine to get six or seven hours of much-needed rest before his alarm clock rousted him before 5:00 a.m. Our grandparents and Aunt Jack went to bed shortly after nine. Mom was always the last one in the household to turn out the lights at the end of the day. She would follow everyone else sometime before midnight. Daily bedtime schedules for everyone in the household never varied much, except on beautiful summer evenings or rare special occasions.

When we first moved to Willow Grove in September 1946, Bob and I were just entering elementary school and too gullible to discount one of our mother's proclamations, which was based on an ultimate "tall tale." I don't know when or where Mom got the idea, but somehow, she learned that one of the engineers on the regularly scheduled 8:10 p.m. freight train knew exactly which bedroom Bob and I shared, and each evening when the noisy train passed our house the engineer checked to see if we were in bed, and our bedroom light was turned off. Every night as the noisy freight train

Bedtime Sheriff

wobbled slowly over the steel rails and approached our farm, the single bright dome light on the front of the panting steam engine would shine directly through the tall window in our bedroom, which faced the oncoming train from the south. For a couple of minutes, our bedroom would burst open with a light show from the locomotive's bouncing bright headlight. It seemed like we were in the center of a continuous lightning storm and had no ceiling or roof over our heads. The enormous bright stream of light from the locomotive, randomly bounced sideways, up and down, and off all four walls in our bedroom. The kaleidoscope theatrics of piercing bolts of bright lights all around our bedroom was quite spectacular. At times, it was a challenge to keep both eyes open. Mostly, Bob and I would just lie on our backs in bed with our eyes closed. Every few seconds, we would squint just enough to grab a quick peek at the amazing lights prancing all around our bedroom.

Bob and I were thoroughly convinced that it wouldn't be any problem for the engineer to know if there was any abnormal activity in our bedroom. He could tell if we were in bed or if the bed was empty. The window that allowed the bright beam of light to enter our bedroom was on the same side of the house as the big twin window in the bathroom, which was next to our bedroom. In our opinion, there was ample opportunity for our whereabouts to be known and understood by any observant engineer on the approaching freight train. If either the bathroom or our bedroom lights were on, the

115

engineer would tell the conductor or attendant in the caboose, and one of them would file a report in Ravenswood with the local public officials. The sheriff would be informed about the report, and you guessed it—an investigation would ensue. I don't recall the fine or penalty, but, rest assured, it was more than sufficient to persuade my brothers and me to be in bed before the freight train's bright headlight began dancing all about our bedroom.

On one particular occasion, my parents, brothers, and I had been in Ravenswood, and we were unwittingly arriving back home at the exact time the freight train was approaching Willow Grove. It only would be a matter of a couple of minutes before the "roving eye" would be scouring through our bedroom window. And of all times, Mom forgot to alert the B&O officials that we would be on a family outing and that her sons had permission to stay up a little past their bedtime. Mom always had a convincing answer to any question my brothers and I had when we were young and apprehensive about any situation. Not this time! We just knew Mom had indeed screwed up, and Bob and I would have to cover for her. At the exact moment Dad stopped the car in the driveway, Bob and I jumped out and sprinted off toward the kitchen door as if some raging animal was chasing us.

After Dad killed the engine, he remained seated behind the steering wheel, chuckling, and enjoying the spectacle as Bob and I raced across the driveway, around the corner of the house, into

Bedtime Sheriff

Mom's unlocked kitchen door. As soon as we climbed the stairs and raced through our open bedroom door, we flopped down on the linoleum, yanked off our shoes, and hustled under the top sheet of the double bed with all our clothes on. The overhead light in our bedroom was off. All the while, Bob and I did not move an inch.

After the light show was over, we lay motionless on our backs in the darkness of our bedroom and stared up toward the ceiling. We were waiting for the familiar sound of the caboose passing by our house. And to make sure we were really safe, we waited a little longer before we slowly climbed out of bed. After what we had just encountered, we were not going to take any chances. We took our shoes and tiptoed into the bathroom. After we hung up our good clothes on our designated hooks, we washed our hands and faces, brushed our teeth, and returned to our bed in our pajamas. We would sleep well tonight, knowing that we had covered for our mother. Now she owed us, big-time!

Night and day for nearly a decade, my brothers and I enjoyed the phenomenal sight and sounds of the giant steam locomotives struggling mightily to keep the wheels on a large number of coal cars rolling over the rails. It would take a few minutes for the slow "mule train" to eventually arrive and crawl across the Willow Grove crossing. The spectacle was delightful!

Grandfather Sam Barber worked as a carpenter for the Baltimore & Ohio Railroad, as did Uncle Charlie Curry, who was a B&O Railroad engineer.

Willow Grove: A Boy, A Family, A Farm

Both told interesting and amusing stories about the "hobo Morse code" and some of the habits and tricks of hobos they encountered during the 1940s and early 1950s. Uncle Charlie and Uncle Floyd Hupp were both B&O engineers and, on a few occasions, tossed comic books, apples, and oranges out the open window onto the lawn beside us.

Occasionally, our mother would accompany us to the edge of the embankment above the train track. We would stand at almost eye level with the seated engineer, fully adorned with his pinstriped hat, practically elbow-length, sturdy gloves, and thick charcoal-colored long sleeved shirt. We were so close that we could almost reach out and shake hands with the smiling engineer. Occasionally, we would enjoy an unexpected treat when Uncle Charlie tossed a ribbon-bound roll of comic books out the engineer's open window for my brothers and me. The western comic books were especially exciting and wonderful for my brothers and me. Comic books cost a dime each, which was too expensive for my mother's budget. Mom probably knew in advance about the delivery of the comic books, which would explain why she was willing to chaperone us to see the big B&O steam locomotive up close.

The Hump

All through our younger years, Bob, John, and I were used to being in bed every night by eight o'clock. There were few exceptions and none during

The Hump

the week when school was in session. Once or twice a year in the summer and usually on a Saturday night, my brothers and I would accompany our parents in the family Chevrolet sedan to a special social event. We wouldn't return home until well after our bedtime. Since our body clocks were set for eight o'clock, all three of us would be sound asleep within minutes after Dad started the car for our return trip home.

Another outing that I remember as a youngster was typical of our trips. We had gone to the movie theater in Ravenswood and had enjoyed a double-feature western. Seeing a western movie was a special treat for my brothers and me. So special that Mom could rely on us to behave like little angels, at least for a week or two before the movie arrived at the Alpine Theatre on Washington Street. The mere suggestion that we might not be allowed to go to the movies was a huge club that Mom held over our heads. Even though the threat was subtle, it worked miracles on three rowdy scamps.

While Mom purchased our movie tickets, we scoured the colorful, action-packed movie posters in the glass cases outside the movie theater that depicted exciting scenes of our "B" western heroes. With the stub from our ticket in hand, my brothers and I rushed to our seats and sat quietly, waiting for the theater lights to dim and the curtain to rise. It was an enchanting moment for three country boys. After movie previews and news clips about ongoing global events, a funny cartoon would grab our undivided attention. Finally, the first movie

Willow Grove: A Boy, A Family, A Farm

would suddenly begin! Magically, our eyes danced and our mouths dropped open as we welcomed the moment we had looked forward to for so long. Seeing our favorite cowboy chasing the bad guys with guns blazing was incredibly exciting.

This is a postcard view of Washington Street in Ravenswood, circa the late 1930s. Note the Alpine Theatre to the right.

Often, little John's spontaneous burst of laughter and giggles was so pronounced that I thought he might be escorted out of the theater. Mom did her best to keep him from laughing so loud. Frog Millhouse was singing one of his hilariously funny, deep raspy songs, and John just couldn't contain his jubilation. Mom muffled John's excitement by holding the palm of her hand over

The Hump

his mouth, which was the only way she could manage to contain a little of his enthusiastic outbursts.

After the movie was over, we walked a couple of short blocks back to where our car was parked. My brothers and I, all the while, went on and on about certain thrilling and funny scenes in the movies. We were so excited, happy, and grateful that we could see our heroes on the big screen. In unison, we thanked our parents for taking us to the movies.

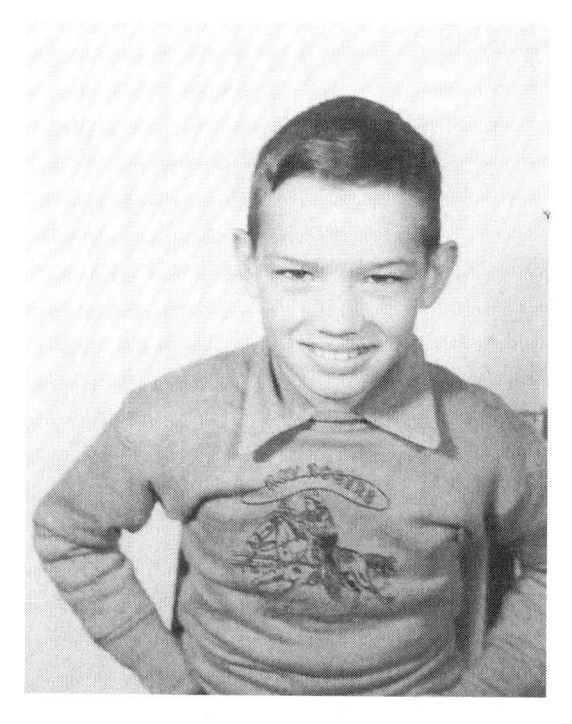

Me, wearing my prized Roy Rogers sweatshirt.

Willow Grove: A Boy, A Family, A Farm

As soon as we reached the car, Bob, John, and I piled into the back seat of our sedan. Still wired from all the excitement, we continued to talk nonstop about our cowboy hero and favorite fight scene. We simultaneously watched the rush of people leaving the movie theater as they walked by our car on the sidewalk. Our parents tolerated the non-stop chatter from the backseat because they knew it would cease very soon after we passed under the last of the bright streetlights in Ravenswood. The asphalt streets in town were smooth and allowed easy conversation in the car. Not so after we reached the noisy gravel road which would take us home to Willow Grove.

About five minutes after Dad started the car, we drove over the rickety steel-frame bridge that crossed over Sandy Creek. The wobbly wood floor was so noisy that it was impossible to hear anyone talking! All four rubber tires sprayed the under-carriage and metal fender wells with a continuous barrage of pebbles hurled up from the roadbed by the tire treads. The dull racket from the constant pummeling under the car quickly lulled three tired bodies into a pleasant daze...and soon afterward into a sound sleep.

Once we crossed the bridge, conversation in the car dropped off substantially. Beyond the rickety bridge, the only light visible anywhere was from our car's headlights and an occasional glimmer in the distance, which pinpointed the presence of a house or one of the accompanying farm buildings. The total absence of outside scenery plus the racket

The Hump

from under the car and the constant mellow hum of the engine were more than enough to force our heavy eyelids to droop slowly and close for good.

As soon as our car had fully engaged the vast darkness of the pitch-black night, John climbed up on the soft shelf underneath the sloping back window and stretched out on his stomach. He was small enough that neither his head nor feet were jammed up against either side of the car. Simultaneously, Bob captured the back bench seat for himself, which left me with the worst spot in the car. I lowered myself down onto the floorboard and draped my body over the round driveshaft hump. Bob and I took turns riding the hump. He reminded me it was his turn to stretch out on the cushy backseat. I argued with him about how awful it was to wrestle with the driveshaft in the middle of my stomach—all the way home. It just wasn't fair! No dice! I was destined to try and get some sleep draped over the awful hump.

After a few minutes of being draped over the hump, I'd had enough! I pushed myself up from the floorboard, straightened my aching back, and peered over the back of the front seat between Mom and Dad. They were talking and enjoying the quiet serenity that enveloped the car. The backseat chatter was long gone. Mom and Dad were both tired, but someone had to stay awake to drive the car. Mom helped by talking with Dad about their day's events.

My eyes were only partially open when I rose up off the hump. I gazed at the muted yellow, white, and red lights, which blossomed below the vehicle's dashboard. The miniature lights were colorful and radiated a festive ambiance. Except for the two beams of light shining straight ahead on the roadbed, and the soft multicolored rainbow from the instrument panel, everything outside the car was invisible. The darkness that completely masked the tranquil countryside and occupied the backseat was so all-encompassing that I could barely keep my eyes half-open. My eyes blinked between closed and half-mast long enough to ponder—how in the world can Dad stay awake long enough to drive home? If my life depended on it, there was absolutely no way I could ever do what Dad was doing! No way! Indeed, I was a young, healthy boy with absolutely no cares or problems in the world. I was living and growing up in a beautiful country with a wonderful family.

As quickly as I raised up off the hump and half-consciously scrutinized the cockpit, my body succumbed and slowly slithered back down over the hard driveshaft. I would fight with the hump until the car's interior lights came on and Mom announced that we were home. Bob and John could easily have spent the rest of the night in their soft nests. Not me! I couldn't wait to get upstairs, brush my teeth, undress, and climb up onto my side of our soft mattress so that I could lie flat on my back. I was so tired that I promptly concluded that I'd just have to double up on my bedtime prayers tomorrow night.

The Hump

Sometime after 1946, Mom took Bob and me to a matinee to see *The Yearling*. Watching such a great movie on a bigger-than-life screen was a thrill. As country boys who loved all animals, the movie had some scenes that broke our hearts. The same was true of *Uncle Tom's Cabin*. Mom did her best to expose us to positive intellectual matters and ethical issues that she thought were important.

When my brothers and I were growing up, the only time books touched our hands was at school and when we had to do homework. We were too energetic and wanted to go outside where we could run and play. There were so many things on the farm that we enjoyed—we were always disappointed anytime it rained.

When an all-day drizzle confined us to the house, we would lie on our stomachs in the middle of the family room and flip through our sparse but well-read collection of colorful Western comic books. Otherwise, reading was not of interest to me or my brothers. The nearest library was eight miles away in Ravenswood and trips back and forth were not practical, even if my brothers and I had had a sincere interest in reading as a hobby.

The only other reading material in our home was the Bible and *Hoard's Dairyman*, the only subscription publication I remember, other than my grandparents' *Ravenswood News*.

After supper, when my father retired to the comfort of the family room couch, he would invariably reach for his handy *Hoard's Dairyman*. Each copy was read from front to back so often that

Willow Grove: A Boy, A Family, A Farm

by the time a new issue arrived, the current copy would be well-used and tattered. Dad would scour the magazine for new information about dairy farming and new products and equipment that would enhance farm productivity. He liked and routinely used squeeze tubes of Squibb's "Instant-Use" penicillin ointment for mastitis. The milk supplement that I mixed with warm water to feed our baby calves was advertised in nearly every issue of *Hoard's Dairyman*.

The Hump

I enjoyed peering over my father's shoulder and asking him questions about the article he was reading, especially if it had a picture of a blue-ribbon cow or a new farm tractor. Dad read every article in the magazine about artificial insemination, which he utilized himself to grow our dairy herd and assist the Jackson County Agricultural Department on appointed Sundays each month.

Fun and Games with Bob

I was 18 months older than brother Bob. We grew up on two different dairy farms and only had each other and, later, little brother John, as playmates. Until I reached the age when I could help my father around the farm, Bob and I were constant companions.

From a very young age, we were often busy inventing new games and new ways of entertaining ourselves. One popular game, mumbley-peg, used a penknife. The game's objective was to perform various maneuvers in chronological order, with the knife always landing blade first in the soft grass. A player lost his turn when the handle didn't stick upright enough to place two fingers between the ground and the knife handle. After losing, the player had to start all over the next time, from the very beginning. I understand the game stemmed from sailors taking turns throwing a penknife at each other's feet. The one who sticks his knife the closest to his opponent's foot is the winner.

Willow Grove: A Boy, A Family, A Farm

If the knife inadvertently stuck in the top of the opponent's foot, the injured player was automatically the winner and won the bet! A dozen or so tricks were performed in order of difficulty. Easiest first, with each succeeding trick increasingly more difficult. Each trick had a nickname. One of the more difficult gyrations with the penknife game was called "spank the baby." It was tough!

We were always either in full view or close by our mother's watchful eye. During an all-day steady drizzle, Bob and I would often crawl under the front porch to play with our toy tractors. Even on rainy days, the beige-colored, soft dirt was always perfectly dry and had the texture of Pillsbury baking flour. We would spend hours bent over under the porch tending to fields of hay and corn on our respective dirt farms. We played in close quarters for hours and rarely had any differences. But "Katy bar the door" when we did have a disagreement! Both of our beautiful and perfectly manicured dirt farms would be blown to smithereens, and dust clouds would erupt from out under both ends of the porch. What a disaster! Our playtime was over!

We had to remove all of our dusty clothes on the outside porch before we could step inside the laundry room. Then we would streak naked through the laundry room door into Mom's kitchen and up the back stairs to a full bathtub of soapy water. By the time we reached the upstairs bathroom, the melee that erupted under the front

Fun and Games with Bob

porch was all but forgotten. Usually, our mother never knew we had been in a scuffle. Because, if she found out, she would assign both of us to a chair in different corners of the kitchen, where she would continue to work and keep an eye on us. Mom would point at the electric clock on the wall and counsel: "When the big hand reaches six, you can get up."

Left to right: me holding Pedro and Tippy, cousin Elsie Jean Barber, John and Bob; with the Ohio River in the background.

Man alive! It was awful! The big hand seemed like it would never move. Our penalty was usually

Willow Grove: A Boy, A Family, A Farm

20 to 30 minutes, which felt like hours to us. Boy, did we hate sitting and waiting for the big hand to reach Mom's punitive number on the clock! And, if we weren't quiet and obedient, the big hand would be extended to the next digit or two before we could get up off of our penalty chairs.

So, mum was the word, regardless of how angry we had been just a short time earlier. We would even get penalized if Mom caught one of us making a face at the other—which we did, whenever we thought she wouldn't catch us! We quickly learned that Mom had 20-20 vision in the back of her head!

Pay Now or Pay Later

Dad was leading my mother and brothers single-file down a narrow hallway in a hospital that was formerly a residential mansion in Ravenswood. We were on our way home after visiting a relative. I was trailing behind when we walked past a hospital bed that was pushed up against the wall in the hallway.

As I passed by the hospital bed, I could see under the edge of a skimpy white sheet that covered the naked body of an old man. His rear end was at eye level and it was not a pleasant sight for a preschool boy. The old man was sleeping.

When we got in our family's Chevrolet sedan and everyone was settled in for our ride home, I asked my mother: Mama, why was that old man sleeping in the hallway?

Pay Now or Pay Later

    Mom chose her words slowly and explained that he was from a poor family and could not afford a hospital room. Mom knew the old man's surname and talked about how he had always struggled to keep his family warm and provide enough food for his wife and children. The house he had lived in for much of his life was considered a shack by most standards: cold in the winter, hot in the summer, and weather-beaten from years of neglect.

    The image of the old man's buttocks and Mom's rendering of his life made an indelible impression on me. So much so, that I concluded at a very young age that I would never let that happen to me. I resolved never to be poor and, sometime during my teenage years, the memory of that sad episode evolved into a metaphor: "Pay now or pay later." That is, work hard when you are young and healthy and become financially secure before it's too late.

    The scene and the consequences of being poor have never escaped my memory.

Willow Grove: A Boy, A Family, A Farm

Chapter Two: Too Young

Willow Grove: A Boy, A Family, A Farm

Muck Brawl!

By early spring, the bulk of hay and straw stored in the dairy barn and smaller calf barn had been fed to the animals, or used as bedding during the winter and cold, spring days. With most of the bales of hay and straw gone, Bob and I would climb up into the open loft in the calf barn and begin moving bales of straw. It was a perfect time to build our annual spring fort or hideout. We would rearrange and stack bales of straw until we had constructed a fairly large room with one side facing the dairy barn. The cracks between the long vertical boards on the side of the calf barn provided ample light and a full view of the barnyard between the big dairy barn and the calf barn. The entrance to the hideout was a long tunnel composed of one or two 45-degree turns. There was enough space in the tunnel to crawl between the bales to the big room, which had a high ceiling but not high enough to stand up. The tunnel entrance to our secret hideout was camouflaged by random bales of hay and straw. From the ground floor of the calf building, there was no visual indication that the hayloft contained a magnificent hiding spot. The extra bales of straw in the loft appeared to be scattered, just as they did before the hideout was constructed.

Willow Grove: A Boy, A Family, A Farm

During the summer, Bob and I would have our mother prepare a picnic lunch, which we would bring to our secret hideout. We would enter the hideout after pushing and sliding the lunch basket ahead of us through the tunnel. After only a few seconds, we couldn't wait to open the basket and devour its contents. In the basket would be a couple of different types of sandwiches cut diagonally, pickle spears, a quart of iced-sweetened tea, and always a surprise dessert. Eating our picnic lunch in our hideout was fun, and the food always tasted extra delicious!

One day, Bob and I had gone undercover and were lying low in our hideout. We'd done something that we knew would precipitate verbal punishment from our grandfather. Grandpa's vocal wrath was almost as bad as the willow switch punishment from our mother. So, we decided to lie low until Grandpa settled down.

It wasn't long before the inevitable occurred. Peeking through the cracks in our hideout wall, we saw Grandpa walking up the lane from the house toward the barn. Shortly thereafter, he opened the gate to the barnyard and walked toward the calf barn. He stopped about halfway between the two barns—calling our names and scanning the horizon for any signs of Bob and me. We were only about 50 feet away, close enough to see Grandpa's face was ruddy with aggravation. Not seeing or hearing a peep from us, he continued toward the calf barn. The door to the calf barn was almost directly below our hiding spot. We listened to the door squeak as

Muck Brawl!

it slowly opened. Grandpa was right below us but couldn't see us! There were no windows in our straw fort, so we couldn't see him, either. After less than a minute, we heard the door squeak once again. Thankfully, Grandpa was leaving the calf pen. We could see him, through the cracks, walking back across the barnyard toward the gate. Wow, were we relieved! Our hideout was camouflaged, perfectly.

Bob and I stayed out of sight for the rest of the day. That evening, Grandpa walked into the kitchen while we were having supper. His complexion was normal, which we were happy to see. Grandpa had had time to cool off and forget about what we had done. At one time, he had been a young boy himself and knew that accidents do happen. All he wanted to know was how we broke his brand-new shovel handle.

We explained that we wanted to build a birdhouse and had found some boards we needed in the machine shed. The best, soft pine boards were at the bottom of a stack of hard oak lumber, which was too difficult for us to cut into short pieces and nail together for our birdhouse.

Then Bob and I had an idea. Instead of removing every board on top of the soft pine and then restacking the lumber, we would raise the top oak boards just enough to slide a couple of pine boards out from under the stack. All we needed was a little help. Instead of a used piece of lumber, I foolishly grabbed Grandpa's brand-new shovel and used it as leverage. One of the men had left it outside, leaning up against the tool shed. The shovel worked fine. I raised several oak boards just high enough for Bob to pull a pine board out from under the stack. We only needed one more board, which was lower in the stack and required more leverage than I could muster. So, together Bob and I both ramped down on the shovel handle as hard as we could. With double leverage, we successfully raised the pile of lumber, but inadvertently cracked the handle of Grandpa's new, long-handled shovel.

Grandpa had far too much experience and understanding regarding how something should be done. It would have been naive for anyone to have ever attempted to refute his condemnation of shoddy work. This was especially true if the issue revolved around the safety or welfare of one of the workers, farm animals, or some expense that would have to come out of the farm bank account. Grandpa could glance from afar and instantly tell if one of his workhorses had been mistreated or worked too hard and too long. He could look at a broken wheel on a wagon, a cracked blade on a plow, or something as simple as a bent prong on a pitchfork and know if the item had been misused or damaged because of carelessness, abuse, or just plain stupidity and laziness. To prosper on a farm, the farmer needed to take care of the plethora of tools and equipment that were mandatory to perform numerous chores. Farming wasn't profitable enough to replace every piece of equipment that might break during the workday. Often, it was too expensive to replace a piece of

Muck Brawl!

equipment. Moreover, even if an item was relatively inexpensive, the farmer couldn't afford to take precious time out of his workday to go buy a replacement. The nearest hardware store was in Ravenswood, a six-mile trip which, before the convenience of automobiles, could take a few hours to travel by horse and wagon.

There are many ways equipment can be inadvertently broken. Some situations are unavoidable and costly, while others can be a nuisance, but still require valuable time to repair. Grandpa recognized that breakage could be anticipated. Accordingly, he kept duplicates of some tools and had spare parts for more expensive equipment.

There was something else that Grandpa would never tolerate...and that was for anyone to lie to him. If anyone needlessly broke a tool, it had better get repaired quickly before Grandpa found out. And if an easy repair wasn't possible, you'd better tell the truth, especially if the equipment broke because of a brain-dead mistake or blatant abuse. Ironically, even if a piece of equipment was broken and repaired without Grandpa's knowledge, all too often, he would eventually find out anyway! He knew his farm equipment like the back of his hand and could recognize a repair job, no matter how minor or how perfectly it was masked.

Bob and I were both apologetic about being so stupid. We could have easily used a scrap two-by-four to accomplish the same objective. Grandpa could see that we had already suffered enough and with a nod of understanding, commented that he would buy a new handle the next time he was at the Rural Supply store in Ravenswood.

We had just left our hideout and were meandering across the barnyard toward the silos at the west end of the dairy barn. Dad and Tommy Speece were in the barn, milking the cows. Mom was in the kitchen preparing supper. Our grandparents were in their living quarters, probably having their usual early supper. Thankfully, it was too early for them to be sitting on the side porch, which they customarily did every evening after supper.

It had been a full day of spirited fun for Bob and me. Besides being a little worn out, it was getting late in the afternoon, and our stomachs were begging for a snack. I don't remember what precipitated our subsequent skirmish, but considering Bob and I both had short fuses, it didn't take much before we were kicking dirt with our bare feet toward each other's ankles and legs. Before long, the kicking accelerated, and dust billowed about our torsos until we were both holding our breath to avoid eating particles of dirt and whirling dust. Immediately, we separated and began scouring the barnyard for perfect clods of dirt and dried cow chips to heave at each other. Usually, any solid contact was on the back, since we instinctively turned our eyes away from any incoming projectile. We never wore shirts in the summer, so when a clod of dirt slammed into a

Muck Brawl!

bare back, it would sting for a few seconds and later reveal a bruised spot.

The skirmish continued to strengthen. After every successful impact, the velocity of each subsequent clod increased on both sides. We were getting angrier at each other by the minute, and neither of us was about to stop and call a truce. The brotherly battle was on!

The clods kept flying until an extra hard one blistered my bare back. That was it! I'd had it! I raced toward a big fresh cow pile and scooped up a handful of dark runny muck. Bob saw what I was doing and took off running as fast as he could. I could outrun Bob, and as soon as I was within striking distance, I hurled a gooey handful of cow manure at his back. Bullseye! On impact, Bob stopped dead in his tracks, and *I* turned and started running. Turnabout was fair play! We traded a few handfuls of the fresh mushy stuff, until Bob turned his head toward me too soon, and *whammo!* a big glob of smelly artillery hit him directly in the face. His face was liberally speckled with smatterings of black, stinking cow manure! When I say fresh...I mean fresh! Still warm! Now... Bob was really, unbelievably furious! Our minor skirmish had morphed into a total, all-out civil war!

It was easy to tell when Bob's irritation was going to upgrade to seething rage! With squinting, almost completely closed eyes, he would stare straight into the eyes of his prey and simultaneously curl his tongue up under the roof of his mouth, bite down on the tip of his acrobatic tongue, and with shoulders and both fists firmly cocked, swagger toward his victim. Trust me! The curled tongue gesture wasn't to be taken lightly! Now, broken bones were on my brother's menu! Translation: scatter and don't look back! A Willow Grove barnyard civil war was on, and the prey had better head for the tall grass. And that is precisely what I did! My bare feet were hardly touching the ground when I executed a half-somersault over the wood railing fence that outlined the barnyard perimeter. Even though I could outrun my brother, the distance between us was way too short for comfort. I shouldn't stop until I crossed the border into the next county!

As soon as I crossed the narrow strip of grass along the cornfield, I began parting thick rows of corn stalks with both hands and ran deep, row after row, into the interior of the cornfield. All the while, I could hear Bob behind me thrashing like rolling thunder through the same rows of corn stalks, hot on my tail. The field of corn was so dense and tall that it was impossible to see beyond two or three rows. After breaking through dozens of rows of corn, I turned 90 degrees and ran between the rows for some distance before I dropped face down on the ground. Lying motionless, I could hear Bob still running straight ahead through the cornfield, which put more distance between the two of us. Bob suddenly realized that I had changed directions. He couldn't hear me and, needless to say, I was far enough away that he couldn't see me, either. Suddenly Bob stopped running. The

Muck Brawl!

cornfield was as quiet as a church mouse. Several seconds went by without a single sound. After a while, I heard Bob walking through the cornfield. He had given up! The rustle of corn stalks was a conspicuous, audible indicator he was leaving the cornfield, and when the familiar sound of corn stalks being smacked stopped, I knew Bob was out of the cornfield. Or...had he just stopped walking and was still somewhere inside the cornfield, staying put and waiting for me to make a move and disclose my hiding spot? I wasn't going to take any chance, whatsoever! I knew I had more patience than Bob and could outwait him.

Sure enough! I was right. Not too much later, I heard rustling corn stalks. Bob was still in the cornfield. Only this time, he announced: "I'm leaving, and if I were you, I'd sleep out here tonight." I didn't trust his threat of leaving the cornfield and remained behind, in my rabbit hole. Bob continued to mutter pejorative advice as he walked between the cornrows. I could tell he was moving in the opposite direction from where I was holed up. The rustling of corn stalks gradually diminished as he walked away. Finally, the rustling completely stopped. I waited a little longer. Then... ever so slowly, I hunkered down and practically crawled on my belly through several rows of corn, until I could peek out of the cornfield. I could see the barn in the distance, and sure enough, Bob was climbing over the barnyard fence. He stopped at the cattle watering trough and buried his face under the pool of water. He cupped handfuls of water with both hands and splashed it all over his bare chest and down his backside, all the while rubbing anxiously to get rid of the dried, stinky muck. Moments later, he opened the barnyard gate and walked by the front side of the barn. Bob was soon out of sight from where I was crouched down in the cornfield.

I waited a few minutes longer, then made my way to the rear door on the east end of the dairy barn where Dad and Jimmy Ice were milking the cows. I knew that once I was inside the dairy barn with Dad, the ruckus between Bob and me would automatically be put on hold—as long as I never left Dad's side!

A few minutes after I hightailed it to the dairy barn and Dad, I looked out the open barn door facing the house, and, sure enough, I saw Bob walking down the vegetable garden path on his way to the pigpen. Safe at last, I walked out of the dairy barn into the milk house and mixed up four buckets of liquid milk supplement to feed the baby calves housed in a pen in one corner of the calf barn. My two primary morning and evening responsibilities were feeding the baby calves and comforting them with fresh bales of straw to bed down on.

Inside the milk house, I grabbed the nozzle on the hose hanging on the wall and walked out onto the open patio, where I sprayed myself from top to bottom with cool water. I washed the dried muck from my stomach and back, which Dad didn't even notice or if he did, he didn't comment. I guess I

Muck Brawl!

looked normal after nearly a full day of escapades on the farm.

Every morning and evening after the cows were milked, Dad and Jimmy would fill up a quart glass container with fresh milk. I walked with Dad to the house, happy to carry our jar of warm milk tucked safely between my arms, up against my bare stomach. I wanted to accumulate some brownie points with Dad, even though I wasn't sure they would help that much.

We entered the kitchen, and Bob was already sitting at the kitchen table, dressed in fresh shorts and a clean T-shirt. He had already taken his evening bath. Usually, we bathed, brushed our teeth, and put on our pajamas a few minutes before bedtime. Evidently, Bob had decided to rid himself of the stench from the barnyard muck before supper and not wait until bedtime. Earlier, I had scrubbed and doused my hands with a disinfectant solution in the milk house. So, I was semi-clean. At least good enough for supper.

Bob and I looked at each other. It seemed as though there was an unspoken truce between us. If Mom had seen or had been aware of our quarrel, she would have punished both of us with chores, which we considered sheer torture. A punishment that we wanted to avoid. We would have to hoe the entire potato patch, weed the vegetable garden, or scrub the porch floor outside the laundry room on hands and knees. Even worse, sometimes Mom's disciplinary training included an extra punitive double whammy: we would have to sit on penalty chairs in different corners of the kitchen for a half-hour or longer and watch her work. None of this contemporary punishment to go to your bedroom.

Bob and me.

Granted, our bedroom was bare bones, but at least we might be able to read a 10-cent Roy Rogers comic book, providing we were able to sneak it past Mom. The penalty chairs were so boring and a terrible waste of good playtime. Half an hour seemed like an eternity! Yet, even when Mom punished us, there was no way we could hold a

Muck Brawl!

grudge against her. Watching Mom work to feed, clothe, and take care of us took the edge off any lingering ire from her strict, no-nonsense discipline.

By the time supper was over and the whole family was enjoying one of Mom's wonderful desserts, our fracas had transformed into mutual, implicit, brotherly forgiveness. We shared the same double bed, and in a couple of hours, we would be dead to the world, and today's battle would be long gone and forgotten.

Harvesting Hair

Every 10 days or so, Mom would reach for her handy box of tools from the bottom kitchen cabinet drawer, unfold a long cape, and then place a stool in an open area away from the kitchen table. Mom would announce: "Who wants to be first?" It was time for a haircut—something that my brothers and I never looked forward to. But rules were rules, and especially during school term: if one hair touched the top of your ear, it was time to harvest some hair.

Dad had a lot of experience cutting hair. He was actually a professional when it came to cutting curly, knotted hair, because every spring on our Silverton farm, Dad would manhandle dozens of sheep during the strenuous shearing process. So, shearing three little country bumpkins' heads while they are sitting on a stool was a piece of cake for Dad.

Willow Grove: A Boy, A Family, A Farm

After Mom chocked us with the tie-string on the barber apron, Dad would oil his manual, hand-held clippers and commence cutting hair. The clippers utilized multiple tiny scissors that cut each time the two handles on the clippers were squeezed together. And, as sure as the rising sun, yelping, twisting, and bending over would start almost immediately. The stainless-steel clippers would cut 10 hairs and seemingly pull out five more by the roots. Mom must have felt sorry for us because she retired the manual clippers after several months of agony and bought new electric clippers.

Dad had one hairstyle that he favored for all three of us boys. Relatively short, but not quite a buzz cut. We didn't care at all what our haircuts looked like. We were young rascals and combing our hair was a waste of time anyway. Besides, there wasn't a convenient mirror anywhere in the house low enough for us to see what we looked like before or after a haircut.

Later, when I was a little older and began scrutinizing Dad's haircuts, I slowly realized that I must have more hair on one side of my head than the other. Dad didn't use a bowl on top of our heads as a guide, which probably would have helped. With the aid of Mom's hand-held mirror, I complained to Dad that one side was longer than the other side. Dad's retort was simple: He would cut the longer side a little shorter. Afterward, the previously long side was too short! Finally, before all my hair was cut off, I just gave up!

Willow Switches

Willow Switches

No child could have had a more resolute mother than my two brothers and I. Mom's three sons' welfare was always foremost in any decisions while we were growing up. Even before we were born, Mom did whatever she could to ensure that her newborns would be as healthy as possible. Mom didn't have much extra money in the family budget to work with, but somehow, someway, she always managed to find a way to stretch our income so that my brothers and I would have what was important to grow up strong and healthy.

Our mother was the principal disciplinarian in our family. Anytime my brothers or I managed to get in trouble, the guilty would have to trek across our long garden to a massive willow tree and select a switch that would psychologically aid Mom during sentencing and ensuing manual punishment. Invariably, the guilty would have to make at least two trips through the garden before the selected willow switch met Mom's punitive standards. The first switch was usually as limber as a wet noodle, which didn't fly with our mother. And the more trips we had to make back to the willow tree—our stalling tactic—only exacerbated the imminent punishment. Mom was busy and needed to get back to her chores. It was easy to discern when Mom was thoroughly finished with our delaying tactics. She didn't have time for foolishness. So, we usually found a suitable weapon after the second trip. Three trips to the willow tree was really playing with fire!

During cold weather, Mom would warm up the naughty son's bottom with a wooden paddle instead of the standard summer-prescribed willow switch. The hefty flat paddle made much more noise than the flimsy willow switches. And, regardless of what artillery Mom used, our feelings were hurt far more than the cursory stinging of our little butts, even though tiny welts would sometimes appear on the back of our legs, caused by jumping up and down, trying to pull away and escape from Mom's tight grip. Our antics would interfere with Mom's aim, and she'd miss her intended target and instead strike the back of our bare legs. Mom's punishments were effective, and each carried an extended warranty. So, any punitive measure from Mom lasted for quite some time.

Using a willow switch to teach discipline wasn't unique to our household. Dolly Parton was disciplined the same way by her Mama and described how she, too, had to pick "out one of those reedy little sting-your-butt-bad switches." During my and Dolly's era, sending kids to their room as punishment would be analogous to eating your Wheaties with vanilla yogurt instead of farm-fresh whole milk. The positive willow switch dogma will linger much longer in the gray matter than a negative, passive trip to a bedroom with all its distractions. The former is quite positive, whereas the latter is counter-effective all too often!

Willow Switches

Until we were old enough to go to school, our mother made it a top priority to know exactly where we were and what we were doing—at all times! This was true whether we were outside playing in the yard or inside the house in our designated play area. If we were playing in the yard, Mom would steadily check on us by coming outside or taking a quick peek through one of the windows. Even when she knew where we were and what we were doing—but couldn't directly see us—she would listen for familiar sounds. If, for some reason, we were too quiet for too long, she would stop what she was doing and check on us to confirm that all was copacetic. Mom was very particular about what we were doing, and her strictness was exactly what any caring mother would do to protect her children.

Mom was the disciplinarian in our family and we knew that there was no need to go to our Dad and seek solace from him. My parents supported each other and always presented a united front, no matter what!

Make do or do Without

Both of my parents were teenagers during the Great Depression. The "Roaring '20s" ended with the stock market crash which ushered in the beginning of the Great Depression in October 1929. Subsequently, many struggling American companies had to lay off employees. My mother's father, Sam Barber, lost his job with B&O, which left the family with no income. Unlike today, there wasn't any federal government unemployment insurance for out-of-work families to lean on. My mother had a difficult childhood and endured a lot of unhappiness. At a very young age, she had to shoulder many household duties that were the sole responsibility of an average housewife. The family income was meager, at best, and my mother was deprived of the basic necessities that most children take for granted.

The Barbers: My grandfather, grandmother, Aunt Helen, and Mom as a child.

As a child, sometimes when my mother's mother, Elsie (who we grandchildren would eventually call "Ma"), baked cornbread for supper, the kids would sit on the bank of the front yard and wait for the milkman to pass by. Ma would give the

Make do or do Without

kids 10 cents for two quarts of skim milk, which was considered a treat for the family. On other special occasions, Mom would walk to the local bakery and purchase a sack of stale donuts for a dime. It was a long walk to the bakery, but worth every step! The adults would warm the stale donuts and relish the rare treat with a cup of hot coffee.

The two sisters didn't own many clothes, and what they did have were mostly second-hand items. A single pair of school shoes—without holes in the soles—was considered a luxury. Aunt Helen was in high school and, like most teenagers, craved new clothing. So, anytime the family budget would permit, Aunt Helen was first to get a new garment. Eventually, Ma would alter the garment to my mother's size. Occasionally, Mom would get her very own brand-new dress and when she did, it was always a momentous occasion!

My mother was attending Lincoln Elementary School when her teacher noticed that the soles of her shoes had holes in them. The teacher gave her a note to give to her father, Sam (who we would eventually call "Pa"), and explained to Mom that the slip of paper would enable her to get a new pair of shoes. Mom was so excited about the prospect of new shoes that she could hardly wait to get home to give the important note to her father.

Pa was still out of work, and the family had no income. Yet, when Mom gave her father the note from her teacher, he became quite angry. Even though my grandfather had no income, he was too proud, and under no circumstances would his

Willow Grove: A Boy, A Family, A Farm

family accept welfare. Her father crumpled the note and threw it in the trash. My mother was an extremely disappointed little girl. Nevertheless, she accepted her father's decision and continued to pad the inside soles of her worn-out shoes with cardboard. My mother longed for the day that she would be happy with her own family, and vowed that her children would not have to experience her deprived childhood.

My mother (center), with friends Juanita Bailey on left and Edna Rau on right, in 1934. They are standing on the huge horseshoe-shaped lawn in front of Parkersburg High.

Make do or do Without

My father, Lawrence Sück, was 14 in 1934 and the only child living at home. His older siblings—Edra, James, and Dorothy—were married and had started their own families. All the work previously shared by the three older children now fell on Dad's shoulders. As many responsible young men did during this era, a 14-year-old often labored just as hard as the adults and sometimes even harder than the hired help. As a teenager, Dad routinely worked side by side with the older men plowing fields, planting crops, mowing hay, and a myriad of other tasks. His responsibility was to make sure the jobs were finished and simultaneously meet his father's strict expectations. Not only did Grandpa expect the work to be done by the time he returned home, he also expected the chores to be done right. Grandpa was adamant about performing a job only one way: the right way! If a job didn't meet his expectations, his response was very clear and direct: "If you are going to do something, either do it right the first time or don't do it at all." Grandpa was a hardworking farmer and, sometimes, during the extra-busy summer months, had several projects going on at the same time. He worked with the local district of the Jackson County Road Department and often left home early in the morning with his team of draft horses. He wouldn't return to the farm until late in the day. While Grandpa was elsewhere working on county road projects, Dad was given work assignments and was expected to have the projects completed by the time his father returned from a full day's work for the county.

Willow Grove: A Boy, A Family, A Farm

Both my parents dropped out of high school in the tenth grade: Dad, so he could work full time on the farm with his father, and Mom, so she could help her family after her mother became pregnant. It was a difficult pregnancy for my grandmother, and the responsibility for the housework, as well as taking care of her little brother, Robert, and her sister Helen's daughter, Ruth Anne, fell squarely on Mom's shoulders.

Pa finally was called back to work by B&O. When he worked in Parkersburg, Mom would rise early and set the kitchen table with biscuits, fried potatoes, eggs, and coffee for her father's breakfast. When he worked out of town, he would leave the house Sunday afternoon, walk to the train station, where he would board the work train and ride to his assigned work site at various locations on the B&O track system. The work crew wouldn't return to Parkersburg until Friday afternoon. All week, while the men were away from home, they lived and slept in a company railroad car.

Aunt Helen was working at the American Viscose Corporation, and my grandfather was away all week working for the B&O. Mom tried to attend school when she could, but anytime her mother wasn't feeling well, she would stay home and care for her mother and the children. It wasn't long before Mom got so far behind in her schoolwork that she decided to quit school. There was just too much work around the house that needed to be done, plus two of Mom's aunts had her scared to death about her mother's condition. Her aunts

Make do or do Without

counseled Mom that at her mother's age—she could die from the pregnancy. So, whatever her mother wanted, day or night, Mom worked feverishly to ensure that her mother was comfortable and that all of the housework was done each day. A lot was expected of the teenager. Her household responsibilities were overwhelming and seemed endless. It was a difficult time for Mom, and at the end of each day, she was exhausted.

Mom in 1937, age 16.

After Elsie Jean was born and Mom's mother had regained her strength, Mom applied for a job at the Viscose and was hired for $10 a week. The job required working all three shifts, which was a challenge but did allow her more time to be a teenager and socialize with her friends. Now Mom even had time to enjoy and sing with a group in Parkersburg and nearby communities. The group sang country and gospel songs at different churches. Mom played the guitar and sang solo with the group. If the group had an engagement that required spending the night away from home, Aunt Helen would accompany Mom. The group performed on local radio stations in Parkersburg and Clarksburg. My mother was with the group for about two years.

Country Boy meets City Girl

Mom and her mother would travel from Parkersburg to Silverton a couple of times a year to visit with Ma's sister Pearl, brother-in-law Perry, and cousins Jim, Virgil, and Floyd Hupp. The trip from Parkersburg to Silverton on the narrow interstate roadway took a few hours during the 1930s. U.S. Highway 21 was a paved road punctuated with multiple meandering curves, steep hills, and sharp bends. Even though cars traveled at a relatively slow speed, flat tires were commonplace. More than one flat tire on a single trip wasn't uncommon. Too often, due to mechanical problems, the trip would end up taking all day.

During one of Mom's trips to Silverton, her older cousin Jim Hupp was having a birthday party. The Hupp residence was located a short distance beyond my grandparents' farm on the road between Silverton and Wilding. On the evening of the birthday party, several teenagers from the community were walking up the road on their way to attend Jim's party. One boy in particular was

Country Boy meets City Girl

dressed entirely in white: white trousers, white shirt, white shoes. He had a generous measure of thick black hair and a dark, honeyed complexion, which highlighted his pearly white teeth and infectious smile. The young man was Lawrence Sück.

Before Mom left with her mother to visit her cousins, her father had gone to Snyder's Department Store on Fourth Street in Parkersburg and purchased a pair of deeply discounted ladies' dress shoes. Her father sawed off the heels so the shoes would appear to be a new pair of slippers, which were fashionable among teenage girls. The girls at Jim's birthday party were all outfitted in stylish, colorful dresses, and everyone was having a good time. Everyone except my mother! She was shy and a bit intimidated by how well the other girls were dressed. Instead of enjoying herself and mixing with the rest of the kids, Mom spent much of the evening aloof and generally secluded. Oil lamps were the only source of illumination and, consequently, the dimly lit atmosphere made it easy for Mom to remain apart, even while surrounded by all the adults and other kids at the party. Even though it was dark outside and only my mother knew the source of her shoes, the darkness wasn't much comfort. Yet, in spite of Mom's effort to maintain a low profile among the joyous birthday attendees, one handsome guest stealthily observed and bookmarked her charming presence: my father, Lawrence Suek.

Willow Grove: A Boy, A Family, A Farm

The next couple years (1936 and 1937) were a challenge for my mother and father. Both were fully committed to their parents' daily demands so much so that any thoughts of a teenage romance had to remain secondary in their young lives. The distance between Silverton and Parkersburg was such a major obstacle that their relationship was surely tested during the two years. My father was a handsome young man from a successful family and had to have caught the attention of many teenage girls in the Silverton and Ravenswood communities. Yet, he worked very hard on the family farm to acquire his father's permission so that he could travel to Parkersburg to see his girlfriend. For the first time my mother was very happy and worked equally hard on their teenage relationship. In my humble opinion, their long-distance courtship would, very likely, never have survived in today's contemporary world.

Before the mid-1900s, rural parents depended heavily on their sons and daughters to help with the workload on the farm and in the family home. Dad was living at home and was indispensable. His father needed him to help run the family farm. My mother did a lot of housework during the days that her father was away each week, and her mother, more than anyone, realized that her daughter's help around the house would be sorely missed.

After Mom had saved enough money working at the rayon plant, she and Aunt Helen hired a lady to help their mother with house cleaning and care for baby Elsie Jean, Robert, and Ruth Anne, Aunt

Country Boy meets City Girl

Helen's daughter. The extra help gave Mom more free time to spend with her friends and with Dad whenever he came to visit. They talked about getting married, but both sets of parents refused to give their permission. They were too young to get married: Mom was only 16 and Dad, 17. They had talked about eloping, but Mom truly wanted to be married at home. Both kept hoping that their parents would eventually acquiesce and honor their request. All Mom and Dad could do was keep asking their respective parents for permission to get married.

As I mentioned before, my mother and I collaborated on many details in this book. We looked forward to our weekly Sunday afternoon phone calls over a period of two decades. Fortunately, Mom was able to read a rough draft of a manuscript that encompassed much of the text in this book and a second book titled *Silverton*.

I inherited my mother's many files that she had assembled over the decades of her life. One of the treasures that she left behind was a collection of 134 letters that she and my father wrote to each other during the latter part of 1936 and all of 1937, beginning just a few months after my father and Jim, Virgil, and Floyd Hupp made arrangements for Dad to pick them up after Sunday School during Mom's next trip to visit with her aunt and cousins in Silverton.

The plan worked like a charm. After Sunday School, the Hupp brothers piled into the back of the pickup truck that Dad was driving. Mom was invited to sit in the front seat, squeezed between Dad and his best friend, Zeldon Combs.

Dad, Mom, Blondine Casto, and Jim Hupp.

The long distance between Silverton and Parkersburg prevented Lawrence and Kathrine from seeing each other very often. Telephone calls were too expensive, so Kathrine and Lawrence wrote faithfully to each other weekly, between December 1936 to New Year's Eve 1937—the day the two teenagers were married. I have 134 letters that Mom and Dad wrote to each other. Mom trumped Dad by two letters. The very first letters revealed that each was deeply committed. It is obvious that both were smitten with each other at Jim Hupp's birthday party. They address each other in their initial letters with loving endearments. Even though they lived a significant distance apart and would not see each other very often, they committed

Country Boy meets City Girl

themselves to each other. It is obvious that my teenage mother was very happy about their courtship. Her prayers were answered, and she was dating a young man who would give her a happy married life.

My parents, around the time of their courtship. I would be willing to bet that the all-white outfit my father is wearing is the same outfit he was wearing when they met.

Willow Grove: A Boy, A Family, A Farm

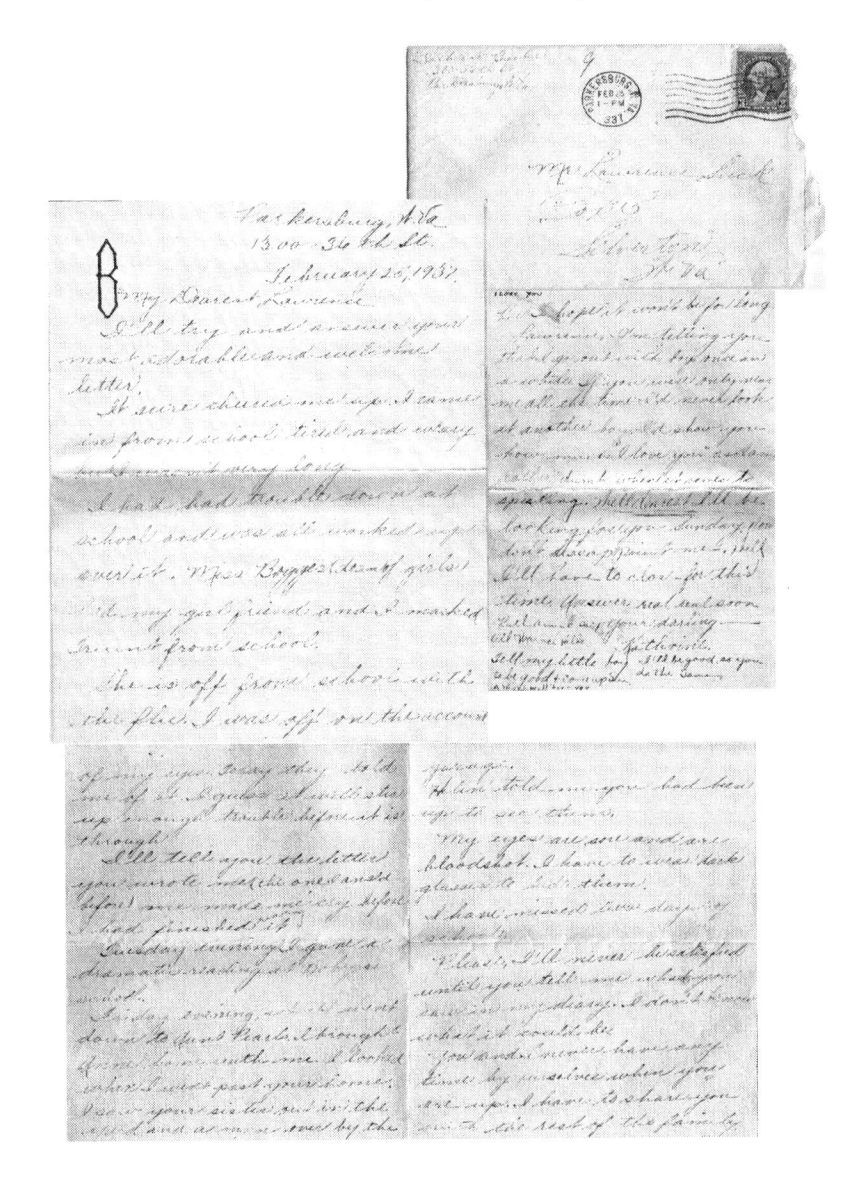

Country Boy meets City Girl

Parkersburg, WVa
1300 36th St.
February 25, 1937

My Dearest Lawrence
I'll try and answer your most adorable and welcome letter.
It sure cheered me up. I came in from school tired and weary but I wasn't very long.
I had had trouble down at school and was all worked up over it. Miss Bogges (dean of girls) had my girl friend and I marked truent from school.
She is off from school with the flu. I was off on the account of my eyes. Today they told me of it. I guess it will stir up enough trouble before it is through.
I'll tell you the letter you wrote me (the one I ans'd before) sure made me cry before I finished reading it.
Tuesday evening I gave a dramatic reading at Boby's school.
Friday evening when I went down to Aunt Pearls, I brought Anne home with me [Aunt Pearl lived in Silverton, just above Dad's home and his parents' farm. Anne is Mom's niece, her sister Helen's daughter]. *I looked when I went past your home. I saw your sister out in the yard and a man over by the garage.*
Helen told me you had been up to see them. [Dad went up to the Hupps when Helen was visiting from Parkersburg. The Hupps' home was a mile or so above my grandparents' farm. Ruth Anne probably accompanied Helen to Silverton and returned with Mom.]
My eyes are sore and are bloodshot. I have to wear dark glasses to hide them.

Willow Grove: A Boy, A Family, A Farm

I have missed two days of school.

Please, I'll never be satisfied until you tell me what you saw in my diary. I don't know what it could be.

You and I never have any time by ourselves when you are up. I have to share you with the rest of the family. [Start of page four. At top of the page, Mom wrote in tiny letters, I love you.] But I hope it won't be for long.

Lawrence, I'm telling you that I go out with boys once in a while. If you were only near me all the time I'd never look at another boy. I'd show you how much "I love you" as I am rather dumb when it comes to speaking. Well dearest I'll be looking for you Sunday. Now don't disappoint me. Well I'll have to close for this time. Answer real real soon. Ruth Anne said your darling—tell "Warnce" hello.

Kathrine

Tell my little boy to be good and come up Sun. Always will love you.

I'll be good so you do the same.

[Ruth Anne was about four years old; old enough to travel from Parkersburg to Silverton with an adult and able to stay alone with her Aunt Pearl in Silverton.]

They had planned to get married on New Year's Day, 1938. Mom's older sister Helen and Jim Banks, a friend of Mom's, planned to stand with the couple during the wedding ceremony. Jim was working in St. Marys, several miles up the Ohio

Country Boy meets City Girl

River from Parkersburg. At the last minute, Jim unexpectedly phoned and informed Kathrine that he *wouldn't* be able to come home for the weekend.

After Jim phoned and while the family was gathered around the kitchen table contemplating what to do about the wedding, Mom's father suggested: "Why wait until tomorrow? Why not get married today!"

Everyone liked the idea!

On Friday, December 31, 1937, at 8:00 p.m., Kathrine Genevieve Barber and Edmond Lawrence Sück were married at her parents' home on Thirty Sixth and Willard streets in Parkersburg. In addition to her parents, Mom's two sisters and brother—Helen, Elsie Jean, and Robert—were present during the wedding.

The next day, Mom's two aunts arrived at her parents' home in time to attend the wedding, which had already taken place the night before. They had invited themselves and were annoyed to learn the big event was over. After venting their frustration, the two ladies were appeased after accepting a cup of coffee and a generous slice of wedding cake delivered by Wier McCutchen from Storks' Bakery. Still, Martha was annoyed enough to proclaim to the family: "Well, I'll give them six months, and she'll be back home." Martha was very wrong. The new couple—my parents—would raise three sons and spend nearly 57 years together as husband and wife.

My parents' marriage was rock solid, never wavered, and was ideal from three youngsters'

Willow Grove: A Boy, A Family, A Farm

points of view. They provided me and my brothers with absolute peace and security and we never questioned how much they cared for us. I never heard them even raise their voice to one another. I never saw them even get close to a common marriage fight. I hesitate to even use the word "fight" in any sentence that includes my parents' marriage. I witnessed their devotion to each other during their natural lives. My brothers and I were so fortunate to have wonderful parents to guide us during our formative years.

Despite my parents' obvious commitment to us and to each other, their marriage was not without its heartaches. During one of my routine Sunday phone calls with my mother, she commented that there is a Sück buried on the family farm where I was born in Silverton, West Virginia. Mom went on to explain that before I was born, she had a miscarriage. Both of my parents were very disappointed, especially my mother. Dad took the fetus, placed it in a shoe box, and buried it somewhere in the meadow on the farm. He never revealed where the baby girl was buried. Mom was 18 years old when she had the miscarriage. She worked especially hard to ensure that her subsequent three sons were born perfect and healthy!

I would be remiss if I didn't admit to the readers of *Willow Grove* and the companion book *Silverton* that my mother left a note with her and Dad's letters that read: "To be burned at my death[.] Do

Country Boy meets City Girl

<u>not Read.</u>" The small 3-M sticky note was signed: "KB Sück Mom."

When I found out about the letters and note, I pondered Mom's request, but not for long. There was no way that I was going to burn over a year of Americana history that had been preserved by my mother. It was too important to me! I wanted to read about how my parents and grandparents lived during the latter part of 1936 and all of 1937. I knew a lot about their lives during that era, yet the 134 letters would give me actual insight that was too valuable to destroy. However, I did wait until almost 11 years after Mom's death on October 11, 2012, to read the first letter.

At the time I wrote this narrative for *Willow Grove*, I had only read one letter that is included in this book. In addition, I had perused another 10 letters and learned information that will be fascinating to my family and friends. During the writing of *Willow Grove*, I had formed an opinion about certain aspects of my father's and mother's teenage personalities and lives. The reading I have done so far has supported my conjecture.

Before *Silverton* is published, I will read all 134 letters and will include my observations in the book. *Silverton* will include a letter written by my father to my mother, as well as more of Mom's writings. All of their letters are going to be digitized and preserved for family history. I can't wait to share more stories about my young parents' lives during the late 1930s. They lived and endured The Great Depression. In summary, I have no remorse for not following my mother's directions. But, to make sure it is okay, I will keep my fingers crossed and behind my back when I read Mom's and Dad's letters!

Immediately after her marriage, Mom moved in with my father and my grandparents. The farmhouse was modern, wonderfully comfortable, and had ample living space for four adults.

Living on an active farm was a huge adjustment for a big-city girl like Mom. Each morning she would rise before dawn and help her mother-in-law, my grandmother Nannie, prepare a hearty breakfast for her father-in-law, husband, and occasionally the farmhands who helped during harvesting season. Every other day, homemade bread was made from scratch and baked in time for the men when they returned from the barn for breakfast. On warm summer days when the windows were open, the men could smell the delightful aroma from the piping hot fresh bread well before they reached the back-screen door, which opened into the mudroom outside Nannie's kitchen door.

Twice a week, Mom's job was to measure the correct amount of flour and yeast and place the mixture on a large flat pan. The flour in the middle of the pile was partially pushed aside to make a small puddle of milk in the center of the pan. Next, the flour and milk were slowly and thoroughly kneaded until the dough was just the right texture to place on individual bread pans or forged into individual bread rolls. The tacky dough was placed

Country Boy meets City Girl

in a warm spot, and after the dough doubled in size, it was baked to a golden-brown color in the oven. Eight loaves of bread and dozens of huge, puffy rolls were baked about every other day for consumption by the family.

Nannie and my mother had breakfast prepared when the men arrived from the barn after milking the dairy cows. They would feast on eggs, pancakes, sausage or ham, fresh-baked bread or biscuits...which the men smothered with homemade butter and grape or strawberry jam. Don't forget the pot of piping hot, fresh-brewed coffee on top of the wood burning stove!

After breakfast, Mom helped her mother-in-law hand-wash and dry all the breakfast dishes, pots, and pans and then commenced thinking about what to prepare for the noon meal. In the interim, other chores kept them busy.

Behind the main dairy barn, along the outer edge of the barnyard was a sizable chicken house. Mom cared for the chickens, which mostly involved daily watering and feeding cracked corn. She gathered the eggs and dutifully washed each one. Most would be sold to the hatchery in Ravenswood. The money from the sale of eggs was used to help buy next week's groceries. Occasionally, Mom would pitch in and help the men whenever they needed an extra pair of hands, if the job wasn't too hefty for a small woman. My grandfather delivered bottled milk in Ravenswood six days a week, and Mom helped by hand-writing the milk bills, which

Willow Grove: A Boy, A Family, A Farm

Grandpa left behind with his residential customers and retail grocery stores.

Mom and Dad standing on the bumper of the Maple Lawn Dairy milk truck, 1937.

    As a young boy, I witnessed how consistently my mother worked at being a good mother, wife, and daughter-in-law. Mom cared deeply for everyone in her family. She also did her best to be a good friend to everyone she met, regardless of whether that person was a close acquaintance or a total stranger. She taught my brothers and me to always show respect for others, especially our elders, whether rich, poor, or oppressed. We were taught to be courteous and sensitive to other people's feelings. As an adult, Mom saved anything that had potential future value. Her rule of thumb was to buy what the family needed, not what the family wanted!

My mother was, without any doubt, the glue that held all these different living endeavors together and the lubricant that made every one of the family's living arrangements a happy experience. My mother was a central part of why I wanted to write this book.

First Winter

During our first winter at Willow Grove, 1946-1947, my parents, Bob, John, and I lived in essentially two rooms on the first floor of the main house. The house had been woefully neglected and needed a lot of work before it would meet my mother's aesthetic and hygienic standards. In between Mom's heavy load of daily chores, she spent many arduous hours on her hands and knees—scraping, scrubbing, and repairing damaged floors and walls. It took most of the winter, but Mom eventually conquered the enormous task. In addition, Mom added two extra plates to her breakfast, dinner, and supper table for my grandparents during the first few months after we moved to Willow Grove.

The first winter at Willow Grove was harsh, and Grandma had to wear insulated boots in the little house to keep her feet warm. The brick walls had no insulation, and, worse, the house was built on a concrete slab. After several days of sub-freezing temperatures, the ground and eventually the hardwood floors in the little house would get cold and stay cold until well after the ground thawed in the spring. In contrast, the main house had thick hardwood floors above a full basement, which kept the floors toasty warm several feet out from the base of the floor-level fireplaces. A single Warm Morning stove in Mom's kitchen and the two fireplaces in adjacent rooms were all that were used to adequately heat the whole downstairs throughout the cold months of the year.

My grandparents lived the first winter in the little brick house next to our house. The only source of heat was one fireplace that didn't keep the concrete floor warm enough for my very thin and dainty grandmother. So, in the spring after enduring an uncomfortable winter, Grandma asked Mom if she and Grandpa could move into the vacant rooms in the "big house." My parents had already lived with my grandparents in their home in Silverton, so living together in the same house was nothing new for either family. Mom wholeheartedly agreed with the idea and encouraged them not to spend another winter in the "little house."

In the spring of 1947, the vacant sitting room was converted into a very functional kitchen, which became part of my grandparents' new living quarters in the main house. They spent their first Willow Grove winter in the small brick house which had no basement and only a single fireplace. As it

First Winter

turned out, the little house was just too cold for my grandparents and, after the first winter, they moved into a section of the big house, which had 10 spacious rooms and five fireplaces. There was plenty of room in the main house for two families. In fact, during the winter of 1950, a dozen people—seven adults and five children—lived happily and comfortably in three different living quarters of the big house.

The two separate downstairs living quarters were also pleasantly comfortable even though the house's exterior walls had no insulation and were composed of two rows of bricks from the ground foundation to the eves. The inside row of bricks was perpendicular to the lengthwise outside row, with no air space in between. The house's exterior walls were a lot different than the brick façade of today's modern homes.

First Summer

During the summer of 1947, Grandma and Grandpa moved into two empty rooms on the first floor of the main house. The rooms were large with high ceilings and located on the north side of the house. A formal sitting room with an early 1900s-era fireplace was remodeled into a roomy kitchen. The second room was already a formal living room. Double windows in the living room looked out over the gigantic front yard and the state of Ohio on the opposite side of the Ohio River. The splendid living room occupied the entire width of the front side of the house. During the summer, my grandparents slept in the front guest bedroom on the second floor, which also afforded the same charming view of the Ohio River.

The two constantly burning fireplaces were in Mom's family room and Grandma's kitchen. Mom's family room, which was sandwiched between her kitchen and Grandma's kitchen, was always aglow from continuous daytime coal and wood fires in both fireplaces. The new living arrangement was perfect for both families. Grandma's kitchen was handily separated from Mom's family room by a tall panel door with adjustable transom glass window above the top of the door. All of the downstairs doors had transom windows that swiveled in the middle of the window frame for good air circulation between rooms. Grandma's kitchen table and chairs were arranged in a spacious alcove composed of three bay windows. The alcove offered a magnificent view of the north lawn and the Wolverton farmhouse and apple orchard. It was deep enough that Grandma could also view the Ohio River to the west and the huge sycamore tree and farm buildings to the east.

On the left side of Grandma's interior kitchen door that opened into Mom's family room was another door that exited onto the side porch ornamented with spindle-spoke railings on two sides. From the porch, they could watch all of the activity around the barnyard, and, during harvesting in the summer and fall, watch the men going to and from the hay- and cornfields. For my

First Summer

grandparents, sitting together on the cushioned swing, enjoying a lazy summer drizzle was as peaceful as it can get.

A striking winding staircase climbed up from Grandma's living room to the second-floor bedrooms, providing easy access to my grandparents' bedroom and a full bathroom. The staircase was wide enough for two people to walk side-by-side and not nearly as narrow and steep as the back stairs that ascended to the bedrooms from Mom's kitchen. When my brothers and I were little squirts, the beautiful wide railing atop the cherry wood banister provided entertainment during boring periods of "cabin fever," brought on by several days of subzero weather. We would take turns sliding backward down from the second-floor hallway to the first-floor foyer. We were not the first kids to amuse ourselves sliding down the banister. In the mid-1930s, cousins Bill, Archie, and June Barber and their siblings straddled the same banister. And likely, they were not the first, either. The banister was a magnet for energetic kids and no doubt entertained several generations of youngsters, dating back to the turn of the century.

Handsome Chariot

Bob and I were too young to be of any help in the hayfields, yet we were old enough to know that in the hayfields was where we wanted to be. We wanted to be with Dad and watch the men with their pitchforks load hay on the wagon, and later unload the mammoth loads in the dairy barn hay loft.

Together, Bob and I considered possible ways to persuade our father to let us go with him and the men to the hayfield. Sitting down on the empty flatbed wagon on the way to the field was okay with our father. His concern was on the way back to the barn. There just wasn't a safe place for Bob and me to sit. We couldn't ride on top of the high load of hay. It was too dangerous. It would be too easy to slide off the slippery hay and get hurt. Moreover, the tractor pulling the loaded hay wagon barely had enough room for one or two adults to stand behind Dad on the tractor drawbar. Bob and I both knew Dad was right, yet we still wished there was some way we could accompany the men to and from the hayfield.

Walking back from the hayfield was an option, but not one Bob and I cared to consider. Walking a long distance on a hot, dusty road with the blistering sun beating down on our bare shoulders wouldn't be much fun. Besides, Dad and the men would have all the hay unloaded by the time we walked back to the barn.

It was exhilarating to watch the long shiny hay forks grab giant gobs of hay and hoist the massive bundle straight up to where it latched onto the steel track, high in the barn's peak. It was even more exciting when Dad yanked the clothesline rope, which triggered the hay forks to break open and allow the hay to fall with a resounding *whoosh* when the big bundle of hay hit the hayloft floor. The

Handsome Chariot

whoosh would create a quick burst of dusty air that would softly smack your face and straighten your hair for an amusing second or two. We didn't want to miss this entertaining spectacle. We just had to find a way!

Just maybe! Yes! Of course! Bob and I had a great idea! We scouted the farm buildings and ended up with several scrap pieces of lumber and a pair of large steel wheels attached to the ends of a sturdy axle. The distance between the two wheels was perfect—just wide enough for Bob and me to sit side-by-side. All we needed to do was construct a flat surface that would fit between the wheels on top of the axle. A sturdy tongue could be affixed to the front of a perfectly engineered, homemade cart.

With our supplies in hand, off we went to our roomy tool shed, where we found nails, a hammer, and a handsaw. Most of the lumber was old, used hardwood which challenged our youthful and amateurish craftsmanship. But we were determined and worked persistently off and on for a couple of days until we could stand back and appreciate our handiwork. The stubborn hardwood lumber didn't succumb easily to the repeated beating that Bob and I leveled at several knotty areas in the two-by-four boards we were trying to nail together. Our masterful cart had more bent nails in it than quills on a porcupine. Regardless, we were determined not to give in to a few pieces of petrified lumber! In several places, we had to drive multiple nails in the same area where one nail would have sufficed, had we been able to drive a nail completely through the

Willow Grove: A Boy, A Family, A Farm

top board into the one below. In the meantime, Bob and I were not sure if Dad was aware of our stealthy project. But if he was, I'll bet he was amused and knew exactly what our plan was for our beautiful, two-wheeled chariot. After all, Dad had grown up on a dairy farm and had built a cart or two himself. He understood why young country boys loved their carts.

A few days later, Dad mowed a huge field of plush alfalfa that was sprinkled throughout with aromatic red clover. The limp hay had to lie fully exposed in the hayfield under the hot sun until all of moisture in the fresh, green grass had evaporated. Afterward, the dry hay would be raked into dozens of rows across the wide field, from one side to the other. As far as Bob and I were concerned, the location of the hayfield where Dad cut down the hay was perfect for our new cart. The field was clear at the far end of the farm, next to the hill pasture. The ride to the hayfield would take about 10 minutes, which was ample time to enjoy a fun-filled, open-air ride in our newly built, homemade cart.

After all the night dew had evaporated from the windrows of hay, Dad climbed up on the red Farmall M and headed across the barnyard, where the long, flat-bed wagon was parked in the grass on the arched driveway beside the dairy barn. Elmer Scarberry and Pop Jett were already standing beside the wagon. Elmer was holding the tongue about waist high with his left hand. He was ready to hitch the hay wagon to the drawbar on the

Handsome Chariot

tractor as soon as Dad backed it close enough to align the twin holes in the wagon tongue to the matching hole in the tractor drawbar. In his right hand, Elmer grasped a three-inch-long, heavy-duty steel pin. Once the steel pin dropped in place, the hay wagon would be securely fastened to the tractor and ready to head for the hayfield.

Not surprisingly, Bob and I were standing at the rear of the hay wagon, proudly erect beside our magnificent chariot. We were all set for our maiden voyage. All we needed to do was attach the tongue of our cart to a large steel ring dangling freely from the back end of the hay wagon. Bob and I had our eyes focused like a laser on Dad, knowing that as soon as the hay wagon was safely tethered to the tractor, he would look up and glance back toward us—standing dutifully beside our cart. And, as soon as he spotted us, he would surely realize from the expressions on our faces that we were waiting for his smiling nod of approval that it was okay to fasten the tongue of our cart to the back of the hay wagon.

By the time Dad got down off the tractor and walked back to where we were, Bob and I had already fastened the cart to the ring on the wagon. Our hooking mechanism wasn't the best. Certainly not state-of-the-art, but it worked okay. Crudely, we had nailed one end of a rope to the tongue on our cart. The other end of the short rope was tied to the hefty steel ring at the back of the hay wagon. Since our cart had only two wheels, it was absolutely imperative that there was no slack in the rope between the tongue of our cart and the ring on the hay wagon. Dad checked the sturdiness of our knot by pushing down on the tongue with both hands. There was hardly any slack. We passed Dad's safety check. We were good to go!

As Dad walked forward to mount the Farmall M, Bob and I jumped on the cart and sat down, side-by-side, facing forward toward the hay wagon and tractor. Bob and I had huge smiles plastered on our faces. We were so proud of our achievement and so happy that Dad allowed us to journey to the hayfield with him and the men. It was exactly what we had hoped for and worked so hard to achieve.

As soon as we arrive at the hayfield, Bob and I would untie our cart from the wagon and wait patiently by the edge of the hayfield while the men hooked the empty hay wagon to the New Holland hay-loader. The hay-loader would gather the dried alfalfa off the ground and load it onto the wagon. Once fully loaded, Dad would pull the load of hay back across the hayfield to where Bob and I would be waiting to refasten our cart to the rear of the hay wagon, ready for the return trip back to the barn. That was the plan!

Before Dad raised his left foot off the clutch on the tractor, he glanced back toward my brother and me one more time. He wanted to make sure we were sitting down and ready to move forward on our first trip to the hayfield in our cart. Satisfied, Dad pushed the throttle forward and steered the muscular Farmall out of the barnyard driveway onto the gravel lane. We were on our way! Our cart

Handsome Chariot

followed obediently and tracked nicely behind the hay wagon. Each time Dad shifted the tractor into a higher gear, the empty hay wagon and our cart picked up speed. Shortly thereafter, our convoy was cruising down the lane at a nice clip. Dad turned and looked back toward us, while keeping one hand on the steering wheel. He wanted to see how the cart was behaving and check on its two beaming occupants. Dad turned around several times during the ride to the hayfield. I knew exactly what he was doing. He wanted to make sure our cart was minding itself and not weaving erratically like an inebriated party-goer as the tractor picked up speed. Weaving is a common problem with some trailers. After a while, Dad was satisfied that our engineering was satisfactory and our homemade cart was roadworthy. The only minor downside was that the low cart didn't have a windshield to deflect the dust kicked up by the wagon and the tractor. No big deal! So what if we had to cope with a little dust and intermittently close both eyes for a second or two. We were having too much fun to worry about breathing or eating a little dust!

Dad took us to a spot inside the hayfield where we untied our cart from the empty wagon. We weren't too far from where Dad parked the hay-loader the previous week when he had used it in a nearby field. There were no shade trees close by, and the sun was baking our bare backs. Yet, Bob and I didn't mind it at all! We both had hats with a bill that shaded our eyes from the bright sun. Plus, my hat had a built-in, fold-down pair of sunglasses, which I could employ with the flick of my index finger. We were both happy to be with our father and the men. Besides, during our ride back to the barn, the breeze would cool us off.

It wasn't long before Dad pulled the loaded hay wagon over to where we were standing beside our cart. As soon as Dad stopped the tractor, Bob and I quickly hitched the cart to the back of the wagon, which was stacked super high with loose hay. It was vital that we didn't waste too much of the men's valuable time. Our cart was fun and great entertainment for Bob and me, but hardly productive and didn't contribute favorably to the bottom line of the farm's income statement!

The load of hay was monstrous and towered high above our little cart. We were completely hidden from Dad's view. After 15 or 20 seconds, Bob stepped out from behind the hay wagon, just far enough to see Dad sitting on the tractor. He waved and yelled: "OKAY, DAD, WE'RE READY!"

Off we went across the smooth hayfield. Dad slowed down to a crawl as he approached the undulating grassy drainage ditch at the edge of the hayfield, alongside the lane. The loaded hay wagon had to be maneuvered through the ditch at the right angle and just the right speed to keep some of the gigantic load of hay from scooting off the wagon onto the ground. Dad was a professional at protecting a load of hay during this tricky procedure. The reason he had to drive the tractor at such a sharp angle onto the lane was that the road was too narrow and too close to the property line.

Handsome Chariot

The practical way to pull a load of hay onto the lane is to approach it head-on, and not at an angle that will cause the wagon or vehicle to tilt each time one of the four wheels enters and pulls out of the grassy drainage ditch.

Bob and I rode to and from the hayfield twice before it was time for our hearty noontime meal. We enjoyed riding in our homemade cart and managed not to waste too much of the men's time hitching and unhitching from the hay wagon.

We were almost halfway down the lane on our last, late-afternoon trip from the hayfield, where Dad and the men had been working since mid-morning. The last load of hay was smaller than usual, but it still completely obscured our cart from Dad's view. The cart was tied so close behind the hay wagon that we couldn't see Dad, and Dad couldn't see us.

We had just crossed over the county road and were a short distance beyond the bus building when I noticed something potentially disastrous and instantly bellowed—"OH, RATS." There was way too much noise for Dad to hear me or have any idea what was happening behind the hay wagon, since we were completely hidden from his view. The knot in the rope—the rope we used to fasten the tongue of our cart to the rear of the hay wagon—was slowing coming untied! Regrettably, Bob and I had been in too big of a hurry! We didn't properly tether our trusty square-knot, which, if tied correctly, is as dependable as an indestructible padlock without a key. Bewildered, I watched the tongue of the cart slowly creep down toward the rapidly moving roadbed underneath our fast-moving cart. The end of the long tongue was too far away for me to reach the knot, plus we were traveling fast enough that all Bob and I could do was hang on and pray we'd make it to the barn—really, really soon!

The prognosis *did not* look good! The rope was hanging down enough for the end of the tongue to slightly kiss the ground, jerking the cart a little and repeatedly skipping up and down a couple of inches off the surface of the road. Soon, the end of the wooden tongue started plowing a shallow rut down the middle of the gravel lane. Yet, the danger Bob and I were in didn't seem too colossal for us. At a relatively young age, we had already experienced plenty of similar situations in which we ended up with only minor cuts and bruises. We were confident that everything would be okay if we just stayed put and toughed it out until we reached the barn! Positive thinking! But unfortunately, only wishful thinking!

With the tongue tilted down and plowing the roadbed, the floor of the two-wheeled cart was also tilted down at a steep angle...so much so that Bob and I were halfway sitting down and standing up. All we could do was brace our feet against the low headboard on the front of the cart and dig our fingernails into the sideboards. Sadly, instead of the tongue continuing to plow a harmless crevice down the middle of the road to the barn, the tip of the tongue finally hit a pothole in the road and dug

Handsome Chariot

in! Instantaneously, the cart went airborne, flipped end-over-end, and Bob and I were catapulted out onto the hard road. The hay wagon and Dad unwittingly journeyed merrily down the lane toward the barn.

After the dust settled and the crash scene was assessed, we saw that our cart had been utterly destroyed. It looked like it had been hit by a freight train. I was lying on my back, framed all around by several pieces of lumber snuggled randomly up against my arms, torso, and legs. Most of the boards had shiny nails sticking up or pushed down into the roadbed. As far as I could tell, I didn't see any blood or feel broken bones. Bob was lying several feet away from me with only one paltry board next to him. Other than stars swirling before our eyes and a few minor scrapes, we were just dusty-dirty from head to toe. Essentially, we were both okay—save one thing! The sharp end of a single long nail sticking out of one measly board lying next to Bob—was embedded deep in his shoulder.

The fun we had riding on our two-wheeled cart was over. Too, Bob and I had no interest in rebuilding. All we wanted to do now was clear the mess out of the middle of the road. We'd be in trouble if one of our nails punctured a rubber tire on one of the farm vehicles. Later, we'd pick up the scattered pieces of lumber from the side of the road and drag them to the woodshed, where the splintered lumber would be used as kindling and firewood. But for now, the only thing we could do was walk down the lane to the house to show Mom the bloody puncture in Bob's shoulder. Bob and I already knew what would happen next. Mom would send us to the bathroom, where Bob would bathe and put on clean clothes so that Mom could chauffeur him to Ravenswood to see Dr. Monroe... and face the dreaded needle. Another tetanus shot was forthcoming for one of the Willow Grove country bumpkins.

Farmall M

I was seven years old when we moved to Willow Grove, and I'd have to wait another three or four years before I could sit on the seat of our Farmall M and reach the clutch and brake pedals. In the meantime, I'd just have to be content riding on the big red tractor with my father. On some occasions when I was allowed to go to the fields with Dad, he would let me stand or sit between his legs and steer the tractor—all by myself. Since the hay and cornfields were big and flat, there wasn't much of a chance that my steering would do any harm to the tractor or farm equipment that the tractor was pulling.

While I was steering, Dad would maneuver the hand accelerator and engage the clutch and foot pedals when necessary. Dad enjoyed my company and would chuckle whenever I attempted to negotiate a sharp turn in a recently plowed field. Instead of the tricycle wheels turning the tractor, as they would easily do on solid ground, the tractor

Farmall M

would sometimes continue straight ahead while the twisted front wheels bulldozed a big mound of loose soil ahead of its two small wheels. When I finally yelled for help, Dad would laugh at the spectacle as he came to my rescue. Sometimes he would wait until the last moment and then salvage my predicament in ample time to keep the tractor from hitting a fence post. On a few occasions, I was almost sure we were going to ram the fence. Yet, deep down, I knew Dad would come to my aid at the right time. After the incident was over, we both laughed about what had just occurred.

Milking Tilly

About the time I was old enough to start school, Mom agreed with me that I was ready to milk our dairy cow. I would take the empty stainless-steel milk pail and skedaddle down the lane to where the Jersey would be waiting patiently by the gate inside the pasture field next to the chicken house. The Jersey's internal clock knew instinctively when it was time to be fed and milked.

As soon as I rewarded Tilly with her designated quart-can of Southern States sorghum-laced mixture of various grains, she would commence immediately to munch on her feast. In the meantime, I had already shoved the empty milk pail underneath Tilly's udder and squatted down on a short three-legged milk stool. Fortunately, for the most part Tilly was easy to milk, but sometimes, I had to use both hands to coax a fine stream of milk

Willow Grove: A Boy, A Family, A Farm

out of one of her more stubborn teats. I didn't have to stop—too often—to rest my tired fingers. Using both hands, I took turns alternating between the four quarters. I alternated because I didn't want to leave the one hard teat until last. My hands would be tired enough! I'm not sure why I alternated, but that's how the farmhands stripped milk from the big dairy herd. I suppose it just took time for the milk to gravity feed into each of the four quarters.

When Tilly had finished eating all her grain, she remained utterly still, patiently chewing her cud. She knew I hadn't finished my job. The milk pail was over half full and would be three-quarters full when I was done. My tired little fingers would continue to squeeze each teat until all four streams yielded only scant droplets of milk.

Even after eating all of her grain, the easy-going, good-natured cow never attempted to move. But the moment I stood up and backed away with my stool in hand, Tilly would gently lift her hind feet, one at a time, and step up and over the pail of warm milk. Standing beside the milk pail, I yelled to Mom, who could hear me through the screen door at the back of the house. I guarded the milk until Mom arrived, and together we walked back to the house, where she strained the milk through a clean, white cloth into a two-gallon crockpot. Mom stored the covered crock in our cool cellar. Any milk not consumed by her three thirsty boys was churned into butter and cottage cheese. Until I left home for college, I never drank any milk that was pasteurized or homogenized; all the milk I ever drank was fresh, whole milk with high butterfat content from our dairy herd.

Third Grade

By the time I entered the third grade, I had ridden the school bus from Willow Grove to Ravenswood Elementary School for two years. I was completely confident of my ability to handle any situation that might occur during the long ride to school. I knew all of the teachers by their full names, what grades they taught, and in what classrooms. I understood and appreciated the principal's strict adherence to safety rules and commitment to elementary learning. I enjoyed school and, sometimes, at my own expense, had too much fun in the classroom.

My third-grade classroom was on the first floor in the front of the building, adjacent to the big kid's playground. Memories of my third grade are plentiful, and I can't adequately express how much I liked and appreciated Mrs. Hughes. She was an exceptional teacher and a wonderful human being. It was obvious that Mrs. Hughes cared deeply for each one of us. I remember how effortlessly she bonded with her students, how she conducted her class, how the classroom was arranged, the location of her desk, and where the venerable American flag hung on the wall cattycorner to her desk.

Willow Grove: A Boy, A Family, A Farm

First Row: Jeanine Ewing, Marilyn Miller, Donna Weekly, James McCoy, Loretta Norman, Irene Kimes, Brenda Pinnell, Dorothy Shockey, NA, me
Second Row: Raleigh Williams, Earl Balis, Linda Bennett, Tommy Zarndt, Chester DeLong, Charles Benson, NA, Merrill Wheaton, Burel Wheaton, Gary Milhoan
Third Row: Joe Rhodes, Ronnie Bare, Robert Vannest, Jimmy Jackson, Paul Jarrett, Edwin Stars, Wayne Fletcher, Iva Jean Crites, Madeline Bigley, Mrs. Nellie Hughes

Mrs. Hughes knew the backgrounds of most of her students well before they ever entered her classroom. And at the appropriate time during the school year, Mrs. Hughes used her prior personal information to instruct and motivate individual students. Mrs. Hughes had taught several of my

Third Grade

cousins and knew my parents. At least a dozen older cousins had all passed through her classroom ahead of me. And as many, if not more, were close behind and would have Mrs. Hughes as one of their elementary grade instructors.

Behind one of the interior walls in our third-grade classroom was a long, narrow coat closet that ran nearly the entire length of the room. Each morning after the school bell rang and each of us was quietly settled in our assigned seat, Mrs. Hughes disappeared into the coat closet behind the wall. After a short pause, she reappeared and gracefully seated herself behind her wooden desk at the front of the classroom. Mrs. Hughes would then ask us to please bow our heads and recite the Lord's Prayer. Before actual classwork commenced, Mrs. Hughes would ask us to rise and stand beside our desks. She would call out a name and then ask the student to come to the front of the classroom. Led by that student, we would face the flag, place our right hand over our hearts, and recite the Pledge of Allegiance to the flag of the United States of America.

Students were assigned seats alphabetically, so each of us knew when it would be our turn to lead the class in the Pledge of Allegiance. Each classmate would lead the pledge six or seven times during the school calendar year. When my turn arrived, I would walk a little anxiously to the head of the class, face the flag, pause, and place my hand over my heart. Standing in front of the class was a solemn moment and I took the responsibility to heart. I would proudly begin the pledge by standing erect and speaking louder than normal so that my classmates would hear me as we recited the pledge together. It was a proud moment and a good feeling walking back to my desk. Pleased with my performance, I was still thinking about how proud I was to lead the pledge of allegiance. Happily, the accompanying good feeling would stay with me all day. Now it was time to concentrate on my homework and Mrs. Hughes' instructions. I hoped I would remember to tell Mom about leading the class in the pledge of allegiance when I got home.

My embarrassing trip up the steep staircase to principal John Hall's office occurred when I was in Mrs. Hughes' third-grade class. Either Raleigh Williams or I had folded a single sheet of notepaper into an airplane, and we decided to amuse ourselves by throwing the airplane across the room to each other. Mrs. Hughes caught us in our mischievous act and promptly sent us to see the principal.

Raleigh and I politely acknowledged our stupidity and, more than a little embarrassed, marched dutifully out of the classroom. We walked slowly down the hallway and steered our wobbly legs up the wide staircase to the second floor, where we could see the principal's intimidating office hovering high above and at the end of a long flight of steps. Before ascending the stairs, Raleigh and I paused and looked up toward the principal's office door. We couldn't tell if Mr. Hall was in his

Third Grade

office. Hopefully not! After a brief pause and a big gulp of air, I grabbed hold of the railing and started trudging up the narrow stairs. Raleigh was close behind. Each step was cumbersome, as if the soles of my shoes were coated with a tacky substance. In a way, both of us hoped the principal was in his office, so we could, as quickly as possible, get the encounter behind us. We had a lot of respect for Mrs. Hughes, and just her instruction to report to the principal's office was more than a sufficient punishment to persuade both of us to mend our inconsiderate behavior. Furthermore, I fully expected to bear additional discipline after I got home from school...and that was *not* a good picture to have to think about for the rest of the school day. I was desperate to get this matter behind me and hoped my parents wouldn't find out about my foolishness. I was ready to be a better student and show more respect for my third-grade teacher.

About halfway up the stairs, we could see a silhouette of Mr. Hall. He was standing in front of his desk in his office. Mr. Hall's hearing must have been fine-tuned to hear a mouse coming up the stairs, for Raleigh and I tried to keep our arrival as quiet as possible. The principal heard us coming and was waiting for our imminent knock on his office door.

Mr. Hall watched us sheepishly open the door after he acknowledged our barely audible peck. The principal stood motionless in a dark business suit, buttoned flawlessly in front of a smart yellow tie. Mr. Hall had a stern boot-camp countenance, which added more weight to my already vulnerable self-confidence. Without saying a word, he pointed toward two chairs in front of his desk. Raleigh and I obediently sat down, locked our fingers together on our laps, and looked straight ahead at Mr. Hall, who was still standing but now behind his desk. From the distressed look on both our faces, he could tell that we were already punishing ourselves.

With Mr. Hall's permission, I explained that I had made a paper airplane and had thrown it in the classroom while the class was in session. Since Mr. Hall had already heard this same narrative many times, he certainly didn't need any further elucidation from me. After shifting his eyes from me, the principal looked directly at Raleigh and, with a daunting expression, demanded: "And why are you here?" Raleigh quickly proclaimed: "Well, sir, you see, I was sitting at my desk, doing my assignment, when suddenly an airplane landed in the aisle right beside my left foot. I picked it up and put it on the edge of my desk." At that point, Raleigh stopped talking.

Mr. Hall, rightly, realized there was more to Raleigh's story and, while still focusing on him, said, "Go on." Raleigh nervously twisted in his chair and then continued, "Well, uh, well...the airplane was on the edge of my desk, and then, all of a sudden, it just took off!"

Still standing at the corner of his desk, Mr. Hall slowly turned around, took a couple of steps, and gradually sat back down in his swivel chair. He had heard enough and told both of us to go back to our

Third Grade

classroom. But, before we left the confines of his office, Mr. Hall made it perfectly clear that he *did not* want to see either of us back in his office! From the steely look in his eyes, Raleigh and I both knew precisely what the implications of his statement were! We were happy to oblige the principal and got out of his office as quickly as possible. Our feet were as light as feathers as we flew down the steep stairs. From now on, we were going to pay close attention to our teacher. We never wanted to climb those stairs again!

Packet *Virginia*

The first steam-powered vessel on the Ohio River was the *New Orleans* in 1811, but the heyday of steam wasn't until 1820 to 1880. By 1920, however, the steam-powered packet trade was replaced by diesel-powered stern-wheeler towboats and conventional diesel towboats. Stern-wheel or paddle wheel steam-powered boats after 1920 were mainly used in the excursion-service business.

Paddle-wheel steamers were still churning the waters of the Ohio River when we moved to Willow Grove in 1946. The front yard was a perfect spot to watch the stern-wheelers push their heavy loads up and down the Ohio River. The big paddle-wheel created rough waves on the river, which was a challenge for a boat following in its wake. The *River Queen, Virginia,* and *Delta Queen* were common sights on the mighty Ohio River. In the late 1800s, the *Queen City, Virginia,* and *Keystone State* from

Willow Grove: A Boy, A Family, A Farm

the Cincinnati-Pittsburgh Packet Line stopped two times each day, every weekday at Ravenswood. Barges that were shoved by diesel engines instead of steam-driven paddle-wheelers were a rare occurrence on the Ohio River before the mid-1950s.

My father told me and my brothers an interesting story about the Packet *Virginia* while we were walking across the river bottom pasture field one summer evening.

During heavy rains, the Ohio River can be treacherous to navigate due to swift currents and dangerous floating debris, such as trees, whole buildings, and chunks of ice. During the 1910 Ohio River flood, the elegant packet steamboat *Virginia* left Pittsburgh loaded with 50 passengers and 500 tons of freight. The 235-foot-long, 40-foot-wide steamer arrived safely in Ravenswood late in the afternoon on Sunday, March 6, 1910. At the Ravenswood dock, the steamboat discharged passengers and freight. One new passenger boarded for a 50-cent fare, along with some new freight, destined for the general store at Willow Grove.

Darkness was rapidly approaching on the river town and the captain of the *Virginia* was advised to spend the night docked at Ravenswood. The captain was told that it would be much safer if he departed for Willow Grove during the early morning, daylight hours. Despite stern warnings and fast-approaching darkness, the captain decided to continue his journey down the swift-flowing river to Willow Grove.

Packet Virginia

When the *Virginia* arrived at the Willow Grove landing on that late Sunday evening, the bank of the river where steamships normally docked to load and unload passengers and freight was completely submerged. The entire mile-long river bottom was underwater and now a vast, muddy expansion of the Ohio River. The captain of the *Virginia* had two choices: either completely pass by the Willow Grove General Store and post office or steer the big steamboat over the flooded cornfield and dock in the grass near the Baltimore and Ohio Railroad crossing.

The captain decided to dock at Willow Grove and discharge the freight and the single passenger who had boarded in Ravenswood. He steered the *Virginia* through the rushing floodwaters and floated the almost football-field-sized paddlewheeler over the cornfield, docking successfully alongside the high ground near the general store. After the sole passenger departed and its new freight was unloaded, the captain commenced backing *Virginia* toward the main channel of the river. The pilot could see the main river channel just beyond the tree tops that lined the river. All was well until suddenly, instead of moving back toward the river channel, the swift current grabbed hold of the steamboat and carried it deeper into the cornfield. The packet completely stopped moving. The massive *Virginia* was stranded in Mr. Williamson's cornfield, 600 feet from the banks of the Ohio River.

Willow Grove: A Boy, A Family, A Farm

All rescue efforts by the captain to dislodge the stranded *Virginia* were unsuccessful. The steamboat's crew pushed desperately with long poles. Heavy bales of steel barbed wire were thrown overboard. All to no avail.

About daybreak the next morning, a towboat stopped by and tied onto *Virginia*. The towboat pulled and jerked, but still, the mighty *Virginia* would not budge. *Virginia*'s passengers ate their breakfast and then were taken ashore in boats, where they boarded a B&O passenger car.

It wasn't long before the previously angry floodwater and docile backwater completely receded. *Virginia* rested high and dry inside Williamson's cornfield for six months, humped up in the middle from a modest swell in the cornfield.

Packet Virginia

Later, when a ditch was being dug to maneuver *Virginia* out of the cornfield, back to the river, the workers found many indigenous artifacts. An archaeologist from the Ohio State Historical Society determined that *Virginia* was stuck on an ancient Indian mound, likely the camping grounds that native Indians used when hunting in the Ohio Valley. Curious visitors from miles away came by special B&O passenger trains and steamboats just to see the powerful lady parked in the middle of Williamson's cornfield. The sightseers strolled through the cornfield and gathered socially around the unusual spectacle, which by now had been invaded by cobwebs and bird nests.

In late summer, a moving crew from Pittsburgh finished a wide ditch and slowly maneuvered Virginia atop logs toward the river. Unexpectedly, on June 20th, about the same time that the steamboat reached the riverbank, a welcomed summer storm raised the water level in the Ohio River, which helped float *Virginia* back out of the cornfield. My maternal grandfather was one of the men in the work crew who nursed the steamboat *Virginia* out of the cornfield and back to the river.

Knapping Rock

Nearly every day, the school bus would stop at the direction of a uniformed guard holding a rifle! From the bus windows we could see several full-bodied, uniformed guards with long rifles and double-barreled shotguns encircling a road gang

Willow Grove: A Boy, A Family, A Farm

from the nearby prison. Several inmates ignored our halted bus and continued knapping rock. A few stopped and looked enviously at us. One prisoner in particular was always standing in about the same area, surrounded by piles of already knapped rock. He was a healthy-looking, handsome young man with thick jet-black, wavy Brylcreem hair that glistened like diamonds in the bright sun. His intensely suntanned face highlighted his ivory-white teeth. From a distance, the young man looked so polite and innocent. I often wondered what grave mistake he made at such a young age and how many years he would be incarcerated. *It must be dreadful to be standing on top of that rock pile in his shoes,* I would think to myself.

The prisoners were housed at the Evans Fairgrounds between Cottageville and Ripley, the county seat of Jackson County. Occasionally, my mother would purchase a block of ice and borrow a couple of one-gallon, hand-crank ice cream churns. Including our churn, Mom would make three gallons of homemade ice cream and deliver the frozen treat in the ice-packed churns to the prisoners at the fairgrounds. Not yet in public school, John accompanied our mother and watched as the appreciative detainees devoured the delicious ice cream. The prisoners even ate the salty ice chips used to freeze the ice cream. Mom was a very compassionate person and was in her element anytime she could help alleviate a little discomfort for a family member, a neighbor, or a complete stranger.

Tatterdemalion

Not too often and principally during summer months, we would see a hobo moseying up or down the railroad track. Hobos traveled the railroad track, and whenever convenient, they would hitch a ride on a slow-moving freight train and ride the railroad car to some destination or until they were spotted by a railroad employee and voluntarily skedaddled from the railroad car.

Typically, hobos traveled alone, and, during their solitary trek, they used signals to communicate with fellow hobos who were also walking the railroad track, either some distance behind them or in the opposite direction. They accommodated each other with various signals placed alongside the railroad track—such as a good place to obtain a nice warm meal. After a charitable source of good food was identified, the hobo would strategically pile lumps of coal alongside the railroad track so that fellow hobos could easily spot and recognize a hobo-friendly kitchen, one without fear of a loaded, double-barreled shotgun or a malicious guard dog that liked to chew on arms and legs.

It was a lazy summer afternoon. My brothers and I were playing in our side yard when we spotted a strange-looking figure wandering erratically and ever so slowly toward the house from the direction of the railroad track. As the figure got closer, we saw that the mysterious person was a hobo. The man's tattered clothes and overall unkempt, ruffled appearance left no doubt. Immediately, my brothers and I raced across the lawn toward the screen door to Mom's kitchen to tell her about the approaching trespasser.

As soon as we opened the screen door and entered the kitchen, we encircled our mother and simultaneously asserted vigorously that a hobo was walking across the side yard. Slowly, with the wave of her hand, Mom swept us aside and told us to stay in the house. She walked to the closed screen door and peered through the mesh toward the railroad track. It took a few minutes for the hobo to shuffle across the freshly tilled soil in the summer garden before he entered the side yard.

The hobo was walking sluggishly, zigzagging across the plowed garden. His fully covered head was tilted forward so much that his shaggy and unbelievably filthy toboggan concealed his face from the chin up. It was evident even at a distance that his clothes hadn't been washed for weeks, maybe even months. Possibly never! His shirt and pants had several big rips in the fabric, and even though it was a hot summer day, the hobo was wearing a long-sleeved shirt, buttoned at the wrists. He was also carrying a grubby, disgusting winter jacket and a soiled brown paper bag stuffed with wadded-up clothes. Every stitch of his clothing was a matching dirty charcoal color. The stench was awful!

Tatterdemalion

Me, John, and Bob. This is where we were standing while we talked with the hobo.

The hobo wandered up close to the house and then stood silently while he gazed over the top of the railing around the perimeter of our miniature concrete stoop, directly outside Mom's kitchen door. The stoop was only two steps above the patio, yet the landing was high enough that Dad, for safety reasons, embedded a steel two-inch pipe

Willow Grove: A Boy, A Family, A Farm

railing along two sides. The hobo stood erect and motionless as if some stealthy drill sergeant had shouted: "Attention!" Still holding his coat and grocery bag, the hobo said nothing and just stared, eyes straight ahead, through the screen door into the kitchen. He didn't utter a word. It appeared as if he was not inclined to move any closer to the house, and instead, he just stood politely regal, watching as Mom, my brothers, and I stared back at him on the inside of the screen door.

After several seconds, the hobo still hadn't moved an inch or uttered a single word. By now, Mom had decided that the hobo was harmless. She asked through the closed screen door, "Can I help you?" All the while, my brothers and I were right at mom's feet, observing every inch of the muted, ragged clown. Finally, the hobo garbled softly, "Habnnt aannyfinng toooate for toooo dwayssss." After a slow pause to inhale, the pitiful soul continued, "Ummm verrrie huunngry." Mom told the hobo to sit down on the steps while she fixed him something to eat.

While Mom was preparing food for the drifter, I slowly pushed the screen door open, and one by one, the three of us—gradually—slunk out onto the landing. The hobo was sitting on the lower step with his back toward us. His head was tilted as if he was half asleep. The steps were wide enough to sneak by the curious-looking specimen without touching him. As softly as a cat on the hunt of a mouse, the three of us hugged the side of the

Tatterdemalion

house, pinching our noses as we tip-toed single file down the concrete steps onto the patio.

Up close, the appearance of his clothes was unbelievable! Actually comical! If the hobo's face was suitably festooned with colorful paint, he could easily have doubled as a funny clown for Ringling Brothers Circus. But yikes, the odor that radiated from him was incredible! I was glad he couldn't see the expressions on our faces. Once on the patio, we stood in a semicircle in front of him, yet far enough away to dilute his pungent and overpowering brand of deodorant.

My brothers and I dutifully remained quiet and just stared. After a short time, I offered: "Where are you from?" By now, the hobo was more relaxed and not nearly as apprehensive as he was when he first approached the house. He replied: "Nuuu Orrlaans." My question broke the ice with the scraggly codger, and right away, we began peppering him with one question after another. He had left New Orleans over six months ago and had been living homeless along the railroad track. He was on his way to an important appointment in Cleveland.

Ten minutes later, Mom walked out onto the landing with both arms overloaded with food. In one hand, she had a dinner plate piled as high as possible with sliced chicken breast, boiled potatoes seasoned with homemade butter and parsley, homemade apple sauce, and fresh red tomatoes from our garden. Staged around the edge of the plate were three warm bread rolls. In the other

Willow Grove: A Boy, A Family, A Farm

hand was a water glass full to the rim with sweetened tea and ice cubes floating on top. Instantly, the hobo jumped up off the step. A super-wide smile of appreciation adorned his dirty face. He extended both arms and reached forward for the plate of food and glass of tea. Large droplets of condensation blanketed the thirst-refreshing beverage. All the while, he was thanking Mom profusely for giving him something to eat.

As quickly as the hobo stood up, he sat back down on the same step and began devouring the food like a starved animal. As he gobbled the food, my brothers and I stood and gazed at the spectacle with amazement. I couldn't imagine how someone could go without food for so many days. The vast quantity of food quickly disappeared from the dinner plate. Equally as fast, Mom was back with more hot rolls, the pitcher of iced tea, and a second fresh plate loaded with more food. I don't recall, but knowing my mother, I would "bet my last buffalo nickel" that before the hobo consumed the last bite of the second full plate of food, Mom was back with a generous piece of her famous angel food cake or delicious peach or blackberry cobbler pie. Probably both!

While the hobo was eating, Bob, John, and I continued to ask questions which the starved mortal attempted to answer whenever he stopped long enough to take a drink or momentarily catch his breath. I asked him, "Why are you going to Cleveland?" He said that he was going to see his dentist. He said he had a bad tooth that needed to

Tatterdemalion

be pulled. I remember thinking how amazing it was that someone would even want to go to a dentist, let alone walk the railroad track all the way from New Orleans to Cleveland...just to see a dentist? I then asked...could we see the bad tooth?

He took a gulp of tea and, after he cleared his throat, opened his mouth wide enough for all three of us to see every tooth in his head. Top and bottom. With his index finger, he pointed in the general direction of the loose tooth. Wow! Unbelievable! His pointing toward the bad tooth was not necessary. Anyone, except maybe a blind person, could easily tell which tooth was loose. Once the hobo opened his mouth, I could've seen the drooping tooth while standing on the other side of the patio with one eye completely closed. One of his upper premolars was cockeyed. All that was holding the badly discolored tooth was a few short strands of partially transparent skin, not much larger than the diameter of number two pencil lead. The tooth was so loose that I was amazed that the hobo hadn't swallowed the hanging enamel while eating the food Mom gave him. We were thrilled and called for Mom to come and see the loose tooth.

The hobo thanked Mom repeatedly for the food. After picking up his coat and bulging grocery bag of smelly clothes, the hobo started walking slowly back across the yard toward the railroad track. My brothers and I stood on the patio and watched every step he took across the yard and potato patch to the edge of the embankment above the railroad track. The last thing we saw of the drifter was the top of his dirty toboggan as it disappeared over the short bank. We stood and watched for a long time, but we never saw the hobo again. Afterward, I mused for days—just how far did the tatterdemalion walk along the railroad track before he inadvertently swallowed his tooth or before it fell out when he sneezed?

Pulling Teeth

The hobo's loose tooth reminds me of an earlier incident when I was younger. Mom, Bob, and I were at my grandparents' house in Silverton. I was five years old and losing my baby teeth. Cousin Dewey Gene Davis was also visiting and gleefully looking for a little ornery excitement. He said he had an excellent idea, although unbeknownst to me, it was a little on the mischievous side. Dewey Gene was four years older than me, and the way he keenly described his simple plan was quite convincing. He was so persuasive that I agreed to sit on Grandma's staircase steps with the door closed and a string tied around my wobbly front tooth. Dewey Gene had cut a piece of string long enough for me to sit on the stair step with one end tied to my loose tooth and the other end around the inside doorknob on the door leading to the attic staircase. With the door completely closed, the string was slightly taut. My part of the procedure was easy. All I had to do was sit quietly in the dark on the staircase. Dewey Gene would yank the door open at an unannounced moment, and, eureka, without any

Pulling Teeth

pain, fuss, or muss, the loose tooth would magically disappear! Dewey Gene masterfully explained that the secret was the "element of surprise."

That moment of "surprise" when Dewey Gene yanked the door open is indelibly embedded in my lifelong collection of youthful memories. The tooth wasn't ready to come out, and when the "rodeo gate" exploded open, the string broke! For a flash, I thought my head had come loose from my shoulders. I immediately jumped up and quickly disappeared. Dewey Gene's tactic, sure as heck, didn't work. Furthermore, I wasn't about to wait around and take note of his explanation as to what went wrong and subsequently be persuaded that the next time it will work "just fine"!

Another episode involving baby teeth occurred one Sunday afternoon at Uncle Conrad and Aunt Edra's Pleasant View farm. My grandparents, their four married children—Edra, Jim, Dorothy, Dad—and their spouses—Conrad, Helen, Homer, and Mom—were there. All 17 grandchildren were there as well.

It was a nice summer afternoon, and the husbands were all sitting outside on the porch, which spanned the complete backside of the historic 1847 house. The noontime meal was over, and the children were running off lots of calories in the roomy yard. Cousin Larry McCoy was losing his baby teeth and was standing on the porch with the men. For no particular reason, Larry moseyed over to where my father was sitting in a lounge chair and stood quietly beside him. Amidst an idle conversation with Larry, Dad learned that he was losing his baby teeth. Always willing to help, Dad offered to scrutinize the annoying situation. Without saying a word, Larry opened his mouth as wide as he could and stood softly while Dad performed his visual examination. Without saying a word, Dad wiggled a loose front tooth a couple of times and then easily extracted it with his fingers. Larry showed no emotion or concern and continued to stand alongside Dad as he examined another loose tooth. It wasn't long before a second tooth was safely in the palm of Dad's hand. Then a third tooth magically appeared in front of Larry's eyes. I don't know if it was after the third or the fourth extracted tooth when Larry realized that he'd probably better speak up. Larry slowly uttered: "Uncle Warrr-ence...I fffink...youuu-ddd...baerrr-er stop." Larry's eventual concern tickled my father and amused the other fathers observing the quiet spectacle. Larry's calm, almost leisurely composure never changed throughout the whole endeavor. No one could tell or even knew that Larry had lost four of his baby teeth—until he flashed a big grin.

Aunt Jack Arrives

In 1948, my grandmother's sister Elfra Belle Carmichael, fondly nicknamed Aunt Jack by me, lived with her older sister Ollie in Vienna, West Virginia, a suburb city upriver from Parkersburg. On one of my grandparents' rare sojourns to Vienna, they visited with sister Ollie and their

Aunt Jack Arrives

youngest sister, Elfra. During the visit, my grandparents extended an invitation for Elfra to move to Willow Grove. Shortly afterward, Aunt Jack moved from Vienna to Willow Grove and lived in the big house, which was already home to my parents and my grandparents. Aunt Jack lived with us until we sold the Willow Grove farm. Afterward, she lived with her sister and brother-in-law in their new home three miles south of Ravenswood. After my grandparents died, Aunt Jack lived on my parents' farm in New England, West Virginia, a rural village along the Ohio River, 12 miles below Parkersburg.

At Willow Grove, Aunt Jack moved her wardrobe into the center bedroom on the second floor of our five-bedroom home. There were three fireplaces upstairs: one in my grandparents' front bedroom, one in the middle guest bedroom, and one in my parents' bedroom. The home had a total of seven grand fireplaces, though, during the near decade that we lived in the house, only two fireplaces on the first floor were ever utilized to heat the whole house during the winter. One was the fireplace in my grandparents' kitchen and the other in my parents' family room. The only other heat source was a chest-high Warm Morning free-standing stove in my mother's kitchen, which burned coal and wood. Bob and I slept in the bedroom directly above the kitchen, and we were the lucky recipients of warm air that escaped up through a one-foot square ventilator in the kitchen ceiling above the Warm Morning stove.

Willow Grove: A Boy, A Family, A Farm

The Willow Grove house was a true brick home, not just a brick façade on the house's exterior, which is common in today's modern brick homes. The width of all of the outside walls of the Willow Grove two-story house was equal to the thickness of two rows of brick. There was no insulation in the outside walls, and over an extended period of extremely cold or blistering hot weather, the inside of the 12-inch walls would become cold in the winter and quite warm in the summer.

Grandfather was not well, and to remain comfortable during cold winter nights, my grandparents slept downstairs in their spacious living room, which was located in the front of the house adjacent to their kitchen. The living room was easily separated from the roomy kitchen by two sliding doors, which represented most of the wall between the two rooms. The carved cherry wood pocket doors were kept wide open during the daytime, which enabled warm air from the kitchen fireplace to heat the living room. Except for my grandparents, everyone else in the household slept upstairs, year round.

Aunt Jack slept in a long woolen gown, heavy woolen socks, and a crocheted woolen nightcap to keep warm during the frigid nights. Heating blankets were available but too expensive and considered a luxury by most people. Instead, Aunt Jack used a little old-fashioned ingenuity to provide extra warmth in her bed during cold winter nights. Every morning, she would leave her chilly bedroom carrying a stone wrapped in a bath towel. The

Aunt Jack Arrives

smooth gray stone was about the size and shape of a slightly deflated football. Once Aunt Jack arrived downstairs, she placed the rock next to the hot burning coals inside the fireplace. The stone would remain all day by the fireplace. When Aunt Jack was ready to retire for the evening, she would carefully pick up the hot stone from beside the floor-level fireplace, wrap it in a heavy bath towel, and carry it upstairs to her bedroom, where it would be strategically placed under the covers near the foot of her bed. Ample heat would radiate from the stone for several hours and, in the interim, keep her elderly, sock-clad feet as warm as toast, all night long.

Aunt Jack.

Willow Grove: A Boy, A Family, A Farm

Aunt Jack spent her life caring for other people. Her boyfriend was killed in World War I and she never married. When her mother broke her hip in 1938, she was there to keep house for her parents. Monnie, another of Grandma and Aunt Jack's sisters, taught school in the mountains and contracted TB, after which she returned home to help Aunt Jack take care of their parents. Monnie died in 1939, one year after her mother's death. Monnie was 47. Aunt Jack died at the age of 77. It is amazing to me that Aunt Jack escaped contracting the dreadful disease.

On April 13, 1939, my mother was gifted with a beautiful baby blanket for my crib. The 31" x 44" blanket was hand crocheted by Aunt Jack. The blanket had to have taken many hours over several months to stitch together. There are 12 large butterflies, all the same size and all with their wings spread, flying in the same direction. The butterflies were anatomically the same, but every butterfly was a different color against a seven-inch-square white background. Besides the striking, finely stitched butterflies, the predominant color of the quilt is an attractive cantaloupe pastel. The baby blanket is such a beautiful color, and especially rich looking for the era in which it was quilted. The blanket was handsomely framed and currently hangs on the wall in our home in Lakewood Ranch, Florida.

It would take remarkable adjectives to adequately describe my paternal grandmother. Without a doubt, Nancy Elizabeth Carmichael Sück

Aunt Jack Arrives

was the most caring, stable, and wise grandmother any grandson could ever hope to have. She was called Nannie by her husband and friends and Grandma by her 17 grandchildren.

Grandma was a trim, exceedingly neat, and very dainty lady. With few exceptions, she wore the same repertoire of clothes every day: a long, charcoal-colored dress, a light-colored apron tied neatly around her petite waist with a embroidered cotton handkerchief judiciously tucked in her apron pocket, and a pair of black leather shoes with flat heels. She wore a pair of simple Benjamin Franklin wire-rimmed glasses with her shoulder-length salt and pepper hair perfectly coiffed in a bun on the top, back part of her head. My grandmother, who possessed an enviable demeanor, was the living model of a textbook grandmother.

Everyone loved living at Willow Grove, but no one more than Grandma. She was the steadiest lady I have ever known. From day to day, her demeanor was as consistent as the sun rises and sets each day. Grandma's character was always calm and sound, regardless of any challenging situation that confronted us throughout our daily lives. Absolutely nothing seemed to alter her always positive character. It was a wonderful and powerful trait that I always admired about my grandmother and one that I have consciously tried to emulate, as often as possible.

Grandmother's youngest sister, Elfra, better known as Aunt Jack by all of her nieces and

Willow Grove: A Boy, A Family, A Farm

nephews, was living in the main house with my grandparents in their part of the big house. We lived in such close proximity that it was easy to observe the symmetry and harmony between the two sisters. It was obvious that Grandma and Aunt Jack were both extremely happy with the quality of life on the Willow Grove farm and that both revered each day to the fullest. They enjoyed the ambiance of numerous activities about the barnyard, activities which were handily witnessed from the spacious bay window in the kitchen and the unobstructed panoramic view from the convenient side porch. The substantial porch was, by far, the primary focal point for family relaxation, and my grandparents and Aunt Jack enjoyed sitting there every day, all year long, during nice weather.

Grandma's kitchen was separated from her living room by two dark cherry pocket doors, which, most of the time, remained recessed in the wall. With the two sliding doors hidden in their respective pockets, the kitchen and living room became a sprawling living area. During the daytime, the airy space was well lighted by six tall windows on the north and west sides of the house and by three identical transom windows over three doors. On each side of the fireplace were identical Lincoln rocking chairs, where Grandma and Aunt Jack sat while they did needlework, relaxed, read their Bibles, and enjoyed casual conversation. The fireplace was a particularly inviting spot in the kitchen during winter evenings. A "Norman

Aunt Jack Arrives

Rockwell" setting—perfect for ending a peaceful day on the farm.

Aunt Jack, Grandma, Aunt Dorothy, and Grandpa.

    I was seven years old in 1946, the year we moved from Silverton to Willow Grove. I honestly don't remember much about my grandmother before 1946, when we lived on two different occasions with my grandparents in their Silverton farmhouse. Fortunately, after moving to Willow Grove, I enjoyed many wonderful years with my grandparents, parents, two brothers, and Aunt Jack. During this stretch of nearly a decade, I saw my grandmother multiple times every day. Until my junior year in high school, I observed her daily

Willow Grove: A Boy, A Family, A Farm

under a variety of enjoyable as well as difficult and sometimes stressful times.

Grandma and Aunt Jack truly enjoyed living in their comfortable living quarters. They spent their entire day together working side by side, cooking, cleaning, and reading their Bibles while sitting on identical oak rocking chairs located on each side of the fireplace. Grandma never went shopping. She made a grocery list and gave it to my mother. The only time she would get in a car was to go to a family gathering at one of the son's or daughter's homes. I have a few pictures of Grandma at distant places, yet I would venture that she never left her kitchen more than three or four times a year over the near decade that I was around her in Willow Grove. She enjoyed a lovely alcove in her kitchen and a roomy covered porch with a picturesque view of the farm buildings and nature's vast beauty in all directions. The double swing on the porch was a great place to relax and watch the activities around the barnyard or to socialize with visiting family and friends. Willow Grove, especially during summer weekends, was a popular destination for a lot of family and friends who lived in Ravenswood and Ripley. In retrospect, I suspect Grandma and Aunt Jack especially treasured their quiet weekdays after hosting a barrage of grandchildren and family during the weekend.

Grandma was an infinitely positive lady, and her quiet, reserved demeanor was steadfast every day of the year. Her language was soft and soothing, yet commanding. She never changed the

Aunt Jack Arrives

tone or inflection of her speech, even during a serious issue or highly stressful situation. On a few extremely rare occasions, I did discern concern in her normally sparkling eyes. Similarly, I occasionally detected a modest hint of disappointment in her facial expression when I did something that didn't meet her standards or expectations of me. Yet, Grandma never raised her voice even under these varied, adverse situations. Not once, in all the years that I was around my grandmother, daily, did I ever hear her come even faintly close to repeating a sour word. Hurtful retorts were never even a tiny morsel of my grandmother's vocabulary. They just didn't exist in any form. She was a strong and quiet lady, and it wasn't in her persona to use anything but correct vocabulary and good grammar—always. Grandma had a lovely and loving presence that made everyone around her feel good and confident about themselves.

I never really thought much about my grandmother's health until I began writing this book. I don't ever remember my grandmother insinuating, let alone saying, that she didn't feel well or was sick. To the best of my knowledge, Grandma was never sick, and if she was during the years we lived in Willow Grove, it certainly wasn't apparent to me.

I have to give my mother a lot of credit for helping to make my grandparents' golden years at Willow Grove so peaceful and enjoyable. After all, we lived in the same house, and Bob, John, and I were healthy and energetic children. Mom had a strict rule. My brothers and I had to ask permission before we could knock on the door and enter our grandparents' living quarters. It was a good rule, which made life simpler and more comfortable for my grandparents.

Surprised by Snuff!

During my youthful years in the latter 1940s and early 1950s, many adults smoked a variety of popular brands of cigarettes. To save precious pennies, some of the men bought loose tobacco in a drawstring cloth pouch. The loose tobacco was accompanied by little slivers of super-thin paper, which the smoker used to roll his homemade cigarettes. Snuff was another tobacco option. I witnessed several of the hired help on the farm partake of homemade cigarettes and powdered snuff.

Before I started elementary school, I remembered how much my grandfather enjoyed his cigars. He only smoked occasionally and only when he was away from the watchful eye of his concerned wife. He had had a heart attack, and no smoking was the doctor's strict order. By the time we had moved to Willow Grove, he ceased even the occasional cigar. His health was too fragile to chance smoking. Both of my parents smoked—Mom smoked Pall Malls, and Dad, Lucky Strikes—which I didn't abhor or condone. Cigarettes were socially acceptable, and many adults smoked. I merely tried

Surprised by Snuff!

to make sure I was upwind of any meandering puffs of smoke. Personally, I never had any desire to smoke. I'd spent enough time around Uncle Conrad to know that if I did, I would be the recipient of a subtle demotion in his eyes...which was something I never wanted to entertain.

Many decades later, when I was working on this book, my mother dropped a family bombshell on me during one of our lengthy, long-distance, Sunday phone conversations. The bombshell was a secret that still amazes me! During my youthful and early teenage years at Willow Grove, I saw my grandmother every day, multiple times, from sunup to sundown. I spent unknown thousands of hours near her—hundreds of hours, elbow to elbow, when we were working together on my school assignments. Also, I had been around enough tobacco users to easily recognize the pungent smell of snuff. Furthermore, the users bulging lower lip conspicuously highlighted the abhorrent habit. Other traits accompanied smokeless tobacco—namely, the cuspidor.

These traits were never, ever remotely apparent to me. Yet, my grandmother used snuff...as did her sister, Aunt Jack. This stealthy bombshell evaded my 20-20 eyesight and excellent sense of smell from 1946 to 1955, the nine years I lived in the same house with my grandmother. When my mother exposed this unbelievable revelation—I was dumbfounded! "How was it possible?" Mom described how Grandma obtained her "medicinal" snuff! Whenever she was getting low, Grandma would stroll into Mom's kitchen and comment: "Kate, the next time you go grocery shopping, would you get me some medicine?" Whenever Mom went to Kelly's market in Ravenswood, she had two grocery lists: one for grandmother and one for herself. Occasionally, grandfather would do a little grocery shopping, but, for the most part, Mom was the designated shopper of foodstuffs for our family and my grandparents. "Snuff" wouldn't be written on Grandma's list—just a bullet point for "medicine." At the time of the revelation, I was bamboozled by Mom's astonishing disclosure. One thing was certain! Grandmother's pinch of snuff was so tiny, a small tin had to have lasted her and Aunt Jack an exceedingly long time!

Midnight Pebbles

It had been a perfect summer day. The serene evening and soothing night breeze gliding across the Ohio River were as equally splendid. Each of the five upstairs bedrooms had two identical double windows, except Aunt Jack's center bedroom, which had only one double window. The bottom half of all of the tall, stately windows would slide up in dual tracks and nest behind the stationary top half of the window. An accordion screen in the bottom half of the window allowed fresh, outside air to circulate throughout the whole upstairs of the house. The six bedroom doors were hardly ever closed, and never on especially warm nights in the peak of summer. The house was large enough that

Midnight Pebbles

every bedroom, except Aunt Jack's, was tucked away in its own private corner upstairs. It was practical to leave all of the upstairs doors wide open during the night so fresh, cool, night air could circulate throughout all of the five bedrooms with ease.

It was almost midnight on a near moonless Friday night, and everyone had been in bed for quite some time. Grandma and Grandpa were in the bedroom in the front of the house. Except for an entrance hallway, the master bedroom spanned the width of the house and featured a magnificent view of the Ohio River. Dewey Gene was settled in the middle guest bedroom across from Aunt Jack. My parents and John were in the corner bedroom, which had a panoramic view of the Ohio River Valley to the north and a view of the dairy barn, silos, and other farm buildings in the east. Bob and I slept in the adjacent corner bedroom on the same eastern side of the house as our parents. Everyone was dead to the world. Life was perfect!

With all of the windows and bedroom doors wide open, the cool air from outside shooed the warm interior air out of the upstairs sleeping quarters. We enjoyed this delightful ambiance almost every night throughout the summer and early fall months. The thick brick walls of the two-story house insulated the first floor during the daytime. The thick walls maintained a comfortable temperature throughout the five active downstairs rooms that my mother, grandparents, and Aunt Jack occupied during the day. Large rooms, tall ceilings, and transom windows above each door permitted air to circulate between all the first-floor rooms.

Even though the thick brick walls of the Willow Grove house insulated the big house during warm summers and cold winters, the same outside walls were not very comfortable after several days of brutally hot weather during the dog days of August. After about a week of scorching weather, the heat from the hot bricks on the outside of the house would eventually penetrate the adjacent bricks on the inside walls of the house. Once the inside brick walls warmed up, the whole house would essentially become a brick oven. The Willow Grove house would remain very warm for several days. Even after the outside temperature dropped precipitously, the inside of our home would remain uncomfortably warm for a couple of days. I remember lying in bed, so hot that beads of sweat would run down the sides of my shirtless body. Dad had to rise and shine very early in the morning and couldn't waste precious time sweating, twisting, and turning all night long. He would remove the screen from the bedroom window and climb onto the slightly pitched porch roof directly outside my parents' bedroom. A pillow and soft blanket were all he needed to rest comfortably under the stars.

Invited and unexpected visitors were always given a cordial welcome at our Willow Grove farm. And we had a respectable number of both, especially during lovely summer and fall weekends. My mother always had plenty of food just in case

Midnight Pebbles

our visitors hadn't had their lunch. Delicious sandwiches and all kinds of fresh, crisp vegetables from our garden were often followed by apple and cherry pies and fluffy angel food cake that would melt in your mouth. Mom knew how to make the best sweetened iced tea ever! And, of course, the farm had an endless supply of chilled, fresh, whole milk for the kids. Ice cold watermelons were always floating in the icy water in the milk house water cooler, used to keep ten-gallon cans full of fresh milk cold until the daily commercial milk truck arrived.

One Friday night Bob and I were slowly aroused from a deep sleep by a strange, very faint sound outside our bedroom. The intermittent pecking continued until I eventually woke up enough to pry my eyes partly open and gather a little of my senses. Soon, I realized that the noise was pebbles striking the windowpane. Tiny pebbles from our driveway were gently tossed from the concrete walkway below our bedroom window. It was after midnight, and everyone in the household had been sound asleep for a couple of hours. All five bedrooms were happily occupied.

Lying in bed and still only slightly awake, Bob and I listened attentively for the next clinking sound on our window. A few seconds later, we heard another restrained clink on the windowpane. Soon, I was aware enough to realize that someone was outside, trying to get our attention without disturbing everyone in the household. Being closest to the beckoning window, I jumped out of bed to see who was tossing pebbles. After removing the accordion window screen, I stuck my head out to scan the sidewalk and driveway directly below. I could see the hazy outlines of two adults standing side by side. There was also a silhouette of a strange vehicle that wasn't in the driveway when we went to bed. Instantly, I heard a familiar whisper that radiated excitement to a young lad, who just moments ago, was sound asleep. "Junior, it's Uncle Bob and Aunt Dee." Immediately, I whispered back: "I'll be right down." Uncle Bob was our mother's younger brother.

Before Bob and I reached the bottom of the stairs, Mom and Dad's bedroom nightlight came on. They had heard our not-so-subtle footsteps as we scrambled down the staircase to happily greet our aunt and uncle. Soon, John lumbered behind, rubbing both eyes with tight fists, wondering what all the downstairs commotion was about.

As soon as the outside door swung open, everyone, equipped with happy smiles, greeted each other with warm embraces and joyful laughter. It was always wonderful to spend time with Uncle Bob and Aunt Dee. They were so much fun to be around and so good to my brothers and me.

We were wide awake. Even though it was well after midnight, no one was even remotely ready to go back to bed—except Dad. Five o'clock would arrive soon enough. About 20 minutes after Uncle Bob and Aunt Dee arrived, Dad excused himself and headed back upstairs to bed.

Midnight Pebbles

The rest of us remained seated around the kitchen table and talked about the trip from Washington Bottom. Motoring a long distance in the 1940s on unpredictable gravel or paved roads—nearly a decade before the beginning of the interstate highway system—was an adventure and always worthy of interesting tales. Mom brewed a fresh pot of coffee and placed a cold pitcher of milk on the table in front of my brothers and me. Then she reappeared from the pantry with a delicious cake, which only she knew about.

After a big chunk of the cake was gone and the coffee cups were empty, Mom turned out the kitchen lights and followed the rest of us to bed. Since both guest bedrooms were already occupied, Aunt Dee and Uncle Bob commandeered our full-size bed while Bob and I climbed into an old, bare-bones, army bunk bed in our bedroom, which Mom kept ready for such an occasion. Bob and I didn't have any problem getting back to sleep. We wanted to be well-rested and ready for tomorrow. After breakfast, Aunt Dee and Uncle Bob would visit with my grandparents and Aunt Jack in their adjacent living quarters. In the interim, seven adults, one teenager, and my brothers and I—almost a dozen—were comfortably lodged in our spacious and hospitable home. We were a truly fortunate and happy family.

We enjoyed Uncle Bob and Aunt Dee's trips to the farm many times from the late 1940s to the early-1950s. Whenever we heard pecking on our bedroom window, Bob and I didn't even waste time going to the window. We would immediately rush downstairs to the kitchen and open the outside door. Lights weren't necessary until we landed at the bottom of the stairs, where we would flip the kitchen light on and warmly greet and hug our aunt and uncle.

Fourth Grade

Mrs. Gillette was my fourth-grade teacher. She was a dynamic, robust lady who wore colorfully flowing, ankle-length dresses and, at all times, maintained complete control of her class. She was an active, bubbly individual—much different than the other more reserved elementary teachers. Mrs. Gillette's teaching style kept our classroom lively and schoolwork interesting.

One morning Mrs. Gillette arrived at school as a passenger on a relatively small motor scooter. It was an amazing scene to witness Mrs. Gillette riding in the open sidecar as her husband maneuvered the tilting, lime-green motor scooter up Henry Street. The sidecar moseyed to a smooth stop in front of the elementary school, where several students watched as Mrs. Gillette opened the miniature side door, stood up, and stepped angelically out onto the sidewalk. A different, engaging, and inspiring lady and teacher.

The elementary students had finished their lunch in the school cafeteria. Now, it was the high school students' turn, and it was best not to be in the path of the big boys when they bolted onto the

Fourth Grade

elementary school grounds. The high school was a mere two blocks away and a short five-minute stroll. The elementary students would stand on the inside of the steel fence and watch as the young men ran down the sidewalk on the opposite side of tree-lined Henry Street and, about halfway down the block, cut diagonally across the street and up onto the sidewalk in front of the elementary school's main entrance. The senior boys would still be running when they bounced up the front steps into the school building. In the interim, observing elementary students made doubly sure they were not in the path of the football players. The high school girls and teachers walked leisurely behind the hungry young men.

Often, cousins John Paul McCoy and Pete Carmichael were leading a small cluster of senior boys. Hastily on their way to lunch, they couldn't wait to feast on the nourishing meals prepared by the cooks in the elementary school kitchen. One of the chief cooks was Pete's mother, Ruth Carmichael, my grandmother's niece. Every Friday Ruth would prepare a huge pot of white navy beans and she made sure that every one of the hungry boys was pleasantly stuffed by the time they exited the lunchroom. Ruth would completely smother their lunch plates with a super-sized portion of navy beans. Accompanied by a generous helping of ketchup, Ruth's was hearty lunch that all the boys looked forward to every Friday.

Willow Grove: A Boy, A Family, A Farm

Playing with Ravenswood Marbles

Recess was a perfect opportunity to escape from the elementary classroom and enjoy a few minutes on the playground before the bell beckoned us back to our solid wood seats and desks.

The first- and second-grade students climbed on the monkey bars, slid down the wavy slide, or enjoyed swinging on one of the chain-link swings on the little kid's playground. The fifth- and sixth-grade boys were busy on the opposite side of the school playing softball on the big kid's playground.

The third- and fourth-grade boys were too old for the monkey bars and too young to play softball with the big boys. But, we had our own favorite game: marbles.

Exterior of the Ravenswood Novelty Works.

Ravenswood was a marble "Mecca" because we had our very own marble factory in town, the

Playing with Ravenswood Marbles

Ravenswood Novelty Works, where one of my classmates' fathers was employed. The Ravenswood factory produced an especially desirable "swirl" marble that was always highly popular with us marble-playing aficionados.

The hard-packed sand on the little kid's playground was perfect for a serious game of marbles. The boys with their small, draw-string bag of marbles would observe while one of the players would draw a big circle on the ground. A dry twig from one of the nearby trees was perfect for drawing a three-foot, diameter circle. If the circle didn't meet the other player's critical eye, he would erase the crooked section with the palm of his hand and redraw that portion of the circle.

Every player would ante up an agreed number of marbles which would be clustered in the center of the circle. Most were dogs unless a new player showed up with a bulging bag of newly minted gems. "Dogs" were marbles that the player didn't mind losing. Compared to the new kid, the rest of us (mostly veterans) had a measly little bag with a sparse number of marbles. We always left plenty of room so that we could go home with a bulging bag of new booty at the expense of our rookie classmates.

The veterans licked their chops when they saw how the newbie (the kid with a big bag of new marbles) held his shooter marble between his thumb and index finger. We looked at each other and indicated with our rolling eyes that this was going to be fun. We tried not to grin too much and give notice of our forthcoming bonanza! We wanted to welcome the newbie and make him feel at home as a new member of our marble gang. We didn't want him to know that his bag full of marbles was going to be lonesome by the time recess was over.

There are two ways to hold the shooting marble. One is a novice way and the other is a method the expert uses. I personally used the expert method. I was pretty good, but certainly not the best. I had to hold my own since I knew Mom would not spring for a new bag of marbles as soon as she learned that I lost all of mine in a marble game at school.

To decide which player goes first, a straight line is drawn on the ground and each boy shoots his best marble from a certain distance to see who comes closest to the line, who is the furthest, and where the other players fall in chronological order in between.

Playing with Ravenswood Marbles

Anytime the pile of marbles in the center of the ring was unusually full of prize marbles, invariably one of the veterans would dig deep in his pocket and pull out the dreadful killer marble. It was a stainless steel, ball bearing that was rare and everyone dreaded. When the steelie hit a pile of marbles, they would scatter like feathers in a windstorm. The steelie was so heavy it would scatter the marbles on impact and then stop dead so that the owner could wipe out most of the remaining marbles inside the ring. The steelie would lose its turn when the shooter failed to knock a marble out of the ring. Afterward, the player picked up all of the marbles that he knocked outside the ring. He had hit the jackpot, while the rest of us ended the game with our tails between our legs. Luckily, recess was over. The newbie flashed a sour grin and mumbled that he would be back tomorrow. The rest of us would go home and pick out some new marbles so we could challenge the steelie tomorrow. It was possible to win the steelie, but it was rare!

After the newbie donated a couple of big bags of prime marbles to the marble game, he voiced his opinion on the rules of the game. The big boys didn't like it too much, but they had to acquiesce in order to keep the newbie coming back with his bag of booty. After the perfect circle was drawn in the sand, Newbie announced: "No steelies and no dropsy!" Wow! Newbie caught on fast! Too fast! The gravy train was about to come to the end of the line. Besides, he had played and had practiced enough that he was almost holding his own during recess marble rumbles. Until he could get his hands on a steelie, dropsy was definitely *non grata*!

Dropsy is a secret method that is analogous to a bomb dropped by a military bomber. The oversized steelie is held horizontally at arm's length over the middle of the cluster of marbles in the middle of the circle. The steelie is dropped and *whammo!* The impacted marbles scatter in all directions and a portion of the cluster ends up on the outside of the circle. The rest of the players wince while watching the steelie's owner jam his bag with plenty of newly won marbles. Furthermore, the steelie has the honor of attacking the remaining marbles in the ring. Sometimes, steelie is the only one that got to take his turn. The rest of us didn't even have a tail to tuck between our legs. Newbie was right! Steelies and dropsy are not allowed!

Playing marbles during recess was a lot of fun. It was a serious game and we played hard and adhered to strict rules. There were usually five or six players and the majority would make the final decision about a close call. As soon as each player anted up, everyone would focus on the best marbles in the ring. A few of the most colorful marbles were nicknamed.

I remember focusing on a beautiful coral-blue marble and immediately named her "blue dolly." She was gorgeous and would look very nice in my bag of marbles. I kept my thoughts to myself until it was my turn to shoot.

Playing with Ravenswood Marbles

I got down on one knee and held my best shooter firmly between my thumb and finger. I had to blast through a tight group of three marbles that were in front of "blue dolly" and at the same time not let my shooter roll out of the ring. I was pumped up and blasted the defending marbles perfectly. I hit them so hard that two scrambled outside the ring. They would go into my marble bag but were not what I wanted.

Now I let the other players know what I was up to! "See beautiful 'blue dolly,' next to that 'red rooster'? She's gonna be mine." I could hardly wait to move around to the other side of the circle so I could get a better shot at "blue dolly."

I knelt down and gave a command performance. *Whammo!* "Blue dolly" was knocked way outside the ring. I was smiling from ear to ear. I knew I could do it! I knew it! I knew it! It was an awesome feeling! I would admire and examine her later, probably tonight just before I said my prayers and crawled into bed.

While I was smiling, everyone else was laughing! My prize marble was indeed outside the ring, but unfortunately so was my shooter, which I had not bothered to watch! The smile was quickly wiped off my face and the only thing left for me to do was pick up the beautiful marble. I held it between my fingers, horizontally at arm's length, and dropped the gem in the middle of the circle. I had lost my turn and by the time it came around again, it would be too late.

Willow Grove: A Boy, A Family, A Farm

Boy, did that hurt! It was a good thing that the next time the bell rang, it will be the end of the school day. For the rest of the afternoon, all I did was kick myself for shooting too hard. With a softer touch, the shooter would have remained in the ring. Darn it! Darn it! Darn it!

Bullies Beware!

The small-town culture was another good quality that permeated the Ravenswood community and its public schools. Not once in a decade did I ever witness a single incident of severe bullying at school or know of any student I would label as a bully. Principal John Hall and sixth-grade teacher Otho Clem would not tolerate any level of misbehavior that came close to a bullying situation. Bullying just wasn't about to occur in their school, not even at a trivial level.

My humble opinion about why there were no bullies in high school is a little less precise. But, maybe not! The number of students in my high school was comparatively small, so, naturally, any bullying was manageable by the faculty. There is another, even better explanation: the model behavior of several senior and junior male students who monitored the younger students on school property—chiefly, outside of the classroom. Jim Brotherton, Eddie McCoy, Charles Rector, Daniel Smith, Franklin Spalding, Bernard Staats, Richard Sück, Dick Vankirk, and Jerry Walters, along with other classmates, were sturdy bodies and accomplished athletes on the football field who could easily squash any skirmish or lingering disagreement—quickly and on the spot! Any wannabe bully was swiftly informed by one of the older boys that his behavior was unacceptable. The selfless students didn't need permission to intervene in a potential one-sided melee. If there had been an incident, the faculty most likely would never have known about it. The seniors would simply waylay an aspiring bully and succinctly counsel the rowdy student that he was out of order and wasn't going to instigate any inappropriate behavior.

I was privileged to follow several of my cousins in both Ravenswood schools. They were good students, good athletes, popular with their classmates and esteemed by their teachers. The older cousins' academic, social, and athletic accomplishments set high standards for successive cousins to try and achieve. Brothers John Paul, Eddie, and James Conrad McCoy; brothers Bill and Archie Barber; Pete Carmichael; brothers Richard and Teddy Sück, and cousin Bill Sück were all good athletes who made noteworthy contributions on the football field as well as in the classroom. In addition, cousins Wilmer Taylor, Darry Fox, Joe McCoy, and my brother Bob were all students during the years I attended Ravenswood High. Brother John, cousins Faye Franklin, Larry, and Connie McCoy, Cecil, Glenn, and Jimmy Sück, attended the nearby elementary school. Even after discounting my personal bias, all my cousins were

Willow Grove: A Boy, A Family, A Farm

good students, attractive, affable, and good friends! Bar none!

Dr. Monroe, Ravenswood's Beloved Doctor

Dr. Loyal McCandless Monroe's medical office and white-frame house on Walnut Street were not far from the elementary school and only a couple of blocks from the high school. Dr. Monroe and his family and the Sücks are mentioned in a history of Ravenswood: "At the time (1947) the Monroes came to Ravenswood, the only industry was the Trendle Blake China Company and Dairying, with the main dairies being the Hughes, Sücks and McCoys..." Dr. Monroe's office was across the alley from Ward's Market and right beside Marsh's Cut Rate, the drugstore-soda fountain. Cousin James Conrad and I occasionally frequented Marsh's Cut Rate after the school day was over, when one of us was packing a buffalo nickel or loaded down with a shiny Roosevelt dime to spend on a candy bar. We had about 20 minutes before we boarded our school bus, which was ample time to walk to the soda fountain and make our big purchase. As soon as we stepped out of the drugstore, we would tear the wrapper off the top of the candy bar and share our tasty Zagnut or Milky Way as we strolled back to the high school to await the arrival of our bus.

Dr. Monroe knew my family well and had spent many relaxing hours fishing in our Willow Grove farm pond. The three-acre pond was in a remote area in the rolling pasture field at the back end of

Dr. Monroe, Ravenswood's Beloved Doctor

our farm. In addition to the pond, there was a cabin, infrequently used by fishermen and my family. Too often, uninvited fishermen would trespass and, after fishing, fail to close the gate behind them, allowing the dairy cattle to wander out of the pasture field. If the cattle ended up in a nearby cornfield, the situation could be tragic, not only for the trampled stalks of field corn but also hazardous for the herd. If not discovered in time, a dairy cow will eat corn until she becomes bloated. I have seen bloated dairy cows lying on their side in total misery, the skin on the ballooned body stretched so tight that it felt like concrete. A dairy cow can die from bloat.

Dr. Monroe had his own personal key to the pasture field and would come and go at his pleasure. Quite often, while working in a nearby hayfield, it was an amusing sight to watch Dr. Monroe drive up the hillside road in the pasture field in his rusty-colored army Jeep. Curls of dust would swirl up from behind the rear wheels as he pushed the accelerator hard, whipping the 4-wheel drive to challenge and mount the high hill. In less than a minute, the distant slow-motion Jeep would disappear behind the apex of the ridge, well on its way to the pastoral pond. Huge snapping turtles would frequently dot the surface of the serene lake as the nylon line from Dr. Monroe's fly rod uncurled and sailed out toward the deep end of the pond near the grass-covered earthen dam. The artificial lure would skip on the water's surface and tease the occupants below, where plenty of splendid bass were lounging deep down in the cool, shaded water.

Dr. Monroe was a treasured family doctor and a highly respected citizen of Ravenswood. He generously donated his time and valuable professional services to the Ravenswood High School sports teams. Often, Dr. Monroe would place his black leather medical valise on the passenger seat of his familiar Jeep and drive to his patient's residence. Once, he was called to Uncle Conrad and Aunt Edra's farm at Pleasant View to care for elderly Bill Scarberry.

Bill Scarberry lived in a tenant house on Uncle Conrad's farm. He was retired, but did light work for Uncle Conrad, mostly during warm summer days. Mr. Scarberry was my grandfather's age and when we drove by the farm on the way to Ravenswood, we would often see him sitting on his front porch, rocking in his chair. Mr. Scarberry was in his golden years and had injured himself riding a bicycle. The medical diagnosis was cracked ribs and possible back injury. I don't recall the exact extent of the injury, but it was severe enough that Dr. Monroe advised Bill to get professional care at the local hospital in Ravenswood. The doctor wanted the injury to be more thoroughly evaluated —surmising that his back would likely have to be immobilized for a few weeks, so the cracked or broken bones would have time to heal. Bill would have nothing to do with Dr. Monroe's recommendation. He was not about to go to the hospital. Even after rigorous discussion and

Dr. Monroe, Ravenswood's Beloved Doctor

admonitions from Dr. Monroe, Bill absolutely refused to leave Uncle Conrad's tenant house.

What was Dr. Monroe going to do with this pugnacious old gentleman? He knew that he couldn't leave him in his current condition. The pain wasn't going to decrease until the injury was immobilized. Pain medication wouldn't stabilize the injury.

After realizing Mr. Scarberry wasn't about to change his mind, Dr. Monroe walked out of the tenant-house without his black medical bag. He wasn't going home, but where was he heading? He walked up the short lane to the machine shed and began scrounging through scrap pieces of lumber stacked in the corner of the building. After leaving the machine shed, he found a saw, hammer, and nails in the tool shed. When the doctor arrived back at the tenant house, he was carrying a wooden cross. By the time the good doctor picked up his black bag, he had taped the top of the cross to Bill's back, from shoulder to shoulder. The cross was secured down his back with a copious amount of wide medical tape, wrapped entirely around his body. The injuries were immobilized, which would help ease the pain and allow his body to heal. Total commitment and creative effort were typical of our esteemed Ravenswood doctor.

Willow Grove: A Boy, A Family, A Farm

Chapter Three: Still Too Young

Willow Grove: A Boy, A Family, A Farm

Ode to the Mighty Sycamore

One of the most wonderful features of our farm at Willow Grove was a tree. Halfway between the dairy barn and the main house was one of the most gigantic sycamore trees I had ever seen. The majestically proportioned sycamore was the only tree along the mile-long lane, which ran nearly the full length of our farm—from the nighttime river bottom pasture field to the daytime hill pasture at the far end of the farm. Other than the mighty sycamore tree, the only other nearby trees were three maples around the perimeter of our house, two shade trees in the yard of the tenant house across the county road, and the apple orchard and shade trees visible from our front yard on the next-door Wolverton farm.

The big sycamore was a remarkable sight, and I often marveled at its massiveness. Justly so: the sycamore was a trophy tree and a tribute to its species. The grand tree stood alone in an open setting and was part of the panoramic view of everyone in our yard or on the side porch. In addition to its greatness and natural beauty, the sycamore was the only source of shade for the farm animals grazing in the adjacent meadow between the house and farm buildings.

In 1950, when I was 11 years old, I "measured" the circumference of the sycamore tree. Standing upright and hugging the tree, I estimated its circumference by reaching around the trunk of the tree as far as I could by stretching both arms and fingertips as far apart as possible. I counted three arm spans around the tree, which I now calculate was a circumference of at least 15 feet and a diameter of about five feet.

Of all the trees in our yard and the hill pasture field near our pond, the trophy sycamore was the only tree that I never had any desire to climb. The first limb on the sycamore was at least 30 feet above the ground, and with its vast circumference —there was no easy way to climb the monster. It would have taken strenuous physical effort to reach any one of the lower limbs. And…an accidental fall from the tree would have resulted in a lot more than a knot on the head!

One particular lower limb on the sycamore extended out into the pasture field. The limb had a very peculiar knot located about 20 feet out from the tree's trunk. The round knot appeared as if Mother Nature had welded a toilet seat in the middle of the long smooth limb, and it wasn't hard to imagine a person sitting on the doughnut-shaped seat, perched like a hawk high above the ground. There was a rumor that, on a dare, one of the Kyle brothers had actually sat on the lofty seat.

Ode to the Mighty Sycamore

When George Washington and his party descended the Ohio River in 1770, he praised the land that would become Ravenswood and Willow Grove. Further south down the river at Point Pleasant, the surveying party turned east and traveled up the Great Kanawha River, where its members observed a sycamore tree that measured 31 feet in circumference. Another measured over 45 feet. The trunks of both trees were measured three feet from the ground. The mighty sycamore, which I measured that day at Willow Grove, was a baby compared to the two trees that George Washington's party had seen more than 180 years earlier. The diameter of the enormous tree along the Great Kanawha was nearly 15 feet or three times larger than the diameter of the sycamore that I enjoyed seeing so often on our farm.

On Blennerhassett Island in the Ohio River at Parkersburg, West Virginia, an estimated 400-year-old sycamore tree expired in the early 1900s. The famous tree was 12 feet in diameter and over 37 feet in circumference. And sycamores weren't the area's only massive trees: A giant black walnut along the Muskingum River in Ohio measured 41 feet in circumference.

The sycamore that I admired so much on our Willow Grove farm was estimated to be well over 200 years old in 1950. In 1770, when George Washington, at the age of 48, descended the Ohio River and surveyed the land at Willow Grove, anecdotally it is very likely that he walked a Native American trail from the Ohio River, and, in doing

Willow Grove: A Boy, A Family, A Farm

so, he would have walked by the same mighty sycamore tree that I walked under as a youngster, 180 years later. The possibility is truly amazing to me!

    I apologize for elaborating so much about the mighty sycamore tree. My humble aim was to pay tribute to a lone monument that both President George Washington and I could have seen with our own two eyes...nearly two centuries apart. Also, I have often wondered how George Washington could have gauged how large, flat, and fertile the land was at Willow Grove. I theorize that until the land was cleared by settlers, it would have boasted dense trees that would have obscured any quick and easy revelation of its acreage and fertility. Notwithstanding, my ensuing thesis is that Willow Grove was possibly clear of any timber when George Washington stepped out of his canoe...for the same reason that the 1800s midwest prairies in Nebraska and Kansas were absent of timber in the days of the roaming buffalo. To provide plenty of grass for 30-60 million buffalo, native Indians set fire to the prairies so grass could thrive and attract herds of buffalo. Buffalo inhabited the Ohio Valley and were indigenous to all of West Virginia at one time. Bottoms along the Ohio River were known by archaeologists to be good camping grounds for the Native Americans when they went on hunting expeditions in the Ohio Valley. So, I advocate that the native Ohio Valley Indians might have also set fire to the thousands of acres of flood-free land at

Ode to the Mighty Sycamore

Willow Grove, just like Native Americans did in the vast prairies of Kansas and Nebraska.

Aunt Dee, Meet Outhouse

Uncle Bob's last remark before he departed for work was: "Dee, don't you dare go near that car." He was gesturing with his index finger and looking straight at his young wife as he reached for the doorknob.

My brother and I were on our annual visit to my mother's parents' farm at Washington Bottom, a community below Parkersburg. The recently wed couple was living with his parents. Not long after Uncle Bob left, Aunt Dee began executing her plan to learn how to drive. I was only 10 years old, but I knew how to steer farm tractors and shift gears on automobiles, pickup trucks, and the farm trucks. So, with Aunt Dee's enthusiasm to learn how to drive and my "driving expertise," we decided that it would be okay to take the coupe for a short drive.

Aunt Dee sat down behind the steering wheel, and I confidently piled in on the passenger side. The coupe was parked on a sandy driveway at the end of my grandparents' house. Directly in front of the car—no more than a few car lengths—was the edge of a steep embankment. More dangerous and even closer behind the coupe was a precarious embankment that descended 20 feet from the flat driveway to a gravel country road. The car's location was *not* a good place to learn to drive, and that is precisely why Uncle Bob voiced his strict

Willow Grove: A Boy, A Family, A Farm

orders before he left for work: "Don't go near the car!"

Also, in front of the car at the edge of the deep embankment was the family privy. The familiar structure was average size and structurally solid; built by my grandfather, who was a lifelong professional carpenter.

Aunt Dee with the Plymouth coupe and one of the family dogs.

The first instruction from the passenger-instructor (yours truly) was to place the right foot on the brake and, with the left foot, push down on the clutch. Then move the gear shift handle on the transmission to the neutral position. Next, move your left foot from the clutch pedal to the brake pedal, and with the right foot on both the accelerator and adjacent floorboard starter, slightly depress both simultaneously. As soon as the engine turns over and the car starts, instantly take your foot off the starter. Starting an early-era, stick-shift

252

Aunt Dee, Meet Outhouse

automobile using both feet was a tricky and a difficult maneuver. It took lots of practice to become proficient.

After Aunt Dee successfully started the car and pushed down on the clutch, she inadvertently shifted the transmission into a forward gear instead of reverse. Then, with the car in gear, Aunt Dee abruptly released the clutch, and, with a heavy foot on the accelerator, the rear wheels spun rapidly, and the coupe lurched forward. In all of five or six seconds—we rammed into the outhouse and twisted the sturdy structure off its foundation. Just that quick, our maiden voyage in the Plymouth was over! We weren't going anywhere! The left front tire was dangling over the edge of the malodorous pit directly below the outhouse floor.

Instantly and in concert, both front doors flew open, and Aunt Dee and I bailed out of the injured Plymouth. We danced around the yard, alternating between jumping up and down and walking in circles. We were in a heap of trouble, and we both knew it.

Shortly, my grandfather came out the kitchen door and stared down from his elevated perch on the back porch, where he could readily see the Plymouth hugging the family privy. He had heard the commotion when the car's heavy steel bumper smacked the corner of the outhouse. After a few choice words, which weren't exactly encouraging or publishable, he quickly realized that we were *all* in deep trouble. When his son got home and saw his car kissing the side of the outhouse, no one would

Willow Grove: A Boy, A Family, A Farm

be spared. Uncle Bob had inherited a hair-trigger temper from his father. What in the world were we going to do?

Pa took his railroad cap off and scratched the top of his nearly bald head. He put his B&O cap back on and just as quickly removed it again—all the while looking down at the ground and pondering the mess we were in. He thought and thought! Finally! "Dee, go in the house and call Harvey! Tell him what happened and ask him to bring his horses as soon as he can. Tell Harvey we need his help, desperately!"

Harvey McKibben's hillside farm buildings and home were in easy eyesight of my grandparents' farmhouse along the same gravel road. Mr. McKibben was my grandfather's age and an experienced, small-time farmer, just like my grandfather. Pa knew Harvey had a team of strong work horses that could pull the car back to where it belonged: in the driveway!

It wasn't long before we saw Harvey walking behind his harnessed team of workhorses: Matilda and Miranda. The horses and Harvey were a welcome sight for three helpless souls.

Fortunately, the rugged chrome bumper on the front of the Plymouth showed no signs of a crash. However, the privy wasn't so lucky. Two of the long vertical boards on the right side of the outhouse door revealed ugly, troublesome cracks right at the spot where the car's bumper rammed the muscular structure. Plus, the narrow horizontal board underneath the bottom of the door was splintered.

Aunt Dee, Meet Outhouse

And, if that wasn't enough, there were several slivers of missing wood caused by the way the outhouse had twisted on its solid foundation. Evidence of a mishap was going to be difficult to mask.

Harvey surveyed the situation. He had pulled many stuck vehicles out of ditches along the country road, but this was his first experience pulling a car out of an outhouse. Harvey was a quiet, old gentleman. He was an intelligent man and knew the Plymouth had to be pulled out of the outhouse on the first attempt, and not allowed to drift back and knock the precarious outhouse entirely off its foundation. If that happened, the privy would quickly end up scattered all over the craggy hillside below. So, even if we returned the Plymouth to its original parking spot, it would still be difficult to explain to Uncle Bob how lumber from the missing outhouse ended up scattered all down the hillside and in the ravine behind the privy.

Pa fastened one end of a heavy log chain around the rear bumper of the Plymouth while Harvey maneuvered Matilda and Miranda several feet up into the yard in front of the coupe. Harvey hooked the other end of the log chain to the singletree behind the two horses' rear ankles. Knowing exactly what could go wrong, Harvey ever so gently encouraged Matilda and Miranda to slowly take up the slack in the long, heavy chain. The calm and powerful team obeyed perfectly! With the chain taut, Harvey paused and treated Matilda and

Willow Grove: A Boy, A Family, A Farm

Miranda with more soft, verbal minutiae, adoring kudos that both draft horses were well familiar with. Then, without any warning and with the log chain still taut, Harvey barked a boisterous, piercing command that rattled both horses and scattered a flock of birds perched high on the top of a nearby maple tree. Harvey was a gentle, mind-mannered man, but when he wanted to, he could cuss the bark off of a white oak tree! His thunderous bellow would've competed with any of the best drill sergeants in the Marines! It was a command that the workhorses readily understood and meant: "Pull you lazy heathens, and don't you dare let up until I say so!"

And that is exactly what the horses did! Instantaneously, Matilda and Miranda bolted forward. The Plymouth lurched out of the outhouse opening, and team was well up into the yard before Harvey could get Matilda and Miranda to slow down and stop. After the horses pulled the car close to the house, Harvey, Pa, and Aunt Dee pushed while I steered the Plymouth back into its original four divots in the sandy parking spot. By the time we swept and feathered the tire tracks in front of the parked car to the outhouse, Uncle Bob would never know his car had ever been touched—let alone taken for the world's shortest joyride!

Pa and Harvey maneuvered the outhouse back over its original foundation using strong timbers and crowbars for leverage. My grandfather was a good carpenter, and by the time he finished, you couldn't tell that the Plymouth had ever touched

Aunt Dee, Meet Outhouse

the outhouse. He re-nailed the loose boards with old rusty nails and even covered all the fresh, bright spots in the cracked boards by rubbing dirt over the shiny areas until they looked weathered, just like the rest of the outhouse.

All that was left now was to thank Harvey for his help and try to recover from the day's turmoil. We stood in the yard and watched Harvey, Matilda, and Miranda amble slowly down across my grandfather's cornfield on their way back to Harvey's barn, which was visible on the other side of the creek at the bottom of the cornfield. Another good deed by a wonderful neighbor.

My grandfather's little farm and Harvey's small hillside property at Washington Bottom were perfect examples of why I loved our dairy farm at Willow Grove so much. Visiting with my maternal grandparents was nice, but a week was a little too long for a boy who loved living on his parents and grandparents' dairy farm at Willow Grove. The hills and valleys that comprised Pa's and Harvey's hill farms didn't appeal to me. I was old enough to know what type of farming topography was necessary for the activities I enjoyed, while at the same time, would enable financial success for my parents. My enthusiasm for Willow Grove stemmed from countless hours walking behind my father and grandfather over rolling terrain in Jackson County.

So many things about our Willow Grove farm were very exciting. The big dairy barn, the several ancillary barnyard buildings, the variety of animals —dairy cattle, calves, horses, pigs—the pond, a

Willow Grove: A Boy, A Family, A Farm

huge front yard, the picturesque view of the Ohio River, and even the huge gravel pit that customers could come to and fill their pickup trucks with loads of clean gravel for a dollar. For a dollar they had to load their truck the old fashion way—one shovel full at a time!

Run Over!

It was a school day in late October 1949. Little brother John wasn't old enough to attend public school and was too young to be venturing out of the safety of the yard into the cornfield, where harvesting was well underway. Bored playing alone in the yard, John was eager to accompany Dad to the cornfield, and, after the noontime meal, Dad acquiesced and let little John go with him. John welcomed the opportunity to ride in the wagon behind the corn picker.

The crispy brown shucks on the golden field corn and the deep dimples in each kernel both confirmed that the ripe ears were ready to be picked and stored in the circular metal storage bins. The two side-by-side, circular metal bins were perforated with one-inch diameter, circular holes, from top to bottom every few inches around the whole circumference of the bin. The numerous holes in the bins aerated the ears of field corn and prevented spoilage.

After a cornfield is cultivated three or four times in the spring and summer to kill weeds and aerate the soil, a high ridge of dirt forms along the base of

Run Over!

the corn stalks. Driving perpendicularly across the ridges after corn has been harvested...is extremely bumpy. Dad was driving the Farmall M, which was hitched to the International Harvester corn picker. Hooked behind the corn picker was a Co-op wagon used to catch the ears of corn hurled down from a conveyor chute on the back of the corn picker. The corn picker's two perfectly meshed circulating rollers stripped the ears from the stalks and deposited the shucked ears into a collection bin. From the bin, the corn dropped onto a continuous conveyor belt and rode up a long chute, which extended about midway out over the trailing wagon. As soon as the ears of corn reached the top of the chute, they dropped into the wagon. John's only job was to watch the airborne ears of corn fly off the chute and somersault into the wagon. John was enjoying the spectacle and had been content sitting and watching for quite a while. Then!

At the end of each row, Dad had to make a wide U-turn. To make the turn, Dad had to drive over several rows of already-picked corn, which acted just like multiple speedbumps on a paved city street. Riding over row after row of raised humps was a challenge for John's soft butt sitting on a hard metal surface in the back of the wagon.

It was getting late in the afternoon and well past John's nap time. After riding in the wagon for a couple of hours, the little man became tired and restless. He had had enough excitement for one day! Luckily, Dad had just returned from the barnyard after unloading a full load of picked corn.

Willow Grove: A Boy, A Family, A Farm

Fully loaded, the wagon weighed at least five thousand pounds!

Dad had picked only a single row of corn and was executing the usual U-turn at the end of the cornfield. He needed to reverse direction and follow a new row of unpicked corn back to the opposite end of the field. The farm tractor, harvester, and trailing wagon formed a long train that required driving over several picked rows of corn. Essentially, Dad had to drive over multiple speed bumps, which were spaced about three feet apart.

Just as Dad was making his U-turn and the front wheels of the wagon were beginning to turn behind the harvester, John decided to climb over the front of the wagon at the exact moment the wagon's front wheels hit one of the speedbumps. The sudden maneuver thrust John out in front of the wagon wheel—which ran right over the middle of his little body. Dad had glanced back toward the wagon just as John was being tossed from the wagon. By the time Dad stopped the tractor, it was too late. John was lying motionless on the ground. Dad picked him up and carried him a few yards to a bed of grass on the edge of the lane. Instead of taking John immediately to the doctor for a professional examination, which today would occur in a heartbeat, Dad was confident that his youngest son would be okay. Yet, being run over by a farm wagon isn't exactly analogous to a bee sting or a knot on the head. John could have been seriously injured. But trips to consult with a doctor just didn't occur that expeditiously! A round trip to

Run Over!

Ravenswood or Ripley would have taken several hours. The emergency had to be readily apparent.

Surprisingly, the degree and tone of John's moaning seemed to indicate that possibly no bones were broken. Convinced that John would be okay, Dad left him lying in the soft grass, remounted the tractor, and continued down the next row of corn to be harvested.

After a while, John picked himself up and staggered down the lane toward the house. The accident happened so fast—and without any doubt, a fortunate phenomenon saved my brother's life. The slightly elevated corn row acted like a launching pad and kept the rubber tire airborne as it passed over John's body, minimizing the weight of the front corner of the wagon. Fortunately, most of the weight from the single harvested row of corn was predominately concentrated in the middle and toward the back of the wagon. The weight of the corn in the back of the wagon functioned as a cantilever and helped lighten the weight over the front wheels. If the wagon had been weighed down with several rows of corn instead of just one row, and that one row concentrated toward the front of the wagon, John would *not* have survived the mishap.

Another Cautionary Tale

The first petrol-powered tractors, which an owner of a small farm could reasonably afford, were built during the latter part of the 1920s. Many of these early tractors were equipped with front and rear *steel* wheels. The two rear wheels were much larger in diameter than the front wheels, and both rear wheels had a series of steel cleats bolted to the outside perimeter of the large wheel. The steel cleats provided traction, which was crucial when pulling heavy farm machinery or a fully loaded wagon over loose soil, a plowed field, or soggy ground.

Newer, more affordable farm tractors were equipped with inflated rubber tires as well as the steel wheels with auxiliary cleats. The early farm tractors were crude and quite uncomfortable. The seats were forged out of hardened steel, and on some models, both rear wheels were exposed entirely and within arm's length of the operator. The driver of the nascent farm tractors needed both powerful arm and leg muscles to steer and manipulate the clutch, brakes, and controls on the rugged machines. Under the best of weather conditions, maneuvering the bulky hunk of steel on wheels was challenging, even for an experienced, muscular farmer.

One afternoon during the dog days of August, Dad was driving his father's farm tractor across the lower pasture on his way to hook onto a wagon parked at the far end of the field. On his way, he noticed a strange object lying in the field. The men had been experiencing occasional transmission problems with the tractor, so Dad decided not to stop the tractor while he investigated the foreign object. He climbed down off the moving tractor and

Another Cautionary Tale

let the lumbering machine continue, unattended, onward through the field. The meadow was completely open, so no harm would come to the slow-moving tractor while he took a quick peek at the object that caught his attention. Dismounting any tractor while it is still moving isn't a wise thing to do, but it wasn't too uncommon. I've done it myself for various reasons. Yet, not really smart!

After Dad reached the object in the pasture field, which had piqued his curiosity, he quickly realized it was nothing of any importance and turned back toward the tractor, which was still chugging slowly ahead through the field. The tractor was moving slow enough that it would only take a few seconds to reach, step onto the rear tow bar and hustle back up onto the tractor seat.

Dad quickly caught up with the tractor and easily placed his left foot on the tow bar and was about to swing his right leg up over the tractor seat when one of the rear wheels hit a treacherous groundhog hole. The tractor was moving at just the right speed, and the hole was deep enough that when the rear rubber tire struck the hole, luckily, it bounced high enough and just the right distance forward. The sudden upward thrust of the tow bar catapulted Dad up and out over the top of the rear wheel. He landed on his back—squarely in front of the moving rear rubber tire. Thankfully, when the tractor tire bounced out of the hole, it landed on the ground right in front of Dad's body. The tractor's massive rear tire had passed over Dad's chest in an upward trajectory—just high enough to dramatically reduce the tons of crushing force moving forward over the top of his stomach and chest. The driverless tractor continued its trek with Dad lying on the ground—dazed but okay. He recovered the tractor before it reached the fence line along the field.

My father was a lucky young man that day. All he received was a sore rib cage and a visible tread impression across his upper torso. Thankfully, he and the men had switched from the rugged steel wheels to rubber tires just before Dad left the barnyard to retrieve the wagon. If the steel wheels had still been on the tractor, there would have been no bouncing when it passed over Dad's body, and he would have been crushed—instantly!

Fifth Grade

The fifth-grade class was too large for any of the classrooms in the school. The solution was a shared classroom with sixth-graders. The class was taught by Mrs. Geren, a soft-spoken, elderly lady who radiated compassion and interest in her students and, in turn, received admiration and respect from everyone. Mrs. Geren's protocol in her classroom showed reverence for her profession.

Fifth Grade

Front Row, left to right: Richard McCoy, David McCoy, Brenda Pinnell, Donna Weekly, Dorothy Tidd, Ronald Bare, John Wildman, Irene Kimes. Second Row: Edna Shamblin, Jimmy Jackson, Earl Balis, Raleigh Williams, Gary Cather, Joe Rhodes, Robert Park, me; Third Row: Helmuts Klingbergs, Burel Wheaton, Delores Groves, Donna Tipton, Patricia Shriver, Loretta Norman, Charles Benson, Donald Vannest; Fourth Row: Linda Mae Bennett, Betty Vankirk, Billie Boggs, Diane Stevenson, Sue Divers, Charlotte Monroe, Eunice Carothers, Larry Jackson, Richard Ward; Fifth Row: Emma Jean Farmer, Miss Geren, Carol Cavender, Margie Rowley, Virginia Lamp, Betty Bennett, Don Bonar, Jeanine Ewing, Roger Nancarrow.

At the beginning of each school day, Mrs. Geren would address the combined classes and convey any general school information from the principal that applied to both grades. Afterward, she would direct the older sixth-grade students to finish their

Willow Grove: A Boy, A Family, A Farm

assigned homework or work in groups on a particular project. While the sixth graders were busy with their assignments, Mrs. Geren would concentrate on the fifth-grade students and give them her undivided attention. During the winter of 1949-1950, the telephone rang in my grandparents' living quarters at Willow Grove. We had one black, plastic Bakelite rotary phone in my grandparents' part of the house. The telephone was connected to a party line that served six or seven of our closest neighbors.

When the phone rang in Grandma's kitchen, it also rang at the same time in every one of our neighbors' homes that were connected to the same telephone line. During the day, the phone would ring often, and before anyone would pick up the receiver, they would listen carefully and count the number of rings, which indicated which neighbor had an incoming phone call. Generally, Grandma answered the phone and, if she couldn't help the caller, she would take a message and track down either her husband or Mom for assistance.

After the telephone rang our designated number of short and long rings, my grandmother picked up the receiver and soon realized that she couldn't help the caller. Politely, she asked the caller to "please hold the line" so that she could give the phone to her husband, who happened to be in the kitchen.

The gentleman on the telephone was calling from the Jackson County Agriculture Department. He explained to Grandpa that a family from Latvia

Fifth Grade

had just arrived in the United States. After they arrived at the port in New Orleans, the family was informed unexpectedly that their sponsor in America would not be able to keep the commitment to provide them with a secure job and a place to live. A father, mother, son, and young daughter had suddenly found themselves in a foreign country with only the clothes on their backs and what luggage they were able to bring with them. Since the Latvian family spoke little English, it was extremely unsettling for them to comprehend how and why they were suddenly stranded and homeless in a foreign country.

I cannot paraphrase the dialogue between my grandfather and the gentleman from the agriculture department. Yet, I know that my grandfather would have listened attentively, with compassion for the Latvian family's situation and the anxiety they must be experiencing in New Orleans. Their future and livelihood in a strange country were not only uncertain but also in the hands of complete strangers.

Grandpa listened as the caller reiterated the Agriculture Department's desire to find an American sponsor for the immigrants so that the family could remain in the United States. Someone who could provide suitable employment and a comfortable place for the family to live.

We already had one full-time employee and his family living on the farm. It was January, and any additional help wouldn't be needed until summer and early fall, when the hay, corn, and wheat crops

Willow Grove: A Boy, A Family, A Farm

were ready for harvesting. In addition to the large two-story main house where my parents, brothers, grandparents, and aunt lived, there were three other smaller homes on the Willow Grove farm, but all were presently occupied by families with children. There was no place for the Latvian family to live!

By the end of the phone call, Grandpa assured the caller that he would seriously consider his sincere plea for help and would call him back before the end of the day. Grandpa needed to consult with three other people—his wife and my father and mother—before he could make any decision.

Grandpa headed for the dairy barn to find my father. He told Dad about the phone call and the Latvian family's dire situation. After a brief but thorough discussion, Dad agreed with his father's opinion about what might be possible. Next, Grandpa needed to talk with the farm's full-time employee.

Robert Moss, his wife, Ruth, and their two children—Everett and Roberta—had been living on the Willow Grove farm for better than a year. Bob was a professional painter and only planned to work on the farm until residential and commercial painting demand picked back up in Ravenswood.

The local economy was improving, and Bob confirmed that he would likely return to painting houses as soon as the weather permitted in the spring. Bob knew and understood that the farm

Fifth Grade

would need hired help after he and his family moved back to Ravenswood in the spring.

In the interim, finding special projects on the farm for an extra employee during the next few months wouldn't be a significant hurdle. Anyone who knew my grandfather knew he could be counted on to help, if at all possible, anytime a deserving individual asked for financial help or was in some minor trouble with the law and needed genuine support. Helping others was something my grandfather did very well many times during his life.

However, until the Moss family moved back to Ravenswood, where would the Latvian family live? As far as grandfather and my parents were concerned, the answer wasn't that difficult! Even though five adults and three children were already living comfortably in our home, there were two spare guest bedrooms with fireplaces. One was a spacious second-floor bedroom with a large handsome bay window and beautifully furnished with an antique, cherry wood, four-poster, canopy bedroom suite, perfect for the Latvian family's first home in America.

But where would the new family prepare and eat three meals each day? Grandpa talked with my mother, and, just as he fully expected, Mom graciously agreed to share her kitchen with the new immigrants. Mom would merely expand her kitchen table to accommodate nine place settings for evening supper instead of the usual five dinner plates. Breakfast and dinner were not an issue since the school kids and adults would be eating at different times.

It was a wonderful and momentous day when Hugo, Valentine, Helmuts, and Helga Klingbergs were welcomed into our Willow Grove home in January 1950. We greeted the family in my mother's spacious family room. Everyone was smiling. It was a splendid moment! Even though we couldn't understand most of what each other said, the room was inundated with gestures of happiness by the Klingbergs.

After several minutes of jubilant greetings, everyone knew each other's first names. Our new friends had traveled halfway around the world, and it was time for them to relax and begin to grasp what had happened to them and fully realize that they were finally safe and secure in their new home in America. My grandfather had done it again! He had helped a deserving and grateful family in a critical time of desperation and need. Of course, this time, Grandpa had a lot of extra help from my always flexible mother!

The Klingbergs were introduced to their roomy and comfortable bedroom through the late-1800s formal staircase, which led to the second floor from Grandma's foyer. The spiral staircase offered a marvelous view of the Ohio River. The serene picture was one of the key reasons the magnificent house was built on this elevated spot.

Opposite Aunt Jack's bedroom at the top of the stairs, the Klingbergs family was led across the hallway to the new living quarters. The room was

Fifth Grade

toasty warm. It was a cold wintry day, and for the next few months, the elegant fireplace would burn incessantly until warm weather arrived in the spring. The Klingbergs were elated and so grateful for the hospitality afforded them by my family.

Helmuts and Helga Klingbergs.

A little before six o'clock on the same day the Latvian family arrived at Willow Grove, my mother sent me to the Klingbergs' upstairs bedroom to tell them that supper was ready and would soon be on the table. Even though I relayed Mom's message slowly and as clearly as I could, not one of the Klingbergs had any idea what I was saying. All the new family did was look at each other curiously, hoping that one of them would have some idea regarding what I was trying to convey. I tried several times to no avail and was about to give up and walk out of the room. Suddenly, I stopped talking and merely pointed my index finger toward my mouth, gesturing by rapidly moving my index finger back and forth toward my wide-open mouth. It worked! Instantly, I saw four huge smiles and everyone happily shaking their heads up and down. They clearly understood my sign language! Well, just maybe their empty stomachs helped a little!

In early 2021, I talked with Helga about her family's life at Willow Grove. We talked about our memories, and one of the things Helga mentioned was my sign language about supper. I was astonished that both of us would remember that seemingly insignificant moment, 72 years later. You could have knocked me over with a feather!

The day after the Latvian family arrived, and well before daybreak, Hugo was out of bed and already working on the farm alongside my father and Bob Moss. Also, before daybreak, Helmuts and Helga ate their breakfast with my brothers and me. After brushing our teeth, the five of us, joined by Everett Moss, all bundled up in warm winter clothes, walked to the bus stop. The walk took about 10 minutes and, on blustery days, we always tried our best to arrive at the bus stop at the same time the school bus arrived. From the bus stop at the Casto farm, the bus driver could see us standing about a quarter mile ahead at our bus stop. If we hadn't already arrived, the driver could

Fifth Grade

spot us running perpendicular up the lane toward the main road. Bob Shockey was a friendly bus driver and a relative on my grandmother's side. If the bus arrived before we did, he would wait patiently until the last straggler had settled safely in one of the bench seats. Mr. Shockey always welcomed us with a smile and a pleasant greeting.

During the winter of 1950, when Hugo, Valentine, Helmuts, and Helga lived with us, 12 people lived in the main house: seven adults and five children. And during this time, I cannot recall a single moment when there was ever an issue, not even a tiny one, caused by so many people living under the same roof at the same time. It certainly helped that the big house had 10 good-sized rooms. The house was built in an era when large families were the norm, and a dozen inhabitants under the same roof wasn't that uncommon. It wasn't even uncommon for much smaller homes, such as our original homestead house in Silverton, which Augustus Fellers Sück purchased in 1885.

After all of us kids left for the bus stop, Mom and Valentine would clear the breakfast table and get ready for the arrival of their hungry husbands. Mom and Valentine had their day organized by the time Dad and Hugo walked through the kitchen door. In another part of the house, Grandma and Aunt Jack were busy preparing breakfast for my grandfather and themselves. Virtually every day, Grandpa would walk from Grandma's kitchen through our living room into Mom's kitchen.

Willow Grove: A Boy, A Family, A Farm

Breakfast was a perfect time for him to discuss the new day's work schedule with my father.

John in front, with (left to right) Everett Moss, Helga and Helmuts Klingbergs, me, and Bob.

Even though Helmuts and Helga could speak very little English, both started elementary school the day after the family arrived in Willow Grove. Helmuts was about my age, 11, when he enrolled with me in Mrs. Geren's fifth-grade class. Helga was a year or so younger. At the suggestion of Mrs. Geren, I partnered with Helmuts in the classroom and assisted him with his English and other subjects, as needed. It wasn't long before Helmuts was doing exceptionally well and needed very little

Fifth Grade

support from me. It was obvious that he had been a good student in Latvia.

Train Whistle Averts Disaster!

An all too familiar, alarming high-pitched screaming in the wee hours of the night woke all the adults in both houses from several hours of deep sleep. Even Bob and I stirred from the endless wailing that accompanied a searing bright beam of white light that lit up our bedroom like fireworks on the 4th of July. Railroad engineers always use their steam whistles to announce a train's imminent arrival at railroad crossings. But, at the Willow Grove crossing, the steam whistle only amounts to a short *toot* during daytime and nothing at all in the middle of the night. The sustained blast was the B&O engineer's way of sending an abrupt signal to a local farmer that a serious problem needed immediate attention.

Soon, and with my eyes still closed, I felt a hand on my shoulder shaking me and a voice saying: "Junior, get your clothes on!" That's all Dad said after he switched the light on and quickly left our bedroom. Even though the single overhead light challenged our squinting eyes, it didn't slow our escape from bed and a night of sound sleep. My brother and I knew every step of the pathway to our hanging clothes and could dress blindfolded. Whatever prompted Dad to wake us in the middle of the night was important and now was not a good time to dilly-dally!

Willow Grove: A Boy, A Family, A Farm

We scampered around the corner into the bathroom and, in a matter of seconds, we were both completely dressed, except for our shoes, which were always dutifully lined up on newspapers at the side door in Mom's kitchen.

As Dad trekked downstairs, he turned on the hall light above the staircase and the kitchen light before he disappeared into the darkness. While sitting on the kitchen floor, lacing up my shoes, I noticed that Dad's flashlight was gone. All Bob and I needed to do was locate a beam of light, and we'd know what direction Dad was heading. Since the engineer on the freight train had made such a ruckus with his steam whistle, I was sure Dad was walking toward the railroad track.

Indeed, and well ahead of us, we saw the beam from Dad's flashlight meandering down the center of the lane toward the railroad crossing. Even though it was nighttime, Bob and I chose to take a shortcut rather than follow the safety of the sidewalk to the lane. Once we reached the edge of the yard, we challenged the slope on our butts and used our hands and heels to slow the speed of our slippery descent down the embankment onto the road below. We gambled that our sliding backsides would miss the thorny gooseberry patch on the side of the bank.

We caught up with Dad just before the railroad track. At the crossing, Dad pointed his flashlight toward the gate leading to the pasture field where he kept the dairy cows at night. The river pasture field was much more convenient than the distant

Train Whistle Averts Disaster!

hill pasture and took a lot less time early in the morning to round up the dairy cows.

The gate was closed and secure. The straight fence line perpendicular to the riverbank looked fine. Dad then turned his flashlight toward the middle of the pasture field. None of the cattle were visible. We couldn't see far enough to tell if the cattle were grazing at the far end of the field next to the irrigation system, where we knew there was plenty of green grass. So, we walked back a few steps to the railroad crossing and started walking south on the railroad track toward Raymond Casto's farm. While we were walking down the track, Dad scoured the terrain on both sides of the rails. He focused his flashlight on the fence line on the right side between the railroad track embankment and the night pasture.

So far, the fence looked good, and we couldn't see any reason why the freight train engineer let loose with such a protracted screaming commotion from the locomotive steam whistle. It was loud enough to awaken everyone in two households and most likely stir the sleeping Ohio residents clear on the other side of the wide river. What was the problem?

After walking some distance down the railroad track, we suddenly noticed several beads of sparkling light reflecting back from Dad's flashlight. The flickering glitter was easy to see against the pitch-black landscape. When we got closer, we knew why the engineer was hell-bent on waking up everyone in the farmhouse. Several of our dairy cows were loitering alongside and in between the rails on the railroad track. The animals were motionless and as curious about a single beam of light approaching them as we were about the multiple beads of glitter clustered in the middle and along both sides of the railroad track.

Hugo and his wife, Valentine, had both been awakened by the blast of the noisy steam whistle, and he was curious about what was going on. A conscientious farmhand, Hugo showed up of his own volition and caught up with us on the railroad track. Shortly after, we spotted the breach in the pasture field fence several yards beyond where we first located the cattle standing on the railroad track.

After corralling all the wandering dairy cows, we herded them back into the pasture field. Extra help was the reason Dad woke Bob and me. He rightly figured that the dairy cattle might be the problem and, if so, he would need both of us to help surround the animals and drive them back into the safety of the river bottom pasture field. Dad told Hugo that he would walk back to the barnyard and get the tools and supplies they needed to patch the fence. Meanwhile, Hugo stood guard at the downed fence and waited for Dad to return with the tractor and supplies. The dual headlights on the tractor would provide ample light for the two of them to temporarily mend the fence. Tomorrow, during daylight hours, Dad and Hugo would return, dig a new post hole, and repair the fence, permanently.

Train Whistle Averts Disaster!

Hugo Klingbergs with Helga on the Farmall M.

The good news was that all the animals seemed okay, at least as far as we could see from the range of the flashlight. It would be awful if the train had struck and killed even one—let alone several—of Dad's good milk-producing cows!

My brother and I walked back to the house with Dad. Before he continued to the tool shed to get a hammer, staples, and wire stretcher, Dad stopped by Grandma's kitchen and informed his concerned parents about the breach in the fence and that all of the cattle were back in the night pasture. While Dad was talking with his parents, Bob and I quickly disappeared upstairs and crawled back into our

Willow Grove: A Boy, A Family, A Farm

unmade bed. Our night's rest was cut a little short, but that was okay. We were both asleep before our heads could sink into the soft pillows.

One month later, Hugo wrote a letter of appreciation to my family. This is what he wrote:

Millwood, 5th Febr., 1950

Dear Mr. E. F. Sück and Family,

When our despair was the deepest, when the anxiety and the care for our future oppressed us mostly, when we did not know where to turn and where find shelter, then came your relief – the nicest deed of your goodness of heart and your assistance.

We are thanking you very heartily for the given possibility to come to this nice country of freedom.

We are in your country and among your people now.

Please, teach us to learn your habits and to understand the rules of your country.

We want to do our duties by the best sense and ability and to become decent citizens of your country.

Please, do not mind our possible error and misunderstanding which can be caused by our imperfect knowledge of your language.

Please, accept our thanks once more.

May God bless your family and us!

Your ever gratefully,

Hugo K. G. Klingbergs
Family

In One Ear...

In One Ear...

 Every year, the fertile soil at Willow Grove would grow a bountiful crop of sweet corn for the kitchen table and booming crops of hay and field corn silage for the dairy cattle. Occasionally, Dad would plant winter wheat in one of the three larger fields between the dairy barn and the hill pasture field. It was a thrill to watch the giant New Holland combine mow down wide swaths of wheat and then completely swallow the spaghetti-thin stalks, each decked on top with healthy kernels hidden in a fuzzy sheath. The hungry machine would devour the standing grain and, without stopping, disgorge the crushed stems out the back of the threshing machine while leaving the winnowed kernels inside the harvester. After a while, the stuffed combine would stop, so the belly full of wheat could be transferred into an empty wagon parked at the end of the field.

 Once the combine disgorged its booty, the full wagonload of wheat was hauled to the Wharton's vacant cattle barn, where it was unloaded and stored in the middle of the empty building. After all the wheat in the field was threshed, tons of loose wheat formed an enormously high pyramid in the middle of our neighbor's barn.

 The huge pile of dry wheat was safe from inclement weather, but not from active kids who couldn't wait to climb to the peak of wheat mountain. My brothers and I had a marvelous time attempting to climb, crawl, or swim to the top of the mutable mountain. We occupied many hours playing and challenging each other to see who would become king of the mountain.

After one of our long playtimes to reach the top of wheat mountain, I realized that something inside my head had come loose. At first, I thought it was my imagination. But, sure enough, every time I shook my head, something inside rattled. After a while, I realized the rattle was in my left ear. I tried tilting my head sideways and then smacking the opposite side. Surely, the cause of the rattle would eventually fall out. No such luck! Finally, I realized I had a kernel of wheat inside my eardrum.

Off to Ravenswood to see Dr. Monroe. As soon as we arrived at the doctor's office, Dr. Monroe led Mom and me into his medicinal smelling room immediately behind the waiting room. Instead of grabbing a few gnarly looking medical weapons, Dr. Monroe washed his hands, filled a squeeze bottle with warm water, and handed me a stainless-steel wash pan to hold under my ear. Within seconds, the single kernel of wheat was flushed out into the pan. It was so quick and easy! I couldn't believe it! I'm sure my mother thought the same and wondered why she hadn't thought of it herself. It would have saved a trip to Ravenswood, and we wouldn't have had to bother the good doctor.

Wasp Warfare

My whitewashed, swollen eyes prompted another memory of smashing mud daubers and

Wasp Warfare

knocking down wasp nests. When Bob and I couldn't think of something to do, we could always stir up excitement by hunting for wasp nests. The hunting expeditions usually occurred after both of us had forgotten who won the last battle—the wasps or us!

Even though we were bored and looking for action, I wasn't keen on Bob's wasp-fighting plan. In the last duel with the wasps, Bob won! The wasps won! I lost—big time! But Bob was determined and wouldn't take no for an answer. His last attempt to talk me into going on the warpath got my attention and changed my pea-size brain when he taunted me: "Cluck, cluck, cluck!" No way was I going to be called a chicken! So, off we went to the barnyard, looking for trouble!

It was late in the afternoon. The dairy barn was the first place we headed to scout for those crazy kamikaze bombers. It didn't take long until we spotted our prey. Ready or not, our four paws were loaded with perfect-sized rocks, which we'd picked up from the side of the road. We had plenty of ammunition and were ready to rumble!

Typically, when one of us ended up getting stung by a wasp, it was on the arm, neck, or shirtless back. When one of us got stung, we'd have to pull the stinger out of the side of our head or cheek. The stinger was painful going in and hurt like heck when it was pulled out. Soon afterward, the ravaged area sprouted a feeling of numbness. Severe swelling would slowly build over the next few hours. And by the time we went to the house for supper, the swelling was enough that Mom didn't have to ask us what we'd "been up to." She could tell with the eyes in the back of her head! Mom could read her sons like a dictionary!

I was especially sensitive to bee and wasp stings. It didn't matter which side of my face was stung. The eye on the same side would swell and remain closed for about 24 hours. During the last wasp fight, I was stung *between* the eyes. Both eyes swelled almost entirely shut. There wasn't much pain, but my face looked horrific. For a while, I had to view the world through two narrow slits, but fortunately, the worst of the swelling only lasted about a day. I was banned from any family photo sessions.

Those vivid memories of past swollen eyes heightened my reluctance to follow Bob into battle with the wasps. Nevertheless, I followed Bob's lead —but this time, Bob's luck ran out when he pelted a nest full of feisty wasps. The mad bombers made three direct hits: lower forearm, cheek, and shoulder blade. The battle was over before I even had a chance to hurl my first rock. The 10-second battle ended in a rout in favor of the wasps. Bob and I hastened from the Wolverton's barn to the house. It was time to borrow Mom's tweezers and plaster Bob's battle wounds with a moist paste of baking soda. The wasps sure mitigated our boredom. We were both content, just sitting in the kitchen, watching Mom prepare supper.

Evening Fun

Many warm evenings after the sun went down, millions of lightning bugs would provide a wealth of enjoyment for my brothers and me. My father would sit on the edge of the wooden porch with his feet planted on the lower step and watch as we ran through the yard, cupping our hands together, trying to capture the flying bugs, whose tails flashed a tiny light on and off in the darkness of the early evening. We each had a glass bottle with a lid, which we used to corral the fireflies after snatching them out of the translucent sky. The more bugs we caught, the brighter our homemade lantern would glow in the dark. Invariably, while we were running and jumping, a surprise collision would occur between one of us and Mom's clothesline pole or one of the trees in our yard. One of us typically ended up on the ground moaning, groaning, and rubbing his head or the part of his body that got hammered. Occasionally, more than one of us would be rolling around on the ground at the same time. The collisions always ignited laughter from our father.

I'm sure there were plenty of times when my parents, especially my mother, wished they'd had at least one compliant daughter to help soothe coping with three rambunctious boys. In the summer, when school was out, it was a rare day when our mother didn't have to go to the pantry where she kept her medical supplies—and garner what she needed to attend to one of her sons or the hired

Willow Grove: A Boy, A Family, A Farm

men working on the farm. It was good that my mother didn't become nauseous when she saw blood, because she certainly saw a lot of it while we were growing up.

Peaceful summer evenings were great occasions for my brothers and me to play in the yard. We would convene in the side yard for one of our favorite hybrid games of hide-and-seek, which we called "kick the can." Most evenings, our father would relax while we played as hard as possible, since our playtime after supper was not unlimited. Our bedtime was eight o'clock sharp!

Kick-the-can was a simple game where all the players, except one, would hide in the yard and cool their heels long enough to lure the player protecting the home plate can away from the can far enough that one of the hidden players could sneak around and kick the can down into the yard. The protector of the can would then have to chase after the can, pick it up, and return it to home base before he could once again start searching for hidden players. The protector of the can had to visually spot someone, then run back and touch the can and identify the player by name—which was all that was necessary to land a player in jail. He had to spot all the players before becoming one of the players to hide. It may sound like a silly game, but it was fun, and we entertained ourselves for hours after dusk, when it was easier to hide.

It was a challenge to kick the can as far as possible, which freed all the jailed players sitting impatiently on the porch steps beside Dad. The real

Evening Fun

aggravating part of the game was catching everyone except one person and then getting outsmarted and allowing the can to go airborne. This enabled everyone in jail to run and hide, which could happen multiple times during the evening. Eventually, the person who was "it" had two options: Get mad and quit or start all over and look for the players who were hiding somewhere out in the vast yard and around the two adjacent residences.

One evening Everett Moss was at the edge of the concrete patio protecting home place, which, this evening, was an empty, upside-down, quart juice can. Everett wasn't having a good evening. He was more than just a little perturbed. Every time he would get close to catching everyone, the very last player would suddenly appear and kick the can, freeing all the players. Clearly, he was ticked off!

Everett finally had had enough! He walked over to where my father was sitting on the porch step and picked up a standard-sized brick from a stack stored underneath the porch. He walked back to home plate, stood the brick upright on the edge of the concrete patio, and placed the can over the brick. The brick was snug and completely concealed. When my father realized what Everett was up to, he started chuckling, and soon the chuckling switched to full-blown laughter. Dad was laughing so hard that he lost any awareness of the consequence of what a brick might do to a tender, adolescent foot. If Dad had only stopped laughing, he might have had time to suggest that Everett use

Willow Grove: A Boy, A Family, A Farm

only half a brick, a piece of firewood, or another lighter material. Cotton balls come to mind...as far as I am concerned!

Lucky, lucky me! I was hiding behind the big maple tree beside the woodshed. Even though I watched every move Everett made, it was too dark for me to see exactly what he was doing. Still, I should have suspected something was up when I heard Dad laughing so hard. Anyway, I couldn't figure out what was going on, and Dad's uncontrollable laughter only hastened my fervent desire to kick that can to the moon.

After placing the can over the brick, Everett... little by little...shrewdly lured me away from my hiding spot by walking slowly with his back toward me, several feet out into the yard. *Man, I thought, this is going to be too easy!* When Everett was just the proper distance from the can, I took off running as fast as my legs could carry me across the concrete patio. Out of the corner of my eye, I could see my father rocking back and forth, laughing his head off, while seated in his favorite kick-the-can viewing spot. I still had no idea why he was laughing so hard. Unfortunately, I was about to find out!

Everett was out of play. No way could he spot me, race back and touch the can and call out my name before I could kick it. If Everett beat me to the can, I would be out. Unbeknownst to me, Everett deliberately gave me all the time and space I needed to kick the can and "hang myself"! When I got close to the quart can, I took a single, stutter-step and

Evening Fun

lined up perfectly with the grapefruit can. I zeroed in on the can with all my might! I powered my right foot forward as hard as possible. On impact, I instantly knew something was wrong. Really wrong! The toe of my shoe bent up and smacked the front of my ankle. I was wearing an old pair of cloth tennis shoes, complete with multiple holes in the vamp. Immediately, I let out a roaring howl and grabbed my right foot with both hands, shouting adolescent expletives and hopping around on one leg. It took a few minutes for the severe pain to subside. Fortunately, I could limp on my foot without sharp pain, so there were no apparent broken bones. By the time Dad had stopped laughing, I'd stopped hopping around and yelling bloody murder. I even chuckled a little myself about how I had been duped. By now, it was close to my bedtime and naturally my foot was still smarting. I was more than ready for a warm, soaking bath. I welcomed the opportunity to go to bed after another full day and eventful summer evening on our Willow Grove farm. Through the two open windows of my bedroom, millions of crickets in the cool night undergrowth lulled me to contented sleep.

Dewey Gene Strikes Again!

Grandpa had just returned from Ravenswood, where he had taken care of business at the Farmers Building and Loan Association. Afterward, he picked up a few items on Grandma's grocery list at

Willow Grove: A Boy, A Family, A Farm

Kelly's Market. He also patronized another Ravenswood business while he was in town.

To our surprise, a new full-size bicycle was lying on the bed of the pickup truck. It was a colorful bike, and my brothers and I agreed to share the gift. We couldn't wait to try out our new pair of wheels.

To learn how to ride our new bike, the loading dock by the milk house was a good launching pad. We would walk the bike to the milk house, where we would lean it up against the concrete loading dock. We would then drop down on the seat from the top of the loading dock and straddle the bike, just like a rodeo cowboy drops down from above to mount a bucking bronco. Once our feet were positioned on the pedals, we would push away from the dock and commence pedaling down the lane toward the house. The gravel lane was smooth and had a modest drop in elevation from the dock to the house, which helped us learn how to ride the bicycle. All we had to do was concentrate on staying upright during the short ride. Once we reached the yard, we could bail out on to the soft green grass. Bob and I were seasoned bike riders after a few trips to and from the milk house dock.

Cousin Dewey Gene was spending the summer with us. One summer day, Dewey Gene was riding our new bicycle up and down the lane between the barn and the main county road, which was about a quarter of a mile from the barn. After a while, Dewey Gene became bored riding all by himself and joined me, Bob, little John, and Everett Moss. The

Dewey Gene Strikes Again!

four of us were playing one of our several "made-up" games, which didn't interest him. He suggested we go for a bicycle ride. Dewey Gene's thoughtful invitation seemed like a good idea. Hauling a bicycle passenger while doing all the pedaling is strenuous work, especially on a gravel lane with a slight incline between the house and barn.

Everett Moss was the first to jump at this generous opportunity and immediately climbed on the bicycle behind Dewey Gene. Up the road they went, past the dairy barn. Soon they were completely out of view from the spot where we were standing in the yard. They were heading for the bus stop at the end of the lane. In the interim, Bob, John, and I were more than a little suspicious of this grand offer to be a passenger on one of Dewey Gene's free rides. We had been around our cousin a lot longer than Everett, and the three of us had a cornucopia of memories etched in our minds of cuts, bumps, scratches, bruises, and knots on our respective heads...from similar superb offers from our older, practical-joker cousin. Being second, third, or the very last to go for a bike ride with Dewey Gene at the helm was just fine with us.

Dewey Gene and Everett had been out of sight for several minutes when we suddenly saw them coming down the lane toward the house. Bob, John, and I were standing along the lane at the end of the sidewalk. Even at some distance, you could tell that the captain of the bicycle and his non-paying passenger were traveling pretty fast. When they got closer, you could see that—just like the early pony express riders—they were "carrying the mail"!

They roared past the machine shed, dairy barn, milk house, and pump house. By the time they were under the sycamore tree—the mammoth monument beside the lane—Dewey Gene's head was bent over and extended well out over the handlebars. Both elbows were higher than his head. Puffs of dust were swirling up from behind both wheels. Pebbles were rattling and ricocheting underneath the fenders. He was pedaling as if a notorious gang of gun-blazing outlaws was chasing them. Dewey Gene was pedaling so fast that his feet were a blur. Everett had his eyes clamped shut and both arms wrapped around Dewey Gene's waist. By the time the duo flew under the shady branches of the mighty sycamore, it was obvious that the pilot and his passenger were close to lifting off. The runaway bicycle was out of control!

The bicycle driver wasn't going to be able to heed the forthcoming danger, which was a few yards straight ahead. Instead of slowing down, Dewey Gene was low in the saddle, elbows high and his chin protruding out over the handlebars. He was pedaling as fast as he could when the bike and both riders sailed past us and continued down the choppy lane toward the railroad track.

The instant the duo passed us, my brothers and I rushed to the center of the lane where we could watch the bicycle hightail it down the road. When the bike passed over the modest drop in the road, it picked up even more speed as it accelerated down

Dewey Gene Strikes Again!

the decline. Somehow, the bike remained upright over the rugged slope. Dewey Gene was fighting the handlebars, trying to keep the front wheel from jerking sideways, which would certainly result in a horrendous wreck. Everett was hanging on for dear life. Half the time, his buttocks were airborne, bouncing up and down on the bicycle carriage as the back wheel recoiled from the surface ruts and protruding stones in the "cow path." My brothers and I knew all about the road's irregular surface and knew that the bicycle would have to slow down sooner or later. The railroad track was only a short distance from the bottom of the decline, and there was no way that they could remain upright and cross over the railroad crossing. The twin tracks were far too rough to cross safely on a bicycle even at slow speed. The only way Dewey Gene and Everett would reach the other side of the railroad tracks would be if they were catapulted over the handlebars.

The railroad crossing proved not to be a challenge for the bikers. Approximately 30 feet before the crossing, the road suddenly changed from a hard, dirt base to a deep, fluffy bed of soft beach sand. When the bicycle's front wheel hit the sand, it twisted sideways and hurtled Dewey Gene and Everett out over the handlebars. The wreck was comical to watch! My brothers and I were certainly glad we weren't crumpled up and buried in the sand, the way the bike, Dewey Gene, and Everett were. From where we were standing, we couldn't determine the extent of damage to our new

293

bike. Grandpa was going to be furious! By the time we reached the crash site, both bodies were beginning to stir, albeit merely! There was enough movement that we could tell they were going to live. The dual litany of ceaseless moans and groans emanating from the partially buried bodies was characteristic of someone who didn't care if he lived or died. It was a sight to behold!

It took a while before the casualties in the pileup felt alive enough to try and sit up. After several minutes, Dewey Gene was willing to stand, but his weak legs weren't quite ready to support his mangled body. Everett wasn't sure when or if he would ever get up! His aching body didn't want to move. Nearly every muscle in his body had been mauled on impact. Fortunately, all the moaning and groaning didn't foreshadow any dire consequences for the two cyclists. Neither Dewey Gene nor Everett had any broken bones. It took a while, but Dewey Gene and Everett finally found enough strength to muster a slight, though contorted grin and muffled chuckle. By then, we could see both were no worse for wear and would live to see another day. Even the bicycle was okay. The glossy fenders survived without any severe scratches, thanks to the fine texture of the sand. Luckily, Grandpa never found out about the wreck of our new bike. Moreover, anytime Dewey Gene offered to take one of us boys for a free ride, we wouldn't even waste time responding "No way, Jose!" before we would turn tail and skedaddle as fast as we could in search of a good hiding spot.

1949 Family Reunion

1949 Family Reunion

    Family gatherings are near the pinnacle of all the countless and rewarding memories that I appreciate so much about growing up in the Jackson County farming community of Willow Grove. My grandfather treasured his family, and every so often during nice summer weather, he would say to his wife that he wanted everyone to get together." Grandmother would telephone Aunt Edra, Aunt Dot, and Uncle Jim's wife, Helen, and tell them that Grandpa wanted everyone to come to Willow Grove the next Sunday for a picnic. Usually, the family received little advance notice. Grandpa's health was waning, and he didn't have the comfort of many good days during the latter years of his life. If he hadn't seen all the immediate family together for several weeks and just happened to be feeling good at the moment, he was prone to make a hasty decision that we should assemble at our farm or one of his children's farms.

    And without fail, everyone would fulfill Grandpa's request and arrive at Willow Grove an hour or so before the noontime meal. All of the ladies would bring a delicious dish for us to enjoy. Unless the occasion happened to fall on a holiday, our social gatherings were always on Sunday. Uncle Conrad, Uncle Jim, and my father were all dairy farmers, and because of their daily workload, they would have about six hours of social time on Sunday. These few hours of relaxation occurred only if everything on the farm was alright. That is,

Willow Grove: A Boy, A Family, A Farm

no problems that needed immediate attention. Otherwise, and with few exceptions, Grandpa was strict about not working on Sunday. Taking care of the dairy cattle was the only labor he would condone on the Sabbath.

In the summer of 1949, my grandfather organized a larger gathering at Willow Grove. Eighty-seven relatives from my grandfather and the families of three of his siblings—Theodore, Joseph Gorby, and Emma—were present for the first of 70 contiguous yearly reunions.

Brother Joseph Gorby was deceased, but his wife, Molly, their children, and grandchildren were present. Two brothers—Cecil and John—both lived quite a distance away in Pennsylvania and didn't attend the reunion. Paul Moore, a professional photographer and renowned resident of Ravenswood, and Jackie Hughes, a schoolmate and close friend of cousin Eddie McCoy, were the only guests who were not direct descendants of my great-grandfather Augustus Fellers Sück.

The big front porch provided a grand balcony for adults to sit, socialize, and enjoy the panoramic view of the Ohio River. The house was adorned with three open-air covered porches and inside with two country kitchens that offered plenty of room to prepare food and keep it warm for the picnic. One of the three outside porches led directly into the first-floor laundry room. Inside the laundry room was a half-bath convenient for everyone attending the picnic. Also, a staircase near the laundry room provided easy access to a second-floor full bath.

1949 Family Reunion

The hardwood floors in the house kept little munchkins with grass-stained shoes from tracking through the main living quarters of the house. Access to both lavatories was ideal for guests, since they didn't have to enter the main living quarters.

The family picnics were grand for the adults and doubly fun for the kids. My brothers and I had 14 first cousins, and we looked forward to socializing with them on our farm. Even when we were together during frigid winter days, the older cousins would remain indoors, talking, laughing, and keeping the adults entertained with their continuous antics.

Willow Grove: A Boy, A Family, A Farm

Key for 1949 Reunion at Willow Grove

1949 Family Reunion

Key for First Sück Reunion in 1949 at Willow Grove, West Virginia

Name	Relationship to Named Person
1. Edmond Fellers Sück	Wife 26
2. Mary Lewis	Father 83, Mother 5
3. Donald Harris	Father 72, Mother 4
4. Wilma Sück Harris	Father Joseph Sück, decd. Mother 20
5. Helen Sück Lewis	Father Joseph Sück, decd. Mother 20
6. Hazel Sück Franklin	Father Joseph Sück, decd. Mother 20
7. Lottie Franklin	Husband 8
8. Lawrence Franklin	Wife 7, Mother 6
9. Virginia Cook Curry	Husband 10
10. Charles Curry	Wife 9, Father 75, Mother 74
11. Janet Paulus	Father 13, Mother 12
12. Mabel Ashcraft Paulus	Husband 13, Father, William Ashcraft, decd.; Mother, Tracy Sück Ashcraft, decd.
13. Warren Paulus	Wife 12
14. Caddie Ashcraft	Husband 16
15. Unidentified Girl Likely an Ashcraft Daughter	
16. Brady Ashcraft	Wife 14, Father, William Ashcraft, decd.; Mother, Tracy Sück Ashcraft, decd.
17. Verna Jean Ashcraft	Father 18, Mother 19
18. Joshua Ashcraft	Wife 19, Father, William Ashcraft, decd., Mother, Tracy Sück Ashcraft, decd.
19. Icie Ashcraft	Husband 18
20. Mollie Coleman Sück	Husband, Joseph Sück, decd.
21. Elfra Carmichael	Sister 26
22. Homer Davis	Wife 27
23. Bessie Sück	Husband 25
24. Kathrine Barber Sück	Husband 70
25. Theodore Sück	Wife 23
26. Nannie Carmichael Sück	Husband 1
27. Dorothy Sück Davis	Husband 22, Father 1, Mother 26
28. Alice Harris	Father 72, Mother 4

299

Willow Grove: A Boy, A Family, A Farm

29. Idonia Ethel (Bunny) Sück Fox Father 25, Mother 23
30. Darrell Fox Wife 29
31. Emma Eleatha Sück Nesselroad Father 25, Mother 23
32. John Nesselroad Wife 31
33. Gail Franklin Earl, Mother 6
34. Willie Franklin Wife 6
35. Carol Jane Sück Father 36, Mother 37
36. Howard Sück Joseph Sück, decd. Mother 20
37. Joy Knapp Sück Husband 36
38. Clarence Franklin Earl, Mother 6
39. Mayford Harris, Jr. Father 72, Mother 4
40. Edward Nesselroad Father 32, Mother 31
41. Bonnie Harris Father 72, Mother 4
42. Dale Nesselroad Father 32, Mother 31
43. Edra Sück McCoy Husband 84, Father 1, Mother 26
44. Connie McCoy Father 84, Mother 43
45. Glen Franklin Earl, Mother 6
46. William (Bill) Sück Father 36, Mother 37
47. Charles Franklin Father, Earl, decd. Mother 6
48. Jackie Turner, Friend of Eddie McCoy 55
49. Joe Lee McCoy Father 84, Mother 43
50. Joe Lewis Father 83, Mother 5
51. John Lewis Father 83, Mother 5
52. Richard Sück Father, Richard, decd. Mother 73
53. John Nesselroad Father 32, Mother 31
54. Dewey Gene Davis Father 22, Mother 27
55. Forest Edmond (Eddie) McCoy Father 84, Mother 43
56. Edmond Lawrence Sück, Jr. Father 70, Mother 24
57. Theodore (Ted) Sück Father, Richard, decd. Mother 73
58. Nancy Nesselroad Father, 32, Mother 31
59. John Earl Sück Father 70, Mother 24
60. David Nesselroad Father 32. Mother 31

300

1949 Family Reunion

61. Mary Helen Harris	Father 72, Mother 4	
62. Faye Franklin	Father 34, Mother 6	
63. Robert Derwood Sück	Father 70, Mother 24	
64. James Conrad McCoy	Father 84, Mother 43	
65. William Larry McCoy	Father 84, Mother 43	
66. Darrel (Darry) Fox	Father 30, Mother 29	
67. Jean Ann Sück Father, Richard, decd. Mother 73		
68. June Sück	Father, 36, Mother 37	
69. James Augustus Fellers Sück	Father 1, Mother 26	
70. Edmond Lawrence Sück	Father 1, Mother 26	
71. John Paul McCoy	Father 84, Mother 43	
72. Mayford Harris	Wife 4	
73. Gertrude Sück	Husband, Richard, decd.	
74. Emma Sück Curry	Husband 75	
75. Charles Curry	Wife 74	
76. Dianne Lewis	Father 83, Mother 5	
77. Doris Jean Sück	Father 69, Mother 85	
78. Dorothy Ann McCoy	Father 84, Mother 43	
79. Joanne Sück	Father 69, Mother 85	
80. Martha Ellen Davis	Father 22, Mother 27	
81. Mary Kathrine Sück	Father 69, Mother 85	
82. Jim Lewis	Father 83, Mother 5	
83. Johnnie Lewis	Wife 5	
84. Conrad Morgan McCoy	Wife 43	
85. Helen Pepper Sück	Husband 69	
86. Tommie Harris	Father 72, Mother 4	
87. James Sück, Jr., Father 69, Mother 85		

301

Willow Grove: A Boy, A Family, A Farm

The 1949 reunion of Augustus Fellers and Catherine Sück's descendants was a tremendous success. Everyone had a wonderful time, and the initial gathering was the first of many which would follow every year on the first Sunday of August. August 4, 2019 was the 70th consecutive reunion. Sadly, the 2020 reunion had to be canceled because of the coronavirus pandemic.

Besides perfect weather, the idyllic setting of our dairy farm in Willow Grove was the principal reason the 1949 reunion was so successful. The spacious yard around three sides of the main residence could accommodate a crowd comfortably. It was particularly inviting for younger kids who needed a lot of room to run off excess energy. Decades-old maple trees were located around the house, providing ample shade for the kids to play under and simultaneously be at a convenient distance from their mindful parents' watchful eyes.

Pony Antics

The Willow Grove farm also afforded the older boys several options to entertain themselves. There was plenty of room to play softball, volleyball, and badminton—all at the same time in different areas of the yard and adjacent, manicured meadow. A three-acre freshwater pond on the farm was a perfect place to fish or go for a nice cool dip.

After we had finished our midday picnic, several of the older boys were talking about the two ponies that we pastured in a meadow next to the house.

Pony Antics

One was an average-sized brown and white spotted pinto. The other was a tall, sleek horse that Grandpa had purchased to help herd dairy cattle. Her name was Nancy. Nancy was a beautiful horse and could have easily passed for an expensive Kentucky thoroughbred, with her long slender legs and striking dark-brown coat. Nancy had been professionally trained to drive cattle, which was apparent to anyone who watched her cut, block, and round up cattle. She could accelerate like a shot out of a gun, run exceedingly fast, change directions on a dime, and while galloping exceedingly fast, instantaneously come to an explosive, abrupt stop with her head high, rump low—all while her four hooves were plowing individual furrows.

Nancy could perform all these feats with ease! The only thing a rider had to do was hang onto the reins with one hand, grip the saddle horn with the other, and at the same time allow the pony to make all the decisions about corralling a disobedient heifer. In essence, the primary challenge for the rider was to remain in the saddle...which was not an easy thing to do!

While we owned and used Nancy to corral and drive cattle, I witnessed more than one adult unexpectedly fly out of the saddle when Nancy made one of her characteristic moves while chasing after one of the lightning-fast, young heifers. Since Nancy had such long legs, the distance to the ground was more than enough to wreck a rider's buttocks and embarrassingly bruise his ego. I

Willow Grove: A Boy, A Family, A Farm

watched many sturdy cowhands, including my father, dust off the seat of their britches after a fall from Nancy.

A group of the older boys had already sauntered across the lawn and drifted down to the enclosed pasture where the pony was standing. Nancy enjoyed the attention she was getting from the teenage boys crowded around her at the entrance, which also opened into the pigpen. Nancy's head was extended out over the top of the metal gate, making it easy for the boys to pat her on the neck, scratch her forehead, and comb through her long mane with their fingers. Dewey Gene Davis, John Nesselroad, Jim Lewis, Jackie Turner, John Paul, Eddie, James Conrad, and Joe Lee McCoy, Richard, Teddy, and Bill Sück, along with my brother Bob and myself, were among the older boys congregated around Nancy. Jim Lewis was one of the most curious and listened attentively to the chatter about Nancy's prowess.

Dewey Gene, Bob, and I knew, all too well, about Nancy's dual personality and her crazy, unannounced antics. The other boys didn't realize that with minimal effort on Nancy's part, several tough cowhands had been surprisingly and harshly thrown out of the saddle. Too, Nancy instinctively knew that any complacent rider was easy prey. As soon as a rider mounted the saddle, Nancy would prance around and act a little jumpy, exposing her spirited demeanor. Then shortly afterward, she would settle down and mosey about—almost mimicking an old, worn-out workhorse. The rider

Pony Antics

would become passive, overly confident, and too comfortable in the saddle atop explosive Nancy. All the while, and unbeknownst to the rider, Nancy's behavior was only lulling her passenger into a false sense of security. The rider would loosen his grip and become too relaxed. Nancy was coy, and her mischievous behavior was as slick as a Popsicle. After the rider became too smug, Nancy would switch personalities and, like a bolt of lightning, let loose with a thunderous, ill-behaved maneuver that would send her rider tumbling.

Nancy's erratic behavior had always been a complete mystery to me! The pony was so unpredictable. Calm and gentle as a lamb one moment and unruly as a lion, the next.

Bob, Dewey Gene, and I deliberately kept our narratives about Nancy's tricks…mellow and brief. There was no need to completely scare off all the big boy cousins from wanting to take Nancy for a spin!

It wasn't long before the prattle led to: "Who wants to be first to ride Nancy?" The older boys scanned the expressions on each other's faces and saw that no one was particularly interested in test driving Nancy. More back-and-forth ensued. It was obvious that no one wanted to risk becoming another notch on Nancy's long list of damaged egos. Soon, the boys were joking, kidding, and daring each other to ride Nancy. Finally, Jim Lewis bravely announced that he wasn't afraid to saddle up! Jim was confident, comically boastful, and didn't show

Willow Grove: A Boy, A Family, A Farm

any trepidation about riding Nancy. Jim humbly swanked: "Riding a pony isn't a big deal!"

While everyone else remained put and continued to pamper Nancy, I ran to the tool shed to fetch the bridle. Soon Jim was leading Nancy down the grassy path in the garden toward the main house, where most of the adults were still lounging around, socializing. Jim paraded Nancy around the front of the house and through the side yard past Grandma's kitchen. As Jim led Nancy past the curious crowd of uncles and aunts, his pride was as conspicuous as any beaming Kentucky Derby trainer walking his prize thoroughbred through the paddock on the way to the oval racetrack. Adults standing under the shade tree in the yard and those sitting on the porch watched as the group of boys marched behind Jim and Nancy up the gravel lane toward the barn. As the parade of boys passed by, one proud mother lovingly announced: "Oh, look, the boys are going to go for a pony ride." The observant mother surely pictured the fun-filled pony rides featured at the local county fair each year. Among the most observant spectators were my father and his brother, who sensed the older boys were up to something—something not too unusual for a group of peppy cousins looking for fun and excitement. Dad and Uncle Jim looked at each other and, with mutually sheepish grins, slowly rolled their eyes as if to say: "This is going to be interesting!" Dad and Uncle Jim knew the pony ride was likely going to be

Pony Antics

more amusing than the other unmindful fathers and adults could hardly anticipate!

Grandpa had purchased a gorgeous western saddle, which we used to ride both Nancy and Pinto. He treasured the saddle and made sure that it was taken care of properly and after each use was hung vertically by one stirrup from a special hook in the tool shed.

After the two girth straps were tightened securely under Nancy's belly, Jim placed his left foot in the stirrup and, just like a seasoned cowboy, swung his right leg high up over the saddle. Comfortably nestled in the saddle with the reins taut in his hands, Jim was in total control of Nancy. At least he thought he was! As usual, Nancy promptly conveyed her "spirited nature"—energetically prancing in circles—revealing that she was ready to take flight just as soon as Jim loosened up on the reins. It was the same scenario that I had witnessed many times when the rider thought he had Nancy at his command.

Across the curved barnyard driveway onto the gravel lane, Jim steered Nancy toward the distant county public road, over a quarter of a mile from where all the cousins were standing and watching with eager anticipation. Jim and Nancy were within plain view all the way to the bus stop. Nancy seemed as if she was a little anxious and ready to more than trot on their way back down the lane to the barnyard. Jim appeared in control, even though it was obvious that Nancy was more than willing to gallop. The duo reached the county road, where Jim

Willow Grove: A Boy, A Family, A Farm

turned Nancy around and headed back down the lane toward the barn. From all appearances, the proud rider was having a good time, yet it was difficult to tell if Jim was still in total control.

Our curiosity was short-lived! Almost immediately after Jim turned Nancy back toward the barn, it was clear she had wrestled control of the reins from Jim. In a split second, the pony bolted and was thundering down the lane. Nancy wasn't trotting or galloping! She was racing as if she was in the final turn on the oval track, heading for the finish line at Churchill Downs! Nancy was on fire! Traveling as if she was trying to outrun a bolt of lightning. There was no stopping her now! The reins were slack and dangling alongside Nancy's neck. Jim had both hands frozen around the saddle horn, and it was obvious that his only purpose now was to try and remain in the saddle. The runaway team flew past where all the cousins were standing. Dust and gravel flew from all four of Nancy's inflight hooves. Jim was still in the saddle —but barely! Leaning back as far as his stretched arms would permit, Jim offered no control over the runaway horse. If Jim had had any fun riding Nancy before, it was all over now! Nancy knew exactly where she was going, and she was scrambling to get there!

With Jim still clinging for dear life, Nancy jumped the concrete sidewalk and rounded the front of the house at a scorching pace. She zoomed past the huge shade tree where a few fathers were still sitting in their lawn chairs. The duo continued

Pony Antics

down through the middle of the garden on the narrow grassy path—which dead-ended at the pigpen gate. It was evident that Nancy was running way too fast to stop. To everyone's amazement—except mine—Nancy screamed right up to the gate and, with an explosive display of agility, abruptly stopped, only inches away from crashing into the closed gate. Jim, on the contrary, didn't stop! He was hurled out of the saddle and sent airborne over Nancy's head. He landed on his derriere inside the pigpen. Luckily Jim wasn't hurt, just a little soiled!

Jim, slowly and without any help from his laughing cousins, rose to his feet. He dug some dirt out of his hip pockets, and glanced down at the front of his smudged, white T-shirt. Staggering in the direction of his amused cousins, Jim spread his dusty fingers on both hands and combed back his long, disheveled, jet-black hair. As the cousins opened the pigpen gate, Jim ambled out of the pen onto the grassy pathway. Jim was a grand sportsman. He joked and laughed with his cousins about his almost successful endeavor to ride crazy Nancy—and the surprise ending at the pigpen gate. The smaller kids enjoyed watching their older cousins jostle with each other and needle Jim about his comical somersault from the saddle. All agreed, including Jim, that his landing wasn't too cool, but it was certainly entertaining.

Willow Grove: A Boy, A Family, A Farm

Uncle Conrad Bears ALL

Uncle Conrad was the uncle I routinely saw when I was growing up in Willow Grove. He was a reticent man, and during all of the years I was around him, it was apparent, though very subtle, that he enjoyed his life as a dairy farmer and treasured his wife and handsome family, above all.

Cousins cutting up, with Dewey Gene as a footstool.

Uncle Conrad was a gentleman of few words. His restrained character engendered reverence. Uncle Conrad also had a good sense of humor.

Uncle Conrad Bears ALL

Notwithstanding, he kept me on the tips of my toes —all the time!

Before television, a story told by a good storyteller was welcomed by lively kids, especially those who chose not to be outside in the damp night weather. Uncle Conrad was a wonderful storyteller. On countless evenings, he would retire to his favorite easy chair, ideally situated in a corner of the family room by the stone fireplace, which kept him warm during winter evenings. Its location also yielded an excellent view of many extracurricular activities, which were always plentiful in a household filled with eight children. It was a weekend, and I had my mother's permission to spend the night with my cousin, James Conrad. We were all in the family room. Uncle Conrad was relaxing in his favorite chair, quietly listening to our chatter. We were sitting on the couch, talking, and absorbing the warmth from the fireplace's sparkling embers.

It was getting late in the evening when Uncle Conrad realized that the tranquil atmosphere was perfect for narrating stories about his college days.

First, Uncle Conrad told a short story about his college and teaching days in Boone County, West Virginia. Uncle Conrad and several boys were lounging on the second-floor porch of a hotel in the town. Deciding to have a little fun, the boys filled balloons with water and began strategically dropping their arsenal onto the sidewalk below, where pedestrians and shoppers were strolling. The water balloons were backed up with ripe

Willow Grove: A Boy, A Family, A Farm

watermelons. To a nine-year-old like me, Uncle Conrad's story was hilarious! He laughed freely and enjoyed recreating the episode almost as much as we enjoyed his humorous narrative.

We listened late into the night to Uncle Conrad's graphic renditions of his funny endeavors as a young college student. One story followed another, keeping us completely mesmerized. I hadn't heard any of the stories before and truly enjoyed the comical episodes. It was way past my usual bedtime, and the soothing warmth of flames glistening from burning coals made it hard to keep my sluggish eyelids open. Uncle Conrad recognized that the moonless night was a perfect backdrop to tell a story about a surprising event that terrorized him and his three brothers.

The scary story took place on a sultry summer afternoon. The four brothers were swimming in their favorite watering hole. The deepest part of the swimming hole was directly under a shade tree along the bank of a creek in the hillside pasture field. One branch of the tree extended way out over the swimming hole and provided plenty of shade for the swimmers. The limb also provided a perfect spot to tie a rope directly above the deepest part of the swimming pool. It was fun to swing high above the water and drop feet first into the cool water. It was especially amusing when one of the brothers was swimming under the rope and would absorb the full impact of a gigantic cannonball shortly after he heard someone above him yell: "Bombs away!"

Uncle Conrad Bears ALL

Uncle Conrad and his brothers had been swimming for a couple of hours, and everyone was getting tired and hungry. They decided to head up the hill toward a blackberry patch in a thicket of scrub brush and apple trees. The berry patch was entirely concealed by underbrush, and unless you knew exactly where it was, the luscious cache of blackberries was impossible to find.

The boys got out of the swimming hole, switched their wet swimming trunks for dry pants, and started climbing up the steep hillside toward the berry patch. By the time the brothers reached the top, they were hot and sweaty from the rigorous hike. Vernon was well behind his brothers and wished he'd stayed back in the cool swimming hole under the shade tree. After the long afternoon of swimming, he was tired and wasn't as hungry as he first thought. Moreover, to get to the berry patch, they had to walk in the opposite direction of their home, which meant they would have to back-track down the hill toward the swimming hole, and then negotiate another mile of rough terrain before they could step on the back porch of their parents' home.

John was the first to reach the top of the hill. At the edge of the underbrush, he bent down and weaved his way on hands and knees through the thick scrub brush to a spot where he knew he would find big, delicious blackberries.

Soon the other three brothers found a good spot in the berry patch and began devouring their share of bigger-than-thumb-sized, sweet-tasting fruit.

Willow Grove: A Boy, A Family, A Farm

Except for an occasional flutter from a spooked grouse, not a sound emanated from the hillside. None of the boys could see each other since all four were secluded in different parts of the berry patch. Other than a periodic faint, cracking noise from a broken twig, not a peep was heard from any of the boys. All four had their mouths jammed full of juicy blackberries.

Then! All of a sudden...a scream from one corner of the blackberry patch was followed immediately by a crashing noise! The lazy afternoon had instantly become a litany of thrashing and bellowing. The four brothers *were not* the only ones eating blackberries: "Get out of here! Run for your life!" Dan headed down the steep hillside toward the distant swimming hole, yelling at the top of his lungs and galloping as fast as his legs would carry him. He was running from the same spot in the blackberry thicket that had just let loose with all the racket.

Vernon and John quickly realized what was going on! A black bear was chasing Dan. Uncle Conrad was running toward all of the commotion when he spotted Dan running in his direction, yelling: "Help! Help! Help!" Uncle Conrad had never seen Dan move so fast! Something had scared him! Uncle Conrad changed direction and ran after his brother.

A few seconds later, Conrad realized what the uproar was about. He had caught up with Dan, and now the bear was chasing both brothers running toward the bottom of the hill. About halfway down

Uncle Conrad Bears ALL

the steep hillside, Dan veered off to the left in the direction of a scraggy old persimmon tree. Conrad continued running straight down the hill, figuring that the bear would continue chasing Dan. Brothers John and Vernon had spotted the bear in time and were roosting up in a hickory tree close to where they had been eating blackberries.

By now, I was sitting on the edge of the couch. I was no longer sleepy, and my eyes were wide open! Uncle Conrad looked around the room. "Wouldn't you know, that confounded bear stopped chasing Dan and took off after me!"

All during the chilling narrative, we hung onto every alarming detail. Uncle Conrad was certainly a superb storyteller. By now, I could hardly believe what a terrible quandary Uncle Conrad was in. I couldn't fathom what I would have done if I had been in such a horrible predicament.

Uncle Conrad continued: "The huge bear was no more than 50 feet behind me...and I was running as hard as I possibly could. Every time I looked back, the bear was getting closer and closer. I never saw so many long, sharp teeth in all my life!"

Uncle Conrad paused for a moment to allow us to realize how dire his situation was. It was dark outside. The inky blackness magnified the scary situation that bedeviled Uncle Conrad. I was sitting straight up...on the edge of my seat, hypnotized by Uncle Conrad's story and how he gestured with a slightly slower rendition and low mellow tone. "By the time I reached the creek, the slobbering bear

Willow Grove: A Boy, A Family, A Farm

was so close behind me, I could feel the ground shaking from the pounding of his enormous paws." Uncle Conrad said the bear was too close to try to scramble up the tree beside the swimming hole. The only choice he had was to keep running. Keep running for his life!

Conrad was exhausted and about to give up when he remembered a massive boulder on the other side of the creek. The boulder was just a short distance up the side of a low bank. If he could just make it to the top of the bank, maybe, just maybe, with an Olympic-style running leap, he could land on top of the boulder, where he would be safe from the furious animal. Bears can climb trees, but they can't climb up the side of a large, smooth rock. Uncle Conrad knew he could make the jump because he'd already made the treacherous leap once before and knew he could do it again—especially with a big bear nipping at his heels.

Realizing that the boulder was probably his last chance to escape the wild bear, Uncle Conrad continued running as fast as his tired legs could muster. Luckily, the bear stumbled when it was splashing across the creek. Uncle Conrad knew where the flat stepping-stones were in the creek bed and how to cross the stream without slowing down. Luckily, the bear didn't and took a tumble in the shallow water!

As soon as Uncle Conrad reached the base of the boulder, he immediately faced an unexpected problem. A major rockslide above the boulder had

Uncle Conrad Bears ALL

uprooted a tree and it was leaning up against the boulder. The tree was still alive, and the trunk was large enough that the bear could easily reach the top of the boulder. Uncle Conrad couldn't stop now! He had to keep running. His only chance now was to try and get to the top of another embankment and hide in an old barn that his father used to store hay. Thankfully, he'd put a little distance between the bear and himself, and the barn wasn't too far away. That was the good news! But the bad news was that the barn was small and didn't have a loft...and Uncle Conrad suddenly remembered that one of the outside doors was permanently stuck—half-open! Wide enough for the ferocious animal to get inside the barn! Uncle Conrad was beside himself with fear!

He had no more than jumped over the trunk of a downed tree, when he inadvertently stepped in a groundhog hole and fell, head over heels. When he tried to get up, the pain in his right foot was excruciating. Instantly, he realized that his foot was either broken or badly sprained. He could barely move, let alone walk. Running was out of the question!

By now, I was convinced Uncle Conrad was a "goner"! Yet there he was! Sitting back in his easy chair, right in front of us, elaborating about a dilemma he found himself in as a young man. I wondered..."How in the heck did he outsmart that bear?"

Uncle Conrad could only limp and drag his right foot—as fast as he could toward the base of the

Willow Grove: A Boy, A Family, A Farm

boulder where he would try to hide behind the big rock under some branches of the fallen tree. He had no sooner started crawling under the tree when he turned around and saw the big slobbering bear, frozen like a statue, watching him crawl on the ground.

This was the end! Uncle Conrad was sure he was going to be severely mauled by the raging beast. He was cornered and had nowhere to go. The only escape path was right through where the bear was crouched, ready to pounce on its prey!

Uncle Conrad continued: "The enormous black bear stood high up on its hind legs, let out a thunderous roar, and, with its mouth wide open, lurched straight toward me. All I could see was a humongous mouth full of sharp teeth! I did the only thing that I could do—I ran my arm clear down the bear's throat, grabbed hold of its tail, and, with a hard yank, flipped the bear inside out. The bear's fur tickled it so much—it ran away."

That was Uncle Conrad! A superb raconteur! Uncle Conrad got a big kick out of the fact that I had hung on to every word of his tale, right up until the very end.

Black Snake!

Uncle Conrad wasn't always pulling my leg. Much of Uncle Conrad's wisdom was very practical. My adolescent cousins and I learned a lifelong lesson from Uncle Conrad about snakes. Black snakes, venomous copperheads, and rattlesnakes

Black Snake!

are indigenous to West Virginia. One afternoon, we had stumbled onto a black snake behind the barn and successfully killed the scary creature with a shovel and rocks. Afterward, we sought out Uncle Conrad so we could show him the dead snake and tell him about our good deed. Instead of the anticipated kudos, we received an immediate reprimand and lecture: "Black snakes are not poisonous and are as afraid of you as you are of them! Don't ever kill a black snake! We need them around the barn to keep mice and rats under control. They also help keep poisonous copperheads and rattlesnakes away from the barnyard and livestock. Don't ever kill another black snake!" Uncle Conrad's stern lecture and important message resonated with my cousins and me...forever!

Not only could Uncle Conrad tell great entertaining stories—he was also a diligent worker and believed in higher education, vital traits which he passed to his sons and daughters, and to me, his nephew. I revere Uncle Conrad's wisdom about the importance of advanced education. And, of course, the importance of black snakes. Indeed, from a beholden and appreciative nephew!

Rattlesnake!

The blacksnake story reminds me of another reptile which is much more dangerous.. Even though I was much younger, the event is still as vivid as our reprimand by Uncle Conrad.

Willow Grove: A Boy, A Family, A Farm

Whenever I overheard Dad and Grandpa talk about going somewhere, I invariably asked if I could go. If it was safe and either Dad or Grandpa would be with me at all times, Mom usually allowed me to go with them. Depending on where we were going and what we would be doing, Mom made sure I was properly attired for the trip. However, her ultimate concern—always—was my safety and well-being.

During extended hot and extremely dry periods in the summer, the pasture field behind the Silverton barn didn't produce enough green grass for all of the up-and-coming young heifers and the core dairy herd. Consequently, to keep from selling a few of the farm animals, Grandpa rented additional pasture from Digg Flinn.

By the way the crow flies, Digg's farm wasn't far from our Silverton farm, but as often was the case, the back-road short-cut that led to Digg's place was so seldom traveled and rough that, most of the time, the road was impassable, except on a horse, farm tractor, or durable four-wheel drive vehicle. The back roads were definitely too dangerous to navigate with a truckload of heifers. The best way to move the heifers from our farm to Mr. Flinn's was to drive them on foot via the same back roads, which Dad and the hired men did early in the spring.

It was late summer. Dad and Grandpa were discussing plans to go to Digg's farm to check on the heifers. Several were old enough to be added to the existing dairy herd just as soon as they had their first calf and began producing milk. Earlier in

Rattlesnake!

the week, Mr. Flinn had called Grandpa and advised him that two or three of the heifers looked as if they would have their baby calves before too long; certainly, within the next week or so. It was essential to bring the "soon-to-be mothers" back to the Silverton farm before their calves were born. The mother would protect her offspring by hiding the newborn in thick underbrush on some remote part of Digg's hilltop pasture field. The newborn might be so well hidden that it could take hours to locate both the heifer and her well-concealed baby calf. And, if the pair weren't found soon enough, the newborn would begin nursing, which wasn't a good thing if the mother was going to become part of the main dairy herd. It was vital that the new mother be milked for the first time using automatic milking equipment...not nursed by her newborn. In fact, a fresh cow should be milked within a few hours after the new calf arrives. After all, it is a waste of valuable time and energy to spend hours locating a fresh cow when the expectant mother could easily be found among the herd of cattle before her new calf arrived.

Mom agreed that it would be okay for me to go with Grandpa and Dad to check on the heifers. We would take the big truck equipped with the tall racks to bring the heifers back to the Silverton farm on our return trip home.

The only practical route to Digg's farm by vehicle was by way of Turkey Run Road, which intersected with Route 2 at Sherman, a remote, wide spot in the county road two miles north of

Willow Grove: A Boy, A Family, A Farm

Ravenswood along the Ohio River. The community of Sherman was no more than a handful of houses clustered close to a dirt road. Digg's farm was a few meandering miles further inland from Sherman along Little Sandy Creek.

It took us close to an hour to reach Digg's farm. We had essentially completed three-fourths of a vast circle that started at our farm in Silverton and ended at Digg's place. The other quarter of the circle was the back roads Dad and the men walked when they drove the herd of heifers from Grandpa's farm to Digg's earlier in the spring.

When we arrived, Digg was standing in the middle of an open area between his pleasant farmhouse on the left and a weather-crusted cattle barn on the right. Digg was about the same age as my grandfather, and as soon as the two men spotted each other, they waved and shouted salutations while the truck was still grinding to a stop, which caused Digg's old bloodhound, Tom, to start to bark in excitement. I had been around my grandfather and his friends enough to know that Dad and I were going to listen to the two men catch up on multiple topics before we would commence checking on the cattle on top of the hill pasture. Grandpa didn't see some of his friends that often, but when he did...well, you just knew they were going to talk and reminisce about family, friends, farming, politics, and other mutual interests—for quite a while.

The very moment we arrived, Mr. Flinn's attire grabbed my attention—immediately! His

Rattlesnake!

appearance was both amusing and somewhat puzzling to me. I concealed my inner wonderment and tried not to stare at his captivating garb. I was in awe of Digg's appearance and quickly grasped that he'd fit right in at any three-ring circus. He was wearing an enormous, wide-brimmed straw hat, and his feet were jammed down inside black rubber boots that hid his trousers clear up to his knees. Why such a crazy outfit? It was an above-average hot summer day with not one drop of water anywhere in any of the dusty potholes in the countryside road that led to Digg's place. Even inside the typically sloppy barnyard, the heretofore muddy ruts made by cow hooves were bone dry.

Digg probably noticed the quizzical look on my face. He even had on a long-sleeved shirt, which was buttoned tight around both wrists and high up under his chin. The rubber boots had to be hot on his feet and legs, and the long sleeved shirt had to be more than a little uncomfortable in such hot weather. But Digg didn't appear hot and looked at ease and comfortable in his bizarre outfit. I had on shorts, a short-sleeved T-shirt, low sneakers, and no hat. One of us was not appropriately dressed for rounding up heifers on Digg's hill farm. We would soon find out who was properly attired!

While Digg and Grandpa stood and talked in the limited shade next to the side of the truck, Digg was gripping a weird-looking and wildly crooked walking stick with an oddly shaped handle. The bottom end of the crazy-looking cane was even more peculiar! It looked like the letter V turned upside down. The rugged cane had been cut from the branch of a smooth bark tree, and the inverted V shape on the bottom of the cane had once been the forks of two twin limbs. I was curious why both sides of the V were no more than one inch in length on the bottom of the cane.

After the three adults stood and talked for several minutes, Digg commenced strolling toward the two-story cattle barn while still chatting with Grandpa and Dad. We trailed behind Mr. Flinn as he opened the barnyard gate, passed by the end of the barn, and headed toward the hill pasture behind the backside of the paint-thirsty barn. Digg was still talking when we reached the iron gate, which opened into the pasture field. After we passed through the wide opening, Digg followed a narrow path that snaked gradually up the side of a hill. The path was the same trail the cattle used when they ventured from the hill pasture to the barn for food and shelter during inclement weather.

Dad walked directly behind Digg. I followed close behind Dad's heels, and Grandpa was the caboose. The side of the hill was too rugged and the trail too narrow for two people to walk side by side. Just as the cattle did when they drifted down from the hilltop, we walked single file.

The hillside behind the barn was primarily thistles, patches of grass, and sparsely populated with various-sized rocks and scraggly, dwarf brush. The barren, dusty hillside was too steep and the bare ground too poor to support even scrubby plant life, let alone good sustenance for the cattle.

Rattlesnake!

Mr. Flinn talked incessantly as we ascended the path. Dad mostly listened while I spent most of my time glancing sideways, alternating up and down the side of the hillside. I also kept a sharp eye on the rocky path since I couldn't see the trail ahead of us. Every once in a while, a perpendicular ditch dug by rapid flowing rainwater from thunderstorms appeared across the path...and if I wasn't careful, I could easily tumble down the hillside and likely land in a patch of thistles. I was very familiar with thistles and landing on one wouldn't have been good. The cow path was super dusty, and the sun was uncomfortably hot, but I was exactly where I wanted to be—with my dad and Grandpa. My only job was not to be a problem or even the slightest aggravation for the grown-ups.

We were close to the top of the steep hill when suddenly Digg stopped, held his crazy cane high above his head, and ever so slowly...tip-toed backward without turning around. He had nearly stepped on a huge rattlesnake that was mostly hidden in underbrush but partially exposed along the edge of the rugged trail. He motioned for us to stop and be very quiet. The head of the rattler was buried under a rock, and its tail was sticking out onto the upper side of the path. The venomous snake was trying to crawl under the bottom of the cool rock and consequently was too busy to notice us before Digg saw the snake's tail and distinctive rattles. After a few startling seconds and with both fists wrapped tight around the top of his walking stick, Mr. Flinn crept softly toward the still unaware snake. The killer was busy slithering underneath the rock, where it would be nice and cool and out of reach of the scorching sun.

In one deliberate motion, Digg lowered the inverted V, the bottom end, of his cane down to just above the snake's body and about five inches behind the rattler's head, which was still hidden under the rock. Then...with a swift, jabbing motion, Digg plunged the walking stick the rest of the way to the ground and wedged the venomous snake's sleek body between the hard dirt and the forks on the bottom of his walking stick. Like a rifle shot, the snake's head blasted out from under the rock, and, with a furious eruption, it began hissing and thrashing, trying desperately to strike one of Digg's legs with its razor-sharp, poisonous fangs.

Fortunately, this wasn't the first time Digg had corralled a rattler with his crazy-looking weapon. He knew exactly how to handle the rattlesnake. Digg had the fighting-mad reptile completely pinned under his sturdy stick and close enough to the snake's head that the deadly fangs couldn't reach either of Digg's legs. Without taking his eyes off the snake, Digg yelled for Dad to grab a rock while he twisted his walking stick back and forth, sinking it deeper and deeper into the snake's nearly severed body.

By now, Grandpa and I had seen enough and moved back down the path where we were safely away from all the commotion. Grandpa and I were content watching at a safe distance while Digg contained the hissing serpent, and Dad found a

Rattlesnake!

good-sized rock. From where Grandpa and I were standing, all we could see was Digg's head leaning forward while steadily holding his walking stick against the ground. Both of Digg's legs were extended backward from his body far enough that the snake's rapidly darting fangs couldn't reach either of his rubber boots. With both hands, Dad raised the rock slightly above his head and then, with a hard thrust, slammed it smack dab onto the snake's rapidly twitching body ahead of Digg's wobbly cane and just behind the whirling head of the desperate killer. The rock stunned the snake, but it was still fighting mad and agile enough to poison Digg or one of us if it was able to escape. Digg kept his cane buried into the snake's back, holding its body firmly against the parched, hard ground.

Still hissing and striking repeatedly at Digg's boots, the penned rattler—though severely wounded—refused to stop fighting. Fortunately, the snake didn't have a chance. After Dad crushed its head with a second rock, the snake succumbed. Yet, its long tail still twisted and shook violently for several seconds. As soon as the tail stopped rattling, I walked close enough to get a good view of the rattler's size. I hadn't realized the potential danger around us until Digg, luckily, spotted the poisonous snake before it had a chance to bury its lethal fangs into one of our legs. Even Digg's ole faithful, floppy-eared bloodhound, Tom, with his nose sniffing close to the ground, scouting ahead of

Willow Grove: A Boy, A Family, A Farm

Digg's toes, hadn't smelled or spotted the deadly critter before the comically dressed Mr. Flinn.

Digg hurled the dead snake down the hillside, and we continued up the winding path toward the spot in the pasture field where Digg was sure we would find the heifers. After the surprise appearance of the rattler, everyone paid a lot more attention to where they placed their feet on the path.

The puzzle was solved! Now, it was clear to me why Digg wore those knee-high rubber boots and carried that crazy-looking, lethal walking stick! Digg was an experienced farmer!

I was 11 or 12 years old when Uncle Conrad surprised us with his remarks and turned our bravery into a stern reprimand for killing the blacksnake. Yet, I'm confident he would have praised my father and Digg Flinn when they killed that rattlesnake on Digg's farm. I was only five or six at the time and certainly glad I was with three experienced adults. It was a lifelong learning experience and why Uncle Conrad made us promise to never kill a blacksnake.

The Seasonal Rhythm of the Farm

Just as the earth has four seasons, so does the dairy farming industry, which is unlike most commercial industries. Because of the cyclical nature of dairy farming, a farmer knows in advance and with reasonable accuracy what he will be doing during each of the seasons.

The Seasonal Rhythm of the Farm

During the spring months, dairy farmers can plan on a bevy of baby calves. Dairy cows are bred to give birth in the spring for a couple important reasons: baby calves have a much higher rate of survival during warm weather than during cold, damp winter days, and dairy cows will produce more milk after giving birth in the spring and early summer, when the pasture fields are rich with nourishing green grass. In the spring, the farmer is busy buying seed, fertilizer, and tilling the soil that will grow new crops of corn and hay. Plowing and preparing the hay and corn fields can take several days. In addition, the ground has to be rather dry before the soil can be tilled. Wet soil sticks to the moldboard and will not turn upside down.

Summer months on an active dairy farm are filled with enjoyable, hard work, harvesting hay crops that are needed to feed farm animals during the winter. Hay fields will be mowed three different times from early to late summer. In between the three various crops of alfalfa, clover, and orchard grass hay, the corn fields are cultivated to stir up the soil around the base of the corn stalk and to kill weeds. Cultivation loosens the soil so that nurturing rain can penetrate the ground and water the roots of the corn. The corn fields are cultivated every couple weeks and until the corn gets too high for the tractor to pass through the field without damaging the stalks. Just as in tilling the soil in the spring, the corn fields cannot be cultivated if the ground is wet. Summer months yield plenty of fresh vegetables and bushels of potatoes.

Willow Grove: A Boy, A Family, A Farm

Watermelons and cantaloupe are enjoyed all summer long.

Fall is full of more dusty harvesting activity. Tall stalks of field corn are cut into silver-dollar-sized pieces of corn silage. Heaping wagon loads of diced, moist corn are hauled to the barnyard, where the silage is manually unloaded using hoe forks and stored in the silo. Like the corn silage harvester, winter wheat is shredded from its limber stem in the field using a combine and is subsequently stored in a dry bin in one of the farm buildings. The last crop harvested in late fall is the yellow corn that was allowed to dry on the stalk. The yellow ears of corn are shucked from the corn stalks in the field using a piece of farm equipment called a corn picker. The corn is stored in circular metal or wooden bins that have ample air circulation to prohibit the corn from decomposing due to the water remaining in the kernels. All of the soil preparation, seeding, and harvesting chores that I have described in the spring, summer, and fall seasons will be performed over several hours each day, sometimes over several days. And as I mentioned earlier, all of the plowing, mowing, and harvesting chores have to be carried out under a clear and preferably sunny sky. Hence, the expression "Make hay while the sun shines," or "You're burning daylight," when a farmer sees one of his farm hands procrastinating! When a farm hand is leaning on his pitchfork instead of working, his boss might comically chide him: "Don't break the fork handle!"

The Seasonal Rhythm of the Farm

Winter time is the harshest time of the year for the farmer and his farm animals: dairy cattle, heifers, and baby calves. The winters can be so rugged that the dairy herd is kept indoors 24 hours a day. If it isn't raining, the cattle might stretch their legs in the barnyard for about an hour in the late morning while the farmer cleans the concrete manure trough with a shovel and wheelbarrow. The dairy cows are fed loose hay three times a day, plus a generous portion of fortified grain sprinkled on top of a shovel of silage right out of the silo. The fermented silage, which the animals really like, is fed to them twice a day.

A farmer's hands really take a beating in the winter. He is constantly removing his warm gloves in inclement weather to complete a task that needs the touch of bare hands. One of the steps mandated by the health department is that the cow's udder and four teats must be cleansed with warm soapy water that is sterilized with an antibacterial solution. The farmer dips his hands in the warm solution constantly during the hour or better that it takes him to milk his herd. I have seen farmers' hands full of cracks, sometimes large enough to place a toothpick in the larger crevices.

During the winter months, the farmer takes the opportunity to repair his farm equipment and get it ready for the forthcoming spring chores. Plowshares—the leading edge of the moldboard—are sharpened so the plow will slice through the soil and turn the soil upside down without laboring the tractor too much. Sickle bars are removed, sharpened, and placed back in the mowing machine, ready to mow the first crop of hay in late spring.

Every moving part on multiple pieces of farm equipment must be lubricated before the farmer can head for the hay or corn fields. Without adequate and timely lubrication, moving parts will get too hot and eventually fail, causing delays, plus there is the replacement cost—which can easily be astronomical. It is unforgivable to forgo greasing your equipment before going to the hay field to cut hay or to the pasture to mow grass. A few minutes with a grease gun can save the farmer a lot of money. He must memorize the number of parts that need to be greased and know where every grease nipple is, since many are hidden by dirt from normal use.

The upside of winters on a farm is that the farmer can take a few more minutes during his two breaks in his 12- to 13-hour normal day. After his hot meal, he can relax a little longer in front of the fireplace before he dons his winter garb and walks back to the barn.

Multi-Talented Uncle Homer

As a young boy growing up in Willow Grove, I saw Uncle Homer, my cousin Dewey Gene's father, a lot. Uncle Homer was a professional painter and worked for the American Viscose Corporation in South Parkersburg. After working all week, he enjoyed escaping from the crowded work

Multi-Talented Uncle Homer

environment. On many weekends and holidays, he journeyed with his wife, Dorothy, and their children, Dewey Gene and Martha Ellen, to Willow Grove, where Uncle Homer treasured the tranquility of the spacious farming community.

Uncle Homer liked to hunt wild game, fish, and enjoyed being alone in the quiet outdoors. When the first day of squirrel season arrived in the fall, Uncle Homer would grab his rifle well before dawn and head for the dense woods in the rolling pasture field near our three-acre pond. If he wasn't having any luck squirrel hunting, he would reach for a ball of string and fishhook in his pocket, cut a pole from a nearby sapling, fashion a bobbin out of a dry twig, and go fishing. The pond was full of foot-long bass, palm-sized bluegill, and large snapping turtles.

At lunchtime, Uncle Homer would sit on the ground and lean back against a big oak tree. Once comfortably seated on a bed of soft grass, he would retrieve a thermos of hot coffee and one of Aunt Dot's homemade sandwiches from his rucksack. His movements during lunch were deliberately slow so that squirrels frolicking high in the tall oak trees would be oblivious to the picnicker down beneath their lofty treetop playground. With his rifle leaning against the tree, Homer would listen for rustling leaves on the ground and watch for isolated moving branches in the tops of the dense stand of timber. Always by himself, he would be gone most of the day and not return home until late in the afternoon.

Willow Grove: A Boy, A Family, A Farm

Another relaxing hobby of Uncle Homer's was to stroll back and forth, many times, over Raymond Casto's and Dan McCoy's recently plowed, river bottom cornfields looking for native Indian arrowheads. After a spring rainfall, the freshly plowed fields would expose pebbles and smooth artifacts lying on top of the tilled soil. Rainwater washed the dirt off the surface and, under bright sunlight, the cleansed fragments were easy to spot. Uncle Homer carried a stout wooden stick, and, as he walked through the plowed fields, he'd continuously swing the stick sideways, back and forth, striking any shiny objects with the end of his staff. Over the years, he found many perfectly shaped arrowheads, which at one time were on the tip of an American Indian hunting arrow. The river bottom shared with our two neighbors to the south had been, in the past, a popular camping ground for native Shawnee, Delaware, and Wyandotte Indians hunting in the fertile Ohio River Valley at Willow Grove.

At family social gatherings, Uncle Homer would quietly blend in with the crowd of teenagers and younger kids. And, more often than not, before we piled into our cars and headed home, he would have pulled some kind of prank on one of the kids. Uncle Homer might not even have been present at the time of the discovery, but everyone knew who was behind the practical joke. Many enjoyable memories can happily be blamed on Uncle Homer.

Multi-Talented Uncle Homer

Uncle Homer, a man of many talents.
Photo courtesy of his daughter, Martha Grisso.

Everyone looked forward to seeing Uncle Homer and Aunt Dot's sedan pull into the driveway at Willow Grove. There were always active projects on the farm that allowed the adults to work and socialize at the same time. If Mom, Grandma, and Aunt Jack were canning a host of fresh vegetables from our bountiful garden, Aunt Dot would don an apron and join the canning party. Working side by side while chatting about family topics and current events was pleasurable and productive. Customarily, Uncle Homer would disappear and be gone for hours. No one knew where he was going

Willow Grove: A Boy, A Family, A Farm

unless someone saw him leave with his rifle or fishing pole. Sometimes, he would be spotted in the distance walking across a plowed field looking for arrowheads and artifacts.

Cousin Dewey Gene, brother Bob, and I would head to the fields with Dad and the hired help. When Martha Ellen wasn't entertaining everyone with her comical antics, she would help in the kitchen or mosey around the house.

Uncle Homer kept a few farm animals on his family's picturesque acreage in Pettyville. A cow and several chickens provided fresh milk and eggs for the family. A fattened pig, butchered each fall, would keep the family well-nourished with pork, ham, and bacon during much of the year. After several sows at Willow Grove had their baby pigs in the spring, Uncle Homer would take a piglet home with him to raise during the summer.

One early spring weekend, Dad and Uncle Homer went to the calf barn where an enormous sow and her newly born baby pigs were housed in a pen. My brother John was only three or four at the time and was sitting on top of the corral inside the calf barn, which also served as a holding pen for the massive sow and her newborn piglets. Dewey Gene, John, Bob, and I were watching Uncle Homer and Dad select a baby pig for Homer to take home. John was sitting high enough above the floor of the hog pen that, normally, he wouldn't be subject to any danger. But not this time! The distraught mother pig did not appreciate the presence of the two men and, without any warning, lunged toward

Multi-Talented Uncle Homer

John's little feet, which were firmly planted on the board below the top railing where he was sitting. Luckily, Uncle Homer was close enough to John to quickly grab him under both arms and hoist him high above the railing. When Uncle Homer put John down on the dirt floor, John was missing one of his rubber boots, which was now firmly ensconced inside the irate sow's mouth and being thoroughly mangled by her sharp teeth. Everyone's face was white with shock. No one uttered a word for several seconds. Uncle Homer's swift action had just thwarted a catastrophe.

Uncle Homer took great care of his farm animals and his lovely, manicured farm. On occasional family sojourns to Willow Grove, he always made sure all of his animals were properly cared for during his two-day absence. Early on, the new piglet needed extra attention, so he made special arrangements to care for the baby pig during overnight visits away from home. He fabricated a wooden cage that fastened to the back of the family sedan. Just before everyone crowded into the car to depart, Uncle Homer put the piglet in the cage where, for the next couple of hours, it would enjoy the sights and swirling breeze as the vehicle traveled down the highway. On their arrival at Willow Grove, Uncle Homer would take the baby pig to the hog pen, where it could mingle with the other pigs until Sunday afternoon, when it was time to get back in its open-air cage and sightsee on the way home. As travelers motored down the highway,

Willow Grove: A Boy, A Family, A Farm

children and adults trailing behind the Davis sedan surely enjoyed the rare spectacle.

A Pig in a Blanket in a Car

Thrifty farmers can be exceptionally ingenious when confronted with a job that needs to be executed with minimum expense and loss of precious time away from the hay- and cornfields. The following event wasn't the first time I saw my father complete a chore using an unusual technique.

Neither of the two farm trucks was available, and Dad needed to take one of his sows to North Ravenswood to mate with a boar. The huge sow was in heat and timing was important. Even without a truck to transport the big pig, the challenge wasn't a big hurdle for my father! Dad simply took the back seat out of the family sedan and left both rear doors wide open. With the help of a couple of ears of yellow field corn, he enticed the hungry sow to follow him to the parked sedan. Obediently, the flabby gargantuan followed Dad and, from time to time, lurched forward in an attempt to bite off a few kernels of corn, which Dad used to tease her as she waddled behind him.

Once Dad got to the car, he turned around and stepped backward into the car through the open rear door, still dangling both ears of corn in his extended arm—tempting the sow to continue to follow him. While hunched over in the back of the car, Dad purposely dropped the ears of corn on the

A Pig in a Blanket in a Car

sheet-metal floorboard behind the front seat, just beyond the reach of the hog's nose. Dad then stepped backward out of the car through the other open rear door on the opposite side. By now, the sow was really slobbering for the corn, and, without any additional coaxing, the obese animal lumbered up into the back of the automobile.

As soon as the sow was inside the car and happily nibbling on the ears of corn, Dad eased the back door shut and then walked hastily around the rear of the car and quickly closed the other door, locking the sow inside the car. The animal was so busy feasting on the corn she wasn't even aware of Dad's sting operation...until it was too late. Actually, the big bruiser didn't mind at all. Hogs are so docile and lazy (unless they're going to grab you, like that mother sow did to John!) that they don't care where they are, as long as they are eating and can lie down in a comfortable spot, preferably in the middle of a mud hole under a shade tree.

After the 300 pounds of lard was safely confined in the car, Dad departed for North Ravenswood. After Dad returned home, Mom listened with amusement as Dad described the humorous incidents that happened on his motor trip with the sow. With teary eyes from laughing so hard, Dad described the puzzled looks on the faces of the Ravenswood onlookers as he drove past. People are used to seeing dogs and cats in vehicles, but not a humongous hog in the back seat of a family sedan, staring at the astonished spectators, with its snout

Willow Grove: A Boy, A Family, A Farm

sticking out through the open window. The passive sow turned a lot of heads that day!

Dad's Summer Birthday

My father's birthday was the fifth of August. Invariably, every year on his birthday, several men would be dragging gunny sacks down through the field between rows of towering sweet corn. Moving at a slow pace, the men would inspect the color of the tassel on each ear of corn. When the tassel was predominately a burnt color, the ear was gripped in the middle, given a quick, quarter-twist turn, and then yanked from the corn stalk. The ears of corn were dropped in a gunny sack, which was dragged over loose topsoil through the cornfield until it was full or too heavy. The men walked back and forth down long windrows until the farm truck was heaped high in the middle with fresh sweet corn. By mid-afternoon, thousands of ears of sweet corn were peeking through the wide cracks and hanging out over the top of the truck's tall racks. The big farm truck was almost fully loaded.

Dad, Jimmy Ice, Dewey Gene, Bob, and I had been working most of the day pulling sweet corn and loading the truck. Brother John couldn't manage a gunny sack all by himself, so he alternated between helping Bob or me drag our sacks through the field. About mid-afternoon, my cousin John Paul McCoy and relative Mayford Harris appeared unexpectedly and joined us in pulling sweet corn. Dad appreciated all the help he

Dad's Summer Birthday

could get since it was getting close to four o'clock and almost time for Jimmy and him to head to the barn to milk the dairy cows.

After the truck was fully loaded, Dad sat down to rest for a moment. He removed his glasses and wiped his forehead with a handkerchief. This was the moment John Paul had been waiting for and why he never missed Dad's birthday. John Paul grabbed hold of Dad and, with a little assistance from Cousin Dewey Gene, wrestled Dad to the ground. John Paul then grabbed a musty, smelly tassel from an ear of sweet corn, which he had been hiding behind his back. The black, greasy muck on top of the ear of corn was a perfect gift for his uncle's birthday. John Paul smeared the gunk all over Dad's face. There wasn't a white spot anywhere by the time John Paul finished. Everyone was howling with laughter...including Dad. He certainly got a birthday gift from his nephew. It was a yearly birthday present that the family enjoyed and talked about for days.

While writing this book, I reviewed and studied many old and revered family photos. I quickly realized that nearly every picture of my father showed him with a million-dollar smile. Thinking back over my teenage and adult years, I recalled how often and spontaneously the distinguishing smile appeared. Anytime he saw a member of the family, a friend, or greeted someone with a hello or warm handshake, his genuine smile always accompanied the salutation.

Willow Grove: A Boy, A Family, A Farm

My dad, always smiling.

A Pox on Christmas

We always had a huge pine tree decorated with lots of ornaments, multicolored lights, and tinsel. Along with the colorful flickering embers from the fireplace, the pleasant pine aroma from the tree embraced the family room with a cheerful and cozy

A Pox on Christmas

ambiance, even though the previously sparse tree had originally resembled what we think of today as a "Charlie Brown" Christmas tree. Every Christmas, we cut our tree from a pine thicket located in the back of the pasture field above the pond. We couldn't be too particular and sometimes had to decide on a tree that had been nursed by a hungry deer or used by a buck to polish its rack of horns. Somehow, Mom always found a way to compensate for missing branches and hide the big bare spots. By the time Mom was finished, the tree was absolutely beautiful, and we enjoyed its vital contribution to a happy Christmas season.

One Christmas, my brothers and I had a serious problem. At least in our minds, the problem was serious. Christmas Eve was only one day away, and we were sick with chickenpox. All five upstairs bedrooms had no heat and were just too cold for three sick boys. Mom had purposely put us together so that all three of us would have the chickenpox at the same time. To keep us as comfortable as possible, Mom spread us out on the couch and two cots in front of the fireplace in the family room. Plus, the kitchen was a few steps away and close enough for Mom to simultaneously be attentive to us and continue with her chores.

The three of us were covered with itchy red bumps and blisters from chickenpox. I was very sick, considerably more so than either Bob or John. I was always the sickest. It didn't matter if it was measles, mumps, flu, or chickenpox—it took me a few days longer than my brothers to recuperate from any illness. My stint with chickenpox was no exception.

I was too sick to care much about Santa Claus. Little John was younger and worried that jolly ole Saint Nick would have to bypass our house this Christmas.

How could Santa possibly deliver Christmas gifts to three sick and, likely, wide-awake little boys nestled only a few feet away from the Christmas tree? Our mother was reassuring and constantly reminded us: "Don't worry! Santa won't skip our house. He'll find some way to get your presents delivered in time for Christmas." Mom's words were encouraging, but doubt persisted, at least in little John's mind.

It was dusk on Christmas Eve. Mom was in the kitchen washing the evening meal dishes. Dad was sitting in the family room with my brothers and me, relaxing in front of the soothing fireplace and perusing one of his colorful *Hoard's Dairyman* magazines. Suddenly, Dad lowered his magazine, raised his head, and looked toward my brothers and me. Everyone stopped what they were doing and focused their attention on what sounded like the soft ringing of bells. At first, the bells were very faint, but the mysterious ringing slowly became louder and louder. No one attempted to move except to gradually sit up in our makeshift beds. We were trying to process "what in the world" was going on outside! It wasn't long before the ringing bells were loud, loud enough that we realized the melodious jangle was very close to our house.

A Pox on Christmas

Suddenly a dull *thump* reverberated from the porch directly outside the entrance to our family room—mere feet from where we remained stone quiet! If our eyes weren't wide enough before, they were even larger now and were accompanied by three big smiles. We had a good idea who was outside and who had caused the mysterious thud on the porch!

John was thrilled that Santa had found a way to deliver our gifts! He was so excited that he jumped out of bed, ran through the family room, and didn't stop until he reached the kitchen. He opened the outside door and started yelling: "I see him, I see him, I see Santa Claus!" He raced back to the living room, all the while yelling that he had seen Santa Claus. He was so steadfast that everyone believed him. How many little boys ever get an opportunity to catch Santa Claus in the act!

With impish glee, our parents monitored our reactions. Shortly after the noisy bump on the porch, the ringing slowly faded in the darkness of the night. Dad looked at Mom and said: "Kate, do you think we should check and see what that commotion outside was all about?" With a grin, Mom followed Dad as he opened the door. For a moment, Dad disappeared. Then, with the door partly ajar, Dad shuffled his feet, heels first, backward into the house, dragging a stuffed burlap sack. The sack was loosely tied with a red bow and partly open at the top—just enough for us to see that the bag was stuffed with wrapped Christmas presents. Once inside, Mom removed the bow and methodically placed each gift under our ceiling-high

Willow Grove: A Boy, A Family, A Farm

Christmas tree. By now, Bob and John had completely forgotten they were sick. I wasn't so lucky. Yet, with all the Christmas excitement, I was feeling a little better and ready to enjoy the festive evening with my brothers and parents. After each one of us reluctantly forced down our respective tablespoon of awful-tasting medicine, our mother began passing out the gifts. Our grandparents, who always retired quite early, ventured into the living room from their living quarters and sat by the Christmas tree. It was a grand Christmas Eve after all!

Grandmother, Grandfather, and Aunt Jack.

Very late in the evening, when my brothers and I were sound asleep, Uncle Bob and Aunt Dee's car

A Pox on Christmas

pulled into the driveway. Only Santa Claus knows for sure, but my adult brothers and I always had a strong suspicion that Uncle Bob was moonlighting as an elf that Christmas Eve.

To this day, brother John is steadfast in his conviction that he really did see Santa Claus those many decades ago.

An Idyllic Life

Our farm at Willow Grove was owned jointly by my parents and grandparents. Grandma kept a legal-sized, hard-bound journal in her antique roll-top desk, which she used to document all farm-related business matters. Revenue from milk sales and salaries paid to the hired help were posted weekly. Grandpa consulted with my father regarding any significant farm expense, and together they decided whether a contemplated expenditure was a good investment for the family business. Grandpa and Dad (who had the highest respect for his father) were an excellent business team, and between the two of them made good investment decisions during the nine years we lived at Willow Grove. The family saved most of the farm profits to make farm improvements and purchase new equipment. In nine years, the operation practically paid off the initial $40,000 loan from the bank, which was used to buy the farm in 1946.

Not only did the farm nearly pay off the entire loan, it also provided a good standard of living for my grandparents, my parents, Aunt Jack, and at

Willow Grove: A Boy, A Family, A Farm

least one full-time hired hand and his growing family. During the busy summer months, when the majority of crops were being harvested, the farm paid for additional part-time employees. Hired help lived rent-free in one of three tenant houses on the farm. Besides ample space for a vegetable garden, employees carried a quart bottle of fresh milk for their breakfast tables every morning after the cows were milked.

In the early 1950s, my grandfather had a serious heart attack, and his doctor advised him to stop driving his car. He was an industrious farmer and enjoyed doing business and socializing with his many business associates and friends in Ravenswood, Silverton, Ripley, and surrounding communities in Jackson County. Since Grandpa was a lifelong resident of Jackson County and a successful dairy farmer, he knew many prominent people. His various business interests and related responsibilities required him to travel often to Ravenswood and Ripley, the county seat. Frequently and on a moment's notice, my mother dropped whatever she was doing and graciously agreed to chauffeur Grandpa to his business appointments. Any trip to Ravenswood or Ripley would generally take two or three hours out of Mom's busy day. My father and the hired help needed to remain in the fields and care for the crops, especially if a hayfield of freshly cut alfalfa was lying on the ground and a rainstorm was forecast.

An Idyllic Life

Regardless of what Mom was doing at the time —washing clothes, ironing, canning, cleaning, and any number of chores—she would always stop, set her work aside, and leave as quickly as possible to drive her father-in-law to wherever he needed to go, so she could return home in time to prepare supper for the family. All the chores Mom had set aside would still be there when she returned. Often her household tasks required working late into the evening since many couldn't be put off until the next day. This was particularly true anytime she was in the middle of canning fresh vegetables from our summer garden. So many jobs on the farm had to be completed in a timely manner. If that meant working past midnight, Mom kept at it until all the work was done. The expression "make hay while the sun shines" is very appropriate for life on a busy farm.

John and Uncle Everett go for a Walk

Grandma's sister, Ollie, and her husband, Everett Browning, visited Willow Grove in the early 1950s. They only made the trip one time. Thanks to little brother John, their sole trip was unforgettable.

Elfra, aka Aunt Jack, was Ollie and Grandma's youngest sister, and she was living with my grandparents at the time of Ollie's visit. The sisters hadn't seen each other for several years, making the reunion an especially happy occasion.

Willow Grove: A Boy, A Family, A Farm

Everett had been blind for several years. He loved to walk, and the lanes and paths on the farm were suitable and safe.

One afternoon, little John, who was six years old, was assigned to take Uncle Everett for his walk. During their outing, John walked close to Uncle Everett, so he could follow John's lead by resting his hand on John's shoulder, or they would hold hands. John liked the idea that he was the leader. He led Uncle Everett past the barn, up the lane to the main county road, where they would turn around and walk back to the house. One time they walked out the gravel pit road and turned around. Mom had forewarned John not to take Uncle Everett down the short but steep incline into the gravel pit.

John was given kudos by the adults each time the two returned from their walk. Uncle Everett gave John high marks for being an almost perfect walking guide. Almost perfect because occasionally, John would let loose of Uncle Everett's hand and stand quietly nearby. Uncle Everett would stop and beckon: "Where are you, you young whippersnapper?" Otherwise, all was well with their daily walk, until John plotted to have a bit of unscripted fun. He realized that Uncle Everett would follow him anywhere he went.

The lane that John and Uncle Everett covered during their daily exercise was the same path covered each day in the summer by the dairy herd when they were driven to and from the river bottom, night-time, pasture field. Consequently,

John and Uncle Everett go for a Walk

there would almost invariably be a splattering of fresh cow manure in the lane, somewhere.

On their next walk, John decided to implement his plan. He saw a prime opportunity ahead of him —lying off to the side of the road. John knew where each of Uncle Everett's feet would land after each step, so he sheepishly steered the elderly, blind gentleman toward a nice-sized, relatively fresh splat of cow manure. Like an aircraft pilot, John guided his passenger's feet toward the new buffalo chip and made a perfect landing. By the time the two got back to the house from their walk, Uncle Everett's shoes were a total mess, visually and otherwise!

After apologizing to Uncle Everett and with John in tow, Mom took the smelly shoes and disappeared into the laundry room. Mom told John to watch her closely, and if this ever happened again, he would clean and polish the shoes all by himself. John got the message, and it never happened again. As usual, Dad got a big chuckle out of the incident, which contributed to the family memories of "serious at the time" but "humorous later."

The Land of Karo

Bob and I were visiting with our maternal grandparents when "The Great Appalachian Snowstorm of November 1950" slammed all of West Virginia and western Pennsylvania with over 30 inches of snow. Coburn Creek, in central West Virginia, reported a staggering 62 inches.

Willow Grove: A Boy, A Family, A Farm

A few days before the snowstorm arrived, Bob and I rode the B&O Railroad passenger train with our mother from Willow Grove Crossing to Parkersburg. Passenger trains were only obligated to stop at Willow Grove if the engineer sighted a prospective passenger standing along the railroad tracks waving a white piece of cloth. A few times during our years at Willow Grove, my brothers and I watched our mother flag down a passenger train. She would walk down the railroad tracks and stand where the engineer could easily see her and have ample time to stop the mammoth steam engine and its rolling tons of railroad cars. Once the engineer spotted a flag-waving passenger, he would acknowledge his awareness by giving a short, obvious *toot* from the steam whistle. Our teenage neighbor, Hazel Casto, would do the same and occasionally stop a B&O passenger train at Willow Grove. She would board the train and be in Ravenswood in a short 20 minutes.

We stayed with our grandparents a few days before Mom left without Bob and me and returned to Willow Grove on the passenger train. She had planned to come back the following weekend with Dad in the family car and take us back home. Regrettably, Mom's plans were interrupted by a slow-moving, powerful snowstorm on Thanksgiving Day, November 23, 1950. The Parkersburg area recorded 34.4 inches of snow. Pickens, West Virginia, had 57 inches over two days.

The big snowstorm was good news for most kids. But not so good for Bob and me. We had to

The Land of Karo

remain at our grandparents for an extra week, much longer than we had planned. It was painful to stay indoors and not be able to go outside and play in the snow. We pleaded with our grandfather to let us go outside and frolic in the snow. No way! He was afraid that we would get sick and refused our incessant pleas.

Bob and I knew that if we were home in Willow Grove, we would be enjoying all the marvels and witnessing the wonderments of a deep snowfall. The dairy farmers in Willow Grove couldn't ship their milk to the commercial creamery, Valley Bell; plus they only had a limited number of ten-gallon cans to store their twice-daily, fresh milk. The snow was so heavy the milk truck couldn't navigate the road to reach the dairy farms. Dad's brother James had a contract to haul milk from Willow Grove to the creamery company in Charleston. Rather than wait for the West Virginia Highway Department to clear the roads, James used a bulldozer and had the main county road plowed from Ravenswood to Uncle Conrad's farm before the county road grader caught up with him. The Thanksgiving snowstorm was a massive challenge for the dairy farmers in Pleasant View and Willow Grove, and they couldn't wait for the government to clear their local road and rescue their milk. Every day that the road was impassable meant lost revenue for the farmers, whose only option was to dump the milk on the ground. Bob and I certainly missed a lot of excitement!

Willow Grove: A Boy, A Family, A Farm

Yet, there was one silver lining in our extended visit with our grandparents: Bob and I finally got our fill of delicious Karo syrup. Ma made plate-sized pancakes every morning for Pa, along with one egg over-easy and hot coffee. She lathered her cast iron skillet with plenty of lard and covered the bottom with pancake mix. The circumference of each super-thin pancake had a delicious crispy edge. Bob and I smothered our hot pancakes with an abundance of homemade butter and drowned them with Karo syrup. What a treat! At home, Mom's pancakes were about the same size but thicker. Her pancakes were also crispy around the edges, but there was no Karo syrup or any brand of an equivalent commercial product on the breakfast table. To save money, Mom diluted dark molasses with warm water, which we poured on our pancakes. Mom's homemade syrup was okay but not as good as the popular, commercial Karo brand.

Big Top, Big Trouble

Grandpa surprised us with our first television. It was a Capehart with exceptional reception, which was rare in the 1950s. We ate dinner promptly at noon, and on Saturday, the "Big Top Circus" TV program commenced at the same time. Bob, John, and I liked to watch the entertaining program and were allowed to enjoy our meal on TV trays in the family room while we watched the show. Mom would often prepare one of our family favorites, a huge plate of spaghetti.

Big Top, Big Trouble

Several of the Big Top Circus acts were so much fun to watch that my brothers and I would attempt to mimic a few of the simpler ones. Acts that didn't require costly equipment or a lot of paraphernalia. One act seemed simple enough. A performer stood on the end of a colorful board while a second performer jumped from a high position onto the opposite end of the board—flipping the person high into the air, while the second performer completed a backward somersault and landed upright on the floor of the circus tent. The act seemed easy enough for my brothers and me to attempt ourselves. Except for the backward somersault!

Bob and I found a long board and an empty 55-gallon drum. The drum was placed on its side near the edge of the woodshed's tin roof, a moderately low building at the end of the driveway directly outside Mom's kitchen window. The board was centered over the side of the drum. One end extended up in the air while the opposite end rested on the ground. John was the smallest and was chosen to stand on the end of the board resting on the ground. Bob climbed on the woodshed roof and cautiously positioned himself at the edge, directly above the board where John was standing. Bob's jump was perfect. He landed squarely on the end of the board and, immediately, John rocketed high into the air. Unfortunately, so did the heavy board since it wasn't fastened to the barrel. The airborne board came crashing down and regrettably struck John on the nose.

Willow Grove: A Boy, A Family, A Farm

The resulting situation *was not* a pretty picture. Blood flowed from an awful-looking jagged tear across the bridge of his nose. Our mother was working in the kitchen and, for some reason, casually glanced out of the window...just in time to see what the three of us were up to, but too late to stop Bob from jumping off the roof of the woodshed. Her emotions ranged between choking Bob and me first or caring for little John.

Before Mom started to work on John's torn nose, she ordered Bob and me to sit on kitchen chairs and not say a word! After Mom cleaned and forced John's drooping nose back to its rightful place, she closed his torn nose with several of her custom-made, medical sutures. Needless to say, Mom was not happy with Bob and me. The crux of her lengthy admonishment was crystal clear: The days of attempting any more circus tricks were over! Mom's edict and formidable punishment were too indelibly etched in our minds ever to attempt another Big Top act.

John's nose healed just fine, save for a slight scar across the bridge of his nose.

Beware Dewey Gene!

Another one of our silly games was called "airplane." One of the participants would lie on his back in the yard, pull his knees up tight against his chest with his feet together, and pointed skyward. The bottoms of his feet would serve as a makeshift passenger seat. Another participant would sit on

Beware Dewey Gene!

the seat so the boy lying on his back could thrust the passenger up into the air as high as possible. It was a senseless game, but we had fun and took turns taking a short airborne ride. The kid going for a ride would land on his feet most of the time, but not always. Sometimes he would land on his buttocks, which was always good for a chuckle from all the playmates.

Dewey Gene saw us playing airplane and made a generous offer to be the pilot. He seemed only too happy to lie on the grass and provide the thrust necessary to rocket his passenger skyward. Since it was easier and more fun to be a rider than the pilot, Bob, Everett, and I, gleefully and wholeheartedly took Dewey Gene up on his offer. Little John was the only one wise enough to pass.

Each of us took our turn, and we were having a grand ole time. Dewey Gene was so nice and gracious, entertaining his younger cousins and family playmate Everett Moss. After the three of us had had several enjoyable complimentary rides, the pilot decided to fly his passengers even higher, so they would have even more fun.

I was the first passenger to mount the unannounced upgraded airplane seat. As soon as I was comfortably settled, Dewey Gene pulled his knees down—really tight—against his chest. He took an extra couple of seconds to pump up his chest with a giant slug of supercharged air. The pilot was determined to be at "full throttle" at liftoff. He was determined to see how high he could hurl his passenger. It was a lot of fun to be tossed skyward! The higher, the better! The rider's objective was to land on his feet, remain upright, and not go tumbling across the yard.

My cousin, Dewey Gene.
Photo courtesy of his daughter, Stephanie Davis Waldron.

Dewey Gene was four years older than me and even older than Bob and Everett. He successfully rocketed me higher than any of us had ever witnessed or thought possible. My body shot

Beware Dewey Gene!

skyward so far and high that I ended up getting tangled up in Mom's clothesline. After I made a revolution around the clothesline, it morphed into a virtual slingshot and slammed me to the ground. The landing wasn't pretty. My brothers and Everett could see how high and far I went and quickly decided that the upgraded airplane ride wasn't a bonus. My flight to the moon was the last one of the day! Bob and Everett had already joined little John, happily seated in the terminal.

Outrunning Indians

Buzz Casto was a year older than me, and we both enjoyed riding our ponies. The Casto residence and dairy barn were within eyesight of our barnyard. After confirming with my grandmother on the community telephone line that I was home, Buzz went to the barn, saddled his pony, and rode diagonally across our harvested cornfield to our barnyard, where I was sitting astraddle Pinto. Buzz's pony, Nancy, was a little larger than mine and was mostly white with brown spots. Several Christmases ago, Buzz had found Nancy under the Christmas tree, a pretty little foal. Nancy had grown to be a sleek-looking horse with a frothy mane. Pinto was an equally nice-looking pony with irregular brown and white patches all over her body. I liked the attractive saddle Grandpa purchased for Pinto and our other pony, who was also named Nancy. The western saddle was a

Willow Grove: A Boy, A Family, A Farm

goldenrod color and still had the pleasant aroma of brand-new leather.

Buzz and I decided to ride down the lane past our house to the river bottom. With every movement Pinto made, the saddle responded with a continuous squeaking sound caused by the supple leather on the saddle rubbing against itself. I enjoyed the squeak of the saddle accompanied by the clacking of Pinto's galloping hooves.

To get the ponies to gallop, all we had to do was simultaneously loosen up on the reins, gently apply pressure to both sides of the pony with the heels of our bare feet, and softly voice a familiar command. Once we reached our bottom pasture field, we raced across the soft grass to the far end, which was the legal property line between our farm and Buzz's father's farm. After racing through the field, both ponies were ready to slow down to a pleasant trot.

Buzz and I led our ponies down the steep river bank to a narrow sandy beach along the river. On our way down, we had to weave around the water maples that shaded the whole bank. The spot along the shoreline where we watered the ponies was beside a commercial sand and gravel bar. I was quite familiar with the gravel bar. One of the windows in my bedroom faced south toward the river where Buzz and I were watering our ponies. With our bedroom window wide open, my brother Bob and I could listen to the continuous hum and associated sounds from the gravel company that dug sand and gravel all night long from the Gosling Bar at the bottom of the river. The constant sound

360

Outrunning Indians

was a soothing, soft monotone that lulled us to sleep sooner than we wanted. We enjoyed listening to the men on the gravel rig carry on a conversation. Even though the gravel boat was quite some distance downriver from our home, their voices traveled up the unobstructed river with ease. A 1929 U.S. Army Corps of Engineers map of the river detailed where the gravel was along the shoreline. The existence of the huge map among my grandmother's cache of important business papers suggested that the farmers who owned land along the river received some kind of royalty from the gravel company.

After the ponies finished drinking, Buzz and I led them back up the riverbank into his father's cornfield. The ponies were rested and ready to race at full speed across the Casto cornfield. After all, we had to outrun the hostile Indians chasing two government pony express riders. Buzz and I raced for our lives across the wide cornfield, jumped the railroad track crossing, and continued up the path to the Casto dairy barn. Luckily, the barnyard gate was open, so we didn't have to slow down as we crossed over the county road into the barnyard. Buzz was ahead of me, leading the way around the corner of a farm building on the way to a safe spot in the barnyard, where we could hide from the Indians. Buzz rounded the corner of the building, but when my pony laid into the same curve at a fast gallop, my pony toppled over on her side. Pinto and I slid several feet through the barnyard muck while I was still in the saddle with my right leg buried underneath the pony's body. What a mess! After Pinto and I managed to disentangle ourselves, it appeared the pony and my leg were both okay. Fortunately, the deep and soggy barnyard muck had cushioned my buried leg from the full weight of the pony's body. The saddle was covered with yuck, and there was no way I could go home until it was restored to its original beauty.

We went to the milk house, where I grabbed the water hose and began hosing down the pony, saddle, and myself. What an ordeal! Buzz and I tackled the wet saddle with gusto. Buzz had leather polish in the milk house, which he used to polish his saddle. It took a lot of elbow grease, but I eventually began to feel better when I saw the original luster of the saddle reappear, and it looked no worse for wear. Grandpa would never know!

For me, it was a different story. I was wearing only shorts, no shoes, and no shirt. I was clean, but no amount of water would eliminate the smell that followed me everywhere I went. Though the odor wasn't nearly as bad as an unfortunate encounter with a skunk, I definitely needed some help from a perfume bottle and a good dusting of baby powder before supper and bedtime! If not, I would probably have to eat my supper sitting alone on the stoop outside Mom's kitchen door and sleep with the cats and dogs in the hayloft. Notwithstanding, I was sure glad our ponies outran those Shawnee warriors.

Outrunning Indians

The Casto family: Buzzy, Grace, Raymond, and Hazel.
Photo courtesy of Hazel Casto Parsons.

Sixth Grade

The sixth grade was my last year at Ravenswood Elementary, and my teacher certainly made the fall of 1950 unforgettable! I still remember witnessing a formidable demonstration of exactly how Mr. Clem maintained strict control of his classroom and, at the same time, sustained the utmost respect from all his sixth-grade students—especially from any of the audacious or vainglorious boys.

Other than Mr. Hall, the principal, Otho Clem was the only male teacher in the elementary school. And, unbeknownst to each new sixth grader, the

Willow Grove: A Boy, A Family, A Farm

two men embodied more than enough male discipline to keep an array of spirited young boys "completely in line" and out of mischief. As sixth graders and elementary school faux seniors, the boys would sometimes erroneously assume that their senior standing would garner more clout and flexibility from the teacher than when they were in the lower grades. This assumption, especially in Mr. Clem's class, quickly proved to be flawed. Terribly flawed!

Otho Clem, by any standards, was a large man. Mr. Clem was always splendidly suited with a starched white shirt, jacket, and matching traditional tie. He had a very thin cover of hair which he combed straight back. He was a good, no-nonsense teacher, yet very humble and friendly with all the students. Just as the principal did, Mr. Clem portrayed an image of influence and authority, and garnered respect in the eyes and minds of every student in the school.

At the beginning of each calendar school year, Otho Clem introduced his unique teaching style and expectations of his students. After welcoming the class and explaining a few perfunctory class procedures and safety rules, he would turn around in his swivel chair and point directly toward a formidable paddle, conveniently and prominently displayed on the wall behind his desk. The wooden paddle was resting on a miniature shelf that accented the enormity of the paddle's flat, oval bottom. The oval part of the paddle was only a little smaller than a hefty sixth grader's buttocks.

Sixth Grade

Dangling from the paddle's handle was a rich-looking strip of rawhide looped through a hole and tied in a meticulous knot at the very end of the handle. The rawhide loop was perfectly tailored for Mr. Clem's weighty right wrist.

While still seated, Mr. Clem addressed the class with the following pronouncement: "See that paddle! Soon after the year begins, I usually have to get the paddle down! That's the bad news! The good news is—I only have to get it down once!" Those three short sentences were his only remarks about the paddle. Mr. Clem had enough experience with rambunctious sixth-grade boys to know that additional comments were superfluous. He knew he would end up paddling one student before his comments about discipline in the class were taken seriously. Oh, I almost forgot! The oval part of the paddle had four or five round holes in it! The thumb-sized holes enabled Mr. Clem to achieve greater velocity, making the paddle more effective when it struck its target.

I enjoyed spelling and the occasional sixth-grade spelling bee. It was a nice change from the typical class routine of constantly sitting and studying at our desks. All the students in the class would stand and form a circle around the perimeter of the room. Mr. Clem would pronounce a word, which a student would repeat and then spell correctly, provided the pupil had done his or her homework. Whenever a word was misspelled, the student would have to sit down. It was fun. I don't recall ever being the first to sit down, but then again, I don't remember ever being the last, either.

First day of school, 1950: me, John, and Bob, with our dog Pedro sitting behind us.

Later in the school year—and as correctly predicted by Mr. Clem on the first day of school—Charles Reynolds and I were misbehaving during

Sixth Grade

class. I don't recall the details of our mischief, but, most likely, we were whispering to each other and not paying attention to the teacher. Mr. Clem spotted Charles first and immediately stopped instructing the class.

Charles was one of the tallest boys in the elementary school. Not only was he tall, but his arms were also quite muscular, and his chest was conspicuously full-bodied, much like a dedicated weightlifter. Charles was likely the toughest boy in the class. He lived on a farm, was used to hard work, and could easily fend for himself. Charles was a friendly and likable classmate.

Charles didn't seem overly concerned when Mr. Clem called his name and directed him to come to the front of the classroom. He rose slowly from his seat and momentarily stood regally beside his desk with an expression on his face that hinted that *This won't be the first paddle that has kissed my rear end, and it probably won't be the last!* He slowly grabbed hold of his wide leather belt on both sides of an oval belt buckle, took a deep breath, and smoothly hiked up his denim dungarees. With his chest still swollen from a big ingestion of air, Charles sauntered like a gladiator to the front of the class where Mr. Clem was standing with the paddle, already looped around his strong wrist and partially cocked in his right hand. Charles appeared ready to be disciplined for something that was as much my fault as his! I was petrified! Motionless and glued to my seat, I was as white as a sheet and enormously grateful that it wasn't me

Willow Grove: A Boy, A Family, A Farm

standing in front of the classroom, waiting to receive my due. Boldly, Charles made no effort to soften his punishment or reveal that I was an equal accomplice in the mischief.

Momentarily, the class would witness why Mr. Clem had the leather strip looped snugly around his wrist. It was essentially to keep the paddle from going dangerously airborne should it slip out of his hand during one of his whirlwind windups.

Mr. Clem took hold of Charles' left arm just above the elbow. With both feet firmly planted on the floor and an extra firm grip on both the paddle and Charles's arm, Mr. Clem slowly raised the weapon back past his body and high above his head. As soon as the paddle was as far as Mr. Clem could reach, he paused for a second and then swung down as hard as he could muster, up under Charles' buttocks. On impact, both of Charles' feet lifted off the classroom floor. The swiftness of the paddle was so furious and powerful that the momentum from the tumultuous follow-through twisted Mr. Clem's body enough that both he and Charles had to quickly right themselves with a quick, clumsy tap dance, in order to keep from ending up all tangled together on the classroom floor.

The loud smack from the paddle revealed how painful the impact was on Charles' buttocks. Never letting go of Charles's arm, Mr. Clem wound up again and again and walloped Charles four or five more times. Throughout the powerful exhibition, Charles didn't resist at all! He didn't utter a word or

Sixth Grade

make any kind of sound—just an anguished grimace after each explosion. Like a brave warrior, Charles willingly accepted his punishment. The room was so quiet that you could have heard a pin drop. Moreover, the intended message was crystal clear in the minds of every student in the classroom —most particularly, *mine*! Mr. Clem was almost as glad as Charles when the paddling ceased. The vigorous workout was more than enough exercise for the teacher for one day.

I sat motionless, since it could easily have been me in front of the class instead of Charles. I realized that if I had gotten the spanking, there was absolutely no way I could have tolerated the punishment as well as Charles did. After the display, it was very apparent that Mr. Clem wouldn't have to discipline any other student for the remainder of the school year. After that, when Mr. Clem *instructed,* his entire class *listened* and *learned*! Especially *me*!

Occasionally when I was in the sixth grade, Mr. Hall would quietly open our classroom door and motion to the teacher to step out into the hallway. After a minute or so, Mr. Clem would return and announce that certain boys would be excused to go with Mr. Hall. Usually, it was two or three boys, and none of us named by the teacher had any idea what was awaiting us when we left the classroom. We would stand up from our desks and promptly leave the classroom! We weren't always perfect "little angels," and consequently, our thoughts wandered to what Mr. Hall might know—that we hoped he *didn't* know! Even worse, if I was disciplined at school by the principal or a teacher, the reprimand had better not reach my parents. If I was punished in school, I could expect the same when I got home. Like many rural parents during the 1940s and '50s, my parents knew the principal and teachers, respected them, and believed that they would always do whatever was best for their students. The teacher's admonishment was never questioned by the parents!

Mr. Hall directed us to follow him, then turned around and walked toward the super-wide staircase that led down to the first floor. On the first floor, we circled back around and continued down to the basement via the narrow, solid stone staircase that dead-ended at the entrance to the school cafeteria on the left and the girls' restroom on the right. At the bottom of the steps, we continued through the cafeteria and entered a storage room in the back of the school.

Our minds were relieved when we learned that Mr. Hall wanted us to help carry foodstuffs and paper products from a service truck down a few outdoor cellar steps to the below-ground storage room. We welcomed the opportunity to get out of the classroom and were more than happy to help Mr. Hall in any way we could…and for as long as he wished! The longer, the better!

As soon as the truck was unloaded, Mr. Hall thanked us for our help and then gave us a few extra minutes to enjoy a package of marshmallow cookies topped with strands of fresh coconut. The

Sixth Grade

cookies were an unexpected treat for three hungry boys, especially in the afternoon after a long school day. Shortly afterwards, we headed back to our classroom with smiles plastered on our faces. We envisioned our classmates still snickering indiscreetly and wondering what kind of trouble we were in and how much "punishment" we netted from the principal. Regarding the delicious cookies —mum was the word.

My six years at Ravenswood Elementary School were enriching. During my adult life, I often recounted how fortunate I was to have been born and reared in a rural community and gone to an elementary school with fewer than 40 students in each class. My teachers were diligent, caring, and interested in their students, which was especially important during the first two or three years of formal education. In this book, I have attempted to highlight memories from 1945 to 1955 that I still appreciate: growing up in a wonderful farming community and attending public schools in Ravenswood. I can't recall a single incident that left a negative thought in my mind during those 10 notable years of my life and education in Jackson County, West Virginia.

But, if I were to distinguish any negative regarding education in small schools, it would be that most young men and women educated in a small, friendly town like Ravenswood were generally not "street-smart," which is more prevalent in urban environments. At least not street-smart enough to recognize and quickly confront countless

Willow Grove: A Boy, A Family, A Farm

negative mores that are ubiquitous in various segments of metropolitan cities in our country. Living in a farming community and attending school there didn't prepare a young person for the reality that too many people in the world are not very amiable or considerate. Such people rarely inhabited a small town in the 1940s and 1950s, and, if they did, they were considered an anomaly.

Very Fine Land

Raymond Casto's dairy farm was our immediate neighbor to the south, and Raymond's neighbor was Dan McCoy. The shape and topography of their two farms and ours were chiefly the same. Each farm had a good-sized river bottom and, more important, much larger and equally flat hay and cornfields at a higher elevation. The river bottoms would occasionally flood, but not the elevated topography that comprised the majority of the farms' tillable land.

Remarkably, all three of the rectangularly shaped farms were bordered on one end by the Ohio River and on the opposite end by a rolling pasture field sparsely populated with mature shade trees. Each farm shared a freshwater ravine, which was an ideal source of drinking water for thirsty dairy cows grazing in the pasture fields. The rolling hills bestowed a unique rural character to each of the farms. It is easy to understand why George Washington was so enamored with this area when he surveyed the land in October 1770. In the

Very Fine Land

1800s, the acreage became known as Warth's Bottom and later in the early 1900s, Willow Grove. George Washington expressed his strong feelings about the rich land during his trip down the Ohio River. On October 29, 1770, the future president wrote in his diary, "...on the east side of the river, appears to be a large bottom of VERY FINE land also [Warth's Bottom]." The 38-year-old future president's observation was astute about Willow Grove!

Two other marvelous farms in Willow Grove belonged to John and Starling Miller. The brothers' farms were adjoining and immediately south of Dan McCoy's farm. Matson King's dairy farm was south of the two Miller farms. North of Willow Grove in neighboring Pleasant View, Wayne Hughes' dairy bordered Uncle Conrad's farm. Just like the Willow Grove farms, both Pleasant View farms had magnificent river bottoms.

From our Willow Grove farm, we not only had a superb, southern panoramic view of the Casto and McCoy farms but also of the Wharton and Walker farms to the north. In all directions, the land was perfectly level and totally unobstructed. The only trees anywhere to be seen were around the neighbors' residences and the uninterrupted row of tall water maples that covered the eastern bank of the Ohio River.

Willow Grove: A Boy, A Family, A Farm

World War II on our Silverton Farm

America and its allies were at war with Germany, Italy and Japan, and as a young kid, I remember the seemingly endless piercing sound from the air raid siren in Silverton. The high-pitched sound was uncomfortably eerie and a bit frightening for Bob and me. As soon as the siren began to roar, Mom would immediately turn out all the lights in the house and pull down all of the window blinds. Then she would light candles, which helped minimize the uneasy feelings my brother and I had during the mandatory black-out. Anytime Bob or I commenced with the "why" questions, Mom always had a reassuring way of explaining what was happening. By the time she ended her explanation, which often took the path of a short story, Bob and I would be wholly satisfied that everything would be just fine. And whatever she concocted, she would never mention a single word about the war or fighting in the European and Pacific theaters. The electricity wouldn't be turned back on until we heard the siren give the all-clear signal.

Mom was a professional at coming up with a soothing explanation for any situation. However, sometimes she took the same liberty as a writer of fiction to stretch the truth or contrive some suitable angle that would pave her storybook explanation into a happy ending for two anxious and curious boys.

World War II on our Silverton Farm

One significant advantage of growing up on a dairy farm during the war was that families living on productive farms never went hungry. Farmers worked extremely hard from well before daybreak until after dusk, which afforded their families a warm bed and plenty of nourishing food. Many farmers raised their own meat, grew their own vegetables, and produced dairy products necessary for a healthy, balanced diet. Farms had apple, pear, persimmon, and walnut trees, and, in remote areas on hillside pasture fields were blackberry, raspberry, and gooseberry patches. Honey, a good sugar substitute, was gathered from beehives in a remote spot along a fence line or robbed from treetops in wooded areas on the farm. Small grape vineyards were common, as were strawberry patches. During World War II, the Amish communities and millions of farmers were rich with ample food in comfortable homes.

Conversely, I'm equally confident there were advantages to living in a municipality, large or small. Still, in my humble opinion, the standard of living on my grandfather's Silverton farm was good and didn't differ much at all from what it was: before the war...during the war...and after the war. I submit that many families living on productive, successful dairy farms had a relatively better quality of life than many city and urban citizens during the Great Depression and World War II.

During World War II, American citizens were issued coupons by the federal government for coffee, sugar, meat, cheese, shoes, gasoline, rubber tires, and ladies' nylons, among others. The nylon was needed for military parachutes. Coupons for certain commodities, such as special food items, shoes, and gasoline, were the main ones received and used by my family. Farmers received extra coupons for gasoline for their tractors and farm trucks. My parents didn't drink coffee, and since Grandpa and Dad butchered several hogs and beef cattle every year, we didn't need meat coupons. Mom would send her coffee coupons to her sister Helen in Parkersburg, who in turn would send Mom her sugar coupons. Mom did a lot of canning, and the extra sugar enabled her to preserve more fruits and vegetables.

Whenever she could, the friendly Silverton general store clerk would sell her loyal customers extra cheese and cigarettes, which Mom would also give to her older sister. During the war, Mom would often welcome a surprise and unannounced visit from family and friends from Parkersburg, which certainly wasn't a simple or inexpensive trip in the 1940s. They would make the round trip not solely for a social visit, but principally because their coffee allowance was gone, and they needed a coffee "fix." The family knew Mom always had a little extra coffee set aside in her kitchen cupboard for just such surprise visits.

The Sunday noon meal was always a feast and particularly enjoyable anytime family members made a special trip to spend a few social hours with their Silverton relatives. Besides freshly brewed coffee, guests could always count on a huge platter

World War II on our Silverton Farm

of fried chicken, plenty of the best mashed potatoes and gravy in the world, as well as ample portions of super fresh vegetables direct from the garden—and I'd be remiss if I didn't mention Mom's delicious homemade pies, cakes, and, sometimes, hand-cranked homemade vanilla, strawberry, and peach ice cream. My parents maintained a flock of chickens, so when one or two ended up on the Sunday dinner table, Mom's loss of revenue from the sale of eggs was hardly noticeable.

Even though rationing was necessary during World War II, and though my extremely industrious parents and grandparents managed quite well, rationing was extra hard on many citizens. Sadly, several small farms were not as fortunate, and many rural families experienced difficult times. After the war, a few returning young Jackson County soldiers had a difficult time readjusting to civilian life, partly due to the severe shortage of good jobs. My grandfather helped several veterans by giving them employment on his Silverton farm or on special projects, which he had with the county government to help maintain county roads.

World War II was an era when many American citizens were still recovering from the decade-long Great Depression of the 1930s. Rural families couldn't afford to purchase all the foodstuffs they needed at the local general store. For the most part, they only purchased the essential ingredients necessary for food preparation and preservation: items such as flour, yeast, sugar, salt, and herbs. Many of the products considered necessities today weren't even available or were considered luxuries during the war. Coffee, fresh meat, and toilet paper are prime examples. Thrifty rural families didn't purchase anything they could grow in their gardens. My family was no exception.

Every summer Mom had a big garden and canned enough food to last our family for more than a year. She always canned extra so she could share with needy neighbors who appreciated her kindness. Mom was a teenager during the Great Depression and witnessed chronic hardships in her family and neighbors. She couldn't stand to see fresh vegetables go to waste. Canning involved long hours and a lot of sweaty work. There was no air-conditioning to keep the kitchen cool. On many days Mom worked from sunrise into the night canning bushels of green beans and vegetables and fruits for the family to enjoy during the cold winter months.

My parents had an account at the local Silverton general store and, each week, they would buy items they needed and couldn't grow or raise on the farm. Dad would pay the bill every month after he received his paycheck. If the bill for the entire month was over two dollars, my parents would sit down at the kitchen table, talk about what they purchased and figure out some way to cut expenses. In the summer, a large chunk of the monthly bill was canning supplies. Dad's salary was $30 a month or one dollar a day for a minimum of 10 to 12 long hours—which on many

World War II on our Silverton Farm

days was very strenuous work. Dad was making a whopping five to six cents an hour.

Hobert and Luta Kaiser, our dear neighbors, lived in the little green house, the same house Dad had rented for a short time. Hobert, who was an electronics wizard, worked for a radio communications company and was responsible for maintaining a radio tower in North Ravenswood. In the late 1940s, Hobert built an oval-shaped, five-inch television. Afterward, Hobert and Luta invited us to their home in North Ravenswood. The evening was fabulous for three young country boys. We watched our hero, the Lone Ranger, and his faithful horse, Silver, ride the western trails, chasing after the bad guys. The video reception was so poor that it looked like it was snowing in the desert. Hobert's homemade TV was the first residential television I ever saw.

Luta was a wonderful lady and always lots of fun anytime she was in the kitchen helping my mother. Everyone just loved her demeanor and sense of humor. Mom could depend on Luta anytime she was challenged with a bumper crop of fresh food from the garden, and it was impossible for her, all by herself, to salvage the vegetables before they spoiled. In our family, as in so many others, it was a "crime" to allow food to go to waste. Every so often, high winds and heavy rains during a thunderstorm would prematurely knock fruit off the apple trees or decimate tomato plants laden with softball-sized ripe tomatoes. When such an unfortunate event occurred, the food spoiled unless it was immediately gathered from the garden and canned within a day or so. Luta would jump in and help Mom, and, whatever they couldn't handle, Mom would hand off to my grandmother and neighbors.

My brothers and I loved it when Luta helped Mom deep fry dozens and dozens of doughnuts. They would make different types, but the one I enjoyed the most was the glossy, sugar-glazed doughnut. Mom's glazed doughnuts were huge, almost as soft as cotton candy, and extra delicious when they were still warm. Mom and Luta knew there was no need to stop until the kitchen table and all the countertops were completely covered with homemade doughnuts. On other occasions, they would make several bottles of homebrew for the adults and a great tasting root beer for the kids. Mom was adept at making special treats on a shoestring budget for me and my brothers.

Another treat came in the fall, after Dad and Grandpa butchered. Mom would pare and season plentiful thin strips of raw beef with salt, pepper, herbs, and special spices. Dad would take a flat platter completely covered with six-inch-long strips of seasoned, raw beef up to the third floor of Uncle Joe's house and hang the strips over a clothesline in the sweltering attic. After a few weeks, the thoroughly dried beef jerky was as rigid as a steel nail and as durable as shoe leather. For a special treat, Dad would take the three of us boys up to the attic, where we would each choose a strip of dried beef. The treat had a unique flavor and though

World War II on our Silverton Farm

tough to chew, was quite tasty and would take a long time to gnaw and completely devour. One strip of beef jerky would keep us busy and quiet for a long time, and by the time it was all gone, our jaws were begging for a rest.

Without exception, Mom always had a dessert for us to enjoy after every evening meal. Most of the time, it was a dessert she prepared from scratch: apple, cherry, blueberry, lemon meringue pies; apple strudel; the best fluffy angel food cake in the world; vanilla and butterscotch pudding; or cookies. She would rarely serve a dessert from a retail store. They were too expensive for her budget, but when she did, you could be sure the treat was purchased at a bargain price.

Basic Yellow Cake — 2-8in layers 25-30 min 375
2 C. sifted cake flour — 1½ C. white sugar
2½ tsp baking powder — 2 eggs
½ tsp salt — ¾ C milk
½ C shortening — 1¼ tsp vanilla
Preheat oven. Grease + dust cake pans.
Sift flour, baking powder + salt together. Cream Short.,
add eggs + beat 2 min. Gradually add flour
mixture alternately with milk. Scrape sides
of bowl as necessary. Pour into cake pans + bake
25-30 min. Test with toothpick. Cool in pans 5 min.

Willow Grove: A Boy, A Family, A Farm

Desserts after supper served as an effective enticement for my brothers and me to eat all the food on our plates. If necessary, at breakfast or during the noontime meal, Mom would remind us: "If you don't clean your plate, no dessert after supper." She wouldn't allow us to forget that hungry children around the world would give anything to have the food we were just pushing around on our plates.

Decades later, I still feel guilty if I waste a spoonful of food.

The Ladies of the Farms

I like this picture of the Willow Grove Farm Women's Club. My mother is sitting on the arm of the couch in our family room at Willow Grove. Mom is joined by eight other ladies. All were wives of dairy farmers except Bertha Wolverton and the two Warth sisters, Irene and Ona.

One of the reasons I like the picture is it shows my mother attired in a nice dress and having a good time socializing with the other club ladies—instead of working, which is what she did seven days a week. Yet, Mom was the host and I know she would have worked feverishly before and during the luncheon to make sure everyone would be comfortable and enjoy herself. Mom was at her apogee anytime she could help someone, either socially or in a time of need.

The Willow Grove Farm Club was an active club. All of the women had a common interest,

The Ladies of the Farms

knew each other well, and enjoyed their club meetings. Each club member took turns hosting the meeting in their home. They invited guests to speak at their meetings, such as the Jackson County Agriculture Extension Agent, and Home Demonstration Agent Rosalee Craft. The county agriculture department was very supportive of the farming community.

The Willow Grove Farm Women's Club was very supportive of the "Willing Workers 4-H Club" and the local Pleasant View Church. It raised money at social events during the year to help pay the expenses for their children to attend 4-H summer camp at Jackson Mills, West Virginia. Jackson Mills had modern facilities to house and entertain a large number of kids. 4-H Club members from 55 counties in West Virginia gathered at the marvelous 500-acre Jackson Mills facility each year for a full week of fun and learning. At the beginning of the week, all of the kids were divided into four tribes: the Cherokee, Delaware, Mingo, and Seneca. I was a proud Mingo. It was fun to sit around the bonfire after the sun went down. Jackson Mills was the site of the first statewide 4-H camp in the nation.

Willow Grove: A Boy, A Family, A Farm

Seated, left to right: Kathrine Sück, Ona Warth McComas, Nannie Sück, Edra McCoy, Bertha Wolverton, Virginia McCoy. Standing: Irene Warth, Grace Casto, Mary Kay McCoy, Constance McCoy King. Note: Nannie is Edra's mother; Bertha is Virginia McCoy's mother. Virginia McCoy is Uncle Conrad's brother Dan's wife; Constance McCoy King is Uncle Conrad's sister; Mary Kay McCoy is Uncle Conrad's brother Vernon's wife. Irene and Ona were sisters and lived on a farm across the road from the Casto's and Virginia McCoy's homes. Dan and Vernon are players in the "Uncle Conrad Bears ALL" tall tale.

Chapter Four: Old Enough

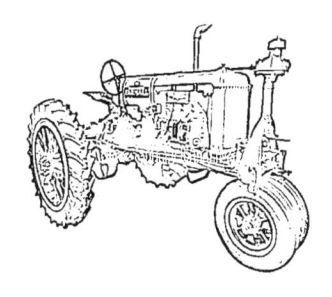

Willow Grove: A Boy, A Family, A Farm

Grandpa's Chauffeur

Even before I had my learner's permit, I chauffeured my grandfather to his appointments in Ravenswood and Ripley. I was a pretty good driver, but operating a vehicle with Grandpa in the passenger seat was a challenge. Regardless, no matter what Grandpa pointed out or how he conveyed his driving preferences, I never once refuted any of his comments—even the trivial ones. I was taught to respect and obey my elders. The thought never entered my mind to question anything Grandpa pointed out regarding my driving. When I was Grandpa's chauffeur, he was well into his golden years and sometimes didn't feel well. Possibly my driving foibles and his subsequent advice took his mind off his health issues for a short time.

The distance from our Willow Grove farm to Ravenswood was only eight miles, but the trip took 25 to 30 minutes on the meandering countryside road. In Ravenswood, I parked the car in a parallel parking spot on the main street in town. My parallel parking had to be accomplished without touching the curb with either of the two passenger-side tires. On countless occasions, an acquaintance would spot Grandpa even before we could feed the parking meter. Instantly, broad smiles would appear on both men, and the salutations, handshaking, and conversation would commence

Willow Grove: A Boy, A Family, A Farm

without delay. It was so evident from the greetings, laughter, and tone of their discussions that the gentleman was one of the countless individuals who admired and respected my grandfather. Grandpa and his friend talked and talked and talked! Quietly, I moved back from their sphere of discussion and proceeded to amuse myself without being annoying or disrespectful. I would count forward and backward from one to a hundred while holding on to the parking-meter pole with one arm and spinning around and around. Before I'd get too dizzy, I'd stop and find some other way to entertain myself.

Me, age 14, 9th grade.

Grandpa's Chauffeur

After 10 or 15 minutes, which seemed more like an hour, Grandpa and his friend would end their social chat, bid each other goodbye, and we would start down the sidewalk on our way to a business office or retail store. Yet, more often than not, before we could get very far down the block and across Washington Street, another gentleman would approach Grandfather with an equally lively and genuinely warm hello! Once again, I would look around for an interesting store window to gaze through for a few minutes or invent another game. I knew the routine and would just relax and make the most of the waiting game. Eventually, we reached our destination, and Grandpa would finally take care of business.

Later, if we happened to stop by the feed store, hardware, grocery, or department store, more chats would ensue about current events and immediate families. Living in Jackson County with so many aunts, uncles and cousins was almost an assurance that we'd bump into other family members running errands. Kelly Somerville owned and managed Kelly's Market, and John McCoy managed The Caldwell Feed and Supply Store. John was Uncle Conrad's brother, and Kelly Somerville was John and Conrad's brother-in-law. Everyone was treated as family!

At least twice a year, Grandpa and I walked down the street in Ravenswood and entered a frosted glass, wood-framed door with an inscription that read "Office: D. E. Cole." Mr. Cole was a banker, town recorder, and a respected citizen of

Willow Grove: A Boy, A Family, A Farm

Ravenswood. My introduction to Mr. Cole was interesting, and Grandpa's business visits with the well-known banker have remained with me since my teenage years.

After a hearty, warm greeting, Mr. Cole turned around and walked back to the swivel chair behind his dark mahogany desk. Simultaneously, Grandpa and I sat down in two solid wood chairs directly in front of Mr. Cole's desk. The top of his decades-old desk was devoid of newspapers, magazines, or stacks of legal documents. There was just an antique desk lamp on one end, a clean perforated yellow legal pad in the middle, a magnifying strip for reading fine print, and a neat row of colored pencils. Seven wood pencils were perfectly lined up, side by side, with the lead end of each pencil pointed straight toward me. They were all different colors and impeccably sharpened to a fine point. I was captivated by how Mr. Cole had the regular graphite, blue, red, and green colors aligned near his right hand. He must have used these pencils more often than the other colors. The orange, brown, and yellow pencils were similarly staged about three inches further to his right but still within easy reach of his fingers. Transfixed, I sat quietly in my chair while Mr. Cole and Grandpa conducted their banking business. Two barrister bookcases, filled with rows of rusty brown books, were framed by several pictures and diplomas hanging on the windowless wall behind Mr. Cole's desk.

Grandpa's Chauffeur

Grandpa's business visits with Mr. Cole were rarely short. The end of their business meeting would quickly evolve into a social dialog. Neither was quite ready to end their mutual enjoyment of conducting business. During the social dialog, their comments and short narratives were often accompanied by bursts of laughter. Even though I didn't grasp much of their discussion, I could discern that Grandpa and Mr. Cole had a productive meeting and were having an enjoyable social visit. Regardless of how antsy I might be at the end of an extended stay, I never said or did anything that would interrupt their conversation.

During the meeting, I watched Mr. Cole add his signature to the bottom of a legal-sized sheet of paper, which he handed to Grandpa to review and cosign. While Grandpa glanced at the signed document, I couldn't help but notice Mr. Cole's disastrous and hilarious signature. Talk about chicken scratch! Mr. Cole's signature looked like someone had dropped a spoonful of cooked, wiggly, angel-hair spaghetti on the bottom of the document. Nearly every letter in his full signature was stacked on top of each other. His first initial, a very fancy D, was on the bottom of the heap. Next came an equally fancy E smack dab on top of the D. His last name was scrambled on top of both initials, all within the size of a silver dollar. Mr. Cole might be a smart businessman, but he definitely would have failed Mrs. Hughes' third-grade calligraphy assignments.

Willow Grove: A Boy, A Family, A Farm

After Grandpa inserted the document inside an accompanying manila envelope, he slowly rose to his feet. It was time to go. Mr. Cole walked around from behind his desk and shook hands long and generously with Grandpa. With their eyes focused like a laser on each other, Mr. Cole cupped his left hand on top of Grandpa's as the two men agreed to meet again soon. Just as he had done when we first entered his office, Mr. Cole extended his hand toward me and kindly shook my hand. I enjoyed the exchange and appreciated Mr. Cole's warm gesture acknowledging my presence.

Whitewashed Eyes!

One summer morning I woke up and *could not* open my eyes. My eyelashes and eyelids were glued together so tight that there was no way that I could open them. Both eyes were swollen and sore. I had a major problem! I anxiously maneuvered my legs out over the edge of the bed and carefully stood up. With my arms extended in front of me, little by little, I inched myself toward the open bedroom door. Simultaneously, I felt around for the walls that I knew were to the left and in front of me. Once I reached the door to my bedroom, I walked through the doorway and reached for the railing that ran along the top of the back staircase. The railing guided me to the landing at the top of the stairs, where I turned and shuffled down the stairs to the bottom of the narrow staircase. As I descended the stairs, I steadied myself by holding

Whitewashed Eyes!

onto the railing with one hand and sliding the other along the wall.

Mom immediately saw that my eyes were matted shut with a nasty, yellow crust, and she knew exactly why.

Every spring, Dad filled a couple of five-gallon buckets with water and a generous amount of lime —a caustic, calcium oxide powder with the texture of Pillsbury flour. After vigorous stirring, the white aqueous mixture was about the same texture as a typical can of house paint. A paint substitute called whitewash is what Dad concocted. Regular white paint was too expensive to cover the concrete block walls inside the dairy barn. Yet, the walls needed to be white and as sterile as possible to mitigate bacteria.

After the inside walls of the dairy barn were scrubbed with soapy water and scraped as clean as reasonably possible, the whitewash was brushed on the walls with a wide-bristled brush. Whitewash is supposed to be treated and applied just like an expensive gallon of white paint, carefully and meticulously. Not for me! I consider the typical painting process way too slow. Lime and water mixture is cheap! My tactic was far more productive. I chose to drown my brush and slap a copious amount of whitewash on the wall in one hasty, haphazard maneuver. And *slapping* on the whitewash is precisely what I did. It didn't matter if some of the whitewash dripped down the wall and ended up in a little puddle on the walkway or found its way onto the window sill. Everything needed to be sterilized. The inside walls of the barn would be nice, clean, and white after the whitewash dried.

However, as I vigorously slapped gobs of whitewash onto the wall and then hastened to spread the gooey mixture before it ran down the wall onto the floor, I sometimes managed to get more than a smidgen on my face. Whenever this happened, I merely stopped long enough to splash my face with clean water, since the lime would sting like crazy if it came in contact with a minor cut or abrasion. Unfortunately, I got more than a few specks of whitewash in my eyes.

Mom took hold of my arm and guided me to a kitchen chair. She filled a wash pan with warm soapy water and placed a warm, soggy washcloth over my eyes. I held it in place with both hands. Mom retrieved the washcloth every few minutes, moistened it with clean soapy water, and placed it back over my eyes. We continued this routine for 20 or 30 minutes. After a while, I could sense that the matted crust over one eye was beginning to soften, which helped lower my anxiety immensely. Soon, when I strained to open my eyes, I saw a flicker of light out of the corner of one eye. The sudden flicker of light encouraged me to try harder. I attempted to gently separate my eyelids with my index fingers. They were not ready! After more soaking, one upper eyelid finally relented and gradually began to separate from the lower. It was painful, but I desperately wanted to see daylight out of both eyes. Finally, the eyelids parted enough to give me hope that my vision would *likely* be okay.

Whitewashed Eyes!

Both eyes were extremely sensitive, painful, and coated with an angry-looking yellow mucus. Mom placed a fresh pan of warm water on my lap and told me to keep soaking my eyes until all the ugly matter was gone.

At first, my eyesight was a little blurry, but not enough to alarm me, especially after my mother's positive smile assured me that I would be fine. Mom encouraged me to keep soaking with plenty of warm water. What an enormous relief! The short time that I could not open either eye was enough grief and fear about my precious eyesight to last me a lifetime. I said a silent prayer and promised myself that I would never take my vision for granted. And in the future, I would whitewash the barn walls with a smaller brush and a whole lot more patience.

Sundays at Willow Grove

After we moved from Silverton to Willow Grove, my family did not attend church. My grandfather's health was not good and the nearest church was 20 minutes from our farm. (Another church was closer but was inaccessible during the freeze-thaw cycles in late winter and early spring, when the road to the church would get so muddy that automobiles were challenged and sometimes helpless.)

My father milked cows twice a day, 365 days a year, and on Sunday did not return from the barn until around 10 o'clock, which was not enough time to bathe, dress, and drive to church. If Dad did go to church, by the time he returned home, he would

Willow Grove: A Boy, A Family, A Farm

only have two or three hours to relax before he would have to return to the barn for the afternoon milking. Men and women who worked in other industries had the whole weekend off, whereas Dad would only have three hours to relax. And since Dad didn't go to church, Mom didn't either, and as follows, neither did I or my brothers, routinely.

A couple of times a year there would be a church fundraising event at the nearby Pleasant View Church. Since the occasion was always in the evening, Dad was able to take us. We always had a grand time. Christmas Eve service was the only opportunity my father had to sit down in a church pew during the time I was growing up in Willow Grove.

Every Sunday I looked forward to the possibility of seeing some of my cousins. We knew we were going to have company anytime Mom informed us not to dress in our regular play clothes, but instead wear the clothes she had laid out on top of the dresser.

On nice summer days and when my grandfather was feeling well, he'd ask my mother if I could go to Sunday School with him. She always said yes and welcomed the opportunity for her sons to attend church. Under his doctor's advice, Grandpa wasn't supposed to drive by himself, and the family felt much better if someone was always with him. The closest practical church was near Flatwoods, about 15 minutes from Willow Grove.

I was glad to accompany my grandfather to church anytime except when I knew it was going to

Sundays at Willow Grove

be a nice sunny day, and my cousins had already arrived or would soon arrive to spend part of a beautiful summer day with us on the farm. Regardless of how much I wanted to stay home and play with my cousins, I always went with my grandfather without any hesitation. Under no circumstances would I ever disappoint him. I would stop whatever I was doing and go to my bedroom in time to dress in my Sunday clothes and my best pair of shoes.

Grandpa and I drove about five miles to the Cedar Run United Methodist Church. The white-frame church was at the fork of the road that continued on to the hamlet of Flatwoods. From the passenger side of the car, I could look down on the roof of the church and see the parking lot at the fork of the road in front of the church.

I don't ever recall Sunday services being overly crowded, but there was always a friendly gathering of churchgoers in attendance. Grandpa and I would usually sit on the right side in one of the wide wooden pews near the front.

There are two things I remember most about attending Sunday school with Grandpa. One was how much he enjoyed talking with his church friends. It was obvious how much he enjoyed the religious camaraderie throughout the services. The other was how much he loved to sing. There were times when Grandpa's singing soared well above all others in the church. He had a rich baritone voice and would enunciate every word in the hymn, from beginning to end. To me, Grandpa was a good gospel singer. Watching and listening to Grandpa sing was the best part of Sunday school for me.

Cedar Run United Methodist Church.

After church, Grandpa would stop and talk with several of his friends. The conversations would start inside the church and slowly trickle out the front door into the parking lot. Grandfather never met a stranger, and if he did, the individual wasn't a stranger for very long. Grandpa also made sure he spoke with the minister Wayne Hughes. Just like my grandfather, the pastor was a dairy farmer and both men enjoyed exchanging information about their respective farms and new ideas in dairy animal husbandry. After several greetings and short conversations, we would gradually mosey toward the car and soon be headed home. Even

Sundays at Willow Grove

though grandfather wasn't in the "best of health," he always felt much better after going to church on Sunday. With all the car windows rolled down, we enjoyed the warm summer breeze and peaceful ride home.

Though Grandpa and I were the only members of our family who occasionally went to church, the Lord was revered in our home. Grandmother and Aunt Jack read their Bibles, regularly. My mother had a Bible in our family room. There was no alcohol in the house and no playing cards, except for "Old Maid." We played Monopoly, checkers, and Chinese checkers. My brothers and I said our prayers every night before we hopped in bed.

My maternal grandfather worked away from home five nights a week during his career with the B&O Railroad. Eventually, his alcohol consumption continued during his weekends at home. After Pa retired in 1947, his son was instrumental in getting his parents out of Parkersburg and away from all of the alcohol establishments. Uncle Bob was newly married and working in Washington Gardens. It was a practical move since Robert and his new wife, Aunt Dee, were living with his parents and DuPont was located in Washington Bottom. Pa did not know how to drive and there were no beer joints in the Washington Bottom. Pa's alcohol dependence problem was solved.

Uncle Bob and Aunt Dee were active in the Washington United Methodist Church and the Washington Lions Club in the community of Washington Bottom. My grandparents attended the same church occasionally and were active in many of the events held at the Washington Bottom Community Building. Every year Pa could be seen sitting outdoors, stirring a cauldron of bubbling apple butter to sell at fundraising events.

During all of our annual trips from Willow Grove to visit with my maternal grandparents, my grandfather always said a short prayer before each meal: "Bless this food to our body's use. In God's name, we pray. Amen." I *never* heard anyone else, ever, say grace in my grandparents' home. Only Pa!

Grandpa, Draft Horses, and Nancy

During my paternal grandfather's childhood and much of his adult life, he worked alongside and cared for horses. When he began his career as a full-time dairy farmer, he always had at least one team of robust workhorses on his Silverton farm. Workhorses were the primary source of power for tilling, planting, and harvesting crops. Petrol-powered tractors were a luxury before the 1940s and used primarily on large, midwest farms.

As a teenager, my grandfather and his brothers spent long hours working in the fields, helping their father raise and harvest crops. As I mentioned earlier, the only practical source of horsepower on the farm, when Grandpa was a young boy, was literally a good team of work horses and a sturdy set of leather harnesses. Every successful farm would have at least one team of powerful draft horses and some farmers would have two teams.

Grandpa, Draft Horses, and Nancy

Otherwise, when a second team of draft horses was imperative, a friendly neighbor would offer the use of his team during the busy harvesting time. The favor would be reciprocated.

Early in the morning and often before daybreak, Grandpa would walk to the barn where the workhorses were housed in their oversized, individual wood stalls. He would feed the team of horses, inspect them for any cuts, bruises, or injuries, and generally make sure they were healthy enough to perform the strenuous chores planned for the day.

Once the team was deemed healthy and ready to go to the fields, Grandpa would place the top section of the bridle over each horse's head and ears, followed by the iron bit, which was carefully placed inside the horse's mouth. Next, the leather strap on the bottom of the bridle would be buckled and pulled snug under the horse's neck. Once the bridles were in place, it was easy to lead the horses, one in each hand, while walking between them, to the tool shed, where the collars and leather harnesses were stored.

Properly harnessing a team of horses was not a quick or easy exercise. The process involved a lot of experience and detailed knowledge about each of the work horse's strengths and weaknesses. A team couldn't effectively pull a heavy steel plow or a wagon loaded with field corn unless each harness was in excellent shape and fit each horse. A properly adjusted, custom-made set of harness was as important to a good team as gasoline is to a combustion engine.

The daily ritual was so routine that the horses knew the exercise almost as well as Grandpa. Each leather harness had a number of complex straps that were placed over the back of both horses and carefully adjusted. After a day in the field, the harnesses were cleaned and then properly coated with oil to keep the supple leather from cracking. When they were not in use, the heavy-duty harnesses were hung on the inside wall of the tool shed, as precisely as a good dress shirt hung in a clothes closet. That was why Grandpa was so strict about how the harnesses were stored when they were not in use. A good set of harness was expensive.

Grandpa spent many days under the summer sun walking behind the horses as they pulled heavy farm machinery through the creek-bottom and over hillside pasture fields. When Grandpa tilled the corn fields, he would walk behind an iron plow and continuously muscle the plow handles with both hands in order to keep the plow moving forward in a straight line. A long, continuous leather strap that extended over the top of his right shoulder and under his left arm was used to maneuver and control the horses. The leather strap was connected to the bridles on both horses and essentially fulfilled the same function as a steering wheel and brakes on a farm tractor or automobile. Plowing a field behind a team of horses was extremely difficult and, moreover, demanded a perfect balance of

Grandpa, Draft Horses, and Nancy

physical dexterity and moment-by-moment communication between the farmer and his horses.

The single-bladed plow had two long wooden handles that Grandpa used to keep the plow upright as the curved plow blade sliced through the packed earth and turned the sod completely upside down. If the horses veered too much to the left or right, Grandpa would tug on the leather reins that encircled his shoulders. A slight tug on the right rein would signal the horses to step slightly to the right, so that the plow would continue to till the ground properly and not leave pieces of soil unplowed. In addition to a gentle tug on the reins to move right or left, a good team of horses would also respond to verbal commands. Grandpa would shout "Gee!," and the horses would react by moving slightly right. If he repeated the "Gee!" command, the horses would continue moving to the right until the command ceased. The horses would react likewise and move to the left if the command "Haw!" was voiced. To stop the team, Grandpa would simply pull back on the reins with both hands and, with strict authority command, "Ho, ho!" Basically, the leather strap around his shoulders was the "steering wheel" that steered the horses across the fields in a near-perfect straight line. The verbal commands complemented the reins and enabled Grandpa to finesse the direction of the horses and communicate with the team without taking his hands off of the plow handles.

After a day or two under the hot sun, the soil in the plowed field was dry enough to crumble into a

Willow Grove: A Boy, A Family, A Farm

granular surface. Grandpa and the team of horses would return to the field with a disc harrow and a tooth harrow. The disc harrow contained several sharp, circular steel discs that would slice through the ground and cut the clumps of soil into pieces. Quite often, depending on the composition and the moisture level of the soil, plowed fields would have to be "worked" more than once before the soil was ready for the tooth harrow, which combed the field, just as a comb goes through a person's hair. Grandpa would walk behind the horses and beside the tooth harrow until the field was perfectly smooth. Often, Grandpa and the horses would have to walk every foot of the field multiple times, behind both the disc harrow and tooth harrow over a period of a few days before the job of preparing the soil was deemed ready for the next phase: planting. Most farmers couldn't afford the luxury of a seat on a disc harrow, but Grandpa was fortunate: he sat on a solid, hard, steel seat atop the disc harrow while the horses pulled it through the field.

Dewey Gene, at it Again!

By the time we moved from Silverton in 1946, affordable farm tractors had completely replaced Grandpa's team of draft horses. However, his lifelong bond and appreciation of horses motivated him to purchase two ponies, Nancy and Pinto, for the Willow Grove farm: Nancy for the men to help corral the dairy cattle from the distant hill pasture, and Pinto for my brothers and me to enjoy riding

Dewey Gene, at it Again!

socially. Grandpa knew that every farm boy needs a pony!

My favorite was a white and polished brown spotted pinto. In contrast to Nancy, Pinto had shorter legs and was an enjoyable pony for both adults and teenagers to ride.

Nancy was a striking and highly spirited dark bay pony with long sleek legs. She reminded me of a thoroughbred racehorse and, at times, acted like one. As soon as the rider threw his leg over the saddle, he'd better have a firm grip on the saddle horn and reins and be prepared for a surge, just like the start of a thoroughbred race at Churchill Downs. With Nancy's long legs, the rider was high enough off the ground that it was wise to remain glued to the saddle and not be jettisoned from the firecracker, involuntarily. Nancy's demeanor was unpredictable. Young boys were advised only to watch and not try to ride her—as Nancy certainly provided plenty of impromptu entertainment around the farm...though not always exciting for the unfortunate rider who was unexpectedly thrown out of the saddle.

One day, I was riding Pinto leisurely around the barnyard and in the lane in front of the machine shed. Meanwhile, cousin Dewey Gene was sitting on the concrete dock beside the milk house, watching me and Pinto mosey back and forth on the arced driveway between the machine shed and the road to the gravel pit.

Dewey Gene decided that he wanted to go for a ride on Pinto and asked me to ride close to the concrete dock so that he could drop down behind me and straddle the pony. Dewey Gene's request seemed simple enough. He would ride bareback while I lolled in the comfort of the attractive, squeaky leather saddle, which still emitted a pleasing, new leather aroma.

As soon as he dropped down on the bare back of Pinto, Dewey Gene grabbed both sides of the leather saddle with his hands and, at the same time, pressed both heels of his work boots into the flanks of Pinto. A horse's flanks are super sensitive areas, right in front of the hind legs. It's the same place on a horse where cowboys tighten a rope when they want a bronco to buck and fight to dislodge its rodeo rider.

The instant Dewey Gene mounted the pony from behind me, Pinto darted forward and began galloping and bucking down the lane toward the house—at a pace much faster than the slow tempo I had been enjoying! Dewey Gene was having fun and, in order to remain astraddle the bucking pony, he buried the heels of his boots even deeper into both flanks, which only made a bad situation worse. I pulled back on the reins, trying vigorously to slow Pinto. My effort was useless! The pony wasn't hindered in the least by my ineffectual attempts. With one hand on the saddle horn and both feet in the stirrups, I remained upright but was unable to slow the runaway. Pulling on the reins with only one hand wasn't enough. I just didn't have the strength to avert the coming calamity. In the meantime, I was so preoccupied I

Dewey Gene, at it Again!

wasn't sure if Dewey Gene was still behind me or if he had already been bucked off. I was about to find out!

Pinto was in full control of the situation, galloping and intermittently bucking high enough to lift all four hooves off the ground. Where were we heading? I had no idea! None of the likely options were good! For all practical purposes, the lane essentially ended at the driveway. The road didn't actually stop but narrowed considerably and forged straight ahead down a rough path toward the river. It wasn't a good idea to head for the railroad crossing. By now, my only real option was to get off this train wreck as soon as possible! Pinto continued to buck aggressively and showed no signs of slowing down or giving up. Then...without any warning, the saddle shifted sideways, tossing me onto the ground. The girth strap had loosened enough to allow the saddle to twist sideways. After my body slammed to the ground, I slid on my left side down the gravel lane—with the full weight of Dewey Gene—right smack dab on top of me.

With no shirt and shoes on, I ended up with an enormous amount of pebbles and dirt embedded in the left side of my body. Mostly in my left arm—all the way from the tips of my fingers to the top of my bare shoulder blade. Dewey Gene was scratch-free. He had essentially gone on a sled ride without any snow—with me as the sled!

I rolled over off of the gravel surface into a thicket of tall grass underneath the sycamore tree. I was in unbelievable pain and just wanted to lie perfectly still in the grass...and die.

To make matters worse, our grandfather was sitting on the porch and witnessed the whole fiasco. He never allowed an animal to be abused and promptly voiced his utmost displeasure with my cousin and me for causing Pinto's highly unusual behavior. I was in incredible pain, and it didn't help to know we had managed to upset our grandfather. None of his grandsons would ever say or do anything to upset him, regardless of the circumstances. But boys will be boys, and any time we disappointed him, it was never intentional. We knew Grandpa had a weak heart, and we tried desperately to conceal any situation that we knew would aggravate him.

Mom was in the house and heard the commotion through her open kitchen window, which faced the giant sycamore tree. She saw Dewey Gene looking down at me. When she arrived, I was lying in the grass, groaning from intense agony. The pain was so deep and severe! It felt like my whole left side was on fire. My mangled arm was completely plastered with pebbles and dirty blood. Though I realized I might live, I wasn't sure I wanted to!

Mom helped me up. Together we walked to the house, where I sat down on a kitchen chair while Mom used warm soapy water to cleanse my arm. My left arm from the shoulder down was a continuous mass of blood with pebbles and sand from the road entrenched in curls of ragged, bloody

Dewey Gene, at it Again!

skin. Mom used a pair of tweezers and meticulously picked each pebble, one by one, out of my arm and my side down to just above my ankle. It was excruciating and took forever! By the time she was through, my whole arm was completely bandaged and my left side and leg were covered with an enormous, homemade pad. Once again, Mom had managed to salvage one of her sons—something she did many times during our young, heedless years. Mom's gentle touch and soothing words helped me feel a little better, which reassured me that the worst might be over.

For several days, each time Mom dressed my wounds, she had to thoroughly soak the bandages before they could be slowly unraveled. The pain was awful all during the daily ritual. My arm was so raw that the bandages were utterly saturated with crusty, dried blood, which made it impossible to remove the gauze without torturous pain. Carefully, Mom removed yards of dried bloody gauze from around my arm, side, and leg. It took several days for the pain to subside substantially and several more before Mom would let me journey outside of the house without a white gauze gauntlet from the wrist to the top of my shoulder.

After my wounds healed, and for a while, I realized walking might be a little boring and take longer. But at least I knew I'd arrive with fewer knots on my head. Hitching a ride with anyone on Nancy or Pinto wouldn't be of any interest to me for quite some time.

Willow Grove: A Boy, A Family, A Farm

Other than giving several cowhands plenty of surprises, Nancy proved not to be a good asset for the Willow Grove farm. No one could comfortably ride her, and it became apparent that Nancy wasn't about to mend her ways. A year or so later, Grandpa decided that the best thing to do was get rid of Nancy before someone got hurt.

Calf Lady

Every dairy cow and all new heifers would have a baby calf once a year. It was rare, but now and then, the mother would have twins. If the newborn was a female from a good, milk-producing cow, we always kept the calf. In contrast, bull calves and the very first calf from young heifers were either sold at the stock market or, more often than not, sold directly to individuals who drove to Willow Grove to purchase baby calves. The small, part-time farmer bought baby calves, fed them for about six months, and subsequently sold the animals at the stock market. For rural people with limited tillable acreage who needed to work full-time at a nearby plant or commercial business, fattening baby calves for sale was a good way to add a few extra dollars to their money pouch.

Calves were born on the farm almost every week, and, in the spring, it wasn't unusual to have three or four baby calves arrive the same week. If we were lucky and none of the new arrivals were bull calves, we would keep and raise all the new calves on our farm. Occasionally, Grandpa would

Calf Lady

sell a female calf to one of his regular customers if the newborn was from a new heifer or happened to be from a mediocre dairy cow that wasn't a particularly good milk producer.

Our dairy had an excellent reputation for producing healthy animals, and we constantly got phone calls from people inquiring about baby calves for sale. Buyers never had to wonder if a new calf from Willow Grove might have a health issue, which was a significant concern with animals purchased from the public stockyard. Grandpa's customers knew they could always count on buying a *healthy* calf at a *fair* price.

I will never forget one couple who came to the farm several times each year to buy calves. During their visits, the couple would stand alongside their bland-colored, aged pickup truck in the barnyard driveway and talk with Grandpa. The thing that amazed me so much about the couple and why I remember them so vividly was their appearance and mannerisms. Both were always dressed alike in men's traditional pinstriped gray bib overalls, men's high-top work shoes, and pastel blue long-sleeved work shirts tucked inside their overalls. The only way I could tell which one was the husband and which was the wife—other than when they spoke—was that the tall, slim individual had a softball-sized bun of very coarse salt-n-pepper hair stuffed up under a lofty railroad cap, the same type of cap that a railroad engineer and fireman for the Baltimore & Ohio Railroad would wear. Also, the woman's shorter husband had a noticeably round

Willow Grove: A Boy, A Family, A Farm

paunch, much like the potbelly of a man who imbibed his share of bottled beer. The intriguing little man, nearly always, had both hands planted deep down inside the side pockets of his overalls.

The lady did most of the talking and made all the final decisions. It was fascinating to watch her carry on a dialogue with my grandfather. She talked, acted, and gestured with her hands, just like a man. She even mimicked her husband with both of her hands tucked in the pockets of her bib overalls. She always contributed worthwhile information about animal husbandry during her conversations with Grandpa. She was also knowledgeable about the local economy and noticeably opinionated regarding local politics. The lady's lively, captivating laugh portrayed her as an all-around happy individual who genuinely enjoyed life and being around people. She certainly enjoyed socializing and purchasing baby calves from my grandfather. I stood quietly, always a short distance behind the trio, staring and listening to the odd, funny couple. I was sort of mesmerized!

The couple was more than pleased with their new Holstein calf. At Grandpa's behest, I ran and obtained an empty feed sack from inside the dairy barn. Working together, the couple carefully hoisted the baby calf up off the ground. Its hind legs were lowered first into the gunny sack, which Grandpa and I were holding wide open. With only the calf's head sticking out of the burlap, the witty lady used baling twine to tie the sack taut around the calf's neck, immobilizing the little animal. Confinement in

Calf Lady

the gunny sack was just enough to prohibit the calf from standing up and possibly hurting itself during transit in the back of the pick-up truck. If the weather was chilly, the burlap bag would ride up front in the cab on the passenger-side floorboard. The black and white spotted baby calf would travel on the floorboard between the husband's feet while his wife drove.

During all the trips that the couple made to Willow Grove over nearly a decade, there was never any discussion or negotiation about the price of the calf they were purchasing from Grandpa. When it was time to load the calf, the happy lady would reach into her pocket and pull out a healthy wad of money wound tightly and ringed with a sturdy rubber band. With the band removed, one bill after another was peeled off and handed individually to Grandpa. When the lady stopped, she would ask: "You surrre that's enough?" Grandpa would nod positively and verbally confirm his approval. Grandpa had one price for new bull calves, and every one of his customers knew the price was firm and more than fair. There was never any need for negotiation!

Farm Chores: Watermelon

One planting season, Dad and Grandpa decided to grow several acres of cantaloupe and watermelon in the field that bordered the main county road. The crop of melons was bountiful. Hundreds of solid green and striped watermelons were lying on the ground, waiting to be picked. Interspersed among the watermelons were hearty, cream-colored cantaloupes.

Watermelon party!

Each day, Grandpa would select dozens of watermelons and cantaloupes that were ready to be picked. He would twist the brown stems off the end of the ripe melons so Bob and I would know which melons to carry to the side of the road. Later, all the ripe melons were loaded onto a wagon. The luscious-looking melons were stacked in a pyramid on the wagon, parked a few feet from the main road. The colorful pile of watermelons was a welcome attraction for hungry motorists. Invariably, the prospective customer would thump the side of the watermelon with one of his middle fingers,

Farm Chores: Watermelon

which confirmed that the melon was ripe and ready for the kitchen table. The price was 10 cents each, and most of the time we worked on the honor system. Grandpa didn't get rich but certainly enjoyed the enterprising spirit and the opportunity to talk with interesting strangers and neighbors.

Almost daily, we would take a couple of big watermelons to the milk house and drop them in the milk cooler, filled to the brim with ice-cold water. Later, we would grab one of the cold melons out of the tank and drop it onto the concrete walkway outside the milk house, where it would break into several pieces. Thirsty and hungry, we would reach for a chunk from the deep-red center of the melon and devour it to our hearts' delight. What a delicious snack on a hot summer day after being in the dusty hayfield under the roasting sun!

High Standards Start at Home

Growing up on a lively, working dairy farm in a rural community was an enjoyable and rewarding experience. It was also pleasing to attend a high school with an average class size of 30 and where several of my cousins excelled, both academically and athletically. The small-school culture and friendly atmosphere provided a solid educational and social grounding, which positively focused and guided me during my developmental years. I'm grateful for having had such a wonderful family, caring schoolteachers, and older cousins who set high academic and social standards for me and our younger relatives.

As a young woman, my grandmother had been a schoolteacher, living away from home in the community where she taught. As a former teacher, she retained a keen interest in education and enjoyed teaching Bob and me. I spent many hours seated beside her while she helped me with my school homework.

My grandmother, Nannie.

During the school term and typically after supper, Grandma often walked into our part of the house and questioned my brothers and me about our homework. Almost always, one of us followed her back to her kitchen to work on our school assignments. I remember spending a lot of time with Grandma going over each of my subjects. She would sit in her rocking chair next to the fireplace while I sat beside her. If I had a spelling test the next day, she would correctly pronounce each word for me, after which I would pronounce and spell it. She made sure I understood the definition, knew its number of syllables, and was able to use the specific word correctly in a sentence. We would go over the entire list of words until my bedtime or until I could correctly spell every word in the assignment.

On other evenings, we worked on my reading and math assignments. Grandma especially liked to show me how to diagram a sentence. Together we dissected and analyzed every sentence in a paragraph. She wanted me to understand the significance and relationship between every word in a sentence. She had me identify the subject, predicate, modifiers, et al., and subsequently showed me how to draw an actual line diagram for every word in the sentence. After seven decades, I still have and occasionally refer to my original copy of the *Plain English Handbook* that my grandmother and I used during those study sessions in her kitchen in Willow Grove in the 1950s.

Working on my homework with my grandmother was a fun way to learn. During our study sessions, Aunt Jack would sit quietly in her twin rocking chair on the opposite side of the fireplace, crocheting, reading, or politely listening to our homework dialog.

High School

I started my seventh year of public education at Ravenswood High School in 1951 and was privileged to attend the school through my sophomore year. I appreciated the opportunity to continue my studies in a small-school atmosphere. A truly rewarding benefit of attending Ravenswood schools was the number of my cousins in elementary, middle, and high school. I had cousins in every one of the six grades in middle and high school. There were four cousins alone in the eighth-grade class.

My four grandparents were natives of Jackson County. All came from large families and, for the most part, resided in Jackson County. My father's parents had a combined total of 17 siblings. My mother's parents had a total of 15 siblings. Consequently, those 32 relatives engendered numerous cousins who attended the same two Ravenswood schools that I did. The teachers in both schools had previously taught several of my older cousins and were already well acquainted with their parents and forthcoming younger brothers and sisters who would eventually enroll in their classes.

Having so many cousins in the same school created an enjoyable atmosphere. Several of my older cousins excelled academically and achieved

High School

respected reputations. Carol Franklin; Bill, Archie, and June Barber; Pete Carmichael; John Paul, Eddie, and Dottie McCoy; and Richard, Teddy, Bill, Joann, and Mary Sück were older cousins who attended the same Ravenswood schools before or during my tenure.

Dottie McCoy.

All the boys were good athletes and excelled in football and basketball—the two most popular sports in Jackson County schools in the 1950s. Cousins Joann and Mary Sück and Dottie McCoy were members of the Ravenswood High School marching band. Dottie was head cheerleader for the Red Devils' basketball and football varsity teams. During her junior and senior years, Dottie was one of the school's homecoming princesses, marching

Willow Grove: A Boy, A Family, A Farm

band president, and a member of the student council.

That's Charlotte Monroe to the left, and the majorettes to the right are as follows: First row: Jigger McGraw, Doris Jean Suck; Second row: June "Sis" Suck, Pat White; Third row: Kay Buffington, Dee Ann Moore; Top: Jean Anne Suck.
Photo of the majorettes courtesy of June "Sis" Suck Hicks.
Photo of Charlotte Monroe is courtesy of Connie McCoy Wright.

The town was equally proud of its school band. In 1952, Head Majorette Charlotte Monroe won the World Junior Two-Baton Twirling Championship. Charlotte led the marching band onto the football field during half-time at Friday night football games. Charlotte's performances in front of Friday night football fans and celebration parades on Washington Street were always proud moments for

High School

loyal Ravenswood students, fans, and spectators. The crowd would stand, cheer, and applaud as Charlotte marched under the goal post, across the center of the field, well out in front of six other majorettes and sixty band members. Her upper torso arched backward so far behind her high-stepping boots that it was amazing how she could remain upright, let alone twirl and toss two batons high in the air at the same time.

Majorettes Jean Ann, Doris Jean, and June Sück were in the same class and all three were popular students among their classmates. Jean Ann was head majorette of the marching band's seven majorettes during her junior and senior years. Mary and Joanne Sück and Dottie McCoy were talented band members. My cousins' athletic and academic prowess, combined with their laudatory reputations in the local community, established high standards and were excellent role models. Cousin James Conrad McCoy and I were in the same class and were lucky beneficiaries of prior accomplishments of his siblings and many other cousins.

I was a freshman in high school before I became more than a little infatuated with the principal's daughter. Mitzi was an all-American young lady. She was distinctively attractive and popular with all of her classmates. Mitzi had two older sisters who were equally attractive and, just as James Conrad had two older brothers, Mitzi and James Conrad benefited socially from having older siblings as role models.

Willow Grove: A Boy, A Family, A Farm

Mitzi was a classmate for only a short time. Her father accepted a new opportunity in the school system in Princeton, West Virginia, and, during our freshman year, the family left Ravenswood. In the interim, Mitzi and I only saw each other in the classroom, hallway, or on our daily walk to the cafeteria.

I lived in distant Willow Grove and did not have my driver's license. I was too young to drive and until I got my license, it was a foregone conclusion that dating was out of the question. Dating never entered my mind and I never questioned the disadvantage while living in Willow Grove. I happily settled for a slumber party picture of Mitzi with a fervent note that was passed to me by another friendly classmate of ours.

James Conrad and I never talked about anything that involved girls. After I left Ravenswood, distance and time slowly morphed our best-friend relationship into memories of the "good ole days," when neither one of us had a care in the world. Life had been so good, I could sleep standing up!

As I was writing about James Conrad and our elementary and high school years, I couldn't help but wonder where his demeanor and the way he carried himself...came from. He certainly had a big influence on me, but who influenced him? There is no doubt that his older brothers John Paul and Eddie were major contributors. I can't prove it, but anecdotally, I believe James Conrad's father, my Uncle Conrad, had a profound influence on his son.

High School

So much so, that I believe James Conrad's teenage years would mirror Uncle Conrad's.

Without question, both James Conrad and his father were important in shaping my character during my formative years. And, at an early age, my best friend must have been exposed, unwittingly, to the Greek philosopher Socrates: "The key to a good reputation is to endeavor to be what you desire to appear." This is a superb character trait that fits James Conrad McCoy, and his father, perfectly.

Coach Bill

I was in eighth grade when cousin Bill Sück volunteered to coach a group of eager boys who wanted to play competitive basketball. The high school varsity team mainly consisted of seniors and juniors, while the junior varsity was chiefly sophomores and freshmen. Both teams had school-sponsored team practices and scheduled competitive Home and Away games. There was no such school-sponsored program for the lower grades. So, with Coach Jones' support, Bill did a big favor for the younger boys and organized a team of seventh- and eighth-grade students.

After the last class of the day, several of us boys would go to the gym, change clothes, and gather on the gymnasium floor. Our practices were scheduled to not interfere with the varsity team practices. But when there was a conflict, we moved to the antiquated former gym located in the back of the main school building. Bill was very conscientious

Willow Grove: A Boy, A Family, A Farm

about his coaching responsibilities, and, to help sustain the team's enthusiasm, he even organized a few competitive games with comparable teams in other public schools in the county.

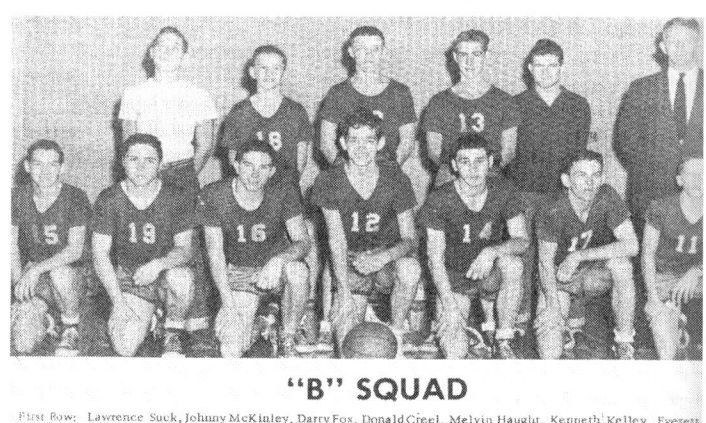

"B" SQUAD

First Row: Lawrence Suck, Johnny McKinley, Darry Fox, Donald Creel, Melvin Haught, Kenneth Kelley, Everett
Second Row: Tom Bish-Manager, Bud Knapp, Bill Rardin, Junior Click, Ward King-Manager, Coach Merrifield

All the boys on Bill's team took the opportunity to play basketball very seriously and worked exceedingly hard during practices. Periodically, Bill would divide the players into red and white teams and organize a regulation game in the modern varsity gymnasium. It was a special time for the team. Bill would get one of his classmates to operate the colorful scoreboard hanging high on the wall above the glistening hardwood floor. The scorekeeper was a senior student who knew how to operate the giant scoreboard, including the timer, buzzer, and the actual score for the Home and Visitor teams.

We never had many spectators in the bleachers, and, when we did, it was usually the parents who

Coach Bill

had arrived early to take their sons home after practice. The fact that we didn't have many spectators didn't matter to us. We enjoyed the camaraderie and the opportunity to play real competitive basketball in the beautiful gymnasium.

Coach Bill.
Photo courtesy of Bill's sister, June (Sis) Suck Hicks.

Coach Bill would frequently be the only referee on the floor during scrimmages. Bill wasn't overweight but did carry an extra pound or two, which slightly hampered his running prowess, since he had to referee both ends of the court. He was constantly sprinting back and forth from one end of the court to the other. Moreover, as he was running, he frequently blew his whistle to stop or start play and give fundamental coaching instructions to his players. In essence, every time our coach refereed a competitive practice—all by himself. He was a busy coach!

During one scrimmage, coach Bill was beginning to show more than normal fatigue. Like the rest of the players, his jersey was completely soaked, and beads of sweat were dripping from his forehead and off the tip of his nose. Bill wasn't running as fast as he normally did, and each successive trip from one end of the court to the other was noticeably slower. Even his whistle was subdued. During scrimmage, a teammate, racing and dribbling the basketball at full throttle, plowed into a defensive player, resulting in a major collision and pileup of three players underneath the basket. The crash resulted in knocked heads and a lot of moaning and groaning from all three players. Suddenly, we realized that our coach was in the mix and was lying on his back on the hardwood floor. Furthermore, he wasn't moving at all. Bill was down for the count.

Promptly, the whole team formed a tight circle around Bill and stood fixated, staring straight down at our coach, lying prostrate on his back. No one had any suggestions about what we could or should do to help—we just stared. Happily, we were relieved when we noticed our coach was beginning to squirm slightly and attempting to open his eyes. The team was thankful that we hadn't killed our coach. Bill was a good sport and didn't make us run laps while he gathered his senses.

Coach Bill

Bill was a committed student-coach and worked hard to ensure the team had a good time, while simultaneously improving as basketball players. He wasn't about to disappoint head coach Jones, nor his small squad of bustling, aspiring basketball players. It wasn't a simple task to organize a team. It took patience, valuable personal time, and sincere commitment to arrange formal games with nearby schools. Bill was a high school student and all the hours he devoted to our basketball team was time he could have spent working on his own priorities, both academic and social. All of his players appreciated coach Bill's generosity. I'm not sure, but I'm confident the team had the presence of mind to show our appreciation with a token bestowal.

Coach Jones

Bill Jones was the head coach for the varsity football, basketball, and baseball teams at Ravenswood High. Coach Jones was a jovial, full-bodied gentleman who expected and received a superior competitive spirit from all his varsity participants. My first memories of Coach Jones were at Friday night football games, which I occasionally attended with my parents and brothers. My father enjoyed watching his nephews John Paul and Eddie McCoy and relative Pete Carmichael play football under the tutelage of Coach Jones.

Willow Grove: A Boy, A Family, A Farm

The home team uniform was all-white with a narrow red stripe on both the jersey and pants. At the beginning of the game, the uniforms were spiffy white under the bright stadium floodlights. Coach Jones made sure the clean uniforms didn't remain snowy white very long! During the Friday night competition, Coach Jones paced incessantly back and forth along the sideline with a rigid roll of paper, wound up tight in his right hand, which he used habitually to strike the palm of his left hand. He often used the paper baton to convey a message to one of his players when he hurried to the sidelines for instructions. Coach would augment his message by thumping the player's shoulder pads or helmet with his paper rod. From time to time Coach Jones utilized his former football prowess to demonstrate a critical point to his team. He was a physical coach and demanded that his team play at full intensity from the very beginning to the end of the game. His coaching style produced many winning football games for the proud Ravenswood residents and loyal fans. The town and school loved their Red Devils and supported them with their financial generosity and faithful attendance.

Five of my cousins—Eddie and James McCoy, Richard, Bill, and Teddy Sück—all played varsity football under Coach Jones during my freshman year. Richard, Eddie, and Bill were seniors; Teddy was a sophomore; and James was a freshman. All were above-average athletes. Richard was the varsity quarterback, and Eddie was a running

Coach Jones

back. Eddie was such an outstanding running back that when a couple of his ribs were cracked during a game, Coach Jones had a special chest device constructed that shielded his rib cage and enabled him to play the balance of the football season.

In 1951, Coach Jones' extra-point team consisted of one player—not like today's typical placeholder and soccer-style kicker. As soon as the football was hiked, Eddie Leeson would catch and instantly drop the football, nose first to the ground. At the exact instant the nose of the football touched the ground, he would kick the football end-over-end through the goal post uprights. A drop kick for an extra point after a touchdown was a rare talent, which was interesting to watch in the early 1950s.

John Paul McCoy.   Eddie McCoy.
John Paul's photo courtesy of Connie McCoy Wright.

Willow Grove: A Boy, A Family, A Farm

I enjoyed football, but didn't weigh enough to compete effectively with many of my peers on the team. To even participate, I had to play with extra determination and enthusiasm. Growing up, I was an active kid and burned a lot of calories running when I could have been walking. I drank too much water and ate too little weight-gaining foods. As a freshman, I weighed 140 pounds and remember asking my mother what I could do to put on some extra weight. I was as lean as a racing greyhound and needed more muscle and a few pounds of body fat.

One afternoon in late August, at the beginning of my sophomore year, the varsity and junior varsity football teams were practicing before the official football season kickoff. I was playing defense on the junior varsity team and having a good practice. Before the scrimmage was over, assistant Coach Virgil Hupp, who was my mother's first cousin, grabbed me by the shoulder pads and walked with me to the other end of the field, where the varsity team was practicing. He spoke to Coach Jones, and, the next thing I knew, I was in the backfield defending against the varsity offense. Even though I had been having a good practice, I now had the distinct feeling that the fun was about to end.

Quarterback and cousin Richard Sück, on the very first play, kept the football and successfully scrambled to his right with a clear field ahead. Unfortunately, I suddenly became the only speed bump between the end zone and the rambling

Coach Jones

quarterback. Richard was an 180-pound-plus senior and for me to tackle him was simply wishful thinking. Regardless, I knew what I had to do, and, despite my mental anxiety that "this was not going to be good," I scampered toward my cousin as fast as I could. I had a good angle and was able to dive headfirst between Richard's colossal legs. I wrapped both arms around one leg and held on with all the strength I could muster. All I did was slow Richard down, but not by much!

Front: Junior Click, me (33), Alan Reynolds, Richard McCoy, John Staats. Standing: Jim Purdy, James McCoy, Bill Rardin, Paul Jarrett, John McKinley.

During the few seconds that I was wrapped around his leg, Richard was still galloping and at the same time trying to shake off a pesky, overzealous "chihuahua." I hung on until help arrived from one of my teammates, which was not nearly soon enough. I felt like I was being run over by a runaway, stomping, six-legged workhorse.

Willow Grove: A Boy, A Family, A Farm

After the whistle blew, I managed to pick myself up off the ground and shake off the consequence of running headfirst into a brick wall. I'm sure the coaches spotted the gaggle of geese whirling around my head. I didn't last long and was sent back to scrimmage with the junior varsity—which was fine with me.

Half-Time Entertainment by Mart Moore

Mart Moore was a favorite personality of the high school students and faculty. He was an extremely polite, shy, older gentleman who worked as the Ravenswood High School custodian and was always willing to help with any extra custodial duties. Mart wore denim bib overalls every day, and did most of his chores when classes were in progress. Between classes, when students were walking the corridors from one classroom to another, Mart would disappear by ducking into an empty room or quietly conceal himself in some inconspicuous spot. Mart had the faculty and student body's genuine respect and admiration.

Mart attended every home basketball game. Clad in his customary charcoal overalls, Mart was an enjoyable part of the half-time entertainment at home basketball games—and the students and citizens of Ravenswood loved every minute of it. Mart would push an extremely wide dust mop over every inch of the polished basketball floor during halftime. The whole time, spectators would watch

Half-Time Entertainment by Mart Moore

his subtle antics. It would take Mart about five minutes to traverse the entire basketball court.

As soon as Mart completed his last round trip with his dust mop, the audience would watch him —with eagerness—as he moseyed over to the end of the gymnasium. Mart would pick up a basketball and walk out to the center court, where he would grip it waist-high between both palms. With a sheepish grin, he would gesture that he was ready to shoot the basketball. All the while, the students raucously encouraged Mart to perform for the audience. At mid-court, with his hands placed on opposite sides of the basketball, Mart would, ever so slowly, with both arms completely extended, lower the basketball down between his legs and then heave it high into the air toward the basket. Mart would make several attempts and often drill the basket from the center court. As soon as Mart scored, his fans roared with blissful approval. Mart would grin, absorb the moment, and then, full of pride, walk off the floor.

Scarred for Life

Running in the high school corridors was strictly prohibited, which was precisely what Earl Balis and I were doing when I came extremely close to seriously severing leaders and arteries on the inside of my right wrist. Earl was chasing me in the basement hallway outside Mr. Rinehart's classroom. As we approached the end of the narrow hallway, I placed the palms of both hands on the

Willow Grove: A Boy, A Family, A Farm

wide horizontal door bar. After opening the door, I planned to hustle up the concrete steps and flee into the schoolyard. Unfortunately, the horizontal bar didn't unlatch the door before Earl caught up with me, and he accidentally bumped my right elbow, forcing my fist through one of the glass panes in the door. As I instinctively pulled my hand back through the broken window, a jagged edge of glass severed my wrist. The cut was in the shape of the letter L and extended about four inches from the joint of my wrist, up the inside of my arm. Instantly, I pressed my left thumb above the cut, which immediately slowed the loss of blood hemorrhaging from the gaping, ugly wound.

 Earl and I walked back to our classroom, where I showed the laceration to Mr. Rinehart, our homeroom teacher, while applying pressure on the cut. I don't recall our excuse, but I suspect that neither Earl nor I revealed precisely what caused the accident. But I remember that Mr. Rinehart wasn't too pleased with either of us and didn't seem overly concerned that I was dripping blood down my pant leg. He must have suspected we'd been horsing around and was politely disgusted with both of us. He had a class to teach and no time for foolishness. After a limited exchange, Mr. Rinehart directed me to go to the doctor's office and charged Earl to go with me.

 So, off we went to Dr. Monroe's office. During our short power walk, I applied pressure with my left thumb and fingers wrapped firmly around my wrist. Earl and I were ashamed of our reckless

Scarred for Life

behavior and just wanted to get to the doctor's office and return to Mr. Rinehart's classroom as more mature and responsible students.

We didn't have to explain why we were in the doctor's office. Dr. Monroe took me by the arm and quickly paraded the two of us into his back office. I remember that one wall was lined with different-sized glass bottles filled mostly with white-colored drugs and various other containers identified as medical supplies. Dr. Monroe cleaned my bloody wrist and advised me that I would be fine. The long L-shaped slash missed the main tendons and, luckily, the primary arteries and veins were spared as well. After Dr. Monroe closed the wound with several stitches, Earl and I left his office and returned to our classroom.

When Earl and I entered the doctor's office, we might have had a total of 10 cents between the two of us, if any silver at all. We left without a bill for the doctor's medical care. I'm sure my mother called his office, and I'm equally confident Dr. Monroe waived the entire medical bill.

Sixty-seven years later, a portion of the scar from the laceration remains legible. Distinct white dots on both sides of the actual cut show the exact spot of a few of the stitches embroidered by Dr. Monroe. Over decades, I have sometimes glanced at the inside of my wrist and thought of the incident, Earl, and Dr. Monroe.

Willow Grove: A Boy, A Family, A Farm

While the Sun Shines

It was a blisteringly hot August afternoon. The year was 1953. My older cousin Dewey Gene Davis had graduated from Parkersburg High School and was living in the big house with my parents, brothers, grandparents, and Aunt Jack. He was comfortably ensconced on the second floor in the historic guest bedroom, with its 1900s-period fireplace. The bedroom was furnished with a handsome four-piece bedroom suite built in 1840 by our great-great-grandfather Justus Fredrick Sück's brother, Fredrick Augustus Sück. Originally, the cherry four-poster bed used manila rope, which crisscrossed horizontally from head to foot and side to side to hold a fabric bag filled with straw or goose down that would have been placed on top of the open-weave rope. By the time Dewey Gene slept on the historic bed, he slept on a box spring and modern-day mattress.

It was early afternoon. Dewey Gene and I climbed up on the back of the big, two-ton farm truck, and dangled our legs off the rear of the truck bed. Both of our hands were braced down against the sides of our hips, ready to firmly anchor our derrieres to the truck bed during the short and sometimes bumpy ride to the hayfield. Along with our pitchforks and Dad behind the steering wheel, we were on our way to the hayfield at the far end of the farm.

Riding on the back of the truck to the hayfield was always fun. We enjoyed the soothing sensation

While the Sun Shines

of the breeze striking our bare backs as the truck sped up the lane. Vapors of dust would swirl up from the parched roadbed as we crossed over the county road and continued straight for another quarter of a mile.

Right after the county road, the lane changed abruptly from a hard-packed gravel base to a sandy surface. During extended periods of dry weather, the beach-like section of the lane would become so soft that Dad would have to shift to a lower gear, unless he was traveling pretty fast, when the truck's front wheels plowed into the sandy spot in the road. When the dual rear wheels hit the sand, the truck's bed would drop abruptly and kick sideways. With our feet dangling down from the rear of the truck bed, our buttocks would go airborne, and land with such a jolt that afterward a little massaging was in order. If you didn't have a firm grip on the edge of the truck bed, you could easily find yourself tumbling off as the truck continued onward. Invariably, one of us would be laughing while the other was groaning and massaging his posterior. Too, occasionally the driver—not Dad, but one of us boys—would amuse himself by deliberately driving over a pothole and, at the same time, glance through the rear-view window as our butts bounced up off the bed of the truck and then came crashing back down with a wallop. Turnabout was fair play, and each of us would remember these shenanigans the next time it was our turn to drive the empty truck back to the hayfield.

Willow Grove: A Boy, A Family, A Farm

As soon as Dad reached the hayfield, he headed to where the New Holland hay-loader, appearing majestically tall and picturesque, waited patiently for our return. As soon as Dewey Gene and I jumped off the truck, we expanded our chests with a big gulp of air, flexed our shoulder muscles, and muttered a low sigh. The fun was over, and now the hard part was about to begin.

The red Ford truck pulled the eight-foot-wide hay-loader while it swept loose hay up off of the ground and flicked it onto a steep incline. Once the hay landed on the incline, alternating columns of steel fingers grabbed it and pulled and pushed the continuous stream to the top of the loader. At the top, the fluffy alfalfa was forced onto a short platform, where it dropped onto the back of the moving truck. From the time the loose hay was flicked up off the ground, it would take about a minute for the hay to reach the top of the hay-loader and free-fall into the truck bed.

The amount of hay scooped up off the ground was determined by how dense the hay was in the windrow and how fast the truck was traveling. The revolutions per minute of the two large wheels on the hay-loader determined the amount of hay the loader would pour down onto the back of the truck. Once the flow of hay started raining down onto the truck bed, it would continue like water over a dam until either the driver stopped the truck or we ran out of hay at the end of the windrow. After each trip to the barn to unload, we would often take turns driving the now-empty truck back to the hayfield.

While the Sun Shines

Positioning loose hay with a pitchfork on a flat surface without tall side racks required patience and skill. The goal was to load as much hay as possible on the truck and then haul the load from the hayfield to the barn without any of the hay slipping off. Cured hay can be slippery, so every pitchfork of loose hay had to be placed carefully. Without exception, the man who positioned the hay had better do a good job. If the chore wasn't done right, too often the truck wouldn't make it onto the road without hay falling off.

Driving the truck was by far the best job in the hayfield. The only thing the driver had to do was straddle the row of hay with the truck's front wheels and proceed slowly down the row. However, not just anyone was allowed to drive the truck to the barn after it was fully loaded. Driving across the flat surface of the hayfield was easy, but driving into and out of the shallow drainage ditch along the lane without some of the loose, slick hay ending up on the ground wasn't. The truck would dip to one side and then to the other as its front and rear wheels gyrated in and out of the drainage ditch. If the driver let the truck dip a little too much or was driving a little too fast, a portion of hay would slide off. A careless driver could easily cause part of the load to end up on the side of the road. If that happened, the driver would endure castigation from everyone. The hay would have to be manhandled back onto the truck, and a lot of hard work would have to be duplicated, which was not a good thing.

Willow Grove: A Boy, A Family, A Farm

Reloading the hay was a hot and sweaty job. We hated to load the same hay twice!

It was getting late in the afternoon, and everyone, including the driver, was getting very tired. Our legs were slightly bowed, and our butts felt like they were dragging on the ground! While ambling up to the hay-loader, we instinctively scanned the hayfield and guessed at how many more loads of green alfalfa were still lying on the ground: Dewey Gene thought there were two full-sized loads left; I guessed there were maybe three; and Jimmy Ice said we were both wrong. I was getting tired and suggested we make this our last load for the day and finish tomorrow, though there was a fair chance of rain within the next 24 hours. My suggestion was not to be! We were going to work in the field until the very last stem of newly cut alfalfa was off the ground and safe inside the barn.

Back at the barn, after hoisting and dropping the last giant fork load of hay in the hayloft, Dewey Gene and I ventured into the milk house—as we always did after every load of hay—and savored a long swig of cool well water. While in the milk house, we noticed that the big hand on the oval clock was sneaking up on four o'clock. This meant that Dad would have to remain behind at the barn so he could assemble the milking equipment and ready the cows for the late afternoon milking. Mom, Bob, and Grandpa had already left to go round up the dairy cows in the distant hill pasture field.

Back in the hayfield, I guided Jimmy to the exact spot so he could fasten the hay-loader to the

While the Sun Shines

truck. After the hay-loader was hooked, Dewey Gene and I rolled back onto the bed of the truck. Dewey Gene took his usual position under the hay-loader chute while I leaned on my four-prong pitchfork directly behind the cab. The truck started down the windrow, and huge gobs of loose hay began to flow like water. The hay dropped onto the floor of the truck, where Dewey Gene would stab a forkful and send it airborne in my direction. My job was to carefully spread the hay evenly over the truck bed. The loose hay continued to flow, and it wasn't long before Dewey Gene and I were standing on top of a perfect load of hay that I had carefully finessed, one slow, deliberate fork-full at a time.

The truck was almost half loaded when we saw a white sedan speeding across the hayfield heading in our direction. When the car got closer, we could see Grandpa driving his four-door Chevrolet. Jimmy stopped the truck, and we watched as the vehicle sped toward us. Grandpa tended to have a heavy foot. He pulled up beside the driver's side of the truck and motioned for Jimmy to get out of the truck. Grandpa said it was time for Jimmy to help Dad milk the cows. Milking is a two-man chore, and Jimmy was Dad's regular sidekick in the dairy barn.

Immediately, Dewey Gene and I grinned at each other and, for a few seconds, believed our day in the hot, dusty hayfield was over. We'd soon be heading back to the barn. Our upper bodies were matted with a thick, brownish-green layer of alfalfa dust. The only white spot on our shirtless bodies was around our lips, which we kept white by periodically licking them with our thirsty tongues.

Surprise! Just as fast as Grandpa arrived in the hayfield, he quickly wiped the hopeful smiles off our faces. He emphasized that there was a good chance of rain showers late tonight and that it was important to get *all* the hay out of the field and into the hayloft before the day was over. We both clearly understood what Grandpa was saying! We would be working in the hayfield for several more hours, well after our usual supper time! And we were already hungry.

Besides being hungry and having to work late, another reason Grandpa's appearance in the hayfield wasn't good—Grandpa would be driving the truck. Without saying a word, Dewey Gene and I looked at each other and rolled our eyes. Our facial expressions revealed more than a little apprehension, and in unison, we thought to ourselves, *We'd better fasten our seat belts*. We had enough experience with Grandpa in the hayfield that we were not looking forward to our grandfather behind the steering wheel. Grandpa had "a lead foot"—which is fine if you are on a racetrack but not so good if you are working on the back of a truck pulling a hay-loader down a windrow of bountiful hay. The reader needs to remember that the amount of loose hay the loader picks up off the ground and deposits like a waterfall onto the back of the truck is directly proportional to the speed of the truck pulling the hay-loader. The faster the

While the Sun Shines

truck, the faster hay will cascade down from the top of the loader onto the truck.

As usual, Grandpa immediately shifted the red farm truck into second gear, instead of the preferred *first* gear, and commenced down the windrow of hay—as if the looming rainstorm would arrive any minute. Grandpa was in a hurry to get the hay in the barn—and at the speed he was traveling, it wasn't going to take long. In a few seconds, like muddy water over Niagara Falls, a nonstop, colossal amount of loose hay began falling at Gene's feet. And almost as fast as the hay fell, Gene hurled a continuous blizzard of hay toward me. Gene's pitchfork never stopped! With his head bent, he was downright slinging hay as if his life depended on it! If Gene didn't remove all the hay falling from the hay-loader, he would quickly find himself buried underneath a mountain of alfalfa. Gene was thrusting hay toward me so fast that the blur of his swinging arms reminded me of a runaway steam locomotive in an old silent movie. His pitchfork was so hot that I'm surprised it didn't catch the hay on fire.

Now get this! My job was to very carefully...and very meticulously...place every pitchfork...precisely in the right spot so that I could build a beautiful, uniform, magnificent pyramid of loose hay high upon the bed of the truck. After a minute or two, it was apparent that I was heading for an absolute disaster. Both Gene and I were moving faster than a "one-legged man at an ass-kicking contest"! There was absolutely no way we were going to stay afloat

Willow Grove: A Boy, A Family, A Farm

in the ocean of hay that we were swimming in. Dewey Gene was in the throes of going down for the third time. And for me—all I could do was either jump off the truck or drown along with Gene under an avalanche of hay. Even though the battle was lost, we weren't about to sound an alarm to abandon ship. Normally, we would bang our fist on top of the cab and yell, "Slow the H down!" But not with Grandpa at the helm!

Dewey Gene and I worked as vigorously as we possibly could. Regardless of how desperately we tried to keep ahead of the hay-loader, it was an impossibility and an absolute fiasco! The hay kept piling up and up! We just couldn't move fast enough to handle the enormous amount of hay thrown at us! Consequently, it wasn't long before I inadvertently hurled a huge pitch-fork full of hay over the top of the cab. Of course, the big glob of hay landed smack dab on the driver's side of the windshield. Immediately, there was a blackout in the cab of the truck. Grandpa couldn't see a thing! The big lump of hay was glued to his side of the windshield, and Grandpa couldn't tell where the truck was heading. He jammed the clutch to the floorboard and stomped hard on the brake pedal. The truck came to an abrupt halt, hurling both of us like a shot out of a cannon against the back of the cab.

Before exiting the truck, Grandpa looked in the outside rear-view mirror and saw airborne hay flying in all directions. At first glance, Grandpa must have reasoned that a mini tornado from the

While the Sun Shines

impending rainstorm had already caught up with us. Yet, if he momentarily believed high winds were the culprit, his assumption changed quickly. Within seconds, Grandpa jumped out of the truck and shouted: "What in the Sam Hill are you two doing back there? That is the sorriest-looking load of hay I've ever seen in my life!"

Gene and I didn't say a word except "Yes sir; No sir; Yes sir." We just hugged our pitchforks and stood motionless on top of the messy pile of hay, catching our breath, grateful that the truck's wheels had stopped turning.

Grandpa realized that the two of us were working as hard as we could and were doing our best. Without looking at us, he whirled around and said, "Now get back to work," as he stepped up on the running board and climbed back up into the cab.

Thankfully, this time Grandpa started down the windrow in first gear. Hay was arriving at the top of the hay-loader at a much more reasonable pace. And, as we fully expected, the slow pace didn't last very long. Grandpa stayed in first gear for a while, then gradually morphed back to his renowned "lead-foot" pace. Ever so slowly, he pressed the accelerator pedal a little closer to the floorboard, and—once again, hay started rolling over the top of the hay-loader at a rapid pace. Fortunately, we were close to having a full load, and the truck would have to stop before too long.

On the way back to the barn with our load of hay, Gene and I agreed we had to sneak a

Willow Grove: A Boy, A Family, A Farm

desperate message to Mom that we needed a replacement driver. We wanted Mom to convince Grandpa that she had supper already prepared and she had time to help Dewey Gene and me in the hayfield. Mom understood Grandpa better than anyone in the family and was always a trooper about helping out, especially when an SOS was being sent from an exhausted hayfield duo. I knew Mom could convince Grandpa that he needed his rest.

We returned to the dairy barn with the load of hay, and, without delay, Grandpa drove the loaded truck up the earthen ramp on the side of the barn and stopped in the center of the sturdy wood floor in the hayloft. Grandpa insisted! No time to waste! We had to unload the truck and head back as quickly as possible. The old adage "Make hay when the sun shines" was certainly apropos today!

Any time we were in the hayloft and it was after four o'clock, Dad was directly beneath us on the ground floor milking the dairy cows. In the floor of the hayloft, next to where the truck was parked, was an opening about three-foot square that linked the hayloft to the first floor of the dairy barn. During the winter, hay was tossed down the hole to feed the dairy cattle. When the opening wasn't being used, the safety cover was always kept closed so that no one could accidentally fall through the portal and land on the concrete walkway below.

Dewey Gene and I had almost decided to wait on Dad to stick his head up through the opening, to see how we were doing. Yet, if Dad happened to be

While the Sun Shines

unusually busy, he wouldn't be able to walk away from the milking machines, even for a couple of minutes. So, before we started unloading the truck, we both raced to the milk house to quench our thirst and hose off our hot heads with cool water. My brothers, Dewey Gene, and I never wore shirts during warm summer days, but we did wear traditional Levi's to protect our legs from the prickly stems when we manhandled bales of hay. Our bronzed, tanned backs were constantly painted with a thick layer of sage-colored dust anytime we worked in the hayfield and hayloft. Our lips and eyes were the only natural-looking parts of our whole body. Our nostrils would be nearly plugged with sweet-smelling alfalfa dust, which required lots of water to remove. This is probably why allergies were essentially nonexistent among many country boys like me and my brothers: From a very young age, our respiratory pipe and digestive tract were exposed to different airborne and dirt particles. As I reminisce about those serene Tom Sawyer summer days, I suspect Mother Nature was immunizing us against dozens of allergies every day, especially when we harvested dusty crops or waded around in muck in the barnyard.

After we drenched ourselves with the refreshing water, Dewey Gene left the milk house and walked back toward the hayloft while I headed straight into the barn where Dad and Jimmy Ice were milking the cows.

I hastily told Dad about our quandary with Grandpa's driving. Dad understood and asked

Willow Grove: A Boy, A Family, A Farm

Jimmy to go to the house and see if Mom could go to the hayfield with Dewey Gene and me. Satisfied, I climbed the ladder up to the hayloft where Dewey Gene was waiting on top of the truckload of hay. One at a time, he would jab each of the four-foot-long, crescent-shaped hay prongs deep down inside the loose alfalfa. Grandpa was outside, sitting anxiously on the tractor that pulled the long rope and hoisted the hayfork bulging with loose hay up to the peak of the barn roof. The hay fork would then latch onto a metal track and travel on wheels across the top of the barn. At just the right place in the hayloft, Dewey Gene would yank on a small rope. The latch would open and allow the bundle of hay to free fall and land in a designated spot, where I would spread the hay in the hayloft. Haymow duty was the toughest job of all. It was a tall order to scatter the entire bundle of loose hay before the next avalanche arrived. Not to mention working under the super-hot tin roof. Up next to the tin roof, the temperature in the hayloft could easily be 100 degrees Fahrenheit.

By the time I climbed down out of the hayloft and walked down the wide ramp out of the barn, Mom was already sitting on the tractor—instead of Grandpa. What a surprise...and, boy! were Dewey Gene and I delighted! Mom had read our minds and knew that Grandpa should be in the house resting and that Dewey Gene and I could use her help.

Mom had talked with Grandpa and told him that supper was prepared and that she had enough free time to help put in the hay. She knew Grandpa

While the Sun Shines

was hot and tired, which wasn't good for his weak heart. Grandpa didn't question Mom's offer and had already headed for the house.

When Mom showed up at the barn to replace Grandpa, she brought a pleasant surprise! A red polka dot cloth-covered picnic basket and a quart of ice-cold sweetened tea. She knew we would be working late into the evening. The tasty sandwiches would satisfy our growling stomachs while we worked well beyond our regular evening mealtime. Rain was coming, and we knew Grandpa wouldn't relax until we opened the screen door and walked into Mom's kitchen, done for the day!

Mom poured us a tall glass of cold tea and Dewey Gene and I jumped up on the back of the empty truck. We began devouring our treasured sandwiches while Mom drove the truck toward the hayfield. We still had a lot of work ahead of us. The rainstorm was coming, and why dally when we could eat our sandwiches on the way to the hayfield. No time to waste! We still had at least two more loads of hay to go, and it was getting close to six o'clock.

It would take about 10 minutes to get to the hayfield, which was enough time to savor our sandwiches. Mom drove slowly, so the truck's dual wheels wouldn't stir up too much dust. Dewey Gene and I were standing, balancing ourselves on the bed of the moving truck while holding a glass of tea in one hand and our sandwich in the other. Since there were no racks on the truck, we stood in the middle of the truck bed with our legs spread wide apart and simultaneously leaned forward to counter the brisk breeze that sought to push us backward. A nice, pre-storm, breeze was blowing in our faces, and the food and drink, which we were thoroughly enjoying, filled both of us with a new burst of energy and enthusiasm.

We knew it would take a couple more hours before all the hay was under cover in the barn. The typical dark storm clouds weren't evident yet, but we could tell from the significant drop in temperature that the rain was on its way. With luck, we would save the remaining hay on the ground from getting wet. If the hay got wet, it would be ruined and a lot of money would be lost!

As soon as Mom pulled up in front of the hay-loader, she scooted over, and Dewey Gene jumped behind the steering wheel. He slowly backed the truck close enough for me to fasten the tongue on the hay-loader to the back of the truck. We were eager to get moving.

Mom did a superb job driving the truck. Not too fast and not too slow. By the time we were almost fully loaded, we noticed Dad and Jimmy coming across the hayfield. Dad was driving the Farmall M tractor, pulling our long flatbed wagon. With Dad and Jimmy's help, it would only take another 10 minutes to finish loading the truck. Dad was sure the wagon would hold the rest of the hay in the field. It would be an extra-large load, but Dad had the expertise necessary to safely maneuver a tall load of hay back to the barn.

While the Sun Shines

Mom watched through the truck's side mirror while we unhooked the hay-loader from the truck and quickly reattached it to the hay wagon. Dewey Gene and I jumped on the wagon and helped Jimmy stack hay. Dewey Gene took over his usual job of pitching hay from under the loader, while Jimmy and I stood near the front of the wagon and placed each fork-full of hay perfectly. With three of us working on the wagon, our jobs were much easier. With a shrieking whistle and a twirling motion of his finger, Jimmy gestured for Dad to "pick up the pace."

It was a good thing Jimmy signaled Dad to drive the tractor a little faster. We had just finished the last windrow of hay when we saw a huge black cloud coming across the Ohio River above Rome Paar's farm. The immense rain cloud was low in the sky and no more than two miles away. We would need a lot of luck to beat the drenching rain.

Dewey Gene jumped in the cab of the driver's side. He was more than ready to start barreling across the hayfield. Dewey Gene was in his prime when he had a good excuse to stir up a little excitement. In the meantime, he couldn't see me and didn't realize that I wanted to ride back to the barn with him and Mom. Luckily, Mom had closed her door just as I caught up with the truck and vaulted onto the passenger-side running board. Normally, I would ride in the cab or on top of the load of hay, but not on this trip! I knew Dewey Gene well enough to know he would be racing to stay ahead of the storm. He was quick to jam the

451

Willow Grove: A Boy, A Family, A Farm

gas pedal to the floorboard anytime he got a chance. Truthfully, Dewey Gene didn't need much of an excuse to push the "pedal to the metal." He liked excitement! He was enjoying the moment! Mom and I knew we were in for anything but a serene ride back to the barn. Not with Dewey Gene at the wheel and a rainstorm looming. That's all the excuse he needed to blast the soot out of the truck's tailpipe.

Sure enough, Dewey Gene smashed the accelerator against the floorboard and shifted from one gear to the next as fast as the fully loaded truck would tolerate. He beat a hasty path across the empty field toward the lane and barnyard. It was okay to speed across the smooth hayfield, but once we reached the edge of the lane, I knew he'd have to slow to a snail's pace. The modest undulation alongside the lane was treacherous for a load of hay, and if he wasn't careful the truck would tilt sideways just enough to cause hay to slide off the truck. The hay would be ruined when the thunderstorm arrived, since we wouldn't have enough time to reload the spilled hay. Fortunately, Dewey Gene had studied how Dad pulled the wagon across the drainage ditch and wisely heeded Dad's example. He crossed at the same angle and slow enough that the truck didn't lean too much and rock hay off onto the ground.

Dad was well on his way toward the barn. I wasn't concerned about Dad's driving or the safety of the hay that he was pulling with the International Harvester tractor. By the time we

While the Sun Shines

arrived at the barn, Dad was already backing his wagon into the machine shed.

The rain clouds had arrived, and it had started to drizzle. The hay on the wagon was safe, but the load of hay on the truck had to be unloaded now! The risk of fire was too great to leave any amount of gasoline in the barn. Even a thimble full! The hay had to be put in the hayloft and the truck backed out of the barn before we could call it a day!

Everyone was more than ready to unload the last of hay. Our growling stomachs were not happy. Dark waves of torrential rain pounded the roof of the barn and splattered on the hard, parched ground. Marble-sized drops of rain hammered the tin roof so hard that you could barely hear the person standing right beside you. After a while, the rain subsided enough that Gene volunteered to drive the tractor used to hoist hay up into the hayloft.

Dewey Gene was soaked by the time all the hay was unloaded. He didn't mind at all! The rain felt good! Cool and refreshing. Moreover, getting soaked was a small matter at the end of a long and productive day. Everyone was tired but pleased that the day ended with several tons of alfalfa safe in the barn. It was awesome to think about all we had accomplished! A wonderful feeling! We knew that Grandpa would be so happy that he would sleep well tonight!

We waited until there was another break in the rain before Dad, Dewey Gene, and I started walking to the house. Jimmy Ice lived in the tenant house

Willow Grove: A Boy, A Family, A Farm

across from the school bus building. It would take him longer to walk home, so Dad told him to drive the pickup.

We had just reached the end of the sidewalk when it started pouring again, and this time, the rain was accompanied by vigorous winds and bolts of lightning. It was a good thing Jimmy drove the pickup home. As soon as we were under cover on our favorite side porch, we paused and looked back toward the barn. We watched the rain blow sideways against the north side of the barn. We were glad we had closed the wide doors to the hayloft, which we left open in the summer. The top of the tall maple tree in our yard was swaying back and forth as the combined gusts of rain and wind continued to build strength. We were tired but at the same time grateful, knowing that the dairy cattle would be eating the hard-won alfalfa during cold winter nights.

Earlier in the evening, Grandpa, Grandma, and Aunt Jack had been on the porch enjoying the summer rainstorm while we were in the barn unloading the last truckload of hay. Gene was the only one they could see as he drove forward and backward several times before all of the hay was safely in the hayloft. Dad was about to open the outside door to our family room when Grandpa came out from Grandma's kitchen and sat down on the porch.

The sparkle in Grandpa's eyes portrayed how pleased he was—it was as if we'd hit the jackpot and already deposited the money in the farm's bank

While the Sun Shines

account. His cheerfulness made our weary bodies and aching muscles feel almost normal. Grandpa's accompanying kudos stressed how fortunate we were to have gotten all the hay off the field before the rain ruined it. Shortly after, Grandma and Aunt Jack came out onto the porch with a folded bath towel for Dewey Gene to dry his rain-soaked head. We all turned our heads while Dewey Gene stripped off his wet Levi's and wrapped the towel around his waist. He would take a quick, warm bath before joining us at the supper table.

The rain stopped long enough for Dad and me to walk around the house to the side entrance that we used many times every day. Before we removed our shoes and stepped into Mom's kitchen, we could smell the delightful aroma of food filtering out through the screen door. Mom had supper on the table, and we were anxious to sit down to a wholesome meal, kept hot by Grandma and Aunt Jack. Dewey Gene normally ate all three meals with our grandparents, but tonight Mom added an extra place plate around our table, since it was so late in the evening.

By the time we sat down at the kitchen table, it was much later than our usual supper time. While we ate our meal, Grandpa stood in the kitchen and reflected on the long day. He had already eaten his supper with Grandma and Aunt Jack and would soon enjoy a good night's rest. We were thankful for another wonderful day on our grand farm in Willow Grove!

Willow Grove: A Boy, A Family, A Farm

Bob hadn't been in the hayfield with us, but he was certainly busy taking care of other chores that had to be done. After lunch, he helped Dad separate some heifers from the pig pen pasture field and drive them to the barnyard. It was time for the soon-to-be mothers to mingle with the main herd, which they would join after their first calf. Around three o'clock, Bob, Mom, and Grandpa drove to the hill pasture and rounded up the dairy cows, and then drove them back to the barnyard in time for the afternoon milking. Then Bob tossed a quart-size dipper of sorghum-laced grain into the cattle trough in front of each stanchion. The dairy cows loved the cracked corn mixture, which made it easier to lock each one in her stanchion while she munched on her treat.

After Bob left the dairy barn, he went to the milkhouse, where he assembled all three of the Surge automatic milking machines, a chore that takes about 20 minutes. Until Jimmy Ice returned from the hay field, Bob helped Dad by carrying pails of fresh milk to the milk house and straining it into a 10-gallon can.

Once Jimmy returned to the dairy barn from the hay field, Bob took care of my twice-daily chore of feeding the baby calves. Bob had helped me feed the calves and knew how much powder supplement and warm water to add to each milk pail. After he fed the calves, Bob would feed the pigs. Everyone had been busy all day and after we were seated around the supper table, each of us took turns talking about certain events that happened during the day. Some of the individual comments were very amusing. Bob said that he liked feeding the calves more than feeding the pigs, and he asked me if I would change chores with him. I didn't even look up from my plate full of food and said, "No way." I knew feeding the baby calves was a more prestigious job than slopping the hogs. Dad didn't say a word, but produced a slight grin, listening to his two older sons talk about the hierarchy of farm life. Since the allowance for both jobs was zero, it had nothing to do with money. My opinion was that we lived on a dairy farm, not a pig farm. I'm a little surprised Dad didn't make us take turns, but then again, Bob really didn't want to switch jobs. He was teasing me and knew "slopping the hogs" was the easiest job. All he had to do was pull a five-gallon bucket, partially filled with food scraps, in our red Radio Flyer wagon to the pig pen and dump the contents into the pig trough. Throw in a few ears of corn and eureka! Bob's chore was done.

Feeding the calves in the afternoon was easy for Bob. During the morning feeding, I cleaned out the calf pen, climbed up in the hay loft, threw down three bales of straw, and spread the dry sheaths all over the calf pen floor. Sometimes, I was tempted to switch jobs with Bob, especially when I had to hump a loaded wheelbarrow across the bumpy barnyard to the manure spreader. Sometimes, Bob was a good brother and helped me push the wheelbarrow; I would have done the same if feeding the calves was his job.

Willow Grove: A Boy, A Family, A Farm

The rain was now a mellow drizzle, which would likely last most of the night. It was getting late, and my sluggish eyelids were becoming heavy and were closed more than they were open. But first, Bob and I had to decide who would be first to take a bath. Before the evening was over, the cast-iron, clawfoot bathtub would be filled and emptied five or six times. A horizontal row of several different neutral-colored bath towels hung on pewter hooks inside the roomy bathroom. Each of us had our own personal hook for a towel and that day's clothes.

Bob and I shared the same bedroom, located directly above Mom's kitchen. I knew I would be sound asleep as soon as my head hit my pillow. With the lower half of both windows wide open, the peaceful patter of the steady, gentle rain on the tin roof of the woodshed quickly lulled me into a deep sleep. For a few seconds, I thought about the fresh-smelling alfalfa hay that was safely under cover in the barn and how the cornfields, pasture fields, and vegetable gardens were getting a much-needed soaking rain. Tomorrow would be another exciting day on our Willow Grove farm, and I was confident it would be as rewarding and productive as today had been.

Mom was always the very last one to go to bed each night. After the dishes were washed, dried, and placed back in the kitchen cabinet, Mom would —finally—have rare, precious time by herself to relax. What errands, chores, and challenges would demand her attention and occupy scarce time starting in the early hours of tomorrow's brand-new day? Three sons, her husband, her in-laws, Aunt Jack, and Dewey Gene were all dead to the world in all five bedrooms on the second floor. For a while, Mom could relax, maybe read a little, work her crossword puzzles, and turn off the remaining lights before midnight and join the quietude upstairs. But, for the moment, she would just absorb the total silence, the peace, that accompanied the waning hours of a wonderful day on our farm. Before Mom turned off the kitchen light, she momentarily reflected on how good life was for her and her family! We were all happy souls!

Little Go-Getter

During my sophomore year at Ravenswood High School, William Vicars, the Vocational Agriculture teacher, invited three of his students to attend an agricultural conference at Duke University in Durham, North Carolina. We motored to the conference in Mr. Vicars' classy, late model sedan, which was proudly protected inside with clear plastic seat covers. The transparent covers didn't cover up the attractive fabric on the bench seat, yet protected it from sundry food and beverage stains.

In 1955, the ubiquitous, present-day President Eisenhower-promoted Interstate Highway System didn't exist, but was under construction in Jackson County and neighboring Wood County. Major U.S. highways were predominately two lanes and often

Willow Grove: A Boy, A Family, A Farm

followed the ancient footpaths of early migrating buffalo and deer, which in turn had been followed by native American Indians, and eventually early settlers in the 1600s and 1700s.

U.S. Route 21 was peppered with multiple twists and sharp turns through the Appalachian Mountains in southern West Virginia. Seat belts were a novelty and rarely evident, if at all, in automobiles in the 1950s. I was constantly amused by Mr. Vicars' antics each time the car accelerated through a sharp left bend in the road. The combo of slick seat covers and centrifugal force produced several entertaining moments while riding over the Appalachian Mountains. On sharp left curves through the crooked mountain highways, Mr. Vicars' stocky body would slide across the slick seat covers and completely occupy the middle of the front bench seat. The only thing that kept him from scooting all the way over to the passenger side was his two extended arms, which clung to the steering wheel. I was his guardrail on the passenger side. Right-hand turns were no problem. I'd just hug the door on the passenger side of the bench seat.

We arrived in Durham early enough for my two classmates and me to stroll through the big city's central business district. It was late afternoon, and the sidewalks were occupied by a few shoppers and commuters. After walking for a while, we were suddenly approached—from out of nowhere—by an African American boy carrying a homemade wooden box. He politely announced that his splendid shoeshine was only five cents. My classmates and I

Little Go-Getter

glanced at each other with a quizzical countenance and then agreed. Why not! We were in a big city, and, besides, even our best school shoes could use a shine.

I was the first to park my shoe on top of the wooden box. The little boy lathered my shoe with a ragged cloth of soapy water, whipped the shoe dry, and then kneaded the vamp and sides with an abundance of black shoe polish using his bare hands. The vigorous massage and coolness of the evaporating shoe polish felt good on my tired, hot foot. After a generous combination of determination and perseverance, the young shoe-shine professional pulled out a long piece of polish-stained cloth and commenced whipping my shoe from a dull, scuffed appearance into a gleaming black leather loafer. I had never had such a great spit-shine! It was grand, and I couldn't wait until my left shoe matched the jewel that crowned my blue-ribbon right foot.

But, before I could even remove my glistening shoe from the shoe-shine box and exchange it for my chafed one, the boy yanked the wooden box out from under my foot and took off like a scared rabbit. After I righted myself, I caught a glimpse of the wooden box as it disappeared down a drab alley between two retail stores. I hadn't paid him for the shoeshine. Very peculiar....I was puzzled by his abrupt departure, but only for a few short seconds!

I had just turned around when I noticed a policeman walking diagonally toward us from the opposite side of the street. The officer walked up to

Willow Grove: A Boy, A Family, A Farm

where we were standing, stopped, and asked a few perfunctory questions. We explained that we were high school students from West Virginia, attending a Duke University agricultural symposium. The officer was very polite, accepted our explanation, and succinctly advised us: "It's against the law to get a shoeshine on the sidewalk in the city of Durham." As the officer fully anticipated, we replied: "We didn't know!" He accepted our sincere innocence, and, as he turned to backtrack across the street, the officer said, with a genuine southern drawl: "Now, you boys have a good visit!"

After pondering what we had just witnessed, my classmates and I decided that we had seen enough of Durham and started back toward the university dorm, where we were lodging for the next two nights.

We hadn't walked more than a block when we heard a hissing noise emanating from a different alley between two commercial buildings: *Pssst. Pssssst. Pssssssst!* Each time, the vocal gesture got a little longer and a little louder! The persistent shoe-shine operator was hunched down close to the ground with his shoeshine box in one hand and the other five fingers around his mouth in the oval shape of a megaphone. As soon as we turned around and saw him, he motioned with his twitching trigger finger to follow him into the alley. I looked at the other guys, and in sync, we all repeatedly twisted our heads from side to side. No way! We were not about to hasten the city officer's reappearance. We completely ignored the little guy

Little Go-Getter

and offered him no encouragement. Off we hurried down the sidewalk on our way back toward Duke University men's dormitory.

Psssssst! Pssssssst! Pssssssssst! Louder than ever! The beckoning signal was from a different location! The shoeshine boy was close on our trail. The persistent little rascal was getting closer and closer. Too close, in fact! He just wouldn't give up! Even though I was sort of repulsed when I looked down at my one ugly shoe, I wanted no part of the wrath that would come with a second conversation with the city's law enforcer. One shoe was highly spit-shined and looked spectacular! The other shoe looked as if it wasn't even a mate and, at one time, must have been homeless. Regardless! We were not about to acquiesce—nor was the shoeshine boy!

Thankfully, the city patrol officer was nowhere in sight. After a couple more blocks, I finally thought to reach into my pocket and pull out a dime. I placed the dime on my thumbnail and clasped it tightly with my index finger. Using my best marble-shooting ability, I flipped the shiny Roosevelt up in the air, tumbling over and over toward the shoeshine box. With a million-dollar smile, the kid snatched the coin in mid-air. He shoved the dime in his front pocket, picked up his shoeshine kit, and, with his free hand, waved appreciatively. He had had a profitable day and was a happy entrepreneur!

On the way back to the dorm, we looked for a store that sold shoe polish. I needed to do something about the appearance of my lackluster and orphaned-looking left shoe. After watching the shoe-shine magician perform his magic, I came to the conclusion that it would not be easy to prove that both of my shoes came out of the same shoe box.

Brother Bob

As teenagers living on an active farm, you could always depend on Bob being involved anytime there was some extraordinary social excitement. I remember one time when several of us boys had been swimming in our farm pond.

After we returned to the milk house to change clothes, John Scott did something to Bob that Bob thought deserved a punitive response. Bob picked up John Scott, stark naked, and dumped him in a 55-gallon barrel of lime in the dairy barn. The dusty, caustic powder has the look and texture of baking flour and is sprinkled inside the barn to kill bacteria. John Scott scrambled out of the barrel and headed for the nearest water hose in the milk house. His derriere was on fire!

On another occasion, we had finished showering in our makeshift, bare-bones shower in the basement. The basement shower saved Mom's second-floor bathroom and kept us from tracking up the back stairs. Located at the bottom of the stairs directly beneath Mom's kitchen, the crude shower was primarily used by us rowdy teenage boys. Our home had a great mudroom, where my

Brother Bob

brothers, Dad, and I removed our shoes and took off any work clothes that were the least bit soiled.

It was near dark by the time we took our showers and climbed the basement stairs into the kitchen. We were on our way to the second-floor bedrooms to put on clean clothes. Instead, for some reason, Bob chased John Scott out of the kitchen, through the mudroom screen door, out into the yard with nothing on but a bath towel wrapped around his waist. John Scott took off running toward the circular porch that protected a portion of one side and the entire front of the house. Two separate sets of wide steps led up onto the wood floor porch. Chuck Grisso was sitting on the first set of steps on the side of the porch, and Mom and a few other women were sitting on the second set of steps, chatting as they enjoyed a marvelous view of the Ohio River.

Bob was close behind John Scott when John Scott raced close enough for Chuck to nonchalantly reach out and unsnap the towel from around John Scott's waist. Still running for his life, with brother Bob right behind him, John Scott, now stark naked, raced passed the second set of steps within a few feet of where Mom and the other women were sitting. With a quizzical look on her face, one of the ladies turned to Mom and said: "I don't think that boy had any clothes on!" She was right! There was always something to laugh about anytime Bob and John Scott were around.

Willow Grove: A Boy, A Family, A Farm

Charles Reynolds, Melvin Haught, Joe Rhodes, me, and Bill Rardin, at the McCoy pond in Pleasant View.

As a teenager, Bob was an excellent operator of all the farm equipment and a good all-around mechanic. His animal husbandry skills in the dairy barn were superior to mine, no matter how hard I tried. Bob went on to enjoy a long and successful career as a tractor-trailer driver. Bob's experience with farm tractors and backing hay wagons into tight spots helped him win several West Virginia Motor Truck Association "Roadeo" titles and the ultimate—the national championship title—which designated Bob as the best tractor-trailer driver in all of America. Truly a supreme accomplishment

Brother Bob

and a remarkable honor. During the latter part of his career, he was recognized for pulling two trailers at a time down the interstates of America. Bob drove tractor-trailers for 34 years. Millions of miles—accident-free. Not even a scratch, let alone a fender bender!

Binder Twine

The next extravaganza is unique and humorous. Hilarious is more accurate! But this time, my brother John was also involved with his sidekick John Scott. Of course, the circus ringleader was Bob; this time, he doubled down!

John Scott and my brothers Bob and John were in the barnyard driveway. This time, Bob was going to teach the duo a lesson. They had been harassing him all afternoon, so Bob went to the barn and cut several long pieces of the binder twine that is used to bind bales of hay together. First, Bob chased down John Scott and wrestled him down on the gravel driveway. Then he tied John Scott's hands behind his back and both feet together at the ankles. With John Scott lying flat on the ground, totally incapacitated, Bob went looking for his other victim. John knew his crazy brother well enough to head for the tall weeds. Bob finally caught John hiding in the barn and marched him, kicking and screaming, over to where John Scott was lying prostrate in the driveway. Bob enjoyed twisting his prey's ear while he walked and contemplated his captive's forthcoming punishment.

Willow Grove: A Boy, A Family, A Farm

Bob pulled out more binder twine, which he had stuffed in his hip pocket. He tied John's hands behind his back and his feet together, and then pushed him down beside John Scott. With John Scott and John lying helpless in the middle of the driveway, Bob bent over and yanked their pants and underwear clear down around their ankles. Bob had one last piece of twine left, which he used to lasso each of their lingams and tie them together —leaving only six inches of slack between the two constrained and screaming boys. Then Bob politely helped both fully exposed, naked boys to their feet, dusted his hands off on the sides of his denim jeans, and walked away.

Shirtless, John Scott and brother John stood in the middle of the barnyard driveway with their pants and underwear scrambled around their ankles. All they could do now was look at each other and yell for help. It was a bright Sunday afternoon, and the married couple who lived in the nearby tenant house was gone and wouldn't return until milking time. Except for Bob, no one else was close by, and he was not about to help the two distressed rascals.

Shuffling sideways, inches at a time, John Scott and brother John slowly scooted their way toward the house. At the same time, they made sure that the six inches of twine between them didn't become too taut, all the while facing each other and scooting sideways. Barely moving at all down the dusty lane—yelling for help!

Binder Twine

Mom heard the commotion and walked over to the window, where she had a clear view of the driveway, all the way to the dairy barn. "Lawrence, you have got to see this." Dad got up and peered over Mom's shoulder. As usual, he started laughing and couldn't stop! His reaction was typical of my father.

After watching the ego-wounded boys for a couple of minutes, Mom grabbed her handy scissors. Out the door she went, walking up the lane toward the spectacle. Dad was still watching from the window and of course, still laughing. The two had only managed to move about a third of the way to the house from where Bob had propped them up in the driveway.

As soon as John Scott and John saw Mom and her scissors, their cries for help changed to cries for mercy! "Please be careful; please, please be careful." Mom cut their hands loose and handed the scissors to the boys to finish the job. When she returned to the kitchen, Dad was still chuckling.

Farms Can Be Dangerous, Part 2

One story Dad told vividly illustrated the need for us to take care in the fields. My father was involved in an accident that resulted in a very painful and protracted injury. During harvest season, September 1937, Dad and Grandpa were busy working in the cornfield. Every single stalk of corn had to be cut by hand, bundled into corn "shocks"—a method of arranging corn stalks into

Willow Grove: A Boy, A Family, A Farm

manageable bundles—loaded onto a flat-bed wagon, and hauled to the barnyard. At the silo, the corn shocks were manually unloaded and placed lengthwise on the silage cutter platform. The chain-link conveyor ferried the corn stalks into high-speed rotating knives, which cut the stalks into pieces and blew the silage up a long, galvanized pipe to the top of the concrete silo.

My mother and father were dating, and Dad had made plans to see Mom over the forthcoming weekend. Their personal contact was primarily through letters and an occasional, expensive telephone call. Mom lived in Parkersburg, and, during the late 1930s, when the two teenagers were seeing each other, a motor trip from Silverton to Parkersburg was a major challenge and not undertaken unless absolutely necessary. A round trip to Parkersburg was time-consuming and expensive, especially if the trip encountered typical car problems, such as an engine overheating or a flat tire. These aggravations and others were not uncommon during the early automobile era.

Early in the week, Grandpa knew Dad and his cousin John Carmichael wanted to go to Parkersburg to see their girlfriends. Grandpa was agreeable, but only if all the remaining corn stalks in the field were cut and in the silo by the weekend.

The opportunity to go to Parkersburg was a big incentive for the boys to work extra hard and have all the corn cut in time to have the whole weekend free. Motivated, Dad and John worked extremely hard from dawn to dusk, cutting the remaining

Farms Can Be Dangerous, Part 2

corn stalks. Like so many chores on a busy farm, cutting sturdy corn stalks by hand—one stalk at a time—in the searing heat of a hot summer day was both strenuous and time-consuming.

Dad had lots of experience cutting corn stalks by hand. Each stalk of corn was cut using a razor-sharp, three-foot-long machete. At arm's length, the left hand grabbed hold of the corn stalk about shoulder high while the right hand gripped the lethal machete. With both hands in place, Dad raised the weapon above his head and then rapidly powered the sharp weapon through the corn stalk about two or three inches from the ground. A large cornfield required swinging the machete thousands upon thousands of times.

Dad was getting tried. Tired enough that he momentarily lost his focus and inadvertently allowed the machete to twist in his hand. It glanced off a corn stalk, striking his left leg just below the kneecap. The injury was very serious! The bad cut ended corn harvesting for my father and the upcoming weekend in Parkersburg had to be postponed. It was a huge disappointment for both of my parents.. Instead of packing a valise, Dad made an emergency trip to the Ravenswood Hospital to see Dr. Priddy.

The laceration was severe and required multiple stitches. Dad had to stay off his feet for several days. Shortly thereafter, his leg began to heal, but a couple of days later, it was apparent that the wound was infected. Back he went to see the doctor. Nothing the doctor did or prescribed eliminated the infection or lessened the pain. Effective antibiotics were not commonly available in drugstores. Instead, the sulfa drugs developed in the 1930s were called "miracle drugs" and were used to treat bacterial infections.

The angry wound persisted for several days. Though his leg was painful and still seriously infected, my father was restless and wanted desperately to make the trip to Parkersburg. Against the advice of his parents, Dad drove to Parkersburg to see my mother. It was obvious to Mom and my grandparents that his leg was causing him a lot of discomfort—so much so that he didn't sleep at all the first night of his visit. The second night, my grandmother opted to try an ancient homemade remedy, which the family had used for generations to treat infected wounds. The salve was called "Uncle A. P. Drawing Salve." The homemade recipe consisted of rendered mutton fat, wild mustard seed, and other natural herbs. Even though the drawing salve had a definite medicinal odor, it was a mild, sweet-mustard aroma. Before my dad retired for the night, my grandmother, "Ma," packed a copious amount of the special drawing salve over the wound.

The next morning Dad announced that for the first time in two weeks, he had slept through the night. After removing the bandage, it was obvious why he had slept so well and why his leg felt so much better. The outside of the wound was completely smothered with a noxious, greasy secretion from the harmful infection that had been

Farms Can Be Dangerous, Part 2

embedded deep in the laceration. The angry redness around the perimeter of the wound was almost gone. The cleansed wound looked much better and afterward, Dad's leg began to heal. The drawing salve was credited with healing his wound and possibly preventing gangrene.

My brothers and I can attest to the great drawing capabilities of the family's homemade salve. Mom often applied the salve to injuries anytime one of us boys stepped barefoot on a nail, sliver of glass, or other rusty items partially buried in the barnyard soil. By the time Mom was through applying globs of the drawing salve and finished wrapping the wound with yards of sterile gauze, the tattered son looked like he had had an unfriendly encounter with a junkyard dog.

Mastery

By the time I was 11 years old, I was experienced enough that Dad would send me to the hayfield to mow down a new crop of alfalfa and timothy. The Farmall C mowing machine was attached to the rear of the tractor, and while sitting on the tractor seat with both hands firmly on the steering wheel, I had to twist my head around more than ninety degrees to see the sickle bar. I didn't like the rear mowing machine setup! I wanted to look ahead and simultaneously watch the six-foot sickle bar topple waves of hay without turning my head around. Dad and Grandpa solved my criticism of the Farmall C rear-mounted mowing machine.

Willow Grove: A Boy, A Family, A Farm

They purchased a brand-new, army-gray Ferguson tractor with a side-mounted mower. The tractor and side mower were perfect! Exactly what I wanted. Even when I was looking straight ahead, the six-foot sickle bar was always in good peripheral view.

I spent many hours over several years mowing hay with the Ferguson tractor. My technique for cutting hay was different than my father's. We both started at the outside edge of the hayfield and progressed around all four sides. When Dad reached the end of a swath of hay, he would lock the right rear brake, spin the tractor 90 degrees to the right, and continue mowing the next long swath of hay. It would take him two or three seconds to turn each corner of the square mowing pattern. It was a professional maneuver, and only experienced operators could make the turn successfully. Inexperienced operators would leave big swatches of uncut hay standing in the field as they maneuvered to make the same turn as Dad. Even Dad would occasionally leave a few stems of grass standing after he made the 90-degree turn. Not me! After I mowed a field of hay, that field looked like it had been cut with manicure scissors. Like a golf course! Not a single stem of uncut grass was left sticking up anywhere in the whole field. If there was, I'd chase it down and remedy the blemish on my picture-perfect field of freshly mowed hay.

My process was different than Dad's. When I came to the end of a swath, instead of locking the brakes on the right rear tire and spinning 90 degrees, I would make a complete circle to the left

Mastery

and approach the new swath straight on—completely opposite of what Dad did when he mowed hay.

Time-wise, my mowing tactic wasn't as fast as Dad's. I was wasting a few seconds and using a tiny bit more fuel. It took me maybe seven seconds longer to make a turn than it did Dad. But I liked my results better! When I approached a new row, I would lower the long sickle bar at the right spot. When I reached the end of the row of cut hay, I would raise the sickle bar at the precise moment so that it wouldn't drag through hay already lying listlessly on the ground. I would attack each swath of uncut hay the same way until the entire field of hay was flat on the ground.

My dad in the fields, drilling corn or a grass crop.
Photo courtesy of Stephanie Davis Waldron.
This photo was taken by my cousin Dewey Gene from a window near the peak of the roof of our barn.

Willow Grove: A Boy, A Family, A Farm

After about 90 percent of the field was cut, I would concentrate and keep my eyes focused several feet in front of the sickle bar. I was watching for any sudden movement in the tall, uncut grass ahead of the tractor, which indicated a little animal was trying to escape the noise and subsequent wrath of the deadly sickle bar. Usually, it was a baby rabbit trying to escape from the small amount of cover—the uncut hay—in the center of the field. The little rabbit was running away and trying to hide from the commotion that destroyed the camouflaged rabbit hole. Once the field was close to being completely cut, the baby rabbits had nowhere to hide. Occasionally, I was disheartened when the sickle bar passed over a rabbit hole, just as several baby rabbits were trying to escape. Afterward, the only thing I could do was stop the tractor and end the tiny animals' suffering. Fortunately, it didn't happen often, but once a summer was still too often.

Sunday Visitors

Sunday was always a pleasant day on the farm, especially on splendid summer and fall days. Even though my grandfather expected the men to work six full days a week, he was equally insistent that no one would work on Sunday. His only exception was caring for the farm animals. They had to be fed and cared for, and the dairy cattle had to be milked twice daily. On Sunday, Dad worked three hours in the morning and about the same late in the

Sunday Visitors

afternoon, leaving him with about six hours to relax and enjoy time with his family between the morning and afternoon milkings. Otherwise, unless an unexpected problem or unusual situation suddenly occurred, Sunday was strictly a day for church, relaxation, and spending time with the family.

Now and then and always on a Sunday when a gradual drizzle looked like it was going to be an all-day affair, my mother would prepare a delicious picnic basket, which the family would take back to the cabin. After a wonderful lunch on the porch, where we watched raindrops disrupt the pond's smooth surface, Mom would stipulate that my brothers and I had to take a short nap. We were never happy about taking a nap, but eventually would capitulate and lie down. Mom's advice was always the same: "The sooner you go to sleep, the sooner you can get up." The soft *pitter-patter* of raindrops tap-dancing on the cabin's tin roof was so soothing that it was impossible to stay awake once your head touched the pillow. Moments after my brothers and I closed our eyes, we were sound asleep.

The peaceful Willow Grove farm was a lovely setting and an ideal place for adults to relax and unwind after spending their workweek indoors in a factory or crowded office. The sweeping environment along the expansive Ohio River, all the way to the rolling hills at the far end of the farm, included a fresh spring-water pond full of bluegill, hearty wide-mouth bass, and plenty of turtles. In the summer, the pond served as a water fountain for the cattle and a swimming pool on the opposite side of the pond, near the earthen dam. The kids had a massive open yard that afforded ample space to play safely near their parents and adults. In addition to an abundance of green grass, there were other enticing opportunities just waiting to soil or even worse, damage good clothes.

Big catch! Mom with her haul; brother John and Roberta Moss with theirs.

My brothers and I knew that nice weather on Sundays was a magnet for relatives and other unexpected motorists during the middle part of the day. Many of our family and friends, particularly those who lived in Ravenswood or Ripley, loved to go for a Sunday drive and often would stop by our farm for a short social visit. Consequently, our mother always made sure she had plenty of extra

Sunday Visitors

food prepared for visitors and that my brothers and I were dressed in clean clothes. Mother would give us strict instructions to remain presentable, at least until after our visitors had arrived. Keeping us respectable all day was a tall order unless my brothers and I were confined to the family room and forbidden to venture outside—where grass stains and rich black dirt were ready to attack our hands, faces, and clothes. More than once, my brothers and I managed to get ourselves in the dog-house with our mother when an ugly tear suddenly appeared in a visitor's brand-new shirt or expensive trousers.

Picnicking at the pond.

Mom knew the best she could hope for was a proper first appearance when the visitors arrived. Shortly after that, Mom accepted the fact that our

Willow Grove: A Boy, A Family, A Farm

neat, clean clothes and combed hair would eventually morph into a disheveled façade, from head to toe.

Not too often, but occasionally on Sundays, Bob and I would become rodeo cowboys and show our guests how to ride a "bucking bronco." We would head for the calf barn with our visiting playmates in tow. We would then "corral" a couple of sturdy, peppy calves and contain them in one of the calf pens. Then, either Bob or I would climb over the top of the wood railing on the side of the pen and straddle one of the calves. As soon as the gate to the calf pen was opened, the calf would dart toward the main door of the calf barn and race out into the barnyard, all the while jumping and swerving to one side or the other. The ride usually lasted no more than 10 to 15 seconds, and, if the cowboy was lucky when he hit the ground, he would land in clean, dry dirt and not in a mud hole or numerous "cow piles" in the barnyard.

The challenge was a lot of fun, and without exception, one of the visiting kids from "the big city" would endeavor to prove his prowess and ride one of the calves. Bob and I were always only too willing to accommodate his wish. Invariably the eager city cowboy would have on a nice outfit and, of course, new sneakers or a polished pair of leather shoes.

Without giving any prior consideration to the likely consequence of a new kid trying his luck at riding a calf, Bob and I, without any compunction, would select one of the liveliest calves—and politely assist our new cowboy hero as he climbed the

Sunday Visitors

wooden fence to mount the spirited bronco. Sitting on the calf in the barn was relatively easy since the animal was confined to a corner of the pen. But, just as soon as my brother and I stepped back from the rider, the calf would bolt for the open door and scamper out into the barnyard. The distance from inside the pen to the calf barn entrance was about 20 feet, and, for a few seconds, everyone enjoyed the rodeo activity. Bob and I shouted kudos to our visitor about his rodeo talent.

The preferred dismounting tactic was to jump off the bucking calf and land feet first on firm, dry ground. On every endeavor, the laughing and howling would be the loudest anytime the rider found himself sitting upright in the middle of a mud puddle or out in the open barnyard on top of a newly minted pile of cow manure. Even then, at the end of our calf riding escapades, the likely outcome was that all of us would be filthy from top to bottom. It was impossible to mask all the evidence from our antics.

After we returned to the house, our mother knew exactly what we had been into and, as politely as possible, admonished Bob and me for getting ourselves and our guests so dirty and in trouble with their parents. Mom was excellent at quickly repairing embarrassing situations and making our guests feel at home. With an ornery grin, my father would comment casually: "Who was riding who?" During a typical summer, more than a few pairs of clothing ended up with various degrees of stains and tears, which Mom would repair. Happily, to the best of my memory, not one of our friends ever got hurt. But their nifty, matching outfits? Now, that's a different story!

On some scheduled Sundays, Dad worked for the Jackson County Artificial Breeders Service as a substitute for the county's full-time employee. Grandma would compile a list of telephone calls from farmers who wanted their cows serviced. Mom, Bob, John, and I, along with a five-gallon tank of liquid nitrogen, would accompany Dad from one farm to another. The stainless-steel tank was filled with tiny glass ampules filled with expensive semen. The ampules of semen were from prize-winning bulls and worth thousands of dollars. Working with Jackson County Artificial Breeder Service enabled Dad to significantly improve our Willow Grove herd of Holstein dairy cows by using discounted, expensive semen and the process of artificial insemination.

Dinner with Robert Park and His Family

Willow Grove was too far away to participate in any teenage activities in Ravenswood. Over a period of nearly a decade, I was only in the town municipal swimming pool once or twice. I never had a date and never complained because I understood why. I didn't have my driver's license and didn't want anyone to drive me to Ravenswood, just for a date. It was too expensive, wasn't practical and, besides, what would my chauffeur do in the meantime? Go to the movies with me and my date? Not going to

Dinner with Robert Park and His Family

happen! Moreover, my best friend and cousin James Conrad and I were blood brothers—no interest in girls was allowed.

Rarely did I get to stay overnight with James Conrad. But when I was allowed, it was so fun and such a wonderful treat. Afterward, Mom could get me to do anything she wanted around the house and in the garden—and I never complained.

Other than James Conrad the only other person I ever stayed overnight with was classmate Robert Park. His father, Robert K. Park, was president and manager of Farmers Building and Loan Association in Ravenswood. It was a lovely evening. Everyone in Robert's family—father, his sister, Sallie Kate, and especially Robert's mother, Sallie—was so nice, which made me feel special.

We ate in a formal dining room with burning candles, which added a glow of happiness to the dimly lit room. I treasured and protected the beautiful, white linen napkin that I smoothed out over my lap. It made such a grand impression on me, one that I have never forgotten.

While preparing the dinner table and during the exquisite meal, Mrs. Park asked me a volley of thoughtful questions. I know I was timid and Mrs. Park wanted me to relax and enjoy my dinner. I was polite and wanted to show my appreciation for a family that was so nice. The evening at the Parks' home made a wonderful and indelible impression.

A few weeks before this book was published, I had a conversation with a dear friend, Hazel Casto Parsons, who also spent a night at the Parks' home with Robert's sister. Unsolicited, we commented about the hospitality of the Parks and what a lovely time we had as their guests. We both talked endlessly about the candlelit dinner, including the white linen napkins. Hazel went on to elaborate about how lovely Sallie Kate's bedroom was. She thought she had died and gone to heaven!

Mom was very protective of me and my brothers and would hardly let us out of her sight. Consequently, we were either on the school bus, in school, or at home. We could bring a dozen kids home for Mom to feed and spend the night, and she would not say a word. In fact, she encouraged it. Notwithstanding, she was reluctant to let us spend the night at one of our friends' homes. My brothers and I accepted her wishes and never gave her a hard time. We knew when no meant no!

Fertilizer Pit

The main barn was ideally situated alongside the only road to our farm and was easily accessed in two directions by a semi-circular driveway. The open space between the driveway and adjacent lane was large enough to provide a suitable spot to park vehicles, a wagon, a set of plows, or other farming equipment used in nearby hay- and cornfields. During the winter months, all the farm equipment was stored, covered, in an open-front shed built by my father and maternal grandfather, Samuel Barber, who my brothers and I referred to as Pa. I

Fertilizer Pit

remember the fun I had pounding nails when the roof of the shed was being completed.

A concrete silo located at the west end of the barn faced the two primary residences. Later, a steel silo was built alongside the concrete silo. Two circular metal corn cribs and a tool shed were positioned at the opposite end of the barn. The tool shed and corn cribs were outside of the wooden fence, which enclosed the east end and the whole backside of the barn. The fenced barnyard had enough open space to conveniently corral a hundred head of cattle at one time.

Every day during the winter, when our dairy cows were confined day and night in their individual stanchions in the dairy barn, the 24 hours' worth of accumulated manure was removed and scattered over the hay- and cornfields. Around mid-morning each day, the waste from the dairy barn was loaded into the New Holland manure spreader and hauled to a designated field for distribution. By the end of the winter, all the crop fields were covered with a thin layer of organic fertilizer from the dairy barn. In the spring, the Farmall M would pull a three-bladed plow through the field, which turned the soil upside down and buried the weathered manure underground, where it would further decompose and enrich the soil.

Uncle Conrad McCoy's dairy farm at Pleasant View managed its winter's accumulation of barn manure differently than my father. Instead of collecting and spreading the manure that same day, Uncle Conrad would store each daily buildup of waste in an open-air pit during the winter months and not spread the organic fertilizer on the river bottom cornfields until springtime.

The distance between the parallel concrete block walls of the open pit was wide enough to drive a tractor through. The twin walls were over six feet high. The top and ends of the long pit were completely open and fully exposed to all the season's elements. At the far end of the pit, a ramp was used to move the manure up an incline and out over the top of a manure spreader, which was parked underneath the ramp. A heavy-duty electric motor and a winch with a steel cable were bolted down on the top of the ramp. Hooked to the end of the cable was a hefty four-prong fork, which was powered by the electric motor. The custom-made fork physically pulled the manure out of the open pit and up the ramp, where the aged fertilizer gravity-fell into the manure spreader parked below.

The crafty operation was quite simple! One of the cousins would operate the winch while the other dragged the fork back over the manure pile and, at the right spot in the mammoth mound, would jab the fork deep down into the compost. Once the four-pronged fork was embedded, the electric motor slowly pulled the big glob of manure across the concrete floor and up to the top of the ramp, where it would free-fall into the spreader below. Trying to keep the steel fork upright as the large mass of matter was being pulled across the manure pit was a hard job and demanded concentration, skill, and strong biceps and legs.

Fertilizer Pit

One spring day, I happened to be visiting with my cousins when the job du jour was the start of the annual chore of cleaning out the manure pit. Cousin Eddie McCoy picked the shortest straw and was awarded his choice of two jobs: winch operator or fork operator. Barefoot and clad in only a pair of swimming trunks, I climbed into the manure pit to assist in manhandling the rugged fork. Out over the pile of manure James Conrad and I tromped, dragging the heavy homemade steel apparatus, while Eddie released the clutch, which allowed the wire cable to unravel from the spool on the winch. Without a doubt, the best job was winch operator, so Eddie and James switched jobs after each load of manure was spread on the river bottom corn field. Operating the winch was touchy, and the operator needed qualified experience to pilot the temperamental apparatus. I didn't have my winch operator's license and was just as happy to assist the fork-operator cousin.

Walking across the partially hardened composite of straw and aged manure while dragging the steel fork was cumbersome and challenging. Every so often, one foot would step on a soggy spot, and your leg would sink into the mucky compost up to the knee, if you were lucky—but sometimes up to the buttocks. Hanging onto the fork's handle and using it as a brace was the easiest way to extract the buried leg.

After multiple times, back and forth over the manure pit, we managed to turn a hard day of work into an amusing manure party. A lot of laughs ensued during the day. Keeping the wide fork upright behind a batch of waste gliding through the long pit was anything but easy. Sometimes, but thankfully not often, the fork operator would lose his balance and topple over, which triggered laughter from the other two cousins. Fortunately, the cow manure was diluted with an abundance of straw, rainwater, and snow, and had been out in the open, fully exposed to fresh air, all through several winter months. Yet, nature's fertilizer still had a noticeable aroma, though not overwhelming, by any means!

After a long day in the manure pit—one thing was for sure! Even though it was the weekend, there wouldn't be any girlfriends within a mile of the fertilizer pit crew. There wasn't enough soap or perfume in Jackson County to combat the reek that lingered for hours—even after going for a swim in the pond and a long, hot scrubbing shower with a stiff brush and Borax soap. I didn't mind at all! Being with my cousins and part of a financially productive endeavor was a perfect way to spend the day. The twinkle in Uncle Conrad's eye revealed his approval and appreciation of his sons *and* nephew's perseverance and hard work. The manure pit was clean, and now it would bake under the hot, disinfecting sun all summer long and be ready for next winter.

Family of the Year!

My McCoy cousins received special recognition in 1956, when their family was chosen "Family of the Year" by *The Ravenswood News*.

Willow Grove: A Boy, A Family, A Farm

Happy Story

The Willow Grove farm wasn't only perfect for dairy farming, it was also a wonderful environment for three healthy brothers during their adolescent years.

The evening supper was over. My brothers and I cleaned our plates, which was mandatory if we were going to enjoy "buzz," our family's moniker for dessert. I don't know where the expression came from, but I imagine it originated from one of us boys not being able to pronounce "dessert" at a young age.

"What's for buzz?" Mom could always expect this question every evening after supper unless her pies, cakes, cookies, or cobblers were in full view on the kitchen counter. Tonight, we had no idea because Mom wouldn't allow us in her food pantry where she hid her tasty sweets. A good way to miss out on buzz was to let Mom catch you in her pantry. My brothers and I would never enter without Mom's permission.

"It's a surprise," Mom announced. Now we were really anxious for buzz! We knew it would be really special. "You boys go outside and I will be out in a little while." Off we went out the kitchen door and around the back of the house to see if our grandparents and Aunt Jack were sitting on the north porch, which was everyone's favorite place to relax. Sitting on the porch you could see across the river into Ohio, see the Wolverton farmhouse on the other side of the lane, and the mighty sycamore

Happy Story

tree, pump house, Wolverton barnyard, our silos, dairy barn, milk house, and calf barn. The view was peaceful and the only sound was a lone whippoorwill in the distance. There wasn't a leaf moving anywhere and the summer evening temperature was ideal.

Grandpa was feeling great and was in a good mood. Grandma had opened up the monthly milk check from Valley Bell and was pleasantly surprised. She knew that the price paid for milk was going up, but no one had known how much. Grandpa and Dad were very pleased with the milk check. The increase would go a long way to paying the installments for the New Holland baler that had been delivered earlier in the day. More hay would enable Dad to increase his dairy herd, which meant the farm would ship more milk. It was a fantastic day!

Bob and I knew Mom and Dad would join our grandparents and Aunt Jack on the porch, so we decided to move our badminton set around to the side yard so we could play and at the same time see everyone. We wanted to play badminton, but didn't want to miss the cheerfulness that was evident on the porch. I was good at badminton and could knock the birdie a county mile. I kept Bob so busy scrambling to try and hit my high birdie that once he tripped and put on a good barrel roll demonstration that had everyone on the porch chuckling. It was the most I had seen Grandpa laugh in a long time.

Willow Grove: A Boy, A Family, A Farm

Mom came out onto the porch with her TV trays. The next thing I knew, Dad was unfolding them in front of his parents and Aunt Jack. *What's going on?* I wondered.

Dad disappeared into the house and soon returned with Mom's six-quart ice cream maker. He set it down on the sidewalk next to the gravel driveway so the salt water wouldn't kill the grass. Bob and I stopped playing, ran over to where Dad was standing, and asked, "Can we turn the crank?"

Me, Bob, and cousin Jimmy, hand-cranking ice cream.

We tried cranking together, but it was too awkward and we didn't last long. The vanilla ice

Happy Story

cream was getting too hard for me and Bob to turn. After a while, Dad came to our rescue.

By now Mom was standing beside the ice maker with a large spoon and several bowls. She knew how much to serve everyone. Grandpa, Grandma, and Aunt Jack were served first. We set the ice cream on the TV trays beside a piping hot piece of blueberry cobbler. Wow! "Mom, this is sure a surprising buzz."

Bob, John, and I sat sideways on the porch steps and rested our cobbler and ice cream bowls on the porch floor. Mom gave us a generous portion and it wasn't long before I stopped eating and was pressing my temples with both hands. Everyone, including my brothers, chuckled at my wincing and moaning. Mom offered, "Don't eat so fast." She didn't have to tell me the second time. The pain was excruciating—for a moment. My brothers didn't listen to Mom and I got my chance to laugh at both of them.

Mom had done it again! She was always looking for ways to make a happy environment even more rewarding. Mom was not skimpy on her portions and my brothers and I ate until we were about to bust. There wasn't an ice cream parlor in Ripley, Ravenswood, or Mt. Alto, West Virginia, that could compete with Mom's kitchen. Eight happy Willow Grove souls would not change places with anyone or anywhere this night!

The whippoorwill was still singing and would likely lull us to sleep before too long. The sun had gone to bed and darkness was approaching. Our

Willow Grove: A Boy, A Family, A Farm

dear mother won't finish her work in the kitchen until after everyone was sound asleep. She didn't mind at all. She would have a few minutes to herself to read, work her crosswords, and reminisce about another marvelous day at Willow Grove. She knew where her loved ones were…and she knew we were in good hands.

Happy Story

Mom and Dad.

Willow Grove: A Boy, A Family, A Farm

Chapter Five: The End

Willow Grove: A Boy, A Family, A Farm

Kaiser

In 1955 my grandfather agreed to sell the Willow Grove farm to the Kaiser Aluminum and Chemical Corporation. Even though my father and one other farmer were against selling their farms to Kaiser, Jackson County certainly needed good jobs for its citizens.

My grandfather and parents owned and operated the farm for nearly a decade until it was purchased by Kaiser Aluminum, owned by Henry J. Kaiser, in November 1955. Kaiser ended up buying much of the Willow Grove community. In defense of my grandfather and all of the Willow Grove farmers, any resistance to selling to Kaiser would have been tantamount to Scrooge in the classic Dickens tale, *A Christmas Carol.*

The farmers of Willow Grove were under extreme public pressure to sell their farms. Businessmen from Ravenswood and Ripley were keeping the gravel road to Willow Grove hot as a little red wagon! They were strong supporters of jobs and beseeched, on behalf of Kaiser Aluminum

Willow Grove: A Boy, A Family, A Farm

Company and Jackson County citizens, the Willow Grove farmers to exercise their options and sell their farms. Truly, my grandfather and the rest of the farmers felt morally obligated to help bring good-paying jobs to Jackson County.

Long before 1955, families had to leave Jackson County and relocate to Parkersburg or Charleston, West Virginia, or as far away as Canton-Akron, Columbus, or Pittsburgh to find good-paying jobs. The exodus continued until Kaiser Aluminum built a new plant at Willow Grove in 1955, and employment at the plant reached 4,100 at its peak. The entire population of Ravenswood in 1950 was only 1,175, less than a third of Kaiser's peak employment. The new aluminum company was a financially prosperous entity for the citizens of Ravenswood, Ripley, and all of the neighboring counties. This is why my grandfather and the other farmers in Willow Grove felt morally obligated to sell their vital farmland to Kaiser Aluminum Company in 1955.

My father was only 35 years old in 1955 and had a wife and three sons to support. He had to replace the Willow Grove farm and traveled thousands of miles searching for new land suitable for dairy farming. Along with my mother and their three sons, my father traveled as far as Albany, Georgia, to appraise a plantation. He evaluated multiple farms in southeastern Ohio, southwestern Pennsylvania, and a rolling hillside farm in Lewisburg, West Virginia. After consulting with my grandfather, they both agreed that the Willow Grove farm was worth far more than what they received from Kaiser. If only my father had found a replacement farm before he and my grandfather signed the option, they could have negotiated with Kaiser to replace the Willow Grove farm. By the time they realized their error, it was too late! The Willow Grove farm was irreplaceable!

My father ended up purchasing a humble farm in Wood County, West Virginia, in 1955. I was not a happy camper but moved to New England, West Virginia, with my parents and brothers. I left behind a school with 50 students in my sophomore class for a high school with 1,000 students in my senior class. It was not an easy transition for a truly spoiled, lifelong Jackson County country boy. "You can take a boy out of the country, but you can't take the country out of the boy" was very apropos at the time!

Humble Stranger

Grandfather was quite ill, and Grandma and her sister, my Aunt Jack, and my grandparents' adult children all knew he wouldn't be with us much longer. My parents, brothers, and I went to see Grandpa at his new home south of Ravenswood. One by one, Mom took us by the hand and walked with Bob, John, and me down the hallway from the living room to the back bedroom to see Grandpa for the last time.

I was the first to go. Grandpa was lying in bed on his back with his head slightly elevated with several pillows. It was obvious he was in pain and extremely weak. It was heartbreaking for me when I stood beside his bed and looked into his partially opened, debilitated eyes. I don't remember what I said when I addressed him for the last time, but I trust it was appropriate. Before I could finish, he reached for my hand. Grandpa grasped my hand as he looked straight into my eyes with a pain-filled countenance. He held my hand briefly before he slowly uttered the last five words that I would ever hear him speak: "Junior, be a good boy." He continued to hold my hand a little longer and then slowly closed his tired eyes. His grip weakened, and his hand slowly opened. Quietly, I left the room with tears in my eyes.

Not long after I saw him for the last time, Grandpa died at home on October 25, 1957, at the age of 70. His wife and family took good care of him until the time he peacefully left us. Funeral arrangements were made by Burl Chambers in the sleepy river town of Ravenswood. I don't recall many details following Grandpa's death, but I vividly remember meeting one stranger among the mourners at the funeral home.

All my grandfather's immediate family and many of his relatives and numerous business and social friends were gathered at the funeral home to pay their respects. Several family members had been in the funeral home for quite some time, and nearly everyone present had known each other all their lives. I was standing alone near the entrance

Humble Stranger

when a total stranger stepped gingerly inside. The man politely stopped near the entrance.

He was wearing a fedora, which he promptly took off and held low in front of him with both hands. What was so noticeable about the uneasy gentleman was that he looked like someone who had had a tough life. He was thin and had the muscular features of a young or middle-aged man, yet his face looked like that of a leathery, wrinkled, much older man. His pants, shoes, and long-sleeved shirt were all a dark, dull color and looked like work clothes. I am confident the clothes he had on were the best he owned, and it was equally apparent to me that he had done his absolute best to dress as well as he could. He wasn't wearing a jacket, but had on a solid drab tie, which was tied too short. His shirt sleeves were too long and covered his hands just above his knuckles. The gentleman was as faultlessly groomed as possible and though his garments had seen better days, his clothes were clean. Very likely his attire had seen many days of hard labor on his or someone else's body. The way his bulky shirt and trousers shrouded his thin frame also suggested that his clothing might have been borrowed, to pay his respects to my grandfather.

The uneasy stranger stood alone, subdued, for several minutes. He purposely waited until no one was standing near Grandpa's casket. Then, the stranger commenced walking slowly, almost tiptoeing, across the wide-open, dimly lit room. The gentleman walked up to the coffin and stood quietly by himself. After a brief period, he meekly stepped back from the casket, turned around, and started walking toward the funeral home entrance.

I had been observing the stranger from the moment he first entered the funeral home. As soon as I realized he was leaving, I walked over and extended my hand to introduce myself. The stranger abruptly stopped and shook hands with me. I introduced myself as one of the grandsons and told him my name. He told me his name, but, regrettably, I don't recall his first name or surname.

After talking for a brief period, we moved away from the entrance, off to the side of the room to a vacant spot and continued our conversation. The stranger was highly complimentary of my grandfather. He conveyed his respect with such compassion that I became glued to every word he uttered about when and how he knew Grandpa. He remarked that "Ed Sück was a good man and friend to me." He told me about an incident that happened when he was a young man. He had gotten in trouble with the law and ended up in the county jail in Ripley. Not a single soul in his own family would help him. No one, including his alleged good friends, went to the jailhouse to see him.

After several days in jail, the sheriff talked to the young man and suggested that he call Ed Sück and ask Ed if he would come to the jail to see him. Grandpa drove to Ripley and listened to the young man explain why he was incarcerated. He asked my grandfather for money, so he could pay the compulsory bail bond and get released from jail. In

Humble Stranger

the end, Grandpa helped the young man and loaned him the money. However, Grandpa made it clear to him that he wanted to help, but he fully expected him to stay out of trouble. Grandpa lectured the young man and told him that if he ended up back in jail, Grandpa "wouldn't help him a second time."

Since the young man didn't have a job, Grandpa offered him a job on the Silverton dairy farm and said that he could stay as long as he wanted to or until he'd paid back all of the money. The stranger didn't have transportation to get to work, but luckily he wouldn't need any. He lived in the Silverton area and could easily walk back and forth each day to the farm, which he did until the loan was paid off.

As I listened to the humble stranger explain how he worked on the farm to pay off Grandpa's loan, I was reminded of similar times when Grandpa had helped other people who were down on their luck. More than once I had watched as people approached him on the streets of Ravenswood and ask for financial help. A few were relatives; others were close friends or acquaintances. Some were just short of being desperate. My grandfather was a good listener and a tough negotiator. Grandpa always listened, offered his advice, and if the disheartened deserved help, they were never disappointed in the end. I saw enough to know that Grandpa was willing to help anyone...but not without a commitment to mend their ways. A sincere handshake, a promise not to

Willow Grove: A Boy, A Family, A Farm

make the same mistake again—that was all Grandpa wanted and needed in return for his financial support. I always knew when an understanding was reached between Grandpa and whomever he was talking with: I would see a big smile on the individual's face as the person extended his hand to Grandpa or give him a big hug and thank him profusely. Grandpa was a good teacher and, most of all, a good man.

My father grew up on a farm, was the youngest, was spoiled by his parents and older siblings and dairy farming was in his blood. He actually had a wonderful life as a youngster and had many pets that he enjoyed, immensely. In his adult years, he planned to work hard and retire early. Dad never had any desire to move from the farm to a residence in a town or urban area. On Sundays in the summer time on nice days we had company that came to Willow Grove to enjoy the peace and tranquility of the countryside.

Conversely, my mother had a very difficult childhood. She worked so hard and had to quit school in the tenth grade because she could not keep up with her schoolwork. As a young girl and teenager, she had more responsibility than most adult housewives. She looked forward and prayed that after she got married, she would live a happy life, which by all accounts, she did.

My parents would tell you that they did not have a hard married life. My father loved farming and would never consider leaving dairy farming for an 8 to 5 plant job. Yes, it was hard work, but dairy

Humble Stranger

farming was hard work that they enjoyed, especially my father.

I loved growing up on a farm, but notwithstanding my experience seeing the poor old man on the roll-away bed, I always aspired beyond what dairy farming could afford me.

RIP of the Mighty Sycamore

After I measured the sycamore in 1950, the hardy specimen lived another 56 years before it was cut down in 2006 by my cousin, Dewey Gene Davis, at the behest of Century Aluminum. The top of the tree was showing its age, and the company wanted it cut down for safety reasons. After my cousin wrestled with his chainsaw for several hours, it turned out that the base of the tree was over seven feet in diameter, was completely solid, and was entirely free of any bad spots. The tree just had a bald spot on its top, and no doubt, the monumental sycamore could have lived many more years, possibly another century or two.

Last Day

The first sentence of *Willow Grove* started with the first day of school on September 2, 1946. It was the day that my family moved from Silverton to Willow Grove. I had planned to end my historical memoir on the last day of school—the same day that I left Willow Grove and Ravenswood High School. I was leaving Jackson County, the place

Willow Grove: A Boy, A Family, A Farm

where I was born and lived happily for the first 16 years of my life. Truthfully, I didn't want to write beyond the decade that I lived at Willow Grove, since my life had changed drastically, and *not* for the best.

Me and James Conrad.
Photo courtesy of James Conrad's wife, Joyce McDermott McCoy.

However, my *Willow Grove* editor and publisher encouraged me to write about my life after Willow Grove. What were my thoughts about leaving Willow Grove? What did I miss the most, etc.? The suggestion forced me to dwell on my teenage years after 1955 and in doing so, I soon realized that I was not the only family member who was unhappy

Last Day

about leaving Willow Grove. For me, it was an amazing revelation and something that I had never entertained, in any manner, until November of 2022, when I was writing the last part of this book —67 years after leaving Willow Grove!

On the last day of school in 1955, I climbed into the family Chevrolet station wagon with my parents and brothers. We had sold our farm at Willow Grove to Kaiser Aluminum Company and I was joining the family who had already moved to a new farm in New England, West Virginia, in neighboring Wood County. I was not happy about leaving Willow Grove and Ravenswood High School but was appeased knowing that I would soon return and continue my education as a junior. Coach Spano had allowed me to take my football cleats with me so that I could work out on my own before football practice commenced in August.

Our new farm was totally different from our Willow Grove farm. The only similarity was that both bordered the Ohio River and both had grand dairy barns and attractive farmhouses. Otherwise, everything else was different. The topography of the new farm in New England was hilly and lacked enough flat land and river bottom for growing feed for a herd of dairy cattle. Just as I had recognized the plethora of positive attributes of our former Willow Grove farm, I realized many were lacking on our new farm. Regardless, I didn't dwell on the negatives, since I was the oldest son and was expected to leave the next generation of farming to my two younger brothers. I was satisfied knowing

Willow Grove: A Boy, A Family, A Farm

that cousin James Conrad McCoy and I had already discussed and decided on veterinarian medicine as our career path.

I enjoyed the summer break and had made plans to return to Ravenswood just before football practice started. I was going to stay with my paternal grandparents at their home and ride the same school bus that I rode when we lived at Willow Grove. At the last moment, I was informed by my mother that Bob wanted to return to Ravenswood High School and stay with my grandparents, as well. The news surprised me and I confronted my brother about his change of plans. I knew that both of us would be too much work for my grandparents and Aunt Jack. I had two more years and Bob had three before he graduated from high school. Two years was long enough!

Bob wouldn't give in and insisted that if I went back to Ravenswood High, he was going too! I couldn't change his mind. Admittedly, I wasn't the best big brother and Mom always gave in to Bob's demands for fairness. Bob had a temper and could interrupt the family's tranquility, whereas Mom knew that I would acquiesce, and, no matter how disappointed, I would accept her decision. I had never given my parents a moment of trouble. It isn't in my DNA to ever cause problems for anyone, let alone my mother.

I was so mad that I turned around, and instead of starting a fight with my brother, I hit the wall of Bob's bedroom with my fist so hard, an ugly bone immediately popped up on the top of my right

Last Day

hand. I had broken my wrist. Dad had to take me to the emergency room in Parkersburg. The incident was the only time I ever saw my father furious with Bob and me.

Parkersburg

My arm was in a cast for six weeks. I missed football practice and didn't return to Ravenswood. Instead, I enrolled in Parkersburg High School, where I was one of 1,000 students in my junior class. I didn't know anyone and was too depressed to even attempt to befriend any of my new classmates. At Ravenswood High School, I was vice president of our freshman class of 52 students.

I always enjoyed public school but did not adjust to the dramatic change from Ravenswood to Parkersburg High. I was miserable and could not shake my love affair with Willow Grove and Ravenswood High School. Admittedly, I was spoiled and the happiness that was ripped from me was accentuated by my selfishness and distant attitude. My parents tried to assuage my unhappiness—without success. I was too macho and remained aloof. I tried to deal with my situation quietly and on my own. In retrospect, someone should have kicked me in the buttocks and shamed my behavior. I should have turned a negative into a positive and taken advantage of the many attributes that a large school had to offer. But I didn't and, as a consequence, remained miserable for far too long! It was my loss! So much so that I never wanted to visit Ravenswood, unless I absolutely had to! It was too painful! I wanted to get my past out of my mind.

Notwithstanding my unapproachable attitude, I was popular with many students at Parkersburg High. Since I was the son of a dairy farmer, I was in the Future Farmers of America organization. My classmates nominated me for president of the club, which I had no interest in, and voiced my negative opinion as forcibly as I could. I was ignored and elected president anyway. It was a nice gesture and I muddled through, somehow.

My father went with me to my graduation ceremony from high school. My mother was not well and her illness only intensified my unhappiness. In my junior year, I had been dating, sporadically, but was not serious about anyone or interested in anything. I wanted to attend West Virginia University and continue my quest to study veterinarian medicine with cousin James Conrad. College was my mental and physical route to revive the awesome happiness and positive attitude that I had enjoyed during the years I lived at Willow Grove.

On graduation night, I went home with my father and was in bed while all the other graduating seniors were enjoying a party on a steamboat cruising on the Ohio River. Peggy, my future wife, was in my class and could never understand why I skipped going on the graduation night cruise. Foolishly, I missed a wonderful evening.

Parkersburg

I often described my life growing up at Willow Grove by interjecting the television show *The Waltons*. The hit TV series was about a family who lived during the depression in the foothills of the Blue Ridge Mountains in rural Virginia. The parents, their seven children, and the paternal grandparents all lived in the same house on a hill farm. At Willow Grove, my family and paternal grandparents, plus my grandmother's sister lived in the same house. There were 11 members in the Walton family and eight in my family. During the winter of 1950, 12 individuals lived happily in our Willow Grove house. Seven adults and five children. Just as was obvious on TV with the Waltons, Willow Grove was a hub of non-stop activity. It was a marvelous way to grow up. At Willow Grove, I was John-Boy, though not nearly as studious as John and Olivia Walton's oldest son. The main difference between our Willow Grove farm and Walton's farm was the topography. Our land was a sizable, flat dairy farm located along the Ohio River. John Walton was in the lumber business and his farm was located near the mountainous Rockfish River.

I mention the TV series because my mother was Olivia Walton in our family. Busy from early morning until late at night taking care of her children, tending to household chores, and aiding her husband and in-laws in any way she could. She loved being needed and helpful! Her time was always in demand. Late at night when everyone was in bed, was the only time Mom had to sit down and enjoy some peace and quiet.

Willow Grove: A Boy, A Family, A Farm

After we sold the Willow Grove farm, our dairy business was shut down and the farm equipment along with the dairy cows were sold at an auction. The hub of activity on the farm completely disappeared. My grandparents and Aunt Jack had moved to a new home. My brothers and I were in school and Dad was away from Willow Grove helping his brother on his farm at Silverton. The Willow Grove farming community became desolate overnight and my mother was all alone, isolated along the railroad track and fearful of the occasional hobo requesting something to eat. To feel a little more secure, Mom brought our pet collie into the kitchen for company and protection. Our pet cats and dogs were never allowed in the house. They had plenty of warm places to live outside and stay warm, year around. Mom was unhappy, afraid, and became lonesome.

When we moved to our new farm in New England, my mother's personal environment was pretty much the same as it was during the latter days at Willow Grove. She was all alone! My brothers and I were in school and Dad was working in the distant fields. There were no neighbors and Mom was alone. All her life, she had lived among family members. Her situation was similar to when my grandfather stopped by the Carmichael house in Silverton and asked Mom and Dad to move back to the farm. Grandpa told her, "It was too lonely for him and Nannie." It was the first time in their lives that my grandparents didn't have several family members living with them.

Parkersburg

Mom eventually had a nervous breakdown. Her depression deteriorated so much that she ended up in a mental hospital in Spencer, West Virginia. The therapy for a nervous breakdown in the 1950s was barbaric compared to today's drug treatments. Mom was in the hospital for six weeks and when she came home, she worked very hard to make sure she never had to return. I remember visiting my mother in the hospital. It was sad to see her in such a depressing environment!

After we moved from Willow Grove my mother's depression was clearly worse than mine. I was too self-centered and spoiled to recognize what was happening to Mom. I never realized that Mom's unhappiness, as well as mine, was caused by the same thing: *We both missed Willow Grove!* If we had not sold our farm to Kaiser Aluminum, my mother would never have had a nervous breakdown. We both paid a heavy price. Especially Mom!

Notwithstanding my beating up on myself, which was the worst of my unhappiness, it only resulted in a few bottles of Maalox for a pre-existing ulcer condition and *one* pill from a two-week prescription for high blood pressure. Fortunately, I wised up early enough as a teenager to remedy both health conditions before it was too late.

Just before I needed to enroll at West Virginia University, my father surprised me with the revelation that he did not have the money to send me to college. I was devastated and couldn't believe my ears. He had known for years that I was interested in going to college, yet, he had never said

Willow Grove: A Boy, A Family, A Farm

anything to me, one way or the other, about the topic. He quit school in the tenth grade and believed that a high school education was all that was necessary to get a good job and live happily ever after. I knew better! For the lifestyle that I wanted, an advanced education was imperative.

My parents were wonderful during our formative years. In fact, too wonderful! My brothers and I never experienced any real hard knocks and were tied way too close to our mother's apron strings. My parents would have been happy if my brothers and I had never married and lived on the ranch like the three sons in the TV show, *Bonanza*. I was not street-smart and didn't have the wherewithal to go to the bank or my grandparents for a loan to go to college, which would have been easy. Without any doubt at all, if we had still lived at Willow Grove, I would have gone to college after high school and followed my intended career path.

While I was working on this book, I began a delightful correspondence with Pastor Chris Skeens, the current pastor of the Ravenswood Free Will Baptist Church. Pastor Skeens was kind enough to share this bit of family history about our wonderful Willow Grove farm:

> My father, Rev. Stanley E. Skeens, a skilled electrician and notable pastor-evangelist, was among the early employees of Kaiser Aluminum Chemical Corporation, Ravenswood Works, Ravenswood, WV. From time to time he would

Parkersburg

recollect and tell our family of a stately, grand red-brick, two-story farm house that once stood empty down from the enormous aluminum smelter and aluminum finishing plant facility toward the Ohio River.

My father described the house as a family farm estate that had magnificent exterior architectural designs and features. He seemed most interested with the beautiful interior wood-trim, especially the stairway to the second floor with its posts, railing, and spindles, and the baseboard and crown moldings. Someone had speculated that the interior wood features were so beautifully rich in appearance that, perhaps, it had been brought to the building site from outside the area. Regardless, my father enjoyed knowing that the grand house was skillfully built for a large family, and the raw materials likely taken not far from its surroundings.

What is important to me, now, is that I understand and accept my father's premise about higher education. Even though my father was wrong—he "didn't know what he didn't know."

In the preface of *Willow Grove*, I highlighted why I felt compelled to write this book. During my hectic, fast-paced career in the Garden State in the early 1980s, many times I recalled my young life in Willow Grove and attending school in Ravenswood. The fond memories of those happy days kept me grounded when I worked for Mobil Chemical Company marketing plastics to the highly

Willow Grove: A Boy, A Family, A Farm

competitive petrochemical industry in metropolitan New York. My Jackson County roots provided the necessary perseverance to never give up and succeed against compelling odds. In the end, I did well and enjoyed over two decades of a very rewarding career, thanks to a lot of people whom I distinguished in the Acknowledgments section of *Willow Grove*. Fortunately, during those rewarding years, I knew how lucky I was and acknowledged my good fortune by appreciating every day of my personal life as well as my career. My advice to anyone who stopped and asked: "Larry, why are you always so happy?" was forever the same: "Have fun, whistle while you work, and enjoy it while it lasts." Life is just a whistle-stop!

In closing, "You can take the boy out of the country, but you can't take the country out of the boy." All through my humble and fortunate life, *Willow Grove was my country*!

Sometimes, when it's very late and very quiet, I think about my years at Willow Grove, and I try to imagine what our farm would look like 65 years after I left the bucolic countryside. In my mind's eye, I see that all of the farms are even more beautiful as a result of modern maintenance and impeccable landscaping by successful dairy and crop entrepreneurs. I envision Willow Grove as a destination for sightseers, similar to those you see driving over the narrow backroads through the Amish farms in Lancaster, Pennsylvania, and Ashland, Ohio.

Parkersburg

And I dream about how great it would be to walk from our farm house to the pasture field pond and throw in an early-morning hook and line.

John and me at our farm pond.

Willow Grove: A Boy, A Family, A Farm

Family Trees

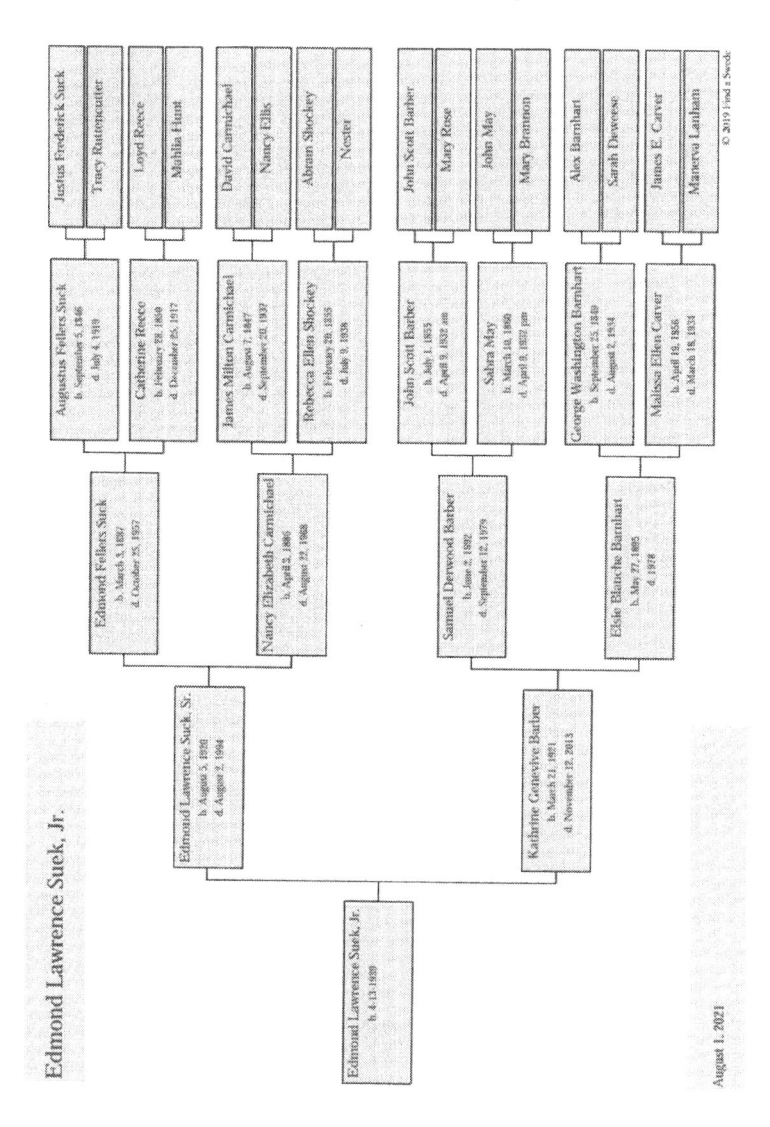

Willow Grove: A Boy, A Family, A Farm

Edmond Lawrence Suck, Jr.

- Justus Frederick Suck
- Tracy Rustenkutter
- Loyd Reece
- Mahlia Hunt
- David Carmichael
- Nancy Ellis
- Abram Shockey
- Nester
- John Scott Barber
- Mary Rose
- John May
- Mary Branson
- Alex Barnhart
- Sarah Deweese
- James E. Carver
- Manerva Lanham

© 2019 Fred a Swcok

- Augustus Fellers Suck
  b. September 5, 1846
  d. July 4, 1919
- Cathrine Reece
  b. February 28, 1860
  d. December 26, 1917
- James Milton Carmichael
  b. August 7, 1847
  d. September 20, 1937
- Rebecca Ellen Shockey
  b. February 28, 1855
  d. July 9, 1938
- John Scott Barber
  b. July 1, 1825
  d. April 9, 1932 am
- Sabra May
  b. March 10, 1860
  d. April 9, 1922 pm
- George Washington Barnhart
  b. September 25, 1849
  d. August 2, 1934
- Malissa Ellen Carver
  b. April 19, 1858
  d. March 18, 1931

- Edmond Fellers Suck
  b. March 3, 1887
  d. October 25, 1957
- Nancy Elizabeth Carmichael
  b. April 3, 1886
  d. August 22, 1988
- Samuel Derwood Barber
  b. June 2, 1882
  d. September 12, 1979
- Elsie Blanche Barnhart
  b. May 27, 1895
  d. 1978

- Edmond Lawrence Suck, Sr.
  b. August 5, 1916
  d. August 2, 1994
- Katharine Genevieve Barber
  b. March 21, 1921
  d. November 12, 2013

- Edmond Lawrence Suck, Jr.
  b. 4.13.1939

August 1, 2021

522

Family Trees

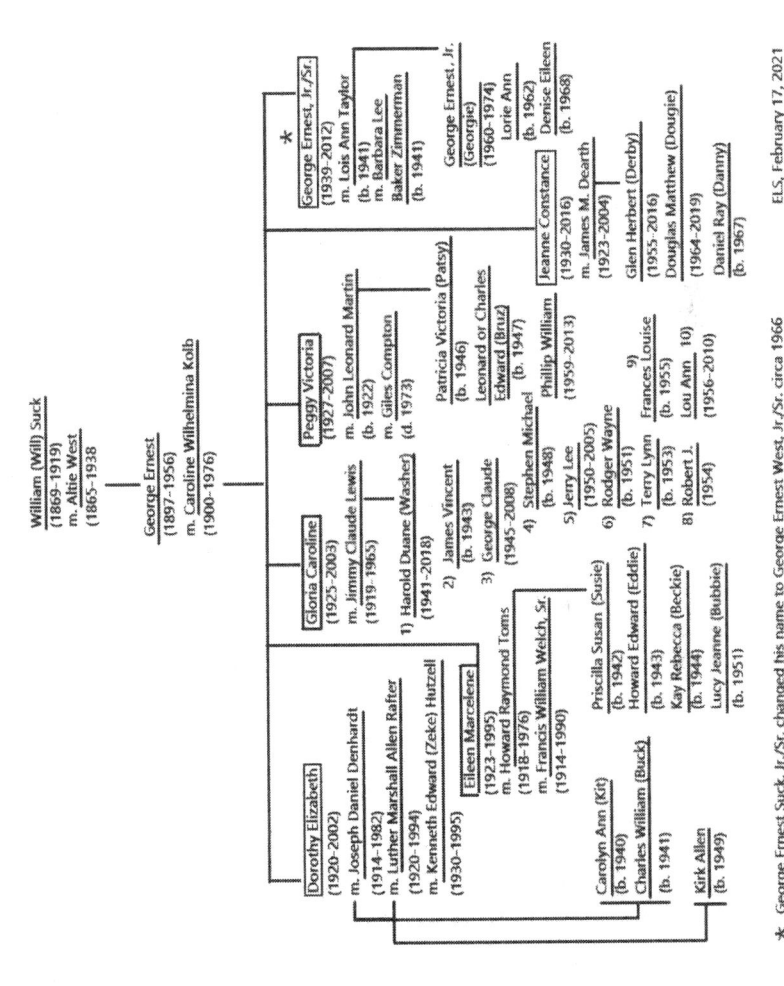

William (Will) Suck (1869-1919)
m. Altie West (1865-1938)

George Ernest (1897-1956)
m. Caroline Wilhelmina Kolb (1900-1976)

Dorothy Elizabeth (1920-2002)
m. Joseph Daniel Denhardt (1914-1982)
m. Luther Marshall Allen Rafter (1920-1994)
m. Kenneth Edward (Zeke) Hutzell (1930-1995)

- Carolyn Ann (Kit) (b. 1940)
- Charles William (Buck) (b. 1941)
- Kirk Allen (b. 1949)

Eileen Marcelene (1923-1995)
m. Howard Raymond Toms (1918-1976)
m. Francis William Welch, Sr. (1914-1990)

- Priscilla Susan (Susie) (b. 1942)
- Howard Edward (Eddie) (b. 1943)
- Kay Rebecca (Beckie) (b. 1944)
- Lucy Jeanne (Bubbie) (b. 1951)

Gloria Caroline (1925-2003)
m. Jimmy Claude Lewis (1919-1965)

1) Harold Duane (Washer) (1941-2018)
2) James Vincent (b. 1943)
3) George Claude (1945-2008)
4) Stephen Michael (b. 1948)
5) Jerry Lee (1950-2005)
6) Rodger Wayne (b. 1951)
7) Terry Lynn (b. 1953)
8) Robert J. (1954)
9) Frances Louise (b. 1955)
10) Lou Ann (1956-2010)

Peggy Victoria (1927-2007)
m. John Leonard Martin (b. 1922)
m. Giles Compton (d. 1973)

- Patricia Victoria (Patsy) (b. 1946)
  Leonard or Charles Edward (Bruz) (b. 1947)
- Phillip William (1959-2013)

George Ernest, Jr./Sr. * (1939-2012)
m. Lois Ann Taylor (b. 1941)
m. Barbara Lee Baker Zimmerman (b. 1941)

- George Ernest, Jr. (Georgie) (1960-1974)
- Lorie Ann (b. 1962)
- Denise Eileen (b. 1968)

Jeanne Constance (1930-2016)
m. James M. Dearth (1923-2004)

- Glen Herbert (Derby) (1955-2016)
- Douglas Matthew (Dougie) (1964-2019)
- Daniel Ray (Danny) (b. 1967)

* George Ernest Suck, Jr./Sr. changed his name to George Ernest West, Jr./Sr. circa 1966

ELS, February 17, 2021

523

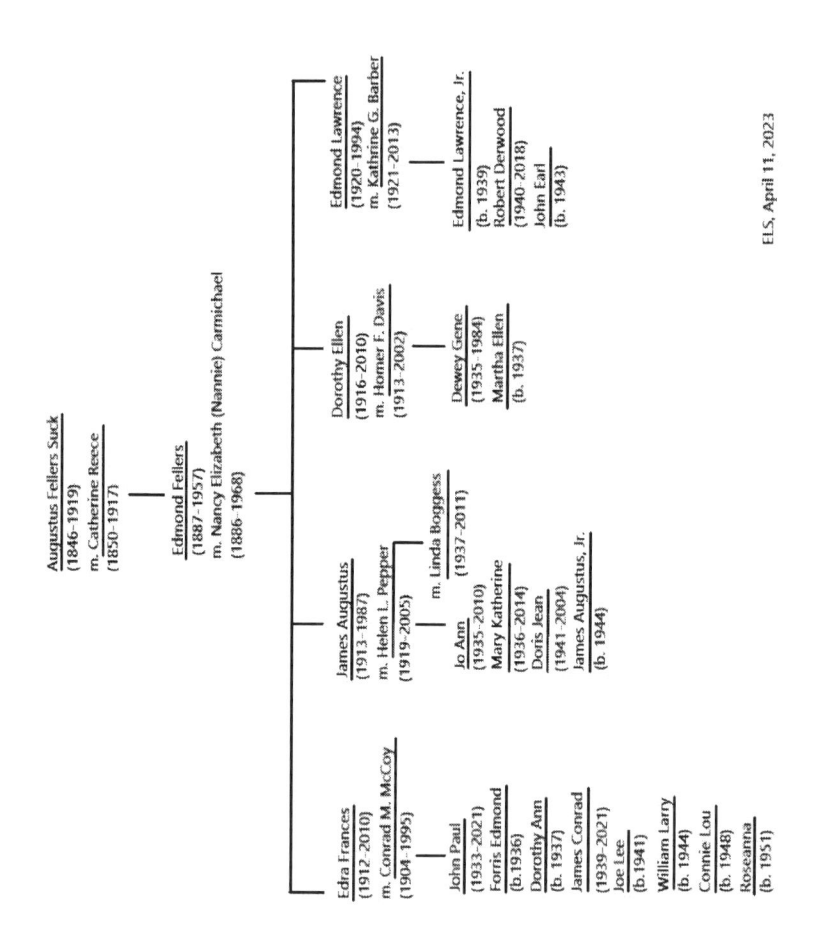

Willow Grove: A Boy, A Family, A Farm

Augustus Fellers Suck
(1846-1919)
m. Catherine Reece
(1850-1917)

Edmond Fellers
(1887-1957)
m. Nancy Elizabeth (Nannie) Carmichael
(1886-1968)

- **Edra Frances** (1912-2010)
  m. Conrad M. McCoy (1904-1995)
  - John Paul (1933-2021)
  - Forris Edmond (b. 1936)
  - Dorothy Ann (b. 1937)
  - James Conrad (1939-2021)
  - Joe Lee (b. 1941)
  - William Larry (b. 1944)
  - Connie Lou (b. 1948)
  - Roseanna (b. 1951)

- **James Augustus** (1913-1987)
  m. Helen L. Pepper (1919-2005)
  - Jo Ann (1935-2010) m. Linda Boggess (1937-2011)
  - Mary Katherine (1936-2014)
  - Doris Jean (1941-2004)
  - James Augustus, Jr. (b. 1944)

- **Dorothy Ellen** (1916-2010)
  m. Homer F. Davis (1913-2002)
  - Dewey Gene (1935-1984)
  - Martha Ellen (b. 1937)

- **Edmond Lawrence** (1920-1994)
  m. Kathrine G. Barber (1921-2013)
  - Edmond Lawrence, Jr. (b. 1939)
  - Robert Derwood (1940-2018)
  - John Earl (b. 1943)

ELS, April 11, 2023

Maryland Family Reunion

Justus Frederick Sück came to America in 1846. Augustus Fellers Sück, one of Justus Frederick Sück's four sons, had twelve children. One son, Augustus Fellers, my great-grandfather, settled in Silverton, West Virginia. Two of Augustus Fellers' sons, William (oldest) and Cecil (youngest), settled in Frederick, Maryland, and Allentown, Pennsylvania, respectively.

Augustus Fellers Sück, my great-grandfather, was very supportive of his family getting together each year for a family reunion. My grandfather, Edmond Fellers Sück, continued the tradition and held the first annual reunion in August, 1949, and, save for the pandemic year of 2020, the family has enjoyed a reunion for 73 consecutive years.

The family of my grandfather's oldest brother, William, has also held a reunion since July 25, 1982. The Maryland family reunion picture was taken on September 17, 2005, near Fairfield, Pennsylvania.

Willow Grove: A Boy, A Family, A Farm

Maryland Family Reunion

Back: Howard Edward Toms, Richard Leo Orndorff with Megan Eileen Orndorff on his shoulders, Chris Fox, Amy Sue Portner, Raymon Eugene Charron, Tyne Kendell, Jeanne Constance Suck Dearth, Glenda Heridia, Kirk Allen Rafter, Arturo Heridia, Wilfred William Plumer, Jr., Kay Rebecca Toms Plumer.

Front: Nathan Ryder, NA, Travis William Plumer, Una Jeeanne Toms Orndorff, Tessa Miller and son Collin, Denise Eileen West Charron, Tabatha Charron with dog, Barbara Lee Baker Zimmerman West, Douglas Matthew Dearth, Prisicilla Susan Toms Portner, George Ernest West, Sr., Lucy Jeanne Toms.

Photo courtesy of Rebecca Toms Plumer.

Willow Grove: A Boy, A Family, A Farm

Acknowledgments

This book has been a work in progress for over two decades. It started as a few bullet points in my personal journal and slowly morphed into a small memoir, mainly for my personal reference. Eventually, over years of long-distance phone calls with my mother every Sunday evening, I became more interested in my ancestral history, which my retired parents worked on while traveling.

After penning so much information over such an extended period, my mother encouraged me to write a book about the family. After I commenced writing, my mission gradually changed from a pure memoir to a hybrid memoir from 1946 to 1955, the years we lived at Willow Grove. The book can serve as a reference for future generations who become interested in their ancestry.

Many people have provided content for this book, especially the reference portion. Numerous invaluable photographs gifted by several family members and friends have helped me immensely. I

Willow Grove: A Boy, A Family, A Farm

studied many photos in such detail that their revelations enabled me to connect many dots, making my writing easier, more interesting and, hopefully as accurate as possible.

Photographs from June (Sis) Sück Hicks, Stephanie Davis Waldron, and Helen Sück have been so helpful and added an exponential value to this book.

I want to acknowledge the effort and time Martha Davis Grisso and Connie McCoy Wright gave to read my rookie tome. I wrote this book for myself, and it's hard to fathom how anyone could endure reading such a reminiscence. I thank Jane and Spencer Dreischarf for their help reading the manuscript.

Many thanks to grandson Ty Ardman, who did the wonderful job colorizing the photo of our Willow Grove farm that graces the cover of this book.

Special appreciation for the three months that Dr. Jennifer C. Jones spent reading, cutting, pasting, and re-reading, multiple times, while editing this book. Jennifer demonstrated a sincere interest and provided a set of unbiased eyes, which I needed to smooth out my rough syntax. I'm sorry that Jennifer did not live to see the culmination of all of her hard work to help me produce a respectable book. What a talent! She died way too early!

The contents of this book are skewed toward my father's side of the family. Growing up, I only spent a fraction of my young life with my mother's family when compared to my father's. I grew up living with

Acknowledgments

my grandparents in the same house at Willow Grove. My maternal grandparents lived a challenging distance, in the 1940s and 1950s, from Willow Grove, plus the Barber family did not have an annual reunion like the Sücks. The same was true for the Carmichael and Barnhart families, my grandmother Sück's and grandmother Barber's maiden names.

The handsome, historic house I lived in from 1946 to 1955 at Willow Grove holds a unique notch on my totem pole of life. Fortunately, I appreciated the home at the time, and even more so with each passing day of my golden years. My mother took many pictures of the Willow Grove farm, including the outside and inside of the first floor. No picture of the interior upstairs exists, except the crystal-clear memories in my mind and that of my brother John. With John's mechanical drawing capabilities and his plethora of varied professional attributes, he has reconstructed accurate dimensions and drawings of both floors of the house. He accomplished this feat by knowing the exact dimensions of the sandstone step on the north side of the house. The step is presently used as a bench in his and his wife, Judy's, front yard in Mineral Wells, West Virginia. John is a stickler for details, especially regarding workmanship. I'm so appreciative of all of John's many contributions.

My brothers and I were taught strict rules about doing everything "right the first time, or don't do it at all." Our formative years of training have stuck with my brothers and me throughout our careers.

Willow Grove: A Boy, A Family, A Farm

All three of us were perfectionists in our own way. However, I always considered myself just average, at most, when writing technical reports and marketing correspondence. Yet, one of the U.S. Steel Company secretaries admitted that I drove her "nuts," typing and retyping my technical reports from dictation tapes. She would correct the report three, sometimes four, times, until it was free of typos. Ruth Adkins shared this bit of office information with me during a "thank you" lunch that I hosted for her when I left U.S. Steel in Baton Rouge and joined Mobil Chemical Company in Edison, New Jersey, in 1981. After we had a nice laugh together, Ruth thanked me and said my rare attention to such detail "was both educational and helped me to be a better typist."

I mention Ruth Adkins and our chuckle together because I thought I was a perfectionist for detail...until I corresponded with relative Beckie Toms Plumer about her great-grandfather Will Sück, the oldest child of Augustus Fellers and brother of my grandfather. Beckie found mistakes in my writing and family tree charts that amazed me. More than once she found a "needle in a haystack" in my work. I was so impressed and grateful for the time she spent helping me write certain facets of this book. Beckie did a tremendous amount of family research, which enabled me to include a lot about her great-grandfather. Without her help, I wouldn't have had more than a paragraph about Will Sück. Thank you, Beckie!

Acknowledgments

"A picture is worth a thousand words!" My dear friend Hazel Casto Parsons shared an aerial picture of Willow Grove with me—worth more than "a million words." The picture perfectly illustrates the era that framed my formative years. The backbone of my book! The years I truly enjoyed so much! I can't say enough about how appreciative I am of the photo and articles about Willow Grove. Hazel, thank you very much!

About 2002, my mother gave me 32 pages of "The Sück Family History" compiled by James E. E. and Patricia Ann Vaughan of Monterey Park, California. The detailed account included a cover letter from James and Pat, dated September 1, 1993, and an address of 5727 Hazelbrook Avenue, Lakewood, California, 90712. The cover letter stated that the 32-page computer printout of family history was updated on 5-16-1993 and that the initial work started in 1988-1989.

James and Pat's work was truly invaluable during the development of this book. I laud both of them for their excellent work, which I perused and referred to hundreds, if not thousands, of times over the past 20 years.

Many business customers, company colleagues, and friends truly enlivened my career at five major international chemical companies. Given that I will certainly miss a few names, the following special people remain very much alive and treasured in my octogenarian mind: Craig Allen, Larry Amos, Don Ashburn, Dr. Toby Avery, Rao Ayyagari, Dr. Jody Belden, Margie Bright, Peter Byra, Dr. Van Canady,

Willow Grove: A Boy, A Family, A Farm

Mitzi Cremeans, Jane Landis Dreischarf, Dr. Eblin, Walt Frazer, Joyce Garlick, John Glass, Dr. Herschel Gross, Pat Jennings, Stan Kulkaski, Dr. Charlie Lancelot, Sue Levine, Al Litman, Dr. Bruce Marion, Len Marouse, Jim Martin, Paul Mastro, Bill Orem, John Pack, Sam Potenza, Glenna Rafeld, Gary Rea, Tom Regan, John Roth, Patsy Ann Schutter, Gary Shepherd, Dr. Jim Song, Dr. Jim Spainhour, Dr. Bäbel Such, Ohio University Language Department, and Tom Wiseman. These esteemed ladies and gentlemen wittingly or unwittingly have enriched my memorable career and life, indelibly!

Ms. Jody Belden was a superb business mentor and contributed enormously to my extremely enjoyable and exciting career in the global petrochemicals industry. Notwithstanding my interest in advanced education in chemistry, Jody absolutely pointed me down the right path, at the right time, early on in my business career. A truly wonderful mentor! Rest in Peace, Jody. I will forever be indebted!

I would like to thank Liz Coursen, owner of OrangeBlossomPublishing.com, in Sarasota, Florida, who edited and published *Willow Grove*. Liz's diligence and commitment to this project was unwavering. Thank you, Liz!

Ultimately, I must credit the humble existence of this book on my mother. The core of this book was inspired by hundreds of hours of conversation with Mom over nearly two decades. Every Sunday, I peppered her with questions, and usually, she had

Acknowledgments

a good answer. If she didn't, she would scan her file cabinet and answer my question the following Sunday. Regarding some topics, I would ask the same question from a different perspective, over and over at different times. I wanted to reaffirm dates and cross-check the accuracy of Mom's synopsis on specific topics, especially the ones I found curious. Without my mother's help, this book would not have been as thorough and forthcoming, notwithstanding the pinnacle of influence from both my beloved wife, Peggy, and my mentor, Uncle Conrad McCoy.

Lastly, I want to distinguish my devoted wife, Margaret Faye—Peggy—Miller Suek for putting up with the hundreds of hours I spent in front of my computer writing this book. She recognized and understood my passion to complete my quest and unselfishly relinquished more than a little of our mutual time together whenever I wanted to write. However, at precisely 4:00 p.m. each day, after Peggy had prepared our usual healthy and sublime entrées for dinner—I had to stop writing! At exactly four o'clock every day, we would sit down together with our books and a glass of wine in hand, put on soft, instrumental music, and read for two hours. Peggy was an enthusiastic reader of novels from a very early age. The librarian at the public library in Parkersburg welcomed Peggy's weekly visit with her father and wholeheartedly encouraged her as a pre-teenager to read educational books. Peggy read every one of the classics! Plainly, I can blame my reading addiction on my best friend and wife!

Willow Grove: A Boy, A Family, A Farm

*Larry Suek, Lakewood Ranch, FL,
April 2023*

For further reading.

Part One

Steam power replaced water power in sawmills in the early 1880s and, by 1909, West Virginia was the largest lumber-producing state in the Union. New and more scientific methods of drilling, introduced about 1890, started a new oil boom, and West Virginia soon became one of the most important oil-producing regions in the world, reaching a peak in 1900 of 16 million barrels from its early beginnings at Burning Springs in 1859. The industrial use of natural gas rapidly increased, and its impact was profound: by 1906, West Virginia ranked first among all states in gas production.

In the number of employees, the glass industry held first place with 9,000. It was followed by car and general repair work, 8,500; iron and steel, 4,300; and grist mills, 3,300. By 1914, thousands of West Virginians had left the farms for work in industry.

During the war, when chemicals couldn't be imported from Germany, chemical plants were established in the Kanawha Valley, which in time became a world center for the manufacture of basic chemicals. The federal government constructed a

Willow Grove: A Boy, A Family, A Farm

high explosives plant at Nitro and a mustard gas plant at Belle. Nitro, a town of about 25,000 people and 3,400 buildings sprang up almost overnight in 1918. The chemical industry later expanded along the Ohio River and into the Northern Panhandle. It depended largely upon rich brines in the Kanawha Valley and great beds of rock salt in upper Ohio and extending eastward to Monongalia County. In addition to chemicals, the plants manufactured many other products, including compounds used to make rubber, plastics, and antifreeze. At Nitro and Parkersburg, raw cotton and wood pulp were processed into rayon. At Belle, beginning in the 1930s, E. I. du Pont de Nemours and Company used coal, water, and nitrogen to manufacture nylon, which replaced silk for many purposes.

World War II (1939-1945) brought renewed prosperity. The war increased the demand for coal, and production mounted steadily to an unprecedented level of about 160 million metric tons in 1947. World War II further encouraged the growth of the state's chemical industry, and from 1947 to 1952 it grew at nearly twice the rate of the chemical industry in the United States as a whole. With the exception of Jackson County, every West Virginia county bordering the Ohio River had at least one chemical plant by the 1970s. That was about to change!

After World War II, Kaiser Aluminum Company built a plant on land that my parents and several other farmers owned and sold to Kaiser. In the years that followed, the rich state of West Virginia

For further reading.

became a paradox of squalor alongside plenty. Its industries prospered, its mineral reserves remained seemingly inexhaustible, and national leadership in coal production continued. However, the increasing mechanization of coal mining brought disaster to miners throughout the Appalachian states. West Virginia was hit the hardest. Scores of small operations closed, and ghost towns grew in number. Conditions resembling the very worst times of the Great Depression developed, as 80,000 unemployed miners with 170,000 dependents lived a marginal existence. State relief laws had no adequate provisions to help them.

West Virginia's industries could not absorb the vast numbers dismissed from the mines. During the 1950s, the state's unemployment rate was the highest in the country, at three times the national average. While most state populations boomed, West Virginia lost 7.2 percent as thousands fled in search of employment. References for the previously mentioned statistics are shown below.

Bibliography.

Hennen, John, *The Americanization of West Virginia: Creating a Modern Industrial State, 1916-1925.* University Press of Kentucky, 1996.

Rice, Otis K., *The Allegheny Frontier: West Virginia Beginnings, 1730-1830.* University Press of Kentucky, 1970. History of politics, economy, and society.

Willow Grove: A Boy, A Family, A Farm

Trotter, Joe William, Jr., *Coal, Class, and Color: Blacks in Southern West Virginia, 1915-32*. University of Illinois, 1990.

Williams, John Alexander, *West Virginia*. Norton, 1976, 1984.

en.wikipedia.org/wiki/Ravenswood,_West_Virginia

WVGES Geology: History of West Virginia Oil and Gas Industry (wvnet.edu)

Part Two

Readers interested in learning more about the 17th century's history of undeveloped land west of the Allegheny Mountains will enjoy these books, which I specifically mention because they have significant references, albeit small, to the rich, flat lands along parts of the Ohio River from Pittsburgh to Point Pleasant, West Virginia. George Washington's and Benjamin Franklin's interest in the Vandalia Colony project is discussed on pages 12, 14, and 25 of Dean W. Moore's marvelous book, *Washington's Woods*.

Bibliography.

Ambrose, Stephen E., *Undaunted Courage, Meriwether Lewis, Thomas Jefferson, and the Opening of the American West*. New York: Simon & Schuster, 1996.

For further reading.

Bordewich, Fergus M., *Washington, The Making of the American Capital*, New York: Amistad, 2008.

Hartford, John, *Steamboat in a Cornfield*, New York: Crown Publishers, Inc., 1986.

Hartley, Audrey Sayre, *"Thresh" Machine A Coming, Memories of Jackson County*, Parsons, WV: McClain Printing Company, 2009.

Jackson County Historical Society, *Jackson County, West Virginia, Past and Present, 1990*, Jackson County: Walsworth Publishing, 1990.

Jackson County Historical Society, *Jackson County, West Virginia, Past and Present, 2012*, Jackson County: Walsworth Publishing, 2012.

Kalish, Mildred Armstrong, *Little Heathens, Hard Times and High Spirits on an Iowa Farm during the Great Depression*. New York, NY: A Bantam Book, 2007.

McCullough, David, *The Pioneers, The Heroic Story of the Settlers Who Brought the American Ideal West*. Simon & Schuster, 2019.

Moore, Dean W., *Washington's Woods, A History of Ravenswood And Jackson County, W.VA*. Parsons, West Virginia: McClain Printing Company, 1971.

Willow Grove: A Boy, A Family, A Farm

Poe, Michael A., *Jackson County, Images of America*. Arcadia Publishing, 2008.

Stark, Peter, *Young Washington, How Wilderness and War Forged America's Founding Father*, New York: HarperCollins, 2018.

Wiencek, Henry, *An Imperfect God, George Washington, His Slaves, and the Creation of America,* New York: Farrar, Straus and Giroux, 2003.

Part Three
    In addition to the sources listed here, there are many interesting books, articles, and reference materials that I read and enjoyed during this decades-long project. I have also included websites that I found and used during my research.

Though this is only a partial list, here are a few.

Baltimore & Ohio Railroad, *System Timetables, Issued October 28,* Page 26, *1946*

Bromfield, Louis, *Malabar Farm*. Echo Point Books & Media, 2022.

Bromfield, Louis, *Pleasant Valley*. Harper & Brothers Publishers, 1945.

For further reading.

Brown, Dorothy Longenette, *Reflections on Growing up Poor in West Virginia.* McClain Printing Company, 2003.

Casto, James E., *The Great Ohio River Flood Of 1937*, Charleston, South Carolina: Arcadia Publishing, 2009

Ferrell, Dave, Parkersburg, West Virginia: *Parkersburg News Sentinel*, November 20, 1980

Moellendick, Cordelia, *Diary of Housewife: Looking Ahead, Parkersburg News and Sentinel*, 1956

Ruben, Mike, *She works at home, but it's not there [anymore]*, Jackson County, West Virginia: *The Jackson Star News*, Wednesday, November 14, 1990

Six, Dean; Metzler, Susie; Johnson, Michael, *Popular American Marbles.* Schiffer Publishing, Ltd., 2007

Swick, Gerald D., *Historic Photos of West Virginia.* Nashville, Tennessee: Turner Publishing Company, 2010

Swick, Ray, and Little, Christina, *Blennerhassett Island, Images of America.* Charleston, South Carolina: Arcadia Publishing, 2005

Willow Grove: A Boy, A Family, A Farm

Thompson, Ali, *Hazel Parsons went "home" to work for 38 years*, Jackson County, West Virginia: The Jackson Star News, Thursday, September 20, 2007

Withers, Bob, *Cornfield Navigation, The Boat Wreck at Willow Grove*, Charleston, West Virginia: Goldenseal

Websites:

www.thelivingurn.com /blogs/news/79236289-how-to-determine-the-age-of-a-tree.

en.wikipedia.org/wiki/Ohio_River_flood_of_1937

www.ncei.noaa.gov/news/great-appalachian-snowstorm-november-1950

en.wikipedia.org/wiki/Great_Appalachian_Storm_of_November_1950#West_Virginia

Made in the USA
Columbia, SC
05 April 2025